A Dictionary of Conservative and Libertarian Thought

A Dictionary of Conservative and Libertarian Thought

Edited by
Nigel Ashford and Stephen Davies

London and New York

First published 1991
by Routledge
11 New Fetter Lane, London EC4P 4EE

Simultaneously published in the USA and Canada
by Routledge
a division of Routledge, Chapman and Hall, Inc.
29 West 35th Street, New York, NY 10001

© 1991 Nigel Ashford and Stephen Davies

Set in 10/12 pt Times, Linotron 202
by Florencetype Limited, Avon
Printed in England
by Clays Ltd, St Ives plc

British Library Cataloguing in Publication Data
A Dictionary of Conservative and Libertarian Thought.
  1. Political ideologies
  I. Ashford, Nigel   II. Davies, Stephen
  320.5

Library of Congress Cataloging in Publication Data
A dictionary of conservative and libertarian thought / edited
  by Nigel Ashford and Stephen Davies.
      p.   cm.
    Includes index.
    ISBN 0–415–00302–4 (h/b)
    1. Conservatism--Dictionaries.   2. Liberalism--
Dictionaries.
  I. Ashford, Nigel.   II. Davies, Stephen.
  JA61.D5   1991
320.5′2′03--dc20 90-47907

ISBN 0–415–00302–4

Contents

Contributors

Nigel Ashford is Senior Lecturer in Politics at Staffordshire Polytechnic

Norman Barry is Professor of Politics at the University of Buckingham

Christie Davies is Professor of Sociology at the University of Reading

Stephen Davies is Senior Lecturer in History at Manchester Polytechnic

Antony Flew is Emeritus Professor of Philosophy at the University of Reading

David Gordon is a freelance writer, based in the United States

R.A.D. Grant is Lecturer in English at the University of Glasgow

Wolfgang Grassl is Director of the Austrian Hoteliers' Association

Paul Helm is Lecturer in Philosophy at the University of Liverpool

Alexander Shand was Lecturer in Economics at Manchester Polytechnic (retired)

Barry Smith is Professor of Philosophy at the International Academy of Philosophy, Liechtenstein

Introduction

In 1960 a reviewer of Hayek's *Constitution of Liberty* described the author as 'a magnificent dinosaur'. The previous year Daniel Bell had published a highly regarded and influential work, *The End of Ideology*. Both articulated a common assumption of the time: that the major ideological or philosophical questions of public policy had been largely settled. This assumption in turn reflected the domination of public debate and policy formation by a 'social democratic' consensus, shared by both left and right, consisting of support for an interventionist form of market economy, a redistributionist welfare state, and a politics dominated by questions of technique and ability rather than theory and principle. To this way of thinking political philosophy of any kind seemed otiose and useless and the traditional philosophies of socialism, conservatism, and classical liberalism such as Hayek's little more than historical curiosities.

The thirty years since then have seen a near revolution in political thought, accompanied by a sharp turn in practice. This has been most marked in the United States and Britain but has affected every major western democracy and much of the rest of the world as well. The once secure social democratic consensus is in disarray, confounded by the stagflation of the 1970s, the ever rising costs of the welfare state, and growing evidence of the incapacity of the state. At the same time political philosophy has been rejuvenated and the 'dinosaurs' have shown unexpected resilience.

This revival of political theory has been most marked in the case of the two established schools of conservatism and classical liberalism. The arguments of both traditions have been articulated and applied to the present with a new vigour. Moreover, neither has stood still; new ideas and arguments have been developed and promulgated by a wide range of thinkers from Nozick to Hayek to Buchanan and Scruton. Consequently, it is conservative and classical liberal arguments which increasingly set the terms of intellectual debate. There is a wealth of writing from the left and from defenders of the social democratic status quo but much of this is defensive, responding and reacting to the theses of the 'new right'. This setting of the intellectual agenda does not mean that a new consensus has emerged – at least not yet. There is, rather, intense debate with ideas and arguments contested and defended by all sides.

However, this intellectual transformation is not fully reflected in the world of scholarly writing and academic publication. There is now a wealth of technical writing on the ideas of the conservative and classical liberal 'new right' but little in the way of informative general secondary literature. This is starting to change and Hayek in particular is now the subject of a considerable body of secondary work. Notwithstanding that, it remains true that the quantity of secondary literature devoted to conservative and classical liberal thought is slight when compared with that available on many socialist thinkers. This is particularly true where general works of reference are concerned. A student of socialist, and particularly Marxist, thought has a number of informative, scholarly reference works to draw on. There are almost no corresponding works for non-socialist thinkers and ideas.

This has several serious consequences. Much of the secondary literature that has been written has severe flaws. There is little awareness of the extent and richness of conservative and classical liberal thinking and limited understanding of the internal complexities of these two traditions. Even otherwise well-informed and perceptive scholars are led to false conclusions. Two in particular recur many times. First, there is the notion that, compared to the 'left', the 'right' is empirical, atheoretical, and unengaged with issues of theory or philosophy. Second, there is the pervasive belief that the 'new right' is a single, ultimately cohesive entity. Even those who show some knowledge of the differences between the various schools of thought lumped together in this way assert that there is an underlying unity. Moreover there is only limited understanding of the historical origin and development of these intellectual traditions.

This dictionary is intended, therefore, to redress the balance somewhat by providing a guide to the full range of conservative and classical liberal thought in all its variety. The dictionary is intended for use by scholars, students, and interested laymen. Technical and abstruse argument has therefore been kept to an unavoidable minimum. The work is concerned, as its title indicates, with *thought*, that is with argument and ideas as they have been developed by thinkers working in a self-aware intellectual tradition. Although some politicians are mentioned (e.g. Guizot, Richter) they only appear in so far as they were also intellectual figures of importance. This is a work concerned more with argument and philosophy than with the application of such argument to public policy. One element of the dictionary is a historical emphasis, on the development of conservative and classical liberal thought through time in various countries. Although the predominant emphasis is upon the United States and Great Britain we have tried to include coverage of other countries as well, particularly France and Germany. The entries in the dictionary show that the traditions of thought covered here are varied, subtle, and profound, raising issues that no one interested in politics and poitical philsophy, from whatever perspective, can ignore.

The most problematic feature of the dictionary, for many people, will be its title. This raises the question of whether the book covers one single school of thought, however internally variegated, or two separate and distinct ones. Why should it be called *A Dictionary of Conservative and Libertarian Thought*? American readers in particular may wonder just what 'classical liberalism' or 'libertarianism' is and how it can be distinguished from conservatism. Why not simply *A Dictionary of Conservative Thought*? The same question would be put, for different reasons, by many socialist commentators, not least those, criticized above, who have written on the subject of the 'new right'.

The problem posed here has two components, one less important and primarily a matter of terminology, the other more profound. The first is simply, though maybe not easily, dealt with. In the United States, and to a lesser extent in Britain, the term 'liberal' has come to refer only to the revisionist or social democratic wing of the liberal tradition. Moreover, because of the stigma which attaches to the term 'socialist' in that country, many Americans pass under the name of 'liberal' who would be described as socialists in any other country. In Europe outside Britain the word 'liberal' retains its old meaning and refers primarily to what political scientists call 'classical liberalism'. Consequently the word 'conservative' has taken on a portmanteau quality in America and now refers both to people who would be described as conservatives in any language and to others who would in any European country other than Britain be labellled as liberals. This leads to a great deal of confusion and misunderstanding. The ideal solution would probably be to adopt the Italian or Danish practice of formally distinguishing between the two varieties of liberalism. However, we have to live to some extent with the actual conventions followed in our own society and many Americans have therefore come to use the term 'libertarian' to distinguish classical liberals from both conservatives and revisionist liberals. In this work the terms 'libertarian' and 'classical liberal' should be taken as describing what Americans call libertarianism in both the narrow sense of pertaining to the sectarian libertarian movement and in the wider sense of the libertarian wing of modern American conservatism.

What, though, is classical liberalism or libertarianism and how may it be distinguished both from other varieties of liberalism and from modern conservatism? Almost every book on liberalism starts by saying that the term 'liberal' is extremely vague and ill-defined. We may respond that, while unable to define a liberal exactly, we all recognize one on sight! More seriously, historical study clearly reveals the broad outlines of the liberal tradition, even if only by showing who cannot be included. Although one can trace an ancestry back to the seventeenth century and figures such as Locke, liberalism as a formal self-aware movement first appears at the end of the eighteenth century. Liberalism was at that time a movement which stood for individualism as against hierarchy, free trade and *laissez-faire* instead of intervention, cosmopolitanism and peace rather than war, and freedom of thought and expression in contrast to the confessional state and the control of speech and writing. This meant that a hostility to the state and to politics as a means of organizing life was a central feature of the doctrine of the movement. Conservatives at that time defended the *ancien régime* and argued for the importance of such values as hierarchy, authority, tradition, and religion. Towards the end of the nineteenth century a fissure developed in liberalism as many liberals came to argue that full freedom required the state to act in a positive way to provide individuals with the ability to make use of formal, legal freedom. It became conventional to describe these as 'revisionist' or 'social' liberals and those who adhered to the older view as 'classical' liberals.

This, however, raises the second, more difficult, point alluded to earlier. Many observers argue that in today's world a classical liberal is *de facto* a conservative. The causes for which they campaigned in the last century have largely been won: only a few hardy eccentrics espouse the hereditarian conservatism of people such as Bonald and De Maistre. Today the classical liberal position of support for a market economy, scepticism towards the welfare state, and advocacy of a minimal role for government is the conservative position, a support for the status quo. Liberalism, on the 'left' in the nineteenth century, when its opponent was reactionary conservatism, is now on the 'right' when old-style conservatism has virtually vanished and the rival philosophy is socialism. As some would put it, the language or discourse of classical liberalism, radical or even revolutionary a hundred years ago, is now one which appeals to, and is used by, conservatives.

This position, however, is false, as many conservatives have argued. Although conservatives and classical liberals agree on many issues and are frequent political and intellectual allies, they still have distinct traditions of thought. There are also still two distinct discourses and, although conservatives may resort to the language of classical liberalism when pressed, this is dangerous for them, as many conservatives have recognized. The distinction is partly historical and partly a matter of theory.

In the first place, it is not true that the classical liberal agenda was achieved during the course of the nineteenth century. Although much was achieved the full programme never came near to being realized. Free trade was never practised by all nations at once, the state was not reduced to its unavoidable minimum, much less abolished, as some of the more radical classical liberals advocated. From about the 1880s classical liberalism was on the defensive against a rising tide of interventionism, imperialism, nationalism, and socialism. The 'ideal state' or *telos* of classical liberalism is still only a far-off goal.

Nor is it a goal which conservatives aspire to. Although they may agree in particulars, conservatives and classical liberals differ on the question of fundamental values. Conservatives value order, hierarchy, tradition, and are hostile to abstract reasoning. Liberals adhere to freedom, individualism, progress, and the use of reason. Classical liberalism is not a conservative doctrine in its conclusions either, since the full elaboration of that doctrine can lead to radical conclusions which often have a revolutionary or subversive flavour. Consequently, there are a number of concrete issues or questions where the two traditions are sharply divided over such matters as victimless crime, the nature and scope of the state, the extent of personal liberty, and the degree of pluralism which is compatible with a free society.

Why then treat these two traditions in one work? The answer lies in the nature of modern political argument and discourse. Here the socialist analysis of the connection between the two traditions has some validity. Since about the 1880s politics in 'western' nations has been primarily about economics. The major questions of public debate and political philosophy have been those concerned with the scale and nature of state intervention in the economy. Planning as opposed to reliance on the market and the question of redistribution of income and wealth by state action have been the key issues. On these questions conservatives and classical liberals broadly agree (so long as one ignores the 'ultras' such as Maurras) with the result that they find themselves on the same 'side' in most debates. In Europe the old conservative tradition articulated by people like Maurras and Gierke, which was sceptical about capitalism and as hostile to liberalism as to socialism, all but vanished in the aftermath of the Second World War with its leading figures disgraced because of alleged or actual collaboration with fascism. Only recently has a conservative (as opposed to classical liberal or christian democrat) right begun to reappear.

Moreover, for the greater part of the last hundred years, socialism in its various forms has set the intellectual and political agenda. Individual actors and theories are defined in terms of their relation to socialism: since conservatism and classical liberalism are both opposed to socialism they have become conflated in many people's view. (This of course ignores the once-flourishing anti-capitalist tradition within conservatism.)

This long alliance between the two traditions has affected both. Many classical liberals, such as Hayek, for example, have taken on board much of the conservative view, particularly its support for 'intermediate institutions' and a scepticism about the capacity of reason. Nor has the traffic been only one way: conservatives are now much more amenable to liberal economics and the classical liberal view of law than was the case a hundred years ago. The intellectual alliance has been reflected in the practical world of politics with political parties and institutes commonly containing both conservatives and classical liberals, while both often contribute to the same journals.

It therefore makes sense, given the present state of affairs both intellectual and political, to cover both of these traditions in the one work. To do otherwise would be to cause unnecessary confusion and would make it extremely difficult to discuss many issues of contemporary concern. However, the editors and contributors have sought to be constantly aware of the differences and tensions between the two traditions and to explore them in the entries. Even brief perusal of the work will reveal the extent of both agreement and sharp dissent between them. The title reflects this intellectual balancing act.

But what of the future? Will the ideas and arguments described in this dictionary continue to gain ground or will there be a revival of socialist thought? Also, will the intellectual and political alliance between conservatism and classical liberalism hold up after the final collapse, which we are surely seeing, of the case for a planned economy?

These two questions are, of necessity, interwoven. In some parts of the world, such as the United States, the two traditions are so close that, for some commentators, a 'fusion' has already taken place. Elsewhere, however, there are still deep divisions, as in France for example. Moreover, individual writers and thinkers remain keenly aware of the distinction between the two traditions and usually have no difficulty in placing themselves in one camp or the other. If, in the aftermath of the upheavals of 1989–90, economic issues become less important in politics and there is a shift to cultural and constitutional questions as the focus of debate then we can expect some kind of realignment, with divisions opening up, or being brought to light, between conservatism and classical liberalism. This seems particularly likely on the continent if the passage of time and the collapse of communist power lead to a revival of old-style conservatism in countries such as France and Germany.

If socialist theory is robust enough to make a comeback (which seems likely), socialist thinkers will still have to take account of the failures of planned economies and welfare states, even when judged by socialist criteria. This may well lead to some kind of *rapprochement* between certain varieties of socialism and classical liberalism. Conversely, a revitalized form of socialism, based perhaps on the idea of an egalitarian market economy with substantial redistribution, could pose a sufficiently formidable intellectual and political challenge to ensure that the alliance between conservatism and classical liberalism continues.

What is certain is this: the ideas and arguments discussed in this dictionary are of vital importance in contemporary debates on almost every topic. What we have here are arguments that are serious, important, and relevant. There can be no doubt that they have had a profound impact on political and intellectual debate over the last thirty years or more and that they will continue to make such an impact in the future.

SD/NA

A

AMERICAN CONSERVATISM

There is considerable difficulty in defining American conservatism because in American intellectual life there are two intellectual streams, traditionalist and libertarian, which have been described (and describe themselves) as conservative, but which perceive themselves as different elements of the same movement. It is this sense of self-conscious conservatism which Nash uses as his criterion in his definitive historical survey. Conservatism can best be recognized in terms of its opposition to the centralizing, all-encompassing, bureaucratic, and utopian state, with its destructive effect on the autonomy of the individual and the natural order of communities. The perennial quest for conservatives is the establishment of both freedom and order compatible with the limited state.

Kirk has attempted to identify six principles of conservatism: a belief in a transcendent moral order, based on divine intent or natural law; social continuity, with value given to the gradualness of change; prescription, faith in tradition and a consciousness of the limits of reason; prudence, a recognition of the complexity and fragility of society, and the disastrous consequences of seeking to construct society anew; variety, a respect and appreciation for the differences in men and societies and a deep distrust of the uniformity of equality; imperfectibility, the acceptance that the imperfect nature of man necessarily leads to an imperfect society and so the impossibility of utopia on earth. While this list has a traditionalist bias and conservatives will differ in their interpretation and emphasis, these principles would be generally accepted by most American conservatives.

Left-liberals in the 1950s, such as Hartz, argued that there was no such thing as American conservatism because America was a liberal society politically, historically, and socially, so American conservatism was an alien import from Europe. The intellectual dominance of left-liberalism led many conservatives to feel themselves to be 'a Remnant' fighting a losing battle against the aggrandizement of the state.

1

However, even as the talk of the nonexistence of conservatism was in the air, it was in the process of intellectual renaissance in two distinct forms. The first was the rise of the libertarians, associated with Hayek, Mises, and the journal *Freeman*. The libertarians were staunch critics of the interventionist left-liberalism of the New Deal, which Hayek argued was the start of the slippery slope to socialism and even totalitarianism. The second sign of intellectual invigoration was the rise of the New Conservatism led by Kirk, Viereck, and Rossiter. This conservatism was more cultural and lamented the decline of standards and traditions in the face of the demand of the satisfaction of wants by either government or business. Particularly significant was the work of Kirk, who identified an Anglo-American tradition based on Burke but firmly rooted in American culture. Among the American conservatives he discussed were Hamilton, John Adams, Calhoun, Hawthorne, Babbitt, and Santayana. This rediscovery of the legitimate American conservative tradition was vital to the self-confidence and assertiveness of intellectual conservatives.

Both libertarians and traditionalists had a sense of alienation from the dominant intellectual and political forces, but there were significant differences between them, with the libertarians celebrating the freedom of the individual and the traditionalists emphasizing the pursuit of virtue. In order to avoid a division between the two camps, Meyer put forward the idea of 'fusionism', that there was no contradiction between the two sides because freedom was the political goal while virtue was the goal of man as an individual. Buckley articulated the political relevance of fusionism in his conservative journal, *National Review*.

Conservatism appeared to be discredited with the massive electoral defeat of Goldwater in the 1964 presidential election. Once again, just as the obituaries of conservatism were being written, it was reinvigorated, and once again from two different directions. First, libertarianism was revived under the leadership of Milton Friedman and the Chicago School of neo-liberal economists. They conducted empirical investigations of the consequences of government policies, particularly those of the Great Society programmes of President Johnson, and found them seriously wanting. Rent control had destroyed the housing market, minimum wages had destroyed low-wage jobs, welfare had created welfare dependency, and regulations on business were destroying jobs and raising prices. Most significant of all was the rapid increase in inflation which the monetarists explained as caused by excessive increases in the money supply. These ideas were expressed in a series of books, articles, and reports and eventually popularized in Friedman's book and television series *Free to Choose* in 1980. The second source was the neo-conservatives who returned to conservative themes of social fragility and order. Libertarianism and neo-conservatism provided the intellectual climate which led to the election of Reagan as president in 1980.

The potential for conflict within American conservatism, both intellectual and political, persists and, some have argued, threatens the possibility of establishing a conservative intellectual hegemony. The sources of conflict can be identified in five basic issues.

Traditionalists take a pessimistic view of human nature, based on the Christian doctrine of original sin, so that the inherent potential for evil must be constrained, by self-restraint or community pressure if possible but by government if necessary. Libertarians take a more optimistic view of man. While man is naturally concerned with the pursuit of his own interests, this is not a source of conflict, providing that there are the correct social institutions to channel that self-interest in ways that benefit others, as expressed in Smith's 'invisible hand' and the desire of the businessman to satisfy the wants of his customers to maximize his profits.

For the traditionalist, government is a natural institution of man. For the libertarian, government is an artificial creation based on a social contract between government and the people in which the people offer their obedience to the state in return for the protection of their life and liberties. This is in the tradition of Locke and the founding fathers, and finds recent expression in Public Choice theory.

Traditionalists, such as the columnist Will, argue that the role of government is the promotion of virtue and so attack the current fashion among conservatives to denigrate the state. This is in the traditionalist vein of Strauss, who distinguished between the ancients, those concerned with creating a society that will promote virtue, and the moderns, those concerned with creating a society based on the satisfaction of wants. Libertarians claim that the role of government should be the protection of the freedom of the individual. It is the betrayal of this role which leads them to be so hostile to big government.

Order is the first requirement of society for traditionalists. While order is most effectively provided through institutions such as the family, ultimately the state is required to impose order on society, by force if necessary. Liberty may sometimes have to be sacrificed to obtain order. For libertarians, freedom is the ultimate value, and the value of order is dependent on the extent to which it protects freedom.

Traditionalists view communities as the basic units of society and seek to protect them from the ravages of the state. This theme has been well explored in the writings of Nisbet. The individual is the basic unit of society for libertarians, and the individual may be oppressed by these institutions as well as by the state.

These intellectual differences are fully reflected in the political debates within the conservative movement. The New Right promotes a stronger social role for the state to combat the damage of the permissive society in areas such as abortion, homosexuality, pornography, divorce, and secularism in the schools, while libertarians see these actions as the legitimate exercise of free choice. In the field of foreign policy, traditionalists urge an active foreign policy against communism, articulated by the neo-conservative Kirkpatrick, while libertarians are critical of America's interventionist role in the world and have, for example, advocated the return of American troops from Europe. Economics might appear to be a source of consensus, but even here there is a dispute between traditionalists who envisage some role for government in the provision of minimum welfare and those who favour the end of the welfare state.

This debate within American conservatism should be seen as evidence, not of its intellectual incoherence, but of its intellectual vitality. While it may be doubted that conservatism will ever come to dominate the intellectuals, particularly in academia, it is now firmly established as a lively and respected force in American intellectual life.

NA

Further reading

Buckley, W.F. Jr and C. Kesler (eds), *Keeping the Tablets: Modern American Conservative Thought*, Chicago, IL, Regnery, 1988.
Carey, G. (ed.), *Freedom and Virtue*, Lanham, MD, University Press of America, 1985.
Gottfried, P. and T. Fleming, *The Conservative Movement*, Boston, MA, Twayne, 1988.
Kirk, R., *The Conservative Mind*, Chicago, IL, Regnery, 7th edition 1986.
Nash, G., *The Conservative Intellectual Movement in America*, New York, Basic Books, 1976.

ANARCHISM

Anarchism is the doctrine that supposes that it is possible for there to be an orderly and predictable social order in the absence of the state. This simple definition, however, conceals a wide variety of anarchist thought. Furthermore, it begs some key questions in political thought. Does anarchism mean that order is possible without government of any kind or merely that it can be achieved without the modern, coercive state? Does it hold that law and rules are required but that an enforcement agency with a monopoly of power is dispensable? Is it the case that anarchism entails a revolutionary change in human nature to be viable or merely the removal of existing, arbitrary social institutions? The differing types of anarchism stem largely from the differing answers given to those, and related, questions.

Anarchism may be conveniently divided into two broad categories: communitarian (or collectivist) anarchism and property rights anarchism. The former is certainly the better-known tradition in social thought. It is a persistent feature of English and European political philosophy: Godwin, Proudhon, Kropotkin, Bakunin, and Marx (in some of his writings) were its most notable exponents. The latter (known in the contemporary world as 'anarcho-capitalism') has led a somewhat furtive existence at the outer extremes of *laissez-faire* economic thought and natural rights individualistic political thought. Historically, there were significant spokesmen for capitalist anarchism in nineteenth-century America, notably Warren, Spooner, and Tucker. In the same century, the Frenchman Gustave de Molinari produced a theory of a 'stateless' market order and, in recent times, 'Austrian' economists have extended catallactic (or exchange) analysis to the supply of public order and defence.

Communitarian anarchism rejects all forms of existing political authority: this would comprise not just the institutions of government but the whole system of law, including common law rules that may have developed spontaneously. Thus no analytical distinction is made between state and law: these are seen as different but complementary aspects of a uniform system of coercion which is not consonant with a true conception of human nature. In this theory even 'legitimately' acquired private property is interpreted as a part of the general system of coercion. The possession of property, guaranteed by coercive law, separates one person from another and destroys that 'natural community' which would emerge spontaneously in the absence of formal legal institutions. However, few collective anarchists have favoured the total communalization of property. Most anarchistic utopias envisage small communities of peasant proprietors, as is exemplified in Godwin's *Political Justice*. To paraphrase Proudhon, property becomes theft when it is the source of socially disruptive inequality and political power.

Communitarian anarchism depends upon an optimistic view of human nature as essentially benign and co-operative. It is the external and coercive institutions of law and state that generate social conflict rather than some innate defect in man's reason and nature. Hence, *contra* Hobbes, man is naturally sociable, it is the artifice of government and law that makes him egoistic and divisive; thus freedom is only possible without political authority. In the words of Proudhon: 'liberty is the mother not the daughter of order'.

Such utopianism is scarcely conceivable in large-scale social organizations. Hence, most communitarian anarchists suggest that an anarchistic society would be a loose confederation of small and independent co-operative associations. When those associations are based on the work-place, we have the doctrine of anarcho-syndicalism (espoused by Sorel): a social theory opposed to both capital and the state. It is from this tradition that the connection between anarchism and the violent overthrow of the state emerged (though this had been implicit in some earlier versions of the doctrine).

The anarchist strain in Marxism emerges in his future communist society which is characterized by the absence of property, law, and state. These are features of the previous capitalist order; its replacement by socialism and, ultimately, communism would eventuate in a new 'man' who would not require coercive regulation. However, since this would be the result of a historical process the state would remain until all the necessary stages had been gone through. This was the cause of his famous dispute with Bakunin, who favoured the immediate overthrow of the state.

Property rights anarchism presupposes no fundamental change in human nature for a stateless society to be viable. It also believes that law and rules (with sanctions) are necessary for order. It simply argues that protection is not a public good and can be delivered privately through competing agencies. It normally holds that individuals have natural rights, which include the right to acquire and exchange property, and that the monopoly state is the fundamental violator of those rights. There is no possibility, according to the theory, of limiting the state by a written constitution since once sovereign power has been granted to a political institution its aggrandizement must be inevitable.

In the anarcho-capitalism of Rothbard there is a fundamental body of individualistic natural law which would be consistent with the spontaneously developing common law only to the extent that the latter honoured the universal right to equal liberty. In the anarcho-capitalism of David Friedman even the content of law is supplied by a competitive market.

Courts and police agencies would be privately owned and the insurance market would provide protection for individuals at competitive prices. The state's power to tax, conscript, compel jury service, provide welfare, and do anything else would be abolished. All wanted goods and services would be provided by the market. This would guarantee efficiency and liberty. The right to property is philosophically underwritten by Lockean natural law: possession is justified in terms of first acquisition ('mixing labour with a previously unowned object'), exchange or gift. However, the familiar Lockean limitations on acquisition are absent.

The conservative objections to all varieties of anarchism tend to spring from Hobbesian sources. Such is the frailty of human nature, it is argued, that without a centralized and sovereign system of power and authority society would collapse into lawless anarchy. Ultimately, then, there can be no distinction between law and state: society, either through altruism or markets, is not stable without force. There is the further, Hegelian, argument that liberty and morality are a consequence of order, not its antecedent. A social and political order can never be the product of individual choice, abstracted from historical circumstances; indeed, individuality itself is a meaningless concept outside some prior system of rules enforced by a coercive state.

Classical liberals accept the state, not out of any reverence for its mystical authority and morality, but merely because it has genuine public good features. That is to say, certain goods, because they are jointly consumed and non-excludable, cannot be provided efficiently by the private market. If one person or group, for example, provides defence then others are protected without having to pay. This encourages people to conceal their preferences so that vital services are under-provided – making everybody worse off. All societies contain 'prisoners' dilemmas' which only a coercive state can solve. Typical public goods are clean air, law and order, external defence, and a system of law relief.

Many classical liberals, such as Buchanan, are contractarians who believe that the state is an artifice constructed exclusively for the delivery of public goods. It has no intrinsic morality or authority and must be limited by higher or constitutional law. Anarchism, however, is regarded as simply impracticable as well as inefficient in a technical, economic sense. People make gains from trade by leaving anarchy since they need to invest less in defence once a central police power has been established.

A classical liberal such as Nozick believes that a monopoly state would emerge spontaneously (without explicit contract) from a normal market in protection. Again, this state is forbidden from transgressing individual rights, including the right to property. Nozick's argument is a kind of dialogue with the individualist anarchist which has the aim of showing that, logically, the state need not arise through force.

NB

Further reading

Friedman, D., *The Machinery of Freedom*, New York, Arlington, 1973.
Martin, J., *Men Against the State*, Colorado, Myles, 1953.
Miller, D., *Anarchism*, Oxford, Blackwell, 1985.
Nozick, R., *Anarchy, State and Utopia*, Oxford, Blackwell, 1974.
Rothbard, M., *For a New Liberty*, New York, Collier-Macmillan, 1978.

ARISTOCRACY

Etymologically the word 'aristocracy' means rule by the best. So when Plato, Aristotle, and other Greek writers refused to commend an actual ruling elite in this way, and its rule was not regarded as necessarily in the interests of the ruled, they put it down as an oligarchy, which meant rule by the few, and carried overtones of disapproval. Members of such elites, denounced by opponents as oligarchs, would speak of themselves as 'the beautiful and good' – a rough equivalent of the contemporary stock phrase 'the beautiful people'.

In more recent, feudal and post-feudal times aristocracies have been taken to be typically, if not essentially, not only hereditary and landholding but also titled. Apologists have always and reasonably emphasized the first two of these three criteria. Before the present century, hereditary titles were rarely if ever awarded to anyone not simultaneously given, or already possessed of, some substantial quantity of real estate. The argument is that such real estate – as something obvious, visible, tangible, and irremovably permanent – is indeed real in a way in which stocks, shares, bank balances, and other forms of property are not. Estates give their owners a very special sort of 'stake in the country'. Which is why Burke pronounced himself 'unalterably persuaded that the attempt to oppress, degrade, impoverish, confiscate and extinguish the original gentlemen and landed property of a whole nation, cannot be justified under any form it may assume'.

The principal justification offered for the institutions of aristocracy is that, given the irremediable imperfection of all human beings and human arrangements, perhaps the best for which the many may reasonably hope is to be ruled wholly or in part by a hereditary elite, bred to the prospect of power, and rewarded with the dignities and privileges necessary to make its members accept the responsibilities of office, with checks and limitations on its powers. Breeding, the breeding both of people and of tamable brutes, has been a main traditional interest – you might almost say the occupational interest – of aristocrats in all countries. (The centrality of this interest to *The Republic* is the best evidence in Plato's writings of his own upbringing as an Athenian aristocrat!)

Again in Burke the emphasis upon the hereditary principle is derived from his vision of society as

> a partnership in every virtue, and in all perfection. As the ends of such a partnership cannot be obtained in many generations, it becomes a partnership not only between those who are living, but between those who are living, those who are dead and those who are to be born.

But 'People will not look forward to posterity, who never look backward to their ancestors'. His argument concludes with a concession, and a characteristically robust counter-attack:

> For though hereditary wealth, and the rank which goes with it are too much idolized by creeping sycophants, and the blind abject admirers of power, they are too rashly slighted in the shallow speculations of the petulant, assuming, shortsighted coxcombs of philosophy.

AF

Further reading

Aristotle, *Politics*, trans. E. Barker, Oxford, Clarendon, 1948.
Burke, E., *Letters to a Member of the National Assembly*, 1791.
Burke, E., *Reflections on the Revolution in France*, Harmondsworth, Penguin, 1968.
Plato, *The Republic*.

ART

A work of art is a device created by a human being for the purpose of giving rise to certain special emotional and other sorts of experience in other human beings, experiences which are in turn found pleasurable by the latter. The experiences in question are not, however, what we might call genuine or bona fide experiences (of love, sadness, terror, etc.). For if they were, then it would be a problem to understand why, for example, tragic art should exist at all, for it would be difficult to see how works of tragic art could be *enjoyed*. Certainly there are some cases, as for instance in the playing of solemn music at funerals, where the experiences brought about by works of art may serve to intensify those genuine experiences which belong to the world of everyday human reality. In general, however, it seems that the experiences which works of art are designed to generate are much rather what we might crudely refer to as 'fantasy' experiences, in the sense that they are experiences which dislodge us from, or are skew to, our normal day-to-day concerns.

We properly ascribe aesthetic value to works of art according to the extent that they are able to give rise reliably to fantasy experiences of a peculiarly subtle or powerful or enjoyable sort. Special disciplines and skills are involved in the production of works with these qualities, and a special genius is required if essentially new ways of instilling fantasy experiences are to be discovered and made concretely effective. Moreover, these disciplines and skills will typically be of the sort which need to be handed down from one generation of artists to the next, and this will imply that the existence of traditions of artistic activity will typically be intertwined with the different sorts of local and national traditions which conservatives hold dear.

From another perspective, however, it must be clear from the above that art and politics need have no intrinsic connection with each other. For the sorts of fantasy experiences which works of art are properly constructed to generate lie precisely outside the normal everyday world to which politics belongs. A genuine feeling of moral guilt fails, to this extent, as a work of art.

These ideas can now be used to distinguish a spectrum of different sorts of conservative attitudes to art. At the one extreme is Plato, for whom the fact that works of art instil fantasy experiences of the sort described constitutes a sufficient reason to place a low value on art as such, precisely because it leads us away from truth and from those genuine feelings and emotions which are alone of value and importance. At the opposite extreme are those conservatives who place a positive value on art precisely because it stands out in this way as a separate ingredient in the natural history of man, a part of that motley collection of non-political human activities which leaven our day-to-day concerns and which are set at a distance from what is a matter of expedience. Such views may see a value in artistic activity that is quite independent of the experiences to which works of art give rise. Thus Hegel conceives art as one of the manifestations of Absolute Mind by which the humdrum concerns of man are transcended in the course of history. Between these two extremes are the views of those, like Tolstoy, who award value to works of art because, and to the extent that, they are deemed able to give rise to genuine experiences of one or other specific sort. A work of art, according to Tolstoy, is a vehicle for the *communication* of emotions, a device by which the artist seeks to infect others with his own emotional experiences. Great art is art which has the power to infect mankind as a whole, and the greatest of all art is art which instils in its audience that feeling of religious compassion which is for Tolstoy the supreme emotional experience. Conservatives may similarly award value to what they conceive as upright or morally uplifting art, or they may see in art a means of energizing and intensifying those national or other sorts of feeling which they deem intrinsically valuable for other reasons.

One further consequence of a broadly political nature would seem to follow from the account presented above. If a work of art is truly a device that is constructed by one human being to give rise to certain sorts of (subtle, and also pleasurable) experiences in the minds of others, then it will follow that those modern developments which tend to thwart this direct contact between the artist and the consumers of the artist's work will tend to have negative consequences for the value of the works of art which are produced. Both conservative and classical liberal theories here predict similar results. Where the artist is confronted with alien tiers of decision-makers, his energies will naturally tend to be deflected away from the construction of objects with properly artistic powers and towards engagement of such activities as will, to put it crudely, impress the members of committees. The careers of those artists will thereby also tend to be furthered who show particular skills or diligence in these activities. 'Thin', conceptually appealing art is what results, subject to the twists and turns of fashion, and owing more to programmes and manifestos than to craftsmanship and properly artistic inspiration.

Conservative and classical liberal theorists can agree, too, that the remedy for this state of affairs would consist in a depoliticization of art, a process which would be expected to lead also to the stimulation of the production of works of art which are on a human scale and which have the power to generate truly aesthetic experiences.

BS

Further reading

Banfield, E., *The Democratic Muse*, New York, Basic Books, 1984.
Smith, B., 'The substitution theory of art', *Grazer Philosophische Studien 17* 1986, 25–6: 533–57.
Tolstoy, L., *What is Art?*, London, Croom Helm, 1985.

AUSTRIAN ECONOMICS

Austrian economics is often thought to be the economic 'ideology' of conservative and classical liberal thinkers. This is because of its implicit individualistic and anti-statist features and because of the crucial role it attributes to private property in the market system. However, it developed out of certain technical innovations that were made in economic theory in the nineteenth century and all of its practitioners, in their pure economics at least, have maintained a resolutely *wertfrei* (value-free) methodological stance.

Austrian economics began with the publication of Menger's *Principles of Economics* in 1870. Along with the work of Walras and Jevons this established the 'marginalist' and 'subjectivist' revolution in economic theory: a new approach which solved certain key problems in the prevailing classical economics associated with Smith and Ricardo. Menger's belief in timeless and universally true propositions in economics led to a fierce *Methodenstreit* (methodological debate) with the German 'historicists' (who understood economics to be the empirical study of historical and sociological categories). Austrian economics was further refined and developed by Weisser and Boehm-Bawerk. Its major twentieth-century exponents were Mises and Hayek; under whom, despite their technical proficiency, it became associated with the politics of liberal individualism. The major contemporary Austrian economists are the American writers Rothbard and Kirzner.

The main concepts that distinguish Austrian economics from other related schools are subjectivism, individualism, time, market process, and entrepreneurship.

Subjectivism is the methodological doctrine that social science deals not with objective 'facts' or rigid regularities but the actions of individuals subject to constraints, e.g. scarcity. Since choice is inherently subjective, economics cannot be a predictive science. The most obvious example of subjectivist economics is the theory of value. In contrast to the Smith–Ricardo tradition, in subjectivist economics price is determined by the preferences of individuals, at the margin, rather than by some objective cost of production. Austrians extended subjectivism beyond the theory of price into all aspects of economic phenomena. For example, Weisser developed the notion of 'opportunity cost'. This is the idea that the cost of producing anything is not the objective value of the resources used but always the forgone value of the next best alternative use of those resources: again, this is a subjective notion. This has the important implication that it is impossible to calculate efficiently the cost of production in the absence of a competitive market.

Methodological individualism is the doctrine that economic processes can only be understood in terms of individual actions and volitions. Collective propositions about 'economy', 'state', and 'society' are only meaningful when they are reducible to propositions about individual motivations. It follows from this that Austrian economists reject 'macro-economics'; where that claims to have discovered regularities between such economic 'aggregates' as the rate of interest, the money supply, the level of employment, and so on. These regularities are of a statistical kind only and therefore cannot be genuinely scientific. This has the policy implication that unemployment can only be reduced by changing an individual price, that of labour: it cannot be eliminated by raising aggregate demand.

Economic action takes place through time. From Boehm-Bawerk through to Hayek, Austrian economists have refined the theory of capital in terms of time. An economy develops through the extension of the length of production. Voluntary savings are invested in capital goods which, although they take longer to produce benefits in final consumption ('roundabout' production processes), will yield more consumer goods in the long run. The level of investment is determined by the 'natural rate of interest' (a function of the saving/consumption ratio of the public) and any attempt to get the money rate of interest below this natural rate will lead to malinvestment in capital goods, i.e. production processes that cannot be sustained by the rate of voluntary saving. Depressions are normally caused by inflationary monetary policies that encourage malinvestments which must be liquidated if the economy is to be co-ordinated.

The idea of a market process can be best understood in comparison with the general equilibrium–perfect competition theory of orthodox neo-classical economics. From Walras, orthodox economists have tried to prove the existence of market equilibrium in which the actions of transactors mesh perfectly. Each factor of production is paid its marginal product, every trader is a 'price-taker' (i.e. no one can influence price but has to accept prices dictated by an impersonal market), there are no profits over and above normal payments to factors, and there are no price differentials to be exploited by entrepreneurs. Many neo-classical economists use this model to criticize and reform real-world markets, which are frequently characterized by monopoly and other market imperfections.

In Austrian market process theory, developed by Mises, Hayek, and Kirzner, the exchange system is never in equilibrium, although there is a tendency towards this. Equilibrium theory is static theory: it never explains how perfect co-ordination occurs. In Austrian theory co-ordination takes place because the price mechanism is constantly signalling information about profitable opportunities to transactors. In a market system knowledge, e.g. of consumer tastes and technical possibilities, exists in a dispersed and decentralized form. Each trader has that information which affects him personally and by following price signals unwittingly produces an overall order. By a process of evolution the competitive order selects out the efficient from the inefficient firms through the discipline of profit and loss. Although equilibrium is described in terms of perfect competition, in fact that competitive process has come to an end precisely because there are no further price discrepancies to correct. Austrians prefer the expression 'rivalrous competition' because this describes a process of constant change and uncertainty.

In market process the entrepreneur plays a crucial role. For it is the entrepreneur's alertness (a term used by Kirzner) to some price discrepancy which can be exploited for profit that nudges a market towards equilibrium. Entrepreneurship is not defined in terms of resource ownership but as a kind of mental sensitivity to possible economic opportunity (or arbitrage). This means that in real-world economies there will always be entrepreneurial 'profit', i.e. income over and above that which is required to keep a factor of production in operation.

In market process theory, monopoly is not necessarily harmful. Monopoly profits may simply reflect a reward for superior alertness. Indeed, without the prospect of windfall profits, particularly risky projects may not be undertaken at all. Furthermore as long as access to all economic activities remains open the monopolist acts under competitive pressure: his supra-normal profits are always likely to be competed away. Finally, it is a fundamental Austrian contention that pure monopoly rarely arises spontaneously: it is almost always the result of a government grant of privilege to particular producers.

Austrian economists have used the above arguments to refute the claims of socialists and interventionists to improve on the market. Their arguments are that governments do not have the knowledge to reproduce the perfect equilibrium of pure theory and that the removal of entrepreneurship, and therefore supra-normal profit, means that there is no incentive for managers to bring about an efficient allocation of resources.

Austrian economics, along with the Chicago School, has become the backbone of classical liberal political economy. Its individualism and recognition of the importance of private property and profit have featured strongly in the revival of anti-statist social theory. It has produced reasons why socialist economic planning will fail rather than made merely empirical observations on its historical mistakes. Even conservatives have admired Austrian economics: largely because its reliance on spontaneous, natural processes betrays an intellectual anti-rationalism which is at the heart of conservative thought. However, some extreme Austrian theorists, who claim that any wanted good or service can be provided by the market, have evinced a distrust of 'politics' and the state which most conservatives find quite inadequate. Conservatives maintain that a political order must logically precede the market if social stability is to be ensured. With the exception of Hayek (and to some extent Mises) Austrian economists have scarcely considered this question.

NB

Further reading

Barry, N.P., 'The Austrian perspective', in D. Whynes (ed.), *What is Political Economy?*, Oxford, Blackwell, 1984.
Dolan, E. (ed.), *The Foundations of Modern Austrian Economics*, Kansas, MO, Sheed, Andrews, & McMeel, 1976.
Mises, L. von, *Human Action*, New Haven, CT, Yale University Press, 1963.
Reekie, D., *Markets, Entrepreneurs and Liberty: An Austrian View of Capitalism*, Brighton, Wheatsheaf, 1984.
Rothbard, M.N., *Man, Economy and State*, Los Angeles, CA, Nash, 1962.

AUTHORITY

Authority is the concept that describes the rightfulness or legitimacy of certain forms of action (normally political). It is contrasted with power in that although both concepts refer to the movement of human beings, power refers to some causality in the process. One obeys authority not because one is caused to obey but because the person in authority has the *right* to issue instructions, and declare that certain things can be done. Although obedience to authority may sometimes appear to have the same features as a response to the exercise of power, and for this reason the two concepts are often used interchangeably, they are analytically distinct. For although compulsion may be associated with authority, we still ask for reasons in connection with its exercise. However, with power we are solely concerned with the prediction of its success (or otherwise). An example of this would be the distinction between the actions of a bank robber and those of the tax authority. Although authority is a normative concept, in the sense of being defined in terms of rules and procedures, it does not follow from this that the actions of authority are right in the sense of being consistent with some substantive moral philosophy.

The one exception to the above analysis is the political philosophy of Hobbes. There is, for him, no real distinction between power and authority. Since all political power, as opposed to the infliction of brute force (i.e. the absence of power), depends upon consent, it must be in some sense 'authorized'; whether consent derives from fear or morality is logically immaterial. Modern conservatives distinguish between power and authority precisely in terms of the differing ways in which obedience is secured.

Political philosophers are interested in the variety of authority relationships: while they all differ from power there are differences between them. Weber, in *The Theory of Social and Economic Organisation*, distinguished three 'ideal' types: charismatic authority, traditional authority, and rational legal authority.

Charismatic authority exists when one person is able to get their way, or seems to be entitled to obedience, through certain personal qualities: they do not derive authority from specific rules. Jesus Christ's authority over his followers is thought to be of this type: in the modern world Hitler, Churchill, and de Gaulle are cited as charismatic leaders. Traditional authority inheres in non-industrial societies where tribal chiefs and hereditary monarchs derive their entitlement from non-articulated rules which appear to have no rational foundation. Rational–legal authority is characteristic of industrial society: relationships are depersonalized and conducted under rules which normally have a specific purpose.

Since these are ideal types no society will exhibit one exclusively. In Britain, for example, the monarchy (and other traditional institutions) exists alongside a complex structure of formal rules. Particular monarchs may also have charisma. However, it is doubtful whether charisma is a separate and logically independent form of authority. Charismatic leaders are obeyed normally because they fulfil some qualifications rather than through the force of their personalities exclusively. Furthermore, if all forms of authority have their source in rules, then the differences between traditional and rational–legal authority become differences of degree rather than of kind. The conservative view of authority, especially as espoused by Burke, is that all authority must be traditional because the human mind is incapable of constructing authoritative rules independently of experience.

The only type of authority not based on rules or some other test of legitimacy is *de facto* authority. Someone may exert authority in the absence of these in, for example, temporary crises. It has been suggested that an anonymous person who directs people out of a cinema during a fire has *de facto* authority. However, this would appear to have no political analogue: political authority is a continuing process in which legitimacy obtains because it is in some sense *de jure*.

Conservatives and liberals maintain that a society cannot be held together by power alone. Although in certain circumstances people may be caused to obey, over time rulership is successful to the extent that it acquires authority and relies less on threat. The key feature in social order is continuity: and this has to be secured by rules rather than power. Also, a society that is held together solely by power would have to invest heavily in the police function and yet the loyalty of the police could not be secured by power. As Hume pointed out, a society based on power alone is a conceptual impossibility. Even power of the most arbitrary ruler depends on some form of consent.

Political theorists differ as to whether authority necessarily conflicts with reason and freedom. It would appear to do so since the existence of authority implies that someone is entitled to make decisions which are not subject to rational argument and which deprive the individual of choice. Political authority relationships clearly contrast with scientific relationships: in the latter no one can make a decision about a proposed theory merely because of their position in the hierarchy.

Classical liberals therefore hope to reduce the area of social life in which authority prevails. They can accept the need for authoritative rules, as in a general system of law, while still claiming that personal authority should be reduced so as to maximize personal liberty. Popper's liberal 'utopia' is modelled on the relationships that obtain in the scientific community precisely because this allows decisions to emerge from free discussion, subject only to the rules of rational argument.

Conservative political theorists maintain that if society is to be stable it requires that a wide range of decisions must be made for which no formal reasons are required. Thus rules ought to be adhered to and decisions obeyed even though on 'scientific' grounds they might be irrational. Since reason cannot predict the consequences of the breach of traditional rules it is reasonable, in an informal sense, to obey authority. Furthermore, there is a Hobbesian strain in some conservative thinking that fears a collapse into anarchy and disorder if individuals can freely question all authority. This implies not just a commitment to traditional authoritative rules but also the necessity of some personal authority of a wide-ranging kind. Conservatism can be identified with authoritarianism when it removes the notion of consent (in a rational choice sense) from the ground of political obligation.

At a more philosophical level it is often argued that authority is not inconsistent with either reason or liberty. In relation to reason it is claimed that because, unlike power, authority is not defined in terms of predictions of success we can always question authority. Irrespective of whether a political authority does the right thing, we can always question whether it had the right to do it. In this view, even 'absolute' authority, such as the Pope's over Roman Catholic believers, is subject to rational criticism by reference to the tenets of the Catholic faith. In a similar way freedom is thought to be consistent with authority because the idea of freedom being increased in direct proportion to the reduction in authority is completely misleading. The very meaning of liberty, it is argued, depends on an understanding of rules and procedures, i.e. authority structures: a person cannot be free without a structure of social rules. Plausible though this may be in relation to authority in general, it is difficult to deny that specific acts of political authority do have liberty-reducing features; and that the authoritative nature of such acts seems to exist independently of reason.

NB

Further reading

Baine Harris, R. (ed.), *Authority: A Philosophical Analysis*, Alabama, University of Alabama Press, 1976.
Friedrich, C.J., *Tradition and Authority*, London, Macmillan, 1972.
George, R. de, *The Nature and Limits of Authority*, Kansas, University of Kansas Press, 1985.
Peters, R.S., 'Authority', in A. Quinton (ed.), *Political Philosophy*, London, Oxford University Press, 1967.

B

BRITISH CONSERVATISM

The English conservative tradition (which includes those who were not native-born Englishmen) is perhaps the richest in the whole of conservative political thought. Although England has produced great political philosophers (Hobbes, Locke, Bentham, Mill, etc.), the country's political tradition is equally important for its long line of conservative thinkers who have reflected on politics, not from a rationalistic and metaphysical position, but from the perspective of history, religion, and the common law and custom. Although a divinely based natural law has inspired much English conservative thought its most notable contribution to politics is a profound scepticism about rational schemes for social improvement. It is secular at least in comparison to much of European conservative thought.

The most articulate spokesmen for a traditionalist and particularist view of man and society were Hooker, Bolingbroke, Hume, Burke, Disraeli, Salisbury, and, in the present day, Oakeshott and Scruton. One should not underestimate the influence of Hobbes, for although his rationalism and contractarianism are alien to most conservatives, his belief in the potential depravity of man is echoed in some traditionalistic thought. There are some elements common to all these writers: anti-rationalism, a belief in the imperfectibility of man, a reverence for the common law and limited government, and an understanding of society in organic terms. Overall is the idea that the explanation of permanence and stability is the proper role of political thought; it is not the prescription of ideal forms of social organization. Whatever goals men might have, such as liberty or justice, they are only meaningful within the context of a prior notion of order.

Anti-rationalism is the doctrine that reason is too fragile an instrument for the construction of a social order. Traditional rules of conduct, which have survived some quasi-evolutionary test, contain an immanent wisdom which cannot be expressed in formal propositions. As Burke puts it: 'The science of constructing a commonwealth, or renovating it, is, like every other experimental science, not to be taught as "a priori".' This has the implication that there are no universally valid political institutions and laws: these must be located within a particular political tradition. All revolutions are therefore dangerous to the extent that they attempt to remodel society in accordance with abstract principles. This applies as much to the 'reactionary right', who wish to restore some past (usually clerical) order, as it does to socialists and utopian economic planners. It also explains Burke's support of the American Revolutionaries of 1776, who merely wished to preserve their traditional liberties against an assertive monarch and his contempt for the rationalists of the French Revolution who were constrained by no tradition.

This scepticism about the possibility of reason prescribing universal values means that most conservative thinkers evince a cautious utilitarianism. This is specifically not a rationalistic Benthamite utilitarianism (which presupposes that a utility function can be determined for society as a whole irrespective of tradition and experience) but one that merely respects the accidental benefits that arise from non-interference with customary arrangements. Nevertheless, some English conservatives have tried to found a political morality on something higher than mere utility. In a conservative tradition that extends from Hooker to Hailsham, the human institution of government is derived from a Christian natural law that prescribes modes of moral conduct. However, few conservative thinkers have derived a specific code of political conduct from this. The demands of prudence normally outweigh the claims of natural law.

The necessity for government, and ultimately coercion, springs from the conservative belief in the imperfectibility of man. Although society does precede the state, and certain pre-political institutions, such as the family, are held to be natural to man, the conservative believes that without political authority a community would collapse into disorder. In Hegel's philosophy, law and morality can only be validated by the coercive state. However, for most conservatives, this belief in imperfectibility tells as much against entrusting too much power to government as it does against utopians who believe that in the absence of authority and coercive regulation men will generate spontaneously a social order.

Hume's conception of human nature is perhaps the most quintessentially conservative. He argued that we should accept men as they are and not as they might be (in some Aristotelian sense) so that schemes for political improvement should not rest on a utopian 'reformation of the manners of mankind' but on the experience of those rules that best serve men's more or less permanent needs. Thus men can recognize, and develop, certain necessary rules of justice and property which are to their advantage. They may be unduly partial to their own interests but they are not so egoistic that they have to be restrained by an absolute sovereign. Hence, conservatism proposes a combination of liberty and authority and a 'mixed constitution' in which rules constrain political actors.

English conservatives propose an organic, rather than a contractarian, conception of society. A social order is a kind of living organism which has not been constructed by artifice and reason but has grown and developed by natural processes. It is an implication of this organicism that a social order in its entirety cannot be comprehended by any one person. The injunction against an interference with this order, even when reason may dictate intervention on grounds, say, of utility, is that the consequences of such action cannot be foreseen. This does not prohibit all reform but is meant to remind us of the fact that a social organism is a delicate entity which cannot stand the strain of a disruptive reformism.

Perhaps the most important feature of an evolving social organism is the English common law. English conservatives have tended to be distrustful of codified law, largely as a consequence of their anti-rationalism. They maintain that the human mind is too feeble an instrument to design a comprehensive set of rules for all circumstances. The common law, because it evolves in a case-by-case manner, will, it is claimed, generate a more complex system than would statute. Many conservatives therefore hold that the common law has a validity independent of the sovereign's command. This was certainly the position of the great judge Coke who held that the common law embodied 'right reason' and could not be overridden by statute.

However, in English legal history, the common law has proved to be an inefficient protector of traditional liberties precisely because it is subordinate to statute. Since English conservatives also believe in the sovereignty of parliament, this has produced an unresolved tension in their legal philosophy.

Property is a crucial element in conservative thought. Although private property is valued both as a right and as a source of independence from the state, its possession (even when legitimate) is never unconstrained. Property has duties as well as rights. This might involve constraints on its free use in order to conserve the national heritage or to redistribute to the poor. Thus property is not a concept descriptive only of the propertied class: it is an institution that benefits society as a whole.

It is for this reason that social justice, as a positive policy of government, has been consistently opposed by conservatives. It is an obligation of the state to preserve order and enforce rules of natural justice but it is not its business to redistribute income and wealth according to some abstract ethical scheme. Not only are such schemes condemnable by conservatism's anti-rationalism, but also they are likely to set in train social divisions based on envy. Societies develop natural hierarchies (inequality is the natural order of things) and egalitarianism is disruptive of the stability these create.

There is some ambiguity about the role of the state in English conservative thought. This has led to at least two varieties of traditionalism: one that limits the state's actions to the enforcement of law and the other more paternalistic that envisages the state having a specific welfare role or at least some moral and political responsibility for the poorest sections of the community. Almost all varieties of conservatism claim Burke as their source but, on this issue at least, he was firmly in favour of a very limited state. In his *Thoughts and Details on Scarcity* he espoused a free market economic system and was highly sceptical of the state's provision of welfare.

Nevertheless, from Disraeli onwards there has been a strong strand in conservative thought that repudiates *laissez-faire*. An untrammelled competitive individualism is held to be destructive of the organic unity of society, and incapable of generating those bonds of allegiance and affection on which, it is argued, continuity and stability depend. In nineteenth-century British history the Conservative Party initiated many social welfare reforms. It was opposed to the commercial philosophy of the Liberal Party not merely because of its close association with the landed interest but also because it believed that *laissez-faire* economics was destructive of national unity. However, the collapse of the old Liberal Party and the rise of socialism has meant that in practice the Conservative Party has absorbed the business community. This tension between the claims of individualism and those of paternalism is present in contemporary Conservative politics in Britain.

Of contemporary conservative philosophers, Oakeshott is the most prominent: although it should be stressed that his thought is disassociated from any sort of ideology. Nevertheless, it evinces just that anti-rationalism and scepticism which is a feature of the English conservative tradition. In his view the error of the twentieth century is the replacement of traditional politics by the politics of 'technique'. His brand of anti-rationalism depends on a distinction between two forms of knowledge: practical knowledge and technical knowledge. Practical knowledge is knowledge of how to do things and is acquired by experience and practical activity rather than by specific instruction. Technical, or engineering, knowledge is precisely that knowledge which can be explicitly formulated. Politics is a practical activity and therefore should be guided by experience rather than reason. Along with many English conservatives, Oakeshott insists that we should not expect too much of politics as a method for bringing about social improvement. It should be limited to 'attending to the arrangements' of a society and making the necessary adjustments to existing rules and institutions, rather than improving schemes derived from abstract principles on a traditional order.

Nevertheless, Oakeshott undoubtedly favours a particular order, which he calls a civil association. This is an order governed by a body of general abstract rules which have no specific purpose or social goal. It is within such arrangements that individuals can pursue their private activities. This idea of civil association has much in common with the classical liberals' concept of the rule of law; and indeed Oakeshott's conservatism is much nearer to individualism than is often supposed.

Scruton's influential *The Meaning of Conservatism*, however, expresses a more authoritarian traditionalism. Although he is hostile to the expansion of the modern collectivist state, Scruton displays a reverence for order and hierarchy that has anti-individualistic overtones. Indeed, much of his fire is directed towards that rationalistic liberalism which supposes that legitimate political institutions are a product of autonomous individual choice. Given Scruton's emphasis on order, and the necessity of a strong state to enforce it, there are few theoretical limitations on the authority of government.

Although classical liberalism and English conservatism have many common features, especially their hostility to collectivism, there are some important theoretical differences. The most important concerns individualism. The classical liberal tends to start political discourse from the inviolable sovereignty of the individual and political institutions are legitimate to the extent that they respect that individuality. Often this ethic is grounded in a universalistic theory of natural rights. While the English conservative is by no means averse to individualism, order is normally thought to be a prior condition for any expression of personal liberty. Certainly, all conservatives reject the notion of natural rights; this is simply a rationalistic error.

This critical attitude towards abstract individualism finds more practical expression in conservative affection for concrete groups within society. This was a prominent feature of Burke's politics. However, in the modern world this has often led to the granting of privilege to favoured groups. The protection that Conservative governments have almost always given the agricultural interest is a spectacular example of this. Nothing could be more alien to free trade classical liberalism than agricultural tariffs.

The conservative attitude to the market is ambiguous. On the one hand it is admired for its efficiency and liberty-enhancing properties: a completely collectivized economy is anathema to all traditions of conservatism. But on the other, conservatives have always distrusted the 'economism' that appears in much of the more extreme market philosophies. To a conservative, a stable society presupposes the existence of rules and conventions that cannot be explained in transactional terms. A society is held together by the less tangible bonds of affection and loyalty. Furthermore, for the traditional conservative, the state is more than an artifice for the production of public goods but is the primary institutional representative of a society's law and morality. It is this that justifies, for example, a more extensive extra-market welfare system than would be acceptable to pure market theorists.

NB

Further reading

Burke, E., *Reflections on the Revolution in France*, Harmondsworth, Penguin, 1968.
Greenleaf, W.H., *The British Political Tradition*, Vol. II, *The Ideological Heritage*, London, Methuen, 1983.
Nisbet, R., *Conservatism: Dream and Reality*, Milton Keynes, Open University Press, 1986.
Oakeshott, M., *Rationalism in Politics and Other Essays*, London, Methuen, 1962.
Quinton, A., *The Politics of Imperfection*, London, Faber & Faber, 1978.
Scruton, R., *The Meaning of Conservatism*, London, Macmillan, 2nd edition, 1984.

C

CAPITALISM

Capitalism is a form of economic organization in which the means of production are in private hands and individuals are free to sell their labour at a price determined by an impersonal market. The goods and services that are produced reflect the desires of consumers (who are assumed to be autonomous) and producers are motivated to satisfy those by the prospect of a positive return on their investment. *Laissez-faire* is associated with capitalism in the sense that under it little or no state intervention is permitted to modify the outcomes of a competitive process. A capitalist system has three factors of production: capital, labour, and land. Capital consists of funds which (when invested) earn interest; labour earns a wage equal to its marginal product; land earns a rental income determined by its scarcity value. Entrepreneurship, although a crucial feature of a capitalist market system, has always been difficult to classify in economics. In theory it is sensitivity to a profitable opportunity (i.e. a price differential), and successful entrepreneurship does not depend upon the ownership of capital. The reward for entrepreneurship is profit; which is not the same as the interest paid to capital.

A capitalist society is sometimes described in terms of three 'classes': landlords, capitalists, and workers. But this is grossly misleading. For example, workers do not merely have their labour to sell: they own 'capital' in the form of houses, insurance policies, personal savings, and so on. In many small businesses, the 'owners' may earn little more than a 'wage'.

In economics, the theory of capital is particularly difficult and obscure. It was developed by the Austrian school, in particular in the economics of Boehm-Bawerk. He showed that capital, as a factor of production, was productive, i.e. the return on capital invested was not reducible to the value of labour inputs. Capital is in essence 'time'. Since it takes time to bring goods to final consumption stage, individuals must refrain from consumption in order to make available funds for investment. Capitalism therefore involves 'roundabout' methods of production: techniques that necessitate 'waiting' but which will generate a greater supply of consumer goods in the long run. In a theoretical sense, then, all economic systems which generate a surplus above mere subsistence, a surplus which is then invested, will display capitalistic features whatever their forms of ownership.

Although the conventional capitalist system is associated with a particular 'stage' or period of economic development (normally post-feudal), capitalistic forms of economy are present in all periods of history. Private ownership and elementary forms of commerce existed in the ancient world and in the Middle Ages. In America capitalism developed spontaneously and did not emerge from a feudal period: it was a product of freedom and limited government rather than some historical process. There are also many forms of capitalism: including commercial and financial capitalism (where the instruments of credit and finance are in private hands), industrial capitalism (characterized by private ownership of large-scale factory enterprises with a well-developed division of labour), and state and welfare capitalism in which government intervenes extensively in the market.

The form most familiar to sociologists and economists is industrial capitalism. This developed first in Britain at the end of the eighteenth century; significantly, it was not the kind of society Adam Smith was writing about in *The Wealth of Nations*. Although at one time economic historians argued that the rise of industrial capitalism brought poverty and urban squalor to the masses, the evidence that it brought a steady improvement in the living standards of the working classes is now overwhelming.

Nevertheless, Marx's description and critique of industrial capitalism remains the source of contemporary criticism of the private enterprise market economy. However, Marx rarely talked about capitalism as such, preferring to dissect the role of capital in the market system. Still, even non-Marxists talk in categories used by Marx in his account of the development of economic systems.

For Marx, the capitalist mode of production has to be understood historically: the laws of market economics are not inferences from universally true propositions about the human condition but are meaningful only in the context of particular historical categories. The point of political economy is to uncover the historical laws that explain the transition from one mode of production to another. Thus capitalism emerges out of feudalism when the social structure of the latter, with its limitations on private ownership, free movement of labour, commercial transactions, and so on, can no longer withstand the pressure of technological development, notably the extension of the division of labour and the growth of factory organization.

Capitalism is depicted as a society divided into classes based on ownership. Capitalists own the means of production and workers have only their labour power to sell. Capital (consisting of the instruments of production) is unproductive: it consists essentially of 'stored up' labour. The capitalist therefore secures 'profit' by extracting surplus value from the worker. The wage paid to labour was said to be equal to the value of the labour time needed to produce subsistence requirements (plus the cost of training workers). However, the value created by labour exceeded this, thus generating a surplus which was expropriated by the capitalist. Wage payments constituted 'variable' capital; raw materials, plant, and equipment constituted 'constant' capital. As the proportion of constant capital increased the rate of profit fell and increasing capitalist concentration created a 'reserve army of unemployed'; this pushed wages towards subsistence. Nevertheless, Marx lavished considerable praise on the capitalist system for its productive powers: indeed the assumption was that it would bequeath a world of abundance for a future socialist order.

Marx's prophecies about the future of capitalism have not materialized. Liberal critics have always argued that since capital is itself productive the return paid to its owners is a reward for abstaining from consumption and not therefore the exploitation of labour. The increased productivity brought about by capitalism increases the demand for labour so that unemployment is not the inevitable result of the competitive process but more likely the result of labour unions keeping the price of labour above its market-clearing price.

Other commentators on capitalism have claimed that, although it may not collapse in the way that Marx prophesied, it still shows a tendency to develop away from the competitive model described in *laissez-faire* theory. Thus the growth of large-scale enterprises is said to lead to 'monopoly capitalism': a phenomenon in which certain industries, because of 'increasing returns to scale', become virtually exempt from competition. Even a critic nominally friendly to liberalism, Joseph Schumpeter, argued that the bureaucratic organization of modern industry was such that it differed little from central planning: socialism would in fact come about peacefully through the demise of the small-scale producer.

Liberals have always denied that capitalism spontaneously develops in the way critics have suggested. They have disputed the alleged 'welfare loss' due to monopoly that is claimed. Unless a monopolist has been granted a privilege by the state (which is in fact the origin of most monopolies) he or she is always subject to competitive pressure as his or her monopoly profits rise. Liberals also dispute the proportion of the output of a modern free enterprise economy that is produced by large enterprises. In all western economies the vast majority of workers are employed in traditional small enterprises. Indeed, it is argued that much of contemporary technological innovation comes from these rather than from large corporations (despite their expensive research departments).

Another common non-Marxist criticism of capitalism is that its development is subject to recurring bouts of prosperity and depression (trade cycles). The most spectacular depression was the great contraction of the 1930s when output and employment plummeted in all western economies, especially that of United States. Keynes argued that unregulated capitalism would generate demand deficiency which causes widespread involuntary unemployment. This could only be cured by high government spending. Western economies, with the notable exception of West Germany, were regulated by such methods during much of the post-war period.

Liberal economists have always been anti-Keynesian. In their view the crises of capitalism are brought about by exogenous factors, mainly the government's control of the supply of money. In Milton Friedman's view, the American Great Depression was caused by a massive fall in the money supply, engineered mistakenly by the Federal Reserve Board. In the liberal view, a capitalist economy is self-regulating through the price mechanism if money is more or less stable. This stability is best brought about by the Gold Standard, or some monetary rule which is immune to political pressure. In the post-war years the major dislocations in the capitalist system have been brought about by inflation: this has been the consequence of Keynesian attempts to manage the economy by manipulating demand.

In the liberal world-view capitalism emerges naturally from the interactions of individuals: in an important sense, all societies that permit exchange are capitalistic. It is the economic order most consistent with freedom, not only in the trivial sense that exchange is itself an expression of liberty, but also in the sense that it allows centres of economic independence of the state to develop. It is also the economic system most consonant with democracy, since choice in politics is the natural counterpart to choice in economics. However, in recent years liberal public choice economists (especially Buchanan and Tullock) have been critical of the effect that unrestrained majority rule has on economic freedom.

Traditional conservatives have always had a more sceptical view of capitalism. Conservatism preceded the rise of capitalist economic institutions and these should always be subordinate to the interests of society. An unrestrained pursuit of profit is not necessarily regarded as socially virtuous and conservatives have always had a paternal attitude towards those who may appear to be the victims of egoistic economic competition. For nationalistic reasons conservatives have been critical of unrestricted international trade. In Britain especially, conservatives have been associated historically with the landed interest. Indeed, in the nineteenth century the divisions in British society were between land and commerce rather than between capital and labour. Although it was a Conservative government that repealed the Corn Laws, agricultural protection has always been the linchpin of conservative economic policy.

In the twentieth century, however, nominal liberal parties have ceased to be parties of capitalism. Since the rise of socialism commercial interests have unavoidably become associated with conservatism. But conservatives were for a long time associated with Keynesian 'managed capitalism' and its social counterpart, 'welfare capitalism'. Genuine intellectual supporters of capitalism, such as Hayek, have hoped to influence opinion rather than political parties in the attempt to maintain the viability of capitalism.

Although conservatives in the west have recently adopted the new philosophy of capitalism espoused by Hayek and Friedman, there is one important reason why this association is likely to be tactical rather than intellectual. A capitalist society is subject to constant change, fortunes rise and fall according to the vagaries of the market, and individuals appear to be held together only by the price nexus. The traditional conservative conception of society as an ordered hierarchy, which the state has an obligation to maintain, sometimes conflicts with the openness and mobility of a capitalist order. The conservative view of social order, then, has something in common with socialism; it is just as eager to condemn the capitalist system for its alleged anonymity and its creation of anomic individuals. It is for this reason, perhaps, that conservatives have acquiesced in the twentieth-century regulation of capitalism by the state.

NB

Further reading

Boehm-Bawerk, E., *Shorter Classics of Eugen Boehm-Bawerk*, Illinois, Libertarian Press, 1962.
Friedman, M., *Capitalism and Freedom*, Chicago, IL, University of Chicago Press, 1962.
Hayek, F.A., *Capitalism and the Historians*, London, Routledge & Kegan Paul, 1954.

CATHOLICISM

The word 'Catholicism' is most commonly construed as referring exclusively to the teachings of the Roman Catholic Church and the practices of those obedient to that teaching. But in another and equally religious sense it embraces all those committed to belief in the Nicene and Athanasian Creeds. The Roman Catholic Church may reasonably be regarded as being, with the Holy Roman Empire which was finally disbanded only during the Napoleonic Wars, one of the two great successor organizations to the original Roman Empire; which once included the entire world of western civilization. Like that empire, this church both makes claims to universality and is authoritarian in its direction. Its head, the Pope, is the

Bishop of Rome – claiming succession in an unbroken line from St Peter: 'Thou art Peter, and upon this rock I will found my Church.'

As members, Catholics are normally expected to accept all of – or at any rate not to deny any of – the everyday teachings of its ministers. But within this broad and not very precisely limited range of teachings there are some doctrines which have been authoritatively defined by one of the councils of the church, occasionally and very rarely summoned, usually in order to settle once and for all some controversial matter. Such definitions standardly begin (in Latin) 'If anyone shall say' and end 'let them be anathema'. To be thus anathematized is to be cast out of the body of the church.

The formidable significance of such pronouncements may well escape those whose knowledge of this church has been confined to the period since the Second Vatican Council. It can be appreciated only when we have grasped the full import of the fundamental claim *extra ecclesiam nulla salus* (outside the church – and what is meant is precisely and only this particular church – there is no safety). When, as so often, the Latin *salus* is rendered as salvation, and the promised saving is thought to be emancipation from the sins themselves; then the promise is one which, however deplorably, will possess little appeal to most case-hardened sinners. But it is another thing altogether when the *salus* is clearly and correctly seen as security against the inconceivably appalling threat of damnation to a literal eternity of excruciating torment, as punishment for those sins.

Ever since the politically motivated and perhaps never quite categorically completed conversion of the Emperor Constantine, the Roman Catholic Church has tried to reach accommodations with established sovereignties on the basis of some sort of separation of spiritual from temporal power. Whenever, and in so far as it has succeeded, the result has been to make possible the maintenance of a major institution separate from and to some degree independent of the state machine. How important this may be can be seen by comparing the Imperial and post-Imperial history of China with that of western Europe, or the experience of Poland since the Second World War with that of other countries in the socialist bloc.

This desire to reach such accommodations with established sovereignties as will ensure respect and protection for the operations of the church in what it considers to be its own proper sphere has until very recently resulted in a tendency to take the politically conservative side, though sometimes this has been only in the strictly relativistic sense in which General Secretary Gorbachev's Stalinist opponents have been described by the western media as conservatives.

In the nineteenth century there were noisy and well-publicized conflicts with and denunciations of liberalism. To understand these we need to remember that in the Latin countries at that time most liberals were staunchly anti-clerical, if not actual unbelievers; while the liberal leadership was often closely involved in the Continental kind of Free-masonry. Also it was the period of unification of Italy, which involved the understandably resented incorporation of the former Papal States.

In our century the Second Vatican Council marks a great divide. At least to outsiders it would seem that its intended rethinkings and modest relaxations have since run out of control, resulting in a widespread and progressive protestantization and even secularization. Certainly many of those still pretending to a Catholic obedience now consider themselves licensed either to pick out for their personal credence, or flatly to reject, items from the traditional deposit of faith, not excluding from their repudiations even items of defined dogma.

There have been substantial changes also in the typical political and social alignments. Whereas for the first forty or more years after the Bolsheviks seized state power the Roman Catholic Church could be relied on to oppose what its spokesmen then always characterized as 'atheistic Communism', today even in the encyclicals of the Polish pope there is at least a hint of 'moral equivalence' between the Leninist regimes and their main opponents. At lower levels it is possible to find – indeed sometimes difficult to avoid – priests who proudly proclaim themselves to be Marxists; and even one or two religious orders which seem to be devoting most of their energies to undermining western defence and supporting various Leninist movements.

There is also the phenomenon of Liberation Theology, strong mainly but not only in some Third World Latin countries. Its proponents claim to be inspired by concern for the poor and the oppressed, and to have become for this reason ready to align with militant Marxist revolutionaries. These claims – which it would be easier to accept at face value if only the proponents were prepared to extend their professed concern to include those oppressed and impoverished by Leninist masters – are, of course, rejected by opponents. They are inclined to put down the whole movement as a misnamed mishmash, having no more to do with God than it does with liberty.

In First World countries, conferences of their Roman Catholic bishops nowadays issue social and political statements which are in tone and substance virtually indistinguishable from those flowing from the main-stream Protestant churches. All support similarly interventionist and compulsorily redistributive proposals, urged in the name of social justice. But Roman Catholics at least should here remember that the economic ideas of classical liberalism were first developed in the sixteenth century by the late scholastics of the School of Salamanca. And these thinkers showed in particular that just prices are not to be determined by hypothetical or actual committees of the wise and good. The just price of anything, including labour, can only be the price which emerges in a competitive market, under standard conditions.

AF

Further reading

Chafuen, A.A., *Christians for Freedom: Late Scholastic Economics*, San Francisco, CA, Ignatius, 1986.
Flew, R.N., and R.E. Davies (eds), *The Catholicity of Protestantism*, London, Epworth, 1959.
McDonald, W.J. (ed.), *New Catholic Encyclopaedia*, New York, McGraw-Hill, 1967.
Novak, M., *Freedom with Justice: Catholic Social Thought and Liberal Institutions*, San Francisco, CA, Harper & Row, 1984.
Novak, M., *Will it Liberate? Questions about Liberation Theology*, New York, Paulist Press, 1987.

CHICAGO SCHOOL

The Chicago School of economics has been a centre of a distinctively free market brand of economics since the 1930s. By no means a monolithic group, on the contrary the Chicago School can best be thought of as a set of influential economists who have been associated with the University of Chicago.

Knight, one of the dominant members of the Chicago Economics Department from the 1930s, stressed the importance of a philosophical grasp of economic principles as opposed to concentration on technicalities. The interests of groups in society necessarily were in partial conflict. Thus, doctrines such as Marxism that believed in the coming of a totally harmonious social order were grievously in error. Attempting to put them into practice would only cause harm.

In Knight's view the market economy was not a panacea that would ensure everyone's happiness. On the contrary, the great advantage of a free market economy was that it recognized the limits of social knowledge. Socialism and kindred systems believe that planning of society is possible. This grossly overrates the amount of knowledge of the workings of society that is available. Capitalism thus is desirable because it works 'less badly' than other systems uncognizant of the barriers to knowledge.

Knight's scepticism about knowledge extended to ethics. Natural law, especially in its neo-scholastic variety, falsely claimed that objective truth was possible in ethics. In Knight's opinion, value was a purely subjective affair. All that there is to value is the preferences of various people. This position, Knight contended, does not lead to a chaos of conflicting claims. Consensus offers a way out: social institutions should be designed to facilitate agreement among people with clashing desires. Knight's advocacy of consensus exerted a strong influence on his student Buchanan, the 1986 Nobel Laureate in Economics. This influence is reflected in Buchanan's work on constitutional agreements.

Knight's work was also marked by two themes characteristic of later Chicago School members. As one might expect from his criticism of natural rights, Knight did not support a pure policy of *laissez-faire* capitalism. Free enterprise economics was a valuable social instrument, no more but no less. His refusal to endorse complete *laissez-faire* by no means made him sympathetic to Keynesian policies. The basic principles of economics survived Keynesian criticism unscathed, and economists knew how to cope with the business cycle, to the extent this was possible, long before Keynes's *General Theory of Employment, Interest, and Money* (1936).

The positions espoused by the school's most famous contemporary figure, Milton Friedman, show strong similarities with Knight's views. Like Knight, Friedman does not appeal to natural rights in his defence of capitalism. He thinks that almost everyone agrees on the ends of social policy, e.g. freedom and prosperity. The question then becomes: how can these ends best be attained? This is a factual, not a moral issue.

For Friedman, the answer lies almost always in the operation of the free market. Wage laws do not promote the welfare of workers but cause unemployment. Medical licensing promotes monopolistic pricing in the medical profession; and so on, through scores of popular nostrums for the market's alleged failings. Friedman is much more concrete and much less philosophically inclined than Knight. He offers many more examples of his views and possesses far more confidence in the ability of a correct social policy to create a good society. He does not emphasize conflict among groups in the fashion of Knight.

Again like Knight, Friedman has been quite sceptical about Keynesian economics. He doubts the ability of government policy-makers to 'fine-tune' the economy according to Keynesian prescriptions. Instead, he supports a constant expansion of the money supply according to a fixed rule.

Another characteristic of Chicago economics appeals much more to classical liberals than to conservatives. For many members of the school, economics cannot be narrowly limited to the 'wealth of nations'. Instead, almost all of life is in this view capable of economic analysis. Becker has aroused some notoriety for his *Treatise on the Family*, which argues that people's decisions to marry, have children, etc., can be explained by the use of the principles of economic rationality. Crudely put, one will have another child if it 'pays' to do so. A natural objection is that many people do not think in these categories.

The Chicagoans, aware of this response, here call into action another basic principle of their approach. The aim of economics is to explain behaviour. Whether it uses 'realistic' hypotheses in doing so is of secondary significance. Thus, whether people think in the terms Becker's model uses counts for nothing, so long as the model does the job. This principle of method was advanced by Friedman in his influential 'An essay on the methodology of positive economics'.

Posner has developed a Chicago model of law. He maintains that the legal system is a means by which national income can be brought to its maximum possible level. Legal and social customs which often appear irrational are in fact reasonable, given the aim Posner imputes to the system. On Posner's analysis, for example, Blackstone comes out far more rational than Bentham. Posner, now a US federal judge, has a chance to have his views incorporated into the United State's legal system.

DG

Further reading

Becker, G., *A Treatise on the Family*, Cambridge, MA, Harvard University Press, 1981.
Friedman, M. and R., *Free to Choose*, Harmondsworth, Penguin, 1986.
Knight, F., *The Ethics of Competition*, Chicago, IL, Chicago University Press, 1946.

CITY

The growth of the sort of cities crucial to the rise of western civilization seems to have occurred first on the shores of the Mediterranean. These cities, populated by Phoenicians or Greeks, depended upon trade and the production of commodities in which to trade. The development of the extended market order relating all these cities through the multiple and various transactions between their citizens presupposes, of course, the institution of private or – better – several property. That in turn presupposes law in the sense of abstract rules enabling any individual to ascertain at any time who is entitled to dispose of any particular thing. The further necessary connection between property and liberty also seems to have been recognized early. Strabo, a Greek geographer of the first century AD, tells us that the constitution of ancient Crete 'took it for granted that liberty is a state's highest good and for this reason alone makes property belong specifically to those who acquire it, whereas in a condition of slavery everything belongs to the rulers'. And, from the period in the high Middle Ages when some commercial cities first began to emancipate themselves from federal overlords, it became proverbial wisdom that *Stadtluft macht frei* (city air makes free).

Such a development of more or less sovereign and independent commercial cities seems never to have been paralleled outside Europe. To be sure that their accounts of the rise of modern science are correct, historians need to be able to show that, and how, these can be extended to explain why, despite China's then technological superiority, this scientific development did not occur there. It is similarly necessary to explain why such commercial cities never arose in China. Presumably the answer must lie somewhere in the facts that China was, while Europe was not, a unified and bureaucratically centralized empire; and that – *pace* the Marxists – it was not during the relevant period, or ever, feudal.

It was in Miletus, one of these Greek commerical cities on the Mediterranean coast of what is now Turkey, that Thales, Anaximander, and Anaximines began the first wholly secular cosmological speculations. It was Pythagoras, first of Samos and afterwards of Sicilian Croton, who, however obscurely, first glimpsed the Galilean truth that 'the book of nature is written in the language of mathematics'. And then, a little later, it was in Athens that almost everything else began.

Thucydides, composing his *History of the Peloponnesian War* in exile after the end of his unsuccessful career as an Athenian general, had no doubts about the preconditions on such development. People 'without commerce, without freedom of communication either by land or sea, cultivating no more of their territory than the exigencies of life required, could never rise above nomadic life' and, consequently, 'neither built large cities nor attained to any other form of greatness'.

In the subsequent century both the Athenian Plato and Aristotle the resident alien propounded their political ideals; their ideals, that is, for the (Greek) city state or *polis*. For both, small alone was beautiful, and both shared an aristocratic contempt and distaste for trade; the trade which was the economic basis for the cultural and political greatness of Athens. These two may, therefore, be seen as founding fathers of a long and evergreen tradition – the alienation of the intellectuals from capitalism and the market order, and the contempt of academics for all those banausic commercial and industrial activities which make possible their own supposedly and self-consciously elevated and spiritual lifestyle.

By constrast, in the eighteenth century it was easy to find intellectuals who were friends not only of the city but also of commerce. Some of Hume's most powerful essays were written to support free trade, while he always insisted that the proper scene 'for a man of letters' was 'the city' – in his case, in particular, Edinburgh. Dr Johnson, too, remarked both that people are seldom so innocently employed as when making money and that anyone who is tired of London must be tired of life.

Once a greater and greater proportion of ever rising populations began to live and work in cities, more and more of which were becoming larger than any had ever been before, a reaction began. You could then hear what had often been heard in ancient Rome – the one mega-city of the classical world – expressions of individual longing for permanent retirement to rural retreats. In the late nineteenth century these coalesced into Ebenezer Howard's Garden City movement. Especially between the wars of the twentieth century, and in those countries of central and eastern Europe which were then permitted a brief period of more or less emancipated political life, the major popular parties usually claimed to represent peasant or agrarian interests; a development which would presumably be paralleled in sub-Saharan Africa if only the grip there of the monopoly ruling parties of the new (Leninist) type were ever to be broken.

Since the 1961 publication of Jacob's *The Death and the Life of Great American Cities* there has been a general counter-offensive against such long-term consequences of the Garden City movement as the separation of different activities into discrete and exclusive areas, doctrinaire decongestion, and other features of the conventional wisdom of town planners. She deployed masses of evidence about low-density public housing to which no one will move save under compulsion, and where under every accepted statistical index of welfare residents are worse off than people still living in unplanned, naturally grown, high-density city centres. As Johnson once remarked to Boswell, 'Men, thinly scattered make a shift, but a bad shift, without many things. . . . It is being concentrated which produces convenience'.

AF

Further reading

Arkes, H., *The Philosopher in the City: The Moral Dimension of Urban Politics*, Princeton, NJ, Princeton University Press, 1981.
Banfield, E., *The Unheavenly City Revisited*, Boston, MA, Little Brown, 1974.
Coleman, A., *Utopia on Trial: Vision and Reality in Planned Housing*, London, Shipman, 1985.
Hayek, F.A. *The Fatal Conceit: The Errors of Socialism*, Chicago, IL, and London, Chicago University Press and Routledge, 1989.
Jacobs, J. *The Death and Life of Great American Cities*, London and New York, Random House and Cape, 1961/2.

CLASS

For the classical liberal, and even more for the libertarian, a class is simply a category, an aggregate of individuals sharing a common market position. Classes are open both in the sense that they have no clear or obvious boundaries and in that the arbitrary category boundaries used by the social observer or market researcher are permeable. Individuals can move up or down from one class to another as they make use or fail to make use of the opportunities the market-place offers for acquiring income, wealth, skills, or qualifications. Income, wealth and, to a large extent, skill and qualification are continuous variables and any boundaries that we choose to draw between classes are merely lines that arbitrarily separate individuals who differ incrementally in their market position no more than they do from adjacent individuals on the same side of the boundary and thus within the same class category.

Such a view of classes is for the liberal both an ideal and a reasonable working description of actual market-based societies in which there are no legal or strong customary boundaries between classes resulting in restrictions on choice of occupation or acquisition of property. For the liberal there is no reason why classes should have any sense of unity, or of shared interests, or possess a common consciousness. If they do, this is because individual liberty and the workings of the free market have been thwarted so that individual achievement and mobility are blocked by legal regulation or strong social convention or because their members have been falsely persuaded that this is the case.

The traditional conservative view of class is much more clearly hierarchical. Classes are seen as having clear boundaries and the members of a particular class have distinctive, clearly recognized rights, privileges, and responsibilities. Social mobility is possible and necessary but is also viewed with suspicion, and a degree of closure involving denial of entry may be seen as justified. Such conservatives have ambivalent and even hostile feelings towards what they see as the anarchy of the market-place. Excessive competition is perceived as disruptive of social order and excessive individualism as the underminer of social solidarity. Individuals who seek to enter the highest strata of a society on the basis of newly acquired market power are feared and excluded because they lack the values, attitudes, and way of life of the established members of that class. The conservative members of such classes would prefer to sponsor and thus to control the upward movement of able and successful members from lower down the hierarchy rather than to leave it to an unregulated contest of the kind favoured by classical liberals. Classes are for the traditional conservative not mere economic aggregates but relatively cohesive social units necessary to the maintenance of social order. Those who enjoy the privilege of belonging to the classes at the top of the hierarchies of wealth and of status are expected to play a major role in the governing of their society and in the maintenance of order, stability, and continuity. At times this may mean that individuals are required not to pursue their self-interest to its full extent but to behave paternalistically so as to retain the co-operation of the members of the other classes in what they see as an integrated and cohesive social order.

Both these views of what classes are and ought to be differ markedly from Marxist or socialist concepts. The latter see classes primarily as economic groups and as in a state of endemic conflict. In its crudest version society is seen as divided into two decisively separate and conflicting classes: those who own the crucial means of production (taken to be land in an agrarian feudal society and capital in an industrial capitalist society) and those who have only their labour with which to earn a living. All the other institutions of a society – political, legal, religious, familial – are an epiphenomenal superstructure whose nature is very largely determined by this single basic economic divide. The liberal view of society as consisting of free mobile competing individuals is portrayed as a delusion since the propertyless proletarians are trapped in a situation of such individual powerlessness that they can only improve their lot by collective action aimed at the overthrow of the capitalist system. This is then said to be a decisive step towards the establishment of a mystical form of pie on earth called communism whose nature and problems are only discussed in an extremely sketchy manner. It is hardly surprising that Marxists have failed to provide a coherent and convincing account of the classes and conflicts between classes that exist in the socialist countries of Eastern Europe and East Asia, partly because their concept of what constitutes a class is too narrow. Their obsession with the impending though frequently postponed demise of a social order prevents them from grappling effectively with the very real questions that divide the liberals from the traditional conservatives. Why is it that societies in the main do cohere and continue? How are the diverse efforts and aspirations of unequal individuals co-ordinated to produce social and economic change and progress?

The conflict between classes defined in economic terms lies at the heart of Marx's systematic analyses of the patterns of change of the past and predictions for the future. Much of subsequent Marxist thought consists of special pleading aimed at explaining away the failure of his predictions and historical trends that do not fit his pattern. Both classical liberals and conservatives have played a major role in the intellectual destruction of the Marxist system but their consequent distrust of historicism and of large-scale model-building has in recent years tended to inhibit them from creating rival dynamic systems of social change rooted in their own distinctive views of the nature of class.

This is a pity because they could have built on the foundations laid by their nineteenth-century predecessors. The best of these cannot be easily classed either as classical liberals or as conservatives. Rather they confronted the tensions between stability and change and between individualism and social cohesion and, knowing that these are irresolvable but not necessarily destructive, used them as a guide to the complex and shifting patterns of interaction between the members of different social classes.

Class necessarily plays a smaller part in the social thought of liberals and of conservatives than in that of their socialist opponents. For the conservative it is but one kind of social unit among many and the complex mixture of co-operation, competition, coexistence, and conflict that makes up social life is to be explained by reference to the activities of national, ethnic, religious, and political groups as well as social classes. For the liberal there are no laws of history, only the laws of the market-place which inexorably regulate the interactions of individuals, however much they try to avoid their consequences by collective action based on a false consciousness of a common class interest.

CD

Further reading

Davis, K. and W. Moore, 'Some principles of stratification', *American Sociological Review*, 1945, 10(2): 242–9.
De Tocqueville, A., *Democracy in America*, Garden City, NY, Doubleday, 1969.
Lipset, S.M. and R. Bendix, *Social Mobility in Industrial Society*, Berkeley, CA, University of California Press, 1966.
Mosca, G., *The Ruling Class*, New York, McGraw Hill, 1939.

COLLECTIVISM

'Collectivism' is defined as the theory and practice which make a collective or collectives rather than individuals the ultimate and fundamental unit of political, social, and economic concern. The term was originally employed to distinguish the kind of anarchistic socialism advocated by Bakunin from the at least initially centralized and statist form promised, or threatened, by Marx and Engels. Collectives for Bakunin were, or would be, associations of individuals. These were not, or would not be, like families, private and natural. Their memberships nevertheless were, or would be, determined at least in part by local associations and involvements. This original narrow sense of 'collectivism', in which collectivists could significantly be distinguished from Marxist socialists, is now obsolete. Perhaps its final appearance, and certainly the most catastrophic, was in the official misdescription of Stalin's agricultural policy as collectivization, rather than as, by merging all privately owned farms into state farms, socialization or nationalization. (The giant farms officially described as state farms were, and are, alleged to be significantly different from the collectives.)

Stalinist collectivization was in truth collectivization in the modern sense, in which social or collective action is construed as action by or under the direction of organizations of the national or local state, and contrasted with actions by individuals acting alone or in voluntary association with other individuals. Although the mainstream churches nowadays constantly demand ever more tax-financed spending upon the state provision of health, education, and welfare services, and appeal to the parable of the Samaritan as their Christian authority for such demands, the Samaritan's conduct was precisely not a paradigm of a collectivist as opposed to an individualist response to human needs. For he bound up the traveller's wounds *with his own hands*, and paid the innkeeper for that traveller's further maintenance *from his own purse*.

Presumably it is on present usage correct to characterize all socialists as being, as such, collectivists: while the nearest approach in our time to any actual realization of Bakunin's ideal of a collective would seem to be the self-managing 'associations of labour' in Yugoslavia, Israeli *kibbutzim*, or the collectives set up by the Spanish anarchists during the Civil War.

Collectivists in theorizing insist that the claims of collectives must, in general and normally, if not always and without exception, override the claims of individual members. What are, surely, remarkable statements of an extreme if slightly covert collectivism are to be found in what is certainly the most discussed work in all the recent literature of political philosophy. Yet this book – even by critics for whom 'liberal' is not a code word for 'social democrat' of 'socialist' – has frequently been praised for presenting a liberal theory of justice. It is also significant of the present pervasive influence of collectivist ideas and assumptions that so many critics seem in their reading of Rawls not to have noticed the implications of such assertions. For in *A Theory of Justice*, although rightly ready to fault all forms of utilitarianism because they do 'not take seriously the distinction between persons', Rawls nevertheless, in explaining and justifying his method, maintains that most if not all such individual differences are 'arbitrary from a moral point of view'.

Thus he says:

> Once we decide to look for a conception of justice that nullifies the accidents of natural endowment and the contingencies of social circumstances as counters in [the] quest for political and economic advantage, we are led to these principles. *They express the result of leaving aside those aspects of the social world that seem arbitrary from a moral point of view.*
>
> (p. 15, emphasis added)

Yet it is and can only be precisely the differences between what different individuals are or are not, and what they have or have not, done or not done which must determine the nature of and differences between their various individual deserts and entitlements; what, that is to say, is justly theirs.

Any hope that Rawls might be intending still to leave room for morally relevant differences of desert or entitlement has to be abandoned when, after arguing that 'the natural distribution of abilities and talents' is the morally arbitrary outcome of a 'natural lottery', he concludes that 'even the willingness to make an effort, to try, and so to be deserving in the ordinary sense is itself dependent upon happy family and social circumstances' (p. 74).

So we ought not to be surprised when, a little later, we read

> that the difference principle represents, in effect, an agreement to regard the distribution of natural talents as a common asset and to share in the benefits of this distribution whatever it turns out to be, those who have been favoured by nature, whoever they are, may gain from their good fortune *only* on terms that improve the situation of those who have lost out'.
>
> (p. 101, emphasis added)

Since, presumably, an argument which thus applies to 'natural talents' must, by parity of reasoning, apply equally both to natural deficiencies and to characteristics which are neither assets nor liabilities, the upshot would appear to be that Rawls is committed to maintaining that every characteristic in respect of which any individual differs from any other individual should be agreed to be, really and ultimately and in every sense, a collective property. It would be difficult to formulate any more extreme kind of collectivism, and that this extreme collectivism is so rarely even noticed, much less challenged, is a formidable index of the current collectivist climate of opinion.

This climate was not formed overnight but came to gradually permeate, to use the favourite expression of one of its leading advocates, every part of intellectual life and all political theory. It is this permeation of all political and philosophical discourse by collectivist assumptions rather than the victory of specific and detailed arguments which accounts for the formidable success of its associated agenda in the modern world.

AF

Further reading

Flew, A.G.N., *The Politics of Procrustes*, Buffalo, NY, and London, Prometheus and Temple Smith, 1981.
Greenleaf, W.E.H., *The British Political Tradition*, Vol.I, *The Rise of Collectivism*, London, Methuen, 1983.
Rawls, J., *A Theory of Justice*, Cambridge, MA, and Oxford, Harvard University Press and Oxford University Press, 1971 and 1972.

COMMUNITY

The word 'community', according to the dictionary, means a feature or quality that is common to or shared by a group of people or, inversely, a group of people having something in common such as place of residence, occupation, religious belief, or ethnicity. However, it is also used, particularly in political discourse, as a reified term so that the group becomes an entity in its own right as in expressions like 'the will of the community'. The question of how far this use of the word is proper and appropriate is the source of much difference between conservatives and classical liberals. They have two very different notions of what a community is and, further, of how important it may be.

The dictionary type of definition given above begs certain key questions. First, can any group of people with a common or shared feature constitute a community? Could people who were tall or blue-eyed constitute a community, for example? The answer must be that in a strict etymological sense one could say so but that in practical political and social analysis such employment of the term would be useless. For an aggregate of people to be a community in the real sense there has to be a common interest deriving from the shared feature; a common social or legal status; the shared feature has to be seen by its holders or others as constituting an important or vital part of their identity. The notion defined this way shares many features with the concept of class, not least the elusiveness of the idea and the importance of subjective identification of and with the community by its members. If that is absent then we may say that objectively there exists a group with common features but it will not form a community in any real sense. Community therefore is both an objective and a cultural phenomenon.

Second, given the importance of subjective identification, how far is membership of a community a matter of choice? Clearly the answer to this question is not fixed. Some communities, e.g. monastic ones, are clearly voluntarist, others much less so. Some types of community are voluntarist in some times and places but not in others or for some groups of people but not all. For instance, in the modern secular west, membership of a religious community is a matter of personal choice but this was not the case in earlier times nor is it the case today for immigrant Muslims or, arguably, for Jews. Membership of an ethnic or racial community is in some senses not a matter of choice.

Third, how has it come about that some shared qualities are constituent of a community and others not? What kinds of factors can make a quality become a defining feature in this way? Fourth, are some kinds of community more important or basic, more inclusive, than others? Lastly, if community is related to identity, can one have an identity outside of a community?

Conservatives and classical liberals give rather different answers to these questions. For conservatives the idea of community is of great importance and it has occupied a prominent place in conservative thought from Burke onwards. It has provided the basis for a hostility to both socialism and liberalism or indeed to modernity in general. Conservatives argue that a society consists of a hierarchy of communities, from the family at the base through ones based on locality and cultural identity to the public community or commonwealth. While allowing for pluralism and overlapping of communities so that, for example, the members of a local community may also belong to several different religious or ethnic communities, many conservatives have thought that such pluralism must be limited and so far as is possible the various subordinate communities should coincide. As the above indicates for conservatives, while there are many forms and types of community, the paramount or pre-eminent one is the political community. While thinkers from Burke onwards have supported the 'small battalions' of family and locality, they have always recognized that these are subordinate to and supportive of the larger political community. A political community is a collection of people who share an allegiance to a common government and political system and, more controversially, a shared culture or way of life based upon language, ethnicity, religion, or some combination of these. Such a community exists as an entity in its own right independent of those individuals who constitute it at any one time. One is normally born into a community and does not chose to be a member of it. A true community in conservative thought is a historical entity, the product of a long process of development and evolution. It is definitely not the outcome of conscious will or action. This is in sharp distinction to the idea, common in classical liberal thought, that a political community is the creation of a mutual contract. For most contemporary conservatives the paradigmatic political community is the nation. This was not always the case, for during the first half of the nineteenth century many continental conservatives, such as Metternich, adhered to the other doctrine which defined the political community strictly in terms of allegiance, usually to a monarch.

This elevated notion of community has important implications for conservative thought. It implies that there are limits to the amount of cultural diversity and freedom of association that may be permissible within a political community; too much and the community will not survive. It is antithetical to individualism. In this way of thinking the individual is not primary and human beings cannot exist or have any real identity outside of a community.

It also leads to a tension between respect for the idea of community and the demands of the market and economic liberalism. This is often overlooked because so many contemporary conservatives are strongly committed to the doctrines of economic liberalism. However, for many conservatives, such as Nisbet, the concept of community leads to a critical view of liberalism and even of modernity in general. They argue that the modern period has seen a decline in true community with the more organic and community-based society of the Middle Ages being replaced by an atomistic social order in which human beings lack the firm identity and security which comes from membership of a community. The political community is undermined by sectionalism and the general individualism so characteristic of modern life. This decline is blamed on several tendencies including the loss of religious faith, the impact of modern technology, and the influence of déclassé intellectuals, but the main blame is put on two factors, the growth of the state and the effects of market forces. This is in the context of a move to a society where an ever increasing part of social life is monetized and governed by the cash nexus rather than other types of social relation such as status, kin, and friendship. This kind of argument is not very common among Anglo-Saxon conservatives because of their support for economic liberalism but it has been very influential on the continent, particularly in

France and Germany. Indeed this analysis derives in great part from the works of continental sociologists, particularly Durkheim, Toennies, and Simmel. For some conservatives such as Maurras it led to a thoroughgoing anti-capitalism. Even in the United States the communitarian approach leads writers such as Nisbet, Kirk, and Weaver to an analysis of contemporary America very similar to that of New Left critics such as Lasch.

Classical liberals take a very different view. Some would agree with most or all of the descriptive and definitive parts of the conservative perspective but then dissent sharply from the evaluation. Others, more radical, would disagree fundamentally and present a different definition of community. The cause of the difference between classical liberals and conservatives on this issue is their opposed view of the individual. For liberals the individual, while a social being, is in some sense primary either ontologically or else in terms of value. Therefore liberals argue that the individual person can exist as an entity outside of a community.

Moreover, liberals from Humboldt and J.S. Mill onwards have feared the capacity of communities to repress the individual through social pressure of one kind or another. The 'close-knit communities' beloved of many conservatives and socialists are seen by liberals in a darker hue as the site of repression, intolerance, and bigotry. They therefore emphasize the importance of pluralism and the need to be able to exit from a community. At the level of practical politics liberals favour policies such as free migration which conservatives oppose because of the threat they pose to the traditional community.

The historical/sociological account of modernity given above is accepted by classical liberals, but instead of bewailing it as a sorry tale they see the move from town to metropolis, from organic to mechanical, and from community to society (*Gemeinschaft* and *Geselschaft*) as being progressive and liberating. The big city, the *bête noire* of conservatives in this connection, is regarded as the place where people can freely associate and express themselves in a way they could not in the closed community of the small town or village. Liberals point out that while conservative intellectuals may sing the praises of community life, all over the world most people are desperate to get out of them and live in the anonymity of the metropolis.

Classical liberals are therefore also often sceptical of the intermediate institutions and communities which conservatives from Burke onwards have lauded as the best defence against oppression. While accepting much of this argument they are also inclined to stress the dangers of these bodies in the possible restrictions they may place upon personal liberty and the extent to which they act as a cover for privilege and power. The more radical classical liberals, from Spencer onwards, have moved on from this to present a quite different definition of community from that offered by the conservatives.

For these thinkers such as Spencer and Heath, the true community is voluntary, its essence being the free association of individuals. They argue further that communities of all kinds are instrumental, that is they exist to serve and meet the ends of their members and do not constitute an end in themselves. There is no question of individuals being instrumental, i.e. existing to serve the ends of the community. The larger public community is not political, i.e. the object of allegiance, but rather a complex of complementary communities, overlapping in membership but with no one type having ultimate precedence and with relations governed by general rules defining procedure. This, strictly understood, implies anarchism or a Nozickian minimal state where the state administrates but does not rule. These thinkers argue that historically the movement is away from closed communities based upon force and status to open communities founded upon trade and contract. The rise of market economy since the Middle Ages is therefore creating a truer, because more voluntary, type of community. Thus the argument of conservatives and socialists that the market system has destroyed community is rebutted by redefining the term and asserting that while one kind of community is being dissolved a better type is replacing it.

These radical liberal arguments were first developed *in extenso* by Spencer in his sociological account of history. They have tended to disappear in much twentieth-century classical liberal writing with some authors, like Roepke, accepting the conservative line *in toto* while others, such as Mises, although critical of the conservatives, do not put forward an alternative model. There were some authors, however, who did extend and elaborate Spencer's ideas, particularly Heath who linked ideas of libertarian community to a sophisticated analysis of the forms and nature of power. In recent years, as 'community' has become *the* buzzword of modern politics, so classical liberals have begun to revive these ideas to defend themselves against assaults from both varieties of collectivism.

The division between classical liberalism and conservatism on this topic has been obscured for much of this century by the domination of political argument by economic issues where the two philosophies broadly agree. As non-economic issues come to the fore things will doubtless change and the question of community will return to the forefront where it was in the last century. The concept of community is at the root of conservative social analysis and is their most powerful weapon against liberalism. It will doubtless therefore see a revival in years to come. The concept is also at the centre of many pressing contemporary political issues, and the way in which it is defined and evaluated has important implications for public policy in a wide range of areas. Among these are such vexed questions as how far economic growth should be pursued if its consequence is to dissolve traditional communities, where and how to draw a line between economic pressures and needs, e.g. for housing and transport, and the wishes of local communities, and what degree of pluralism is possible in a traditional political community.

SD

Further reading

Heath, S., *Citadel, Market and Altar*, Baltimore, MD, Science of Society Foundation, 1957.

Hiskes, R., *Community without Coercion*, Delaware, Delaware University Press, 1982.

Nisbet, R., *The Search for Community*, Oxford and New York, Oxford University Press, 1960.

CONSERVATISM

'Conservatism' may refer either to a political and social attitude, or to a more or less well-defined set of political policies designed to preserve the best of what has been inherited in the light of changing and unanticipated circumstances.

Because of its strong historical sense and interests, conservatism focuses upon particularities, and eschews theory. Thus it seeks the preservation of the literature, institutions, and characteristic ways of thinking and doing that have grown up in a nation or culture, and offers no prescription for change or for national development. As such it often appears quirkly or even irrational to those, socialists and others, who have a theory of how society ought to progress and who are bent on devising means for the attaining of the goal. But to say that the conservative does not have a theory of political development is not to say that he does not have reasons for the stance he takes, though these reasons are often surprisingly difficult to articulate. This in itself leads overt political theorists to be suspicious of the conservative attitude.

The distrust of theory, and the desire to conserve what nourishes and satisfies, is defended by several overlapping arguments. In the first place, a view of human nature which stresses human ignorance, in particular ignorance of the future. Because the future cannot be known, it cannot be planned for, except negatively.

The most striking application of such reasoning is in conservative economic doctrine where it has been argued that no human agency, and certainly not the state, can approach to a satisfactory degree of knowledge the range and change of human preferences in that society, and that the best mechanisms for dispersing such knowledge are the impersonal forces of the market which bring people together solely on the basis of what is demanded and what can be supplied.

Not only are people ignorant of the future, but they are liable to act corruptly. All conservatives have in common this pessimistic view of human nature, based either upon common observation, or on Christian teaching, or both. It has led conservatives to oppose tyranny, whether that of kings and princes or of fascist and socialist dictatorships, and to favour a system of constitutional checks and balances. Under such a system the judiciary is separated from the executive and the legislature, either by explicit constitutional provision, as in the United States, or through the processes of historical growth, of trial and error, and of established precedent, as in the United Kingdom. In the face of modern dictatorships in particular conservatives have held fast on the importance of the rule of law. Law is not the plaything of the government of the day but the government is itself subject to law. Such law is in turn supported either by an appeal to antiquity, or to natural law, or to the law of God.

Paradoxically, perhaps, conservatives have coupled the stress on both ignorance and corruptibility with an emphasis upon the responsibility of the individual for his own actions. This stress is, however, qualified in two respects. Unlike the case with liberalism, individualism is not the dominant conservative motif. But the conservative characteristically stresses that individual duties and responsibilities are intelligible only within a social, or even a socially organic, context.

The fundamental question of political theory concerns the legitimacy of political authority; there are two broad answers, one which stresses the explicit choice of the individual, either mythical (in a 'state of nature') or real. The other, conservative one rejects any social contract approach to political problems, any appeal to a Rawlsian original position, because it supposes that the individual exists prior to any social relations that he or she may enter into. This is criticized by the conservative on both historical and philosophical grounds, most notably by Hegel. (Such an approach is also rejected because it attempts to circumvent the *de facto* character of political life, refusing to start discussion from where we are, and preferring instead to seek inspiration from an ideal but unreal starting point.)

Instead the conservative looks for political legitimation not in any original position and what has transpired there, but in the *de facto* angularities and particularities of existing society, in tradition and convention which are in turn supported by an appeal either to the moral values of Christianity or to natural law and natural rights.

Such an attitude links to what is perhaps the last dominant characteristic of the conservative, that he or she eschews the abstract, whether a concept, such as 'human rights', or a theory, such as the social contract theory, in favour of the concrete and the particular. Thus the conservative does not appeal to human rights as such, but to *these* rights, enshrined (but not necessarily created) in particular pieces of legislation. He focuses on the importance not of 'the community' in the abstract, but on the multifarious, more or less voluntary groupings that make up society – families, churches, clubs, universities, trade unions, and the like.

The role of the government is not to usurp or to bridle such institutions but to provide them with space, under the law, to flourish in accordance with their members' plans and preferences. Conservatives are therefore suspicious of the growth of 'big government', of government bureaucracy and regulation (except in the vital areas of external defence and internal law and order), and of laws passed on some a priori view of what is appropriate but which it is impossible to enforce in practice. In international relations great stress is laid on the balance of power between nations and, provided that balance is not upset, on persuading nations to live up to the ideals that they profess.

Both nationally and internationally the conservative has great respect for the institutions that exist and flourish. To do so they have had to struggle, and must therefore (it may be assumed) be fitted to continue. This is coupled with the fact that institutions exist in delicate interrelationships, and a belief in the unwisdom of tinkering with those relationships unless forced by changing circumstances to do so.

Historically, it is possible to detect various phases of modern political conservatism, and for convenience these can be distinguished as three phases. In the era before Burke, conservatism was often associated with the preservation of rural interests and ideals, and the structure of the landed aristocracy and the squirearchy, against the commercial and banking interests of the cities, of London and Bristol in particular. (This distinction roughly corresponded to the social differences between the Church of England and Dissent.) The writings of Hume, both philosophical and historical, are characteristic of the conservatism of this period, though an earlier, less secular but perhaps more influential version, based upon natural law rather than on custom and engrained habit, is to be found in Hooker.

The French Revolution, and Burke's writings on that momentous event and on other themes, marks a great watershed. The Revolution was the temporary triumph of abstract reason, and in Burke's eyes the bloody unanticipated upheaval was the inevitable price for that triumph. In the face of such a calamitous overturning he argued for the importance of the continuity of institutions, of tried and tested practices, of settled ways. This conservative appeal became transmuted to (at least) an extreme suspicion of, and outright opposition to, 'progress' in any of its forms, but most notably in the rise of industrialism and in attempts at parliamentary reform. For it is a characteristic of conservatism to distrust the idea of development, and to be hostile to the idea of *inevitable* progress, and instead to meet political and social problems in a minimalist and *ad hoc* way. During this period there was a tension in conservatism between the more liberal and more national–cultural wings as epitomized, for example, in the controversy over the repeal of the Corn Laws.

The latest phase in the evolution of political conservatisms identified with the death of liberalism in its characteristic, *laissez-faire* form and with the rise of theories of state socialism and, later, of Stalinism and fascism. During this period conservatism incorporated liberalism's emphasis upon personal liberty and responsibility, and the freedom of markets to provide a range of goods and services, though it was sidetracked from this by the Keynesian consensus of the 1950s and 1960s. During this period conservatism as a political force has changed from being rural, aristocratic, and Anglican in character to being markedly commercial and industrial; in fact, to occupy much of the ground of classical liberalism as against state socialism.

While in the popular mind conservatism is linked with capitalism there is no intrinsic connection. But the fact of such a connection gives rise to cultural and political tensions between those who construe political effectiveness in terms of economic success in the narrow sense, and those conservatives for whom a wider set of values, together with the creation of wealth to sustain and enjoy them, is important.

Unlike liberalism, however, conservatism continues to lay stress on the importance of strong central government, and justifies the state's provision of basic health care and education in terms of precedent, the need to secure the culture, and to keep in place a safety net of basic standards. For all their differences, from the late nineteenth century onwards conservatism and liberalism share a common commitment to representative parliamentary institutions and the paramountcy of the rule of law.

Such an emphasis upon the rule of law does not extend to conservatism's view of relations between nations, quite simply because law implies the power to enforce the law and punish breaches of it by a recognized, legitimate authority. Such an authority is singularly absent in international affairs. Rather than pursue such a chimaera a nation ought to secure its own interests by appropriate alliances and trading arrangements, draw attention to international hypocrisy and the existence of double standards (e.g. the rhetoric over human rights), and as far as possible ensure the continuing stability of international relations.

Conservatism is often thought of as promoting a series of rearguard actions in the face of change. But this would be a mistake, both as an understanding of conservative attitudes, and the actual outcome of events. Given its distrust of theory, and stress on human ignorance, conservatism is intensely resistant to any efforts to extrapolate present happenings into the future under the guise of 'historical inevitability'. It is critical on these grounds both of the progressivism of liberalism and the secular eschatology of Marxism. Assertions of conservatism are never pure reaction, a turning back of the clock, but a renewal of conservative attitudes and values transposed by the pressure of current events. Thus what links conservatives of succeeding centuries is not so much policy as attitude, temper, and overall philosophy.

Conservatism is, in turn, criticized on the grounds that it expresses an elitist and class-dominated view of the world, has often relied upon the sanctions and prescriptions of religion, and gains the consent of men and women only because they are deceived, that is, because they are suffering the effects of false consciousness derived from their class position. It is characteristic of conservative responses to such criticisms that it refuses to join in any such theoretical analysis of society and its travails but emphasizes the surface commitments, loyalties, and enjoyments which are characteristic of a people's life together.

NB

Further reading

Kirk, R., *The Conservative Mind*, Chicago, IL, Regnery, 1953.
Mannheim, K., *Conservatism*, London, Routledge & Kegan Paul, 1986.
O'Sullivan, N., *Conservatism*, London, Dent, 1976.
Scruton, R., *The Meaning of Conservatism*, London, Macmillan, 2nd edition, 1984.

CONSERVATIVE THEORY

The very idea of a conservative theory, or conservative philosophy, is paradoxical. For the conservative is one who likes to take as it comes the given order of worldly affairs, and the very idea of expressing a theory of these matters, even a theory to the effect that it is a Good Thing to take as it comes the given order of worldly affairs, seems already to constitute an interference in that order of precisely the sort that the conservative spurns. Some conservative theorists like Tolstoy and Wittgenstein have been willing to shoulder the full weight of this paradox, and have insisted that conservatism cannot be said, but only shown, or hinted at darkly, or borne in silence. Conservatism, as Scruton expressed it, is characteristically inarticulate.

A further reason for this inarticulateness lies in the fact that whenever conservative attitudes have enjoyed a historical importance they have been characterized by a certain conditionality. Where the classical liberal is able to claim unconditional validity for the theories in which he believes, a validity that would be independent of time and circumstance, the thinking and attitudes of the conservative have tended to arise in reaction to specific political or historical events wherein something that is (or is seen as being) especially valuable in and of itself – and something that has hitherto been taken for granted as such (and hence not seen as requiring a theory) – comes under threat.

Conservative theorizing, too, therefore has been often part and parcel of the reaction to specific social or political developments. Hence such theorizing is often marked also by a certain particularism: it is infused by the spirit of a particular place and time and culture, and claims validity only in relation thereto. Above all, conservative theorizing has been associated with nationalism, and it has tended to come to full force where the nation is seen as being under threat from without. Such theorizing is, however, riddled with impurities of a non-theoretical sort, as is seen not least in the fact that it derives much of its vocabulary from the language and symbolism of national defence (glory, loyalty, patriotism, treachery, sanctity of national boundaries, etc.). The conservative sentiment that is brought to expression by such impure theorizing may be further intensified by appeals to political or social arrangements of the past, arrangements which were (or which are now perceived as having been) superior to those of the present. Typically, however, conservative attitudes that have come to play an important political role are, for all the backward-looking rhetoric, very much of the present day and arise in reflection of shifts in the relative economic strengths of particular groups in society. Conservative attitudes have typically arisen among the members of one group as arrangements which are valuable to its members come to be threatened by the aspirations of other groups who have suddenly become relatively more articulate or more powerful. The threatened arrangements will then be identified as essential to the order of society itself, or to the very survival of the nation.

Some modern-day conservative thinkers have, however, sought to transcend the particularism and self-seeking nature of conservative theorizing of this sort, and conservatism has to this extent become to different degrees articulate: it has been brought to the level of a theory in the strict and proper sense.

We can imagine, first of all, a purely theoretical conservatism of someone who sees all political (and other, related sorts of) institutions, and all changes therein as being, like the weather, inevitable and unavoidable, and as being valuable as such. Even proponents of this, the purest of all forms of conservative theory, are not, therefore, against change as such. Change, they reason, will come in any case. Rather, they are uncomfortable in the face of exertions on the part of their fellow men designed to bring about further, avoidable change, as they would be uncomfortable in the face of exertions designed to bring about changes in climatic conditions or in the velocity of rotation of the earth.

Hayek, perhaps, has come closest to expressing a theoretical conservatism of this sort. He has argued in his writings that many, if not all, of the institutions of society have grown up over long periods by processes about which the participants have in every stage understood little, so that we, in particular, cannot know how these institutions achieve their results. In some cases, perhaps, we may have quite mistaken notions as to what these results are. Hence ideas which might be brought forward as to how these institutions might be improved, through more or less drastic changes, are to be treated with the utmost suspicion.

Another, closely related idea, which has been articulated especially by Oakeshott though it is to be found in different forms also in the writings of Wittgenstein, Polanyi, and Hayek himself, consists in the idea that many of the most valuable human institutions and practices rest not on rules and recipes and theories that can be conveyed explicitly from one generation to the next, but rather on what can be transmitted only through enculturation. True culture presupposes a rich and complex established order, it presupposes disciplines which take time to develop, both on the level of the individual and on the level of society as a whole. And disciplines, or ways of doing things (of speaking, reasoning, cooking, violin-playing), cannot be acquired through explanations of what is right and wrong; they must, rather, be internalized, through practice and example, empathy and intuition.

The conservative theorist is generally suspicious of explanations, and of the role of explanations, in the workings of society. He is suspicious also of the cult of science, especially in the field of politics (which explains why political science departments contain so few theorists of conservative disposition). He stresses in contrast the importance of slow, gradual development and of what is tried and tested, and points out how it is in effect the wisdom of the ages that has contributed the most complex and valuable institutions of society, including language, the arts, the family, and the law. The same principles have been at work in the development of these institutions as have brought about the evolution of biological species and of man himself.

BS

Further reading

Hayek, F.A., *The Fatal Conceit*, London, Routledge, 1988.
Nyiri, J.C., 'Wittgenstein's later work in relation to conservatism', in B.F. McGuinness (ed.), *Wittgenstein and His Times*, Oxford, Blackwell, 1982, 44–68.
Nyiri, J.C. and B. Smith (eds), *Practical Knowledge. Outlines of a Theory of Traditions and Skills*, London, Croom Helm, 1988.
Oakeshott, M., *Rationalism in Politics*, London, Macmillan, 1962.
Scruton, R., *The Meaning of Conservatism*, London, Macmillan 2nd edition, 1984.

CONSTITUTION

A constitution is no more than a set of rules and procedures for determining the legitimacy of government and of the acts and policies of governments. Legitimacy of government action under a constitution is not a function of the intrinsic 'rightness' or desirability of that action but whether constitutional rules permit it. Thus, the aim of a constitution is to be, as far as is possible, neutral between policies and social philosophies. Nevertheless, the specific content of a constitution will to a large extent reflect particular views of politics and society: a 'liberal' constitution will include special protection for individual rights while an 'authoritarian' constitution will allow wider discretion to government. However, the existence and enforcement of any constitution will *ipso facto* limit the discretion of whoever is in government.

A distinction must be drawn between the existence of a constitution and an attitude, on the part of rulers, or 'constitutionalism', i.e. an acceptance of the normative principle that government should be restrained. Most governments in the contemporary world operate under some formal, written constitutional rules yet very few are constitutional governments: they act arbitrarily. In contrast, Britain has never had a formal written document yet government in Britain is constitutional; although, recently, commentators have been critical of that country's lax and flexible constitution and the decreasing effectiveness of its informal contraints.

The idea of constitutionalism really derives from the natural law tradition in European thought. Although it does not depend on a rationalist idea that there is a universal body of moral norms against which we can test all municipal law for its validity, there is nevertheless an assumption in constitutional thought that there ought to be a clear distinction between two types of law. One body of laws is concerned with the substantive ends of government (statute law); the other is that 'higher' set of rules to which statutes should conform, i.e. the constitution. In constitutional democracies, it is normally permissible for bare majorities to pass statutes, but usually a special procedure is required for the changing of the constitution. This can take a variety of forms: perhaps a weighted majority (two thirds) in a referendum or an amending process that takes account of all parts of the community. The aim of liberal constitutions is to provide permanent protection for individual and minority rights from arbitrary political action.

The idea of a constitution in principle refutes the notion of sovereignty associated with the English command theory of law (formulated by Hobbes, Bentham, and Austin). In this jurisprudence, because all law must emanate from a determinate source, the sovereign rules, and since the sovereign must be illimitable and indivisible, there can be no room for a separate body of constitutional law that binds legislators. Irrespective of the known inadequacies of this theory as an explanation of the logic of a legal order, its normative implications have been criticized by constitutionalists precisely because it sanctions unlimited power. Indeed, the British 'constitution' has been subject to much critical analysis because the existence of a sovereign parliament, which cannot be limited, destroys the vital distinction between ordinary law and constitutional law. This position has been only slightly modified by the fact that British courts now enforce 'European law' as a consequence of Britain's accession to the European Community.

In all ongoing constitutional orders, judicial review is a key element. This is the doctrine that courts (which are independent of all political pressure) are charged with the responsibility of interpreting ordinary law for its consistency with the constitution, and with the oversight of government and administrative action. Germane to the idea of judicial review is a distinction between law and politics. This means that at least some of the actions of government should be tested for their lawfulness or legitimacy rather than for their political efficacy.

The most successful constitution is the US Federal Constitution (inaugurated in 1789). Its separation of powers, divided sovereignty, complex amending process, and independent Supreme Court embody the familiar principles of constitutionalism. However, its 'neutrality' has been questioned throughout American history. It is often claimed that the Supreme Court's decisions often seem to reflect the prevailing political and economic opinion rather than a more or less unchanging body of norms.

Not all political philosophers have favoured constitutionalism. In Plato's *Republic*, philosopher kings, because of their possession of knowledge, are not constrained by law. Aristotle, however, not only was the first political theorist to recommend a 'government of laws rather than men' but also studied existing constitutions. Rousseau argued that the 'general will' should not be restrained precisely because it represented common values; and Marx believed that the transformation of man that the abolition of capitalism would bring would make constraint unnecessary.

The need for constitutionalism that liberal thinkers stress derives from that infirmity and fragility of human nature that makes the grant of absolute power to any one person, group, or institution dangerous. Madison put the point succinctly in *The Federalist Papers* (No. 51): 'If men were angels, no government would be necessary. If angels were to govern men, neither external nor internal controls on government would be necessary.'

Liberal and conservative political economists have shown great concern with the apparent collapse of the 'constitutional attitude' in recent decades, especially in those countries with, historically, strong constitutional traditions. The process of politics under simple majority rule democracy has extended into areas of private (especially economic) life which the bulk of the population probably do not welcome. No constitution (not even 'liberal' ones in West Germany) has proved strong enough to prevent this.

The most prominent liberal-conservative writer on constitutionalism is Buchanan. From a contractarian perspective he has argued that a new constitutional order should be constructed. The state should be limited to two activities. In its 'protective' role it must enforce objective and unanimously agreed basic law (e.g. of property and contract) in a neutral manner. Thus bodies like the Supreme Court in the United States should be precluded from 'creating' law. In its 'productive' capacity it will respond to the people's subjective wishes, i.e. for the supply of public goods and services, but only under the constraint of something like a two-thirds majority rule.

What is original about contemporary liberals is their analysis of the breakdown of the 'monetary constitution' in western democracies. This normally comprised the Gold Standard (or some other method of preventing money creation) and a rule, explicit or implicit, forcing governments to balance their budgets. The advance of Keynesian macro-economics and pressure group politics, operating in democratically elected and unconstrained legislatures, have effectively destroyed the 'monetary constitution' so that inflation and government deficits have become endemic. Therefore, in addition to the traditional demands for a constitution that protects individual and minority rights and constrains majorities, liberals now insist that it should contain anti-inflationary monetary rules and procedures to enforce government to balance its budget.

NB

Further reading

Buchanan, J., *Freedom in Constitutional Contract*, Austin, TX, A & M University Press, 1977.
Marshall, G., *Constitutional Theory*, Oxford, Clarendon Press, 1971.
Pennock, J. and J.W. Chapman, *Constitutionalism*, New York, New York University Press, 1979.
Siegan, B., *Economic Liberties and the Constitution*, Chicago, IL, University of Chicago Press, 1980.

CORPORATISM

A term with two related but distinct meanings.

1 'Corporatism' refers to a prescriptive political doctrine current in the earlier part of the twentieth century. According to this, society should consist not of isolated individuals nor of hostile classes but rather of corporations, vertically organized bodies which would structure the social

order on the basis of economic and social functions. Each corporation would represent a group which had a common function in the social division of labour, and individuals would act socially and relate to each other through the corporation to which they belonged. At the level of politics the state should be organized on a corporate basis with representation of citizens not as individual electors but indirectly through the corporations. The corporations would also exercise controlling and regulatory functions in addition to their representational one. Corporatism was thus hostile towards both liberal capitalism and socialism, the one being attacked for excessive individualism the other for promoting class hatred. In economics, corporatists advocated a system which combined private property with a rejection of market forces, which were seen as socially disruptive. This was presented as a 'third way', an alternative to both capitalism and socialism.

Corporatism arose as an offshoot of social Catholicism, developing the ideas found in the encyclicals of Leo XIII, particularly his *Rerum Novarum* of 1891. The other primary source was a romanticized view of the nature of medieval society and the role within it of guilds and other corporate bodies. The most influential proponent of this was the French thinker La Tour du Pin. Corporatism was influential among many conservatives in the early part of this century, especially in France where it was taken up by Maurras and the Action Française. However, it has come to be associated with fascism due to its being adopted as the official philosophy of both Italian fascism and the Dollfuss regime in Austria, as well as the Estado Novo of Salazar in Portugal. Corporatism can be seen as a type of extreme conservative doctrine but its antipathy to individualism and market economy renders it anathema for individualist conservatives and classical liberals. The radical nature of its prescriptions makes it in practice a revolutionary doctrine, hence its adoption by fascists. This shows the dilemma facing ultra-conservatives today, adhering to a doctrine which, if its prescriptions are to be realized, requires a social and economic revolution – hardly a conservative posture!

2 'Corporatism' means a descriptive account of modern capitalist societies. According to this account there are intermediate interest groups which occupy the space between the state and civil society. In pluralist theories such as Maitland's these are voluntarist, the product of free association. In corporatist accounts they are monopolistic and closely linked to the state. Examples of such corporate interests are large business firms, trade unions, professions, and major institutions such as universities. Theorists of corporatism such as Schmitter and Drucker argue that the corporation is the key institution of advanced societies and that corporations are the primary actors in the political process. In some states this is given institutional recognition with corporate

interests involved in both the formation and the execution of policy, so combining representative and administrative roles. The clearest examples of this are Austria and Sweden, with the United States furthest from this model. In Britain an attempt was made during the 1970s to adopt a corporatist system of economic management but this broke down in 1978/9.

The theorists of corporatism purport to be giving an objective account of the workings of contemporary societies, but in reality many are proponents of it (e.g. Drucker). Many conservatives and classical liberals accept the descriptive element but are highly critical of corporatism as an actual system of politics, first for its collectivist emphasis, second for assuming a false harmony of interests between the members of various groups, but mainly because a corporatist system will entrench established interests, so inhibiting change and development, and will politicize large areas of life which should be in the private sphere. This makes politics into a struggle for resources and control of the state between various groups in which weaker groups and isolated individuals lose.

SD

Further reading

Berle, A.A. and G.C. Means, *The Modern Corporation and Private Property*, New York, Macmillan, 1933.
Cawson, A., *Corporatism and Political Theory*, Oxford, Blackwell, 1986.
Drucker, P., *The Concept of the Corporation*, New York, New American Library, 1965.
O'Sullivan, N., *Fascism*, London, Dent, 1983.

CRIME AND PUNISHMENT

Crime and punishment is a topic of great interest to many conservatives and classical liberals. The most vexed question for writers on the subject is the seemingly simple one of what crime may be. The standard positivist definition, followed by most lawyers, defines crime as being any act of omission which is prohibited by law. Crime is thus an arbitrary category: anything can be a crime if the legislature so decides. Consequently, most modern lawyers also adhere to the doctrine of *mens rea* (criminal mind) which holds that a crime cannot be said to have been committed unless there was an intent to do so, since the essence of crime is the breach of a law and this can only be punishable if done knowingly. Thus the criminal deed, or *actus reus*, is of secondary importance. Crime, for modern lawyers, is sharply distinguished from tort, or civil wrong. The main differences are that crimes are prosecuted by the state rather than private individuals with conviction resulting in punishment by the state rather than compensation to the injured party. All of this, however, is a relatively recent historical development, being the outcome of what some historians have come to call the 'judicial revolution'. Under the *ancien régime* the distinction between crimes and torts was vague or nonexistent, with compensation the typical penalty even for most homicides, and most prosecutions being undertaken by the victim or the victim's kin. Crime was then defined as an action which caused harm or violated rights.

Most modern criminology has tended to minimize the importance of personal responsibility on the part of criminals for their actions. Crime is explained as the product of environmental factors such as housing or of economic conditions such as the level of employment. Alternatively it is accounted for by reference to ideological or cultural factors or inadequate socialization. All of these theories have shared features. They are methodologically collectivist, assuming the existence of a collective entity called crime when in fact what actually exist are criminal actions (however defined) carried out by individuals. They explain individual criminal acts committed by individual people in terms of impersonal structures. This eliminates personal responsibility on the part of the criminal – how can one be responsible for a criminal act if it was caused by one's 'inadequate socialisation'? They also make the whole concept of punishment inherently dubious – how can punishment be justified if people are not responsible?

They also mostly assume that crimes are unnatural and require explanation; in theory there should not be any so reality is defined as a deviation from the theoretical state. The only partial exception to this is the deviancy theory of Durkheim and others which has it that all societies need to define certain actions and groups as deviant so as to promote social solidarity. Crime (i.e. the definition of certain acts as criminal by the law) is therefore necessary and functional. This does show another shared concept, that the category of crime is arbitrary, purely a matter of definition by people with power, and has nothing to do with the actual nature of the acts so defined or with any notion of morality.

All of this runs counter to common sense and is strongly rebutted by most conservatives and classical liberals. A great deal has been written on this subject in recent years because of the clear failure of modern penology and the relentless and massive growth of recorded crime in most developed societies. Conservative authors are concerned to revive the notion that certain acts are inherently criminal. This means establishing some standard or principle by which criminality can be defined. The most popular is that outlined earlier, that criminal acts are ones which violate another person's rights and are deemed worthy of a particular kind of punishment. This can have interesting consequences for certain categories of offence, particularly victimless crimes. Another concept which conservative authors have sought to revive is delinquency in its classic sense of a failure to perform a duty or obligation. This makes criminality a failure to meet legal or traditional obligations which include respect for the property and persons of others.

Many writers are particularly concerned to reaffirm the moral element in accounts of criminality, the assertion that crimes are moral as well as legal wrongs. This is linked to the reassertion of the doctrine of personal responsibility on the part of criminals. The modish accounts of the present crime wave are rejected in favour of one which explains it as a product of a process of demoralization, part of the breakdown in modern societies of the very concept of right and wrong and its replacement by an ethos of self-gratification and hedonism. According to this thesis, order is maintained in civil society not by force or police but by mores, generally accepted standards of behaviour, and by informal institutions which enforce them. The last century saw a strengthening of these and a process of moralization resulting in a decline in recorded crime. This has been reversed in the present century in most countries, though not in Japan or Switzerland. Conservatives in particular stress the decline of the family as an institution and the more general undermining of authority in all areas of life as causes of delinquency. The decline of religious belief is also often cited.

Yet another argument, made with especial force by Van den Haag, is that, given man's fallen nature, criminal acts are inevitable and do not require explanation in themselves, although the type and number of them may. The question for those in authority is primarily one of how to deal with crimes when they are committed and how to minimize such occurrences. On this subject, that of practical policy, there are a variety of positions, some strongly opposed to each other. In general, however, they all argue for a reduction in the role of the state and its agencies and more emphasis on other institutions as well as voluntary action. This can extend in some cases to advocating the replacement of a statutory state police force by private law enforcement agencies and self-help groups like the New York Guardian Angels. Measures to remoralize society are also advocated although this is seen as being more a matter of spontaneous action than a government responsibility.

In penal policy, the commonest position adopted is to argue for a return to the philosophy of Beccaria, first put forward in the eighteenth century. In this view the main purpose of penal policy is to deter potential criminals by making them perceive crime as too costly/risky to be worthwhile. This is achieved *not* by severe punishment but by the certainty of punishment, i.e. mandatory penalties for crimes and a high probability of detection and conviction. This may involve opposition to the recent tendency of American courts grossly to favour the defendant, so reducing the possibility of conviction. A rather different view is that punishment should be exemplary in so far as its main purpose is the reassertion of common values by the punishment of those who flout them. This has been used in the past to justify public punishment.

A very different approach is advocated by those like Barnet who call for a move to restitution rather than retribution as the central feature of penal policy. This implies a return to the pre-modern concept of crime and the removal of the distinction between crimes and torts. In general most conservatives and classical liberals are critical of the modern, Benthamite penal system with the reformatory prison as its main institution. This is attacked as ineffective, inhumane, and corrupting rather than reforming. There is strong support for alternatives to prison such as tagging, fines, or corporal punishment. In their analysis of the prison conservatives and classical liberals have much common ground with radical leftists such as Foucault.

The one aspect of crime and punishment which has most divided conservatives from classical liberals is that of victimless crimes such as the sale and use of drugs and prostitution. Authors such as Szasz argue that to criminalize such activities is wrong in itself because it violates personal freedom by restricting actions which only harm the people involved, not third parties, and ineffective because the result of prohibition is to make the problem much worse than it would otherwise be, as happened in America in the 1920s with alcohol. If crime is defined as an action which harms someone else then such actions cannot be crimes, however objectionable. Conservatives argue, first, that there is harm to third parties in terms of imposed costs and other externalities and, second, that the public authority has a responsibility to maintain a shared morality in society which duty precludes the toleration of wicked or immoral actions by individuals, however self-regarding.

SD

Further reading

Barnet, R.E. and Hagel J. (eds), *Assessing the Criminal*, Cambridge MA, Ballinger, 1977.
Berns, W., *For Capital Punishment*, New York, Basic Books, 1979.
Van den Haag, E., *Punishing Criminals*, New York, Basic Books, 1975.
Wilson, J.Q., *Thinking About Crime*, New York, Basic Books, 1983.

CULTURE

In the social sciences, 'culture' denotes indifferently all manifestations of social life (such as customs, religious observances, habits of association) which are concerned not simply with the reproduction and sustenance of human beings. Culture is all those activities which endow the world with meaning and it thus has an important role in the process by which individuals come to understand and to accept social order.

In a narrower (and more normative) sense, 'culture' denotes the set of habits, customs, and attitudes that are specific to human creativity and to leisure. One can here distinguish 'high' from 'low' culture. The first term refers to 'refined' forms of activity (such as music, literature, and art) in which true aesthetic interest is exercised and which require educational attainments for their performance and understanding; the second term refers to activities like dancing, entertainment, and sport, in which relaxation and social contact are the principal aims.

Conservative thinking has typically been concerned with preserving and supporting 'high' culture as a means of permitting the outlook of the educated class (or of elites in general) to shape the expectations, customs, and values of society as a whole. 'High' culture conveys a sense of historical continuity and permits individuals intuitively to understand their place in the social order.

In the wake of cultural conservatism, the main interest of neo-conservatism centres on a critique of contemporary culture; its target is particularly the system of values (such as the cult of 'authenticity') associated with the 'counter-culture' typical of the 1960s. From a conservative point of view, much of contemporary culture amounts to an irretrievable dwindling of the accepted authority of traditions and thus to an erosion of some of the most vital bonds sustaining the social fabric. It is the task of education, particularly that of humane learning, to convey values and ideas in tune with traditional culture. Conservatives are therefore concerned with the defence of traditional university education as the custodianship of general culture.

Whereas liberalism typically reduces cultural manifestations to individual talent, both Marxism and conservatism regard them as dependent upon basic forces constituting society. While Marxists, however, view culture as a mere 'superstructure' expressing, enforcing, and consolidating the economic base upon which it rests (with 'high' culture being the ideology of the ruling class), conservatives see culture as a web of practices, customs, and traditions constituting and preserving historical continuity. If culture helps individuals to understand their social environment, such understanding is provided not through choice, but rather through concepts and perceptions embodied in the social fabric, practices (such as those of greeting and of marriage) which it does not make sense to think of as the products of individual will or as the outcomes of some 'social contract' whose terms no one can state or remember.

It was, particularly, German conservatives like Hegel and Fichte who explicitly identified state with culture, making cultural purity, expressed by a shared language, a vital goal in the struggle for national unification. Much of British conservatism, on the other hand, embracing Hobbes's dissociation of state from community, could make substantial concessions to cultural pluralism and placed less emphasis on cultural purity within a state.

In the wake of Mandeville and Hume, the formation of complex cultural institutions has been seen as a process of selective evolution. Hayek asserts that culture is neither natural nor artificial, neither genetically transmitted nor rationally designed; it is a tradition of learnt rules of perception and of conduct which have never been 'invented' and of whose functions individuals usually are not even aware. According to Hayek, the evolution of culture may be fruitfully investigated in terms of the competition between vital traditions or practices. A natural selection among such traditions then occurs which is at least partly to be explained by the relative efficiency of some as opposed to others as bearers or embodiments of (tacit and abstract) knowledge. The traditions, practices, and rules that make up the culture of a society were not deliberately chosen but have spread because they were the ones that most enhanced the prosperity and expansion of certain groups. There is thus a wisdom immanent to the surviving rules or practices, since they encompass the experience of generations and have proven successful in regulating social life. It is from this conviction that many conservatives derive their attachment to 'traditional' or 'established' culture.

WG

Further reading

Arnold, M., *Culture and Anarchy*, Cambridge, Cambridge University Press, 1960 (first published London, 1869).
Eliot, T.S., *Notes Towards the Definition of Culture*, London, Faber & Faber, 1948.
Hayek, F.A., *Studies in Philosophy, Politics and Economics*, Chicago, IL, University of Chicago Press, 1967.
Hayek, F.A., 'The three sources of human values', in *Law, Legislation and Liberty*, Vol. III, London, Routledge & Kegan Paul, 1979.

CUSTOM

The word 'custom' may be defined as referring to a sort of repeated rational action, in which past performance provides the reason for present repetition. The customary is 'what is done' as opposed to 'what is not done'. It is important to recognize that in this kind of context the rational is not opposed to the irrational but to the non-rational. So the term 'rational' here is not necessarily commendatory.

The present usage is that followed by Aristotle when he defined man as the rational animal. His point was that we are uniquely capable both of rationality and of irrationality; as presumably the brutes, and quite certainly things which are inanimate, are not. Throughout his long life Bertrand Russell used to make cheap and unfair fun of that Aristotelian definition; objecting, irrelevantly, that most people much of the time are very irrational.

Without prejudicing any questions about the rationality or irrationality of any particular customs, we must go on to distinguish custom both from law and from habit. Thus, whereas prescriptive law must be enforced by definite and regular penalties, customs are not necessarily enforced by any sort of penalties at all. People protest that 'there ought to be a law against it', however, precisely and only because laws are intended to be, and typically are, enforced. Again, whereas habits may be attributed to brutes, customs are things which only humans can have. For to do what is customary is to act intentionally; and, at any rate typically, for one specific reason – the reason, namely, that that is 'what is done'.

Laws may emerge, and in fact often have emerged, through the formulation and sovereign ratification of those customary practices and procedures which had previously served as more or less acceptable substitutes for statutory laws. The notoriously unwritten and therefore unjustifiable British constitution constitutes perhaps the most familiar instance in the developed world of customary practices and procedures continuing to serve as a generally accepted substitute for codified law, even in matters of the ultimate importance to all citizens. But it might perhaps also be argued that countries like the USSR, which have written constitutions containing clauses which are not and were never intended to be observed, in fact possess also unwritten constitutions consisting of the established and actually observed customary practices and procedures.

Attachment to custom and the traditional is an important conservative ideal. For Roman political orators under the Republic perhaps the most powerful and acceptable appeal was to the *mos majorum*, the custom of our ancestors. Cicero's speeches are full of it. This appeal is taken to show that some sort of behaviours can be wholly justifiable, even though its justification necessarily possesses only a local and parochial validity. It cannot, therefore, be appreciated by outsiders – those breeds without the custom.

Such appeals to custom and to tradition are sometimes extolled as the conservative alternative to doctrine. Compare with this the Roman Catholic contention that what is to be believed is *quod semper, quod ubique, quod ab omnibus, creditum est* – what was believed always, everywhere, and by everyone. His insistence upon this principle constitutes, no doubt, one of the main reasons why John Henry, Cardinal Newman became one of the chief conservative thinkers of this century.

Again, although custom has to be and has been distinguished from habit, it is no doubt in large part because Hume presented people as primarily and above all creatures of habit that he too became one of the great conservative thinkers. Indeed it is now often argued that Hume rather than Burke should be seen as the founding father of the modern conservative intellectual tradition.

AF

Further reading

Flew, A.G.N., *David Hume: Philosopher of Moral Science*, Oxford, Blackwell, 1986.
Hume, D., *Essays Moral Political and Literary*, ed. E.F. Miller, Indianapolis, IN, Liberty Classics, 1985.
Livingston, D.W., *Hume's Philosophy of Common Life*, Chicago, IL, Chicago University Press, 1986.
Wolin, S., 'Hume and conservatism', in D.W. Livingston and J.T. King (eds), *Hume: A Re-evaluation*, New York, Fordham University Press, 1976.

D

DEMOCRACY

The word 'democracy' was invented in classical Greece. Its original meaning was literally 'rule by the people'; where the people (*demos*) meant one section of the community, the poor and numerous. Thus it could be easily and uncontroversially contrasted with other forms of government, e.g. monarchy (rule by a single person) and aristocracy (rule by the wise and virtuous). However, in the modern world it is much less frequently used to describe a particular form of government – almost all regimes describe themselves as democratic in some sense or other – but has become something of an honorific label designed to persuade people of the value of a particular political system. Its descriptive content has almost entirely been replaced by its emotive meaning. A partial resurrection of democracy's descriptive meaning may be achieved by using an adjective to indicate the type of democratic regime that is under consideration. Thus we may legitimately speak of 'liberal democracy', 'people's democracy', 'majoritarian democracy', 'totalitarian democracy', 'constitutional democracy', etc.

A further point of clarification may be helpful. In the great variety of contexts in which the word democracy is used two very general senses may be distinguished: a 'procedural' sense and an 'end-state' sense. In the procedural sense democracy is no more than a method, normally by some form of voting, for generating collective decisions and choosing rulers. From such a procedure there is no necessity that desirable outcomes, e.g. liberalism or egalitarianism, will emerge. 'End-state' democracy refers to particular qualities a society must have, e.g. popular participation, liberty and equality, minority rights, if it is to be called 'democratic'.

The original meaning of democracy was almost entirely procedural: indeed, democratic processes were often regarded as a threat to individual liberty. In English political thought perhaps the first reference to democratic ideas was made in the famous 'Putney Debates' in the Civil War.

But it was the utilitarians, Jeremy Bentham and James Mill, who produced the first systematic defence of the democratic method. For them, (almost) universal suffrage, majority voting, and representative institutions that 'mirrored' the opinions of the people were the only ways in which utility or the public interest could be maximized. Given their axiom that all human action was motivated by self-interest, any other form of government would simply generate minority or 'sinister' interests. It should be noted that no intrinsic value was attached to 'participation' or equality; democracy was no more than a mechanism for maximizing utility. There was also no recognition of the possibility that democracy might generate private and group interests rather than the general interest.

That majoritarianism might well threaten liberty, the rule of law, the rights of property, and civilization itself was first recognized by Macaulay. Such fears were put in a sophisticated form by John Stuart Mill. In perhaps the first demonstration of *liberal* democracy Mill proposed a variety of complex institutional devices, such as plural voting, proportional representation, and limitations on the majority will of parliament, in order to protect minority interests and 'higher' social values. In fact, Mill was less enamoured of democratic processes implementing popular decisions than he was of their educative value. He thought that involvement in politics was a valuable training in citizenship. Other Victorian critics of majoritarian democracy included Maine and Fitzjames Stephen. A prevailing theme was that majoritarian procedures would in practice lead to the manipulation of the 'people's will' by organized minorities.

The idea that representative democracy was an impossible ideal was given some scientific credibility in the twentieth century by the theorists of elitism, notably Pareto, Mosca, and Michels. In their work, democracy appears not to be the description of a specific form of government but a convenient ideological symbol. Michels had in fact studied the most democratic political organization at the time, the German School Democratic Party, and detected an 'iron law of oligarchy'. Despite impeccable democratic procedures he noticed that the same people regularly were in control of the major offices of the party. This was because their control of information, and their political commitment in the face of general apathy, made them natural leaders irrespective of constitutional rules.

Pareto saw all human history as the story of the rise and fall of elites. The democratic ideal of equality was an illusion since men possessed certain psychological properties (or 'residues') to an unequal degree. Government would always be carried on by minorities who possessed the dominant residue: such as 'courage' or 'cunning'. Government was necessarily irresponsible, whatever its form, since the apathetic masses were incapable of controlling their leaders. Mosca held not dissimilar views, although the foundations of his elites were sociological and class-based rather than psychological. Governing involved technical skills and elites were successful to the extent that they could recruit able personnel rather than through their accountability to the people.

The economist Schumpeter produced the first 'realistic' theory of procedural democracy. He was critical of what he called the 'classical theory' of democracy largely because it erroneously presupposed that voting procedures reflected the people's will in the outputs of government. He argued that there was no coherent public opinion or popular will and that, anyway, people's behaviour in politics was largely irrational (at least in comparison to their behaviour as individual transactors in markets where the presence of constraints enforced some degree of rationality). Nevertheless, democracy, in the sense of responsible government, was not impossible. By drawing an analogy between, on the one hand, consumers and voters and, on the other, producers and party leaders, he showed that democratic voting procedures allowed the people to choose which minority would rule over them. In his famous words democracy is 'that institutional arrangement for arriving at political decisions in which individuals acquire the power to decide by means of a competitive struggle for the people's vote'.

Thus democracy is possible, not in the 'classical' sense, but in the sense of securing some notion of responsible government via the mechanism of party competition. As long as the extent of political activity is kept relatively small, and a governing class is imbued with a certain kind of professionalism, it is likely to work better than other forms of government.

The contemporary economic theory of democracy builds on Schumpeter's market analogy. Downs argued that if voters were arranged on a left to right political spectrum then self-interested competition for votes between parties would drive them towards the centre: the outputs of government would tend to reflect the opinions of the median voter. However, other theorists are less sanguine: it is argued that the political market-place is unlike an economic market in that there are few constraints on government action. The competitive struggle for the people's votes is likely to result in excess public spending and also in coalitions of interest groups forming which seek government privileges and therefore undermine the public interest.

Nevertheless, most classical liberals accept the democratic procedure as the best available method of producing necessary government services. However, it should always be limited by strict constitutional rules to protect minority and individual rights. They reject the idea that there is any necessary connection between democracy and liberty. In fact, they would maintain that in Britain the main features of a liberal order were achieved before the movement towards universal suffrage began. What they oppose most of all is unconstrained majoritarianism.

Classical liberals are particularly critical of the contemporary tendency to define democracy as an end-state, or way of life, rather than as a simple decision-making process. It is this, they claim, that has allowed communist states to masquerade as 'people's democracies', even though these forbid party competition and genuine choice in voting. The source of most non-liberal theories of democracy is Rousseau. He was particularly critical of a system of democracy that permitted voting once every five years and favoured a democratic ideal of constant citizen participation in law-making so that the General Will can emerge. Since the General Will is unlimited in its power there are no protections for individuals who may find themselves in conflict with it. It is also the case that the General Will may not be perceived even by a majority within a community. It is claimed that the modern theory of 'totalitarian democracy', a phenomenon described first by Talmon, in which absolute power is granted to an elite by virtue of its possession of the knowledge of the true ends of society, derives ultimately from Rousseau. This monist view of society, in which all political values are subordinated to a single collective end, may be contrasted with the pluralism of ends and purposes which is valued by liberal procedural theorists of democracy.

Liberals and conservatives tend to be sceptical about the value of too much political participation. Apathy may be a virtue in a political system since it reflects a fundamental agreement in society. The encouragement of active involvement in political affairs leads to the transfer of private activities to the public sphere; it is argued also that there are fewer incentives to rational action in politics than there are in economics.

Historically, conservatives have been sceptical of many of the familiar forms of democracy. The egalitarian impulse in the creed runs counter to the conservatives' vision of an *ordered* society in which hierarchy is essential for stability. Conservatives have been especially critical of majoritarianism, seeing this as a potent threat to property and the rule of law.

However, in western democracies this has not proved to be a real danger. Existing electoral systems ensure that a majority in a representative assembly is unlikely to represent a majority of the electorate. Not only that, but in western democracies it is unlikely that the same party will regularly control the representative assembly. When parties alternate in office the system is known as pluralism or, following Dahl, polyarchy. In this, democracy is not defined in terms of majority rule at all but as 'minorities rule'. It should be noted that polyarchy can only be effective if a country is not sharply divided on racial, religious, or any other sociological ground that is likely to be permanent.

Despite its considerable distance from majoritarianism neither liberals nor conservatives are happy with pluralist democracy. For liberals, individual rights are still vulnerable since majority principles still operate in the representative (legislative) assembly. Buchanan accepts that in a democracy government activity must respond to the subjective wishes of the people but argues that under simple majority rule the outputs of government will impose heavy costs on minorities. The ideal rule would be unanimity since under this rule nothing would be produced which was not desired. However, it has the disadvantage that bargaining costs to secure unanimous agreement would be very high. Buchanan suggests, therefore, that a weighted majority (two-thirds) would be the appropriate democratic decision rule. Almost all classical liberals accept the necessity of weighted majorities.

The conservative argument against pluralism does not normally extend to the construction of elaborate constitutional rules. These objections to pluralism centre largely on the fact that alternation between political parties is likely to lead to a factionalism that distorts the true public interest. For some conservatives a direct appeal to the public may often generate conservative values. It was Disraeli who extended the vote to the working classes in Britain in 1867 in the confident belief that they were conservative. In twentieth-century America, the conservative political theorist Kendall believed that genuine majority rule would always defeat collectivist elitism. On the whole these views are exceptional: the typical conservative response to democracy is to accept it as undesirable but inevitable and to mitigate its effects by recommending qualifications for voting (e.g. property and education).

NB

Further reading

Lively, J., *Democracy*, Oxford, Blackwell, 1975.
Pennock, J.R., *Liberal Democracy*, Westport, CT, Greenwood Press, 1978.
Savton, C., *The Theory of Democracy Revisited,* New Jersey, Chatham House, 1987.
Schumpeter, J., *Capitalism, Socialism and Democracy*, London, Allen & Unwin, 1942.
Tullock, G., *The Vote Motive*, London, Institute of Economic Affairs, 1976.

E

EDUCATION

For the conservative, education is one of the most important means of introducing the child or young person to the interlocking forms of culture in that person's society. Education is, in essence, a parental responsibility, though one largely discharged through delegation to schools and colleges. Through education a child or young person, in so far as he or she is capable, is introduced to characteristic forms of thinking and enquiry, to distinct disciplines with standards of excellence and established bodies of knowledge.

Two matters stand out in this account. Great prominence is given by the conservative to the social aspect of education, in the sense that the forms of thinking and bodies of knowledge are themselves social products, and also because the means of induction into them is social. So it is of the essence of education that it is directed; the pupil or student is not a free-floating agent, much less a solitary re-occupier of the state of nature. The educational ideal is that the pupil be taught the best of what has been thought and discovered, along with the methods that have made such thought and discovery possible, and which hold out the best, if not the only, prospect of further thought and discovery.

Teaching aims not merely at a surface acquaintance with a body of general knowledge of the sort that a multiple choice questionnaire might reveal, but at the mastery of appropriate methods of enquiry. To be achievable such a goal requires two things of the student: discipline (in the first instance, acceptance of the authority of the teacher and, later on, self-discipline) and an interest in the subject matter for its own sake.

So education is to be distinguished from training, for training is concerned with the imparting of marketable skills. So the justification of education in intrinsic terms is to be sharply distinguished from its justification in instrumental terms.

This can most vividly be illustrated in the attitude to science education. For a concern for science to be education, both the teacher and the student must be interested in it because of the intrinsic intellectual power and captivation of its problems and of the strengths developed to address these problems. So science education is to be distinguished both from training (in, for example, the use of certain machines or experimental routines) and from the technological or commercial exploitation of the science. Without an interest in the discipline for its own sake, whether science or something else, the intellectual tradition will wither, and the prospect of educating new generations will vanish.

Conservatism is thus opposed to justifying education in utilitarian terms, in terms of the Gross National Product or job opportunities. A distinction is drawn between a liberal education and both professional and technical training which do have such a justification. This is not to say that a liberal education does not have useful by-products, e.g. in developing lines of intellectual and therefore personal attachment to the culture of a nation, in the growth of an 'educated public', and in developing marketable powers of specialist knowledge, mental sharpness, and intellectual curiosity. Nevertheless, the goal of education will not be intelligible without a firm grasp of things worthwhile in themselves.

Such attitudes give rise to a large number of political and policy consequences from primary to higher education. They embrace discipline and punishment, the importance of knowledge, the nature of the curriculum, the education of ethnic minorities in the national culture, the place of religion in education, elitism, and the state funding of education. Whether there ought to be state-funding of education has been a matter of some controversy within conservatism, and reveals a tension between those who wish to maintain competitiveness between different sorts of educational institution (and the reality of parental choice) and those who stress the importance of education for national as well as individual well-being.

By contrast, and as might be expected, the liberal view of education is both more permissive and more individualistic than that of the conservatives. In fact, two distinct strands in liberalism can be identified, the pluralist and the progressive, each respectively justified in terms of a rather different view of human nature.

According to the pluralist the nature and type of education is simply the outcome of preferences, social, ethnic, religious, and family. The state has no part in education as such (and it is interesting to observe that in England liberalism is now strongly associated with moves to secularize education), but is a neutral ring-holder. It follows that education is not regarded as a precious commodity, the key to unlocking and maintaining the national culture (and much else) for future generations, but is a set of arrangements whose character and justification move at the behest of the wants of individuals, and particularly the demands of the market-place for 'trained manpower'. (Both liberalism of this kind and conservatism are light-years away from the justification of education in terms of socialist 'manpower planning', however).

According to progressive liberalism, education is a means of individual and social emancipation from tradition (particularly religious tradition) and from any other factor that might cramp the individual human spirit. And so education concentrates upon providing a context for 'free expression' and for 'experimentation' in matters otherwise regarded as private and personal, notably sex. Little emphasis is placed on the content of a curriculum, or on structured learning of any kind, which is widely but mistakenly taken to be equivalent to 'rote-learning', but the child is encouraged to do what he or she chooses to do.

Such a view, characteristic of educationalists such as Neill and Russell, in fact tacitly supposes an education middle-class set of values. Where such a background cannot be presupposed the results of such regressions to Rousseauesque primitivism have been both ridiculous and tragic.

PH

Further reading

Newman, J.H., *The Idea of a University*, London, 1873.
Oakeshott, M., *The Voice of Liberal Learning*, New Haven, CT, Yale University Press, 1989.
Shils, E., *The Academic Ethic*, Chicago, IL, University of Chicago Press, 1984.

ELITES

Etymologically 'elites' are sets of people who have been selected, typically for some purpose and/or upon some principle. (By Cantor's Axiom for Sets the sole essential feature of a set is that its members have at least one common characteristic, any kind of characteristic.)

1   Ruling elites. In a political context the term 'elite' has been used to refer to a set of persons in a position to see themselves and to be seen by others as chosen to govern: either chosen by some other more or less identifiable set of individuals, such as 'the people' or 'the proletariat', or chosen by some hypostatized abstraction, such as Nature or History. Sometimes a distinction is made between government by an elite, defined as a set of people the members of which actually have been in some way chosen, and government by a ruling class, which has somehow emerged over the years without any deliberate and demonstrable selection. Thus Eliot distinguishes power elites in Marxist–Leninist regimes from traditionalist ruling classes. These latter, he argues, cannot be described, in the same literal sense, as elites.

In the context of political and of more general sociology there are also the doctrines, described as scientific elitism, propounded by Pareto, Mosca, and Michels. Pareto distinguished governing elites from non-governing elites, and both from non-elite remainders. He argued that all regimes, including democratic regimes, cannot but generate both kinds of elite, the one dominating politics, the other society. No official formulation was in fact ever provided by its eponymous discoverer for Michel's famous, or notorious, Iron Law of Oligarchy. He confuses the logically necessary truth that in all hierarchical organizations those above must be considerably less numerous than those below with various much more dubious allegations about the practical impossiblity, in all kinds of hierarchy, of movement from lower to higher and from higher to lower positions.

Some more recent sociologists have extended Pareto's theory, arguing that in all developed societies there is a plurality of competing elites, which rise to eminence through the several systems of control. Politics is only one such system; others include management, trade unions, military organizations, and cultural and educational institutions.

2   Achievement elites. Wherever there is room for superior and inferior levels of achievement there is room too for the emergence of an elite; the set of people, that is, consisting of all, but only, those who in this particular area, although perhaps nowhere else, are high achievers. And wherever, too, there actually are higher and lower achievers the former are – in respect of whatever kind of achievement is in question, if in no other – superior to, and hence perhaps offensively unequal to, the latter. The concepts of elites, of excellence, and of inequality are thus necessarily connected. In consequence, and equally necessarily, principled egalitarians are bound to be upset by any favourable references to actual elites or to actual excellence in any sphere.

There have perhaps been places and periods in which 'elitist' was a neutral word for a person favouring rule by an 'elite', and there, presumably, an elite neither answerable to nor ejectable by the governed. In that understanding Plato's Guardians – the philosopher-kings of *The Republic* – are the original paradigm case of such an absolute and irresponsible ruling elite; while, as advocating a system of this kind, Plato himself must be scored correspondingly as the philosophical founding father of all elitism. And in the same understanding, in our own time, by far the most common and most important of such elites are the ruling Marxist–Leninist parties; while the most numerous and powerful elitists are members, fellow travellers, or other sympathizers of such parties.

In Britain in the 1970s and 1980s, however, 'elitist' seems to have become for every kind of egalitarian a favourite term of abuse; and one almost as empty of definite descriptive meaning as 'fascist' on the lips of those too young to remember what was actually believed, and done, by fascists (in Italy) and National Socialists (in Germany). Because these abusers of elitism are rarely if ever successfully challenged to try to make plain either what it is that this term is supposed to mean or why we are being asked to renounce its referent, those who live and work in the educational world are from time to time deafened by a hubbub of disclaimers and denunciations of elitism. Even in universities and other institutions supposedly striving to become centres of excellence, we too often hear vice-chancellors and principals shamefacedly explaining that, while not of course being elitist, they do nevertheless rather feel that some standards of academic quality ought to be maintained; and perhaps – greatly daring – the better, the better.

What should amaze us is the effrontery of those who, while eschewing excellence, present policies requiring and promoting this eschewal as policies for the improvement of state *education*. Anyone inclined to join the chorus against excellence should be invited to reconsider an obituary tribute to Wittgenstein from two Australian philosophers, A.C. Jackson and D.A.T. Gasking: 'There are many sorts of human excellence. Not least among them is the excellence of one who devotes his whole life, giving up all else, to the attempt to do one thing supremely well.'

AF

Further reading

Eliot, T.S., *Notes Towards a Definition of Culture*, London, Faber & Faber, 1965.
Michels, R., *Political Parties: A Sociological Study of the Oligarchical Tendencies of Modern Democracy*, Glencoe, IL, Free Press, 1915. German original 1911.
Pareto, V., *Mind and Society*, New York, Harcourt Brace, 1935. Italian original 1923.
Parry, G., *Political Elites*, London, Allen & Unwin, 1969.

THE ENLIGHTENMENT

The Enlightenment was an intellectual and cultural movement of eighteenth-century Europe but deriving from earlier developments in the field of ideas. It was particularly associated with France, Scotland, and albeit ambiguously, Germany. A fundamental distinction must be made between the Continental Enlightenment and the Scottish, the two being quite different in several respects. The Continental Enlightenment can be distinguished from the Scottish by its greater confidence in the power of abstract reason and its emphasis upon design and intent in human affairs as opposed to the Scottish thinkers' stress upon the spontaneous and unplanned. However, the division was one of ideas rather than geography with several French and German thinkers espousing ideas similar to those of the Scots.

Although located in the eighteenth century the Enlightenment was a product of the scientific revolution of the seventeenth century and can be seen as the application to general issues of the cosmology and methodology of Newton. Most adopted the Newtonian model of an automatic, self-regulating, and mathematically definable cosmos as their starting point, so abandoning the medieval notion of Macrocosm/Microcosm with its stress on Divine intervention and detailed correspondences between the natural and human worlds. In methodology and argument the Enlightenment followed the example of scientists such as Newton, applying the style and forms of argument of the natural sciences and mathematics to social and political analysis while relying where possible upon empirical fact and investigation rather than appeals to authorities such as scripture. Consequently the rhetorical and metaphorical form of argument which had been common during the Renaissance fell out of favour. This shift began as early as the seventeenth century, e.g. in Hobbes's *Leviathan* (which explicitly uses the methodology of geometry), but was only completed in the eighteenth.

In the first half of the eighteenth century several factors – the start of a long period of relative peace after 1715, widespread political stability, a general growth of prosperity and the appearance of a truly international community of scholars being the most prominent – produced an intellectual movement which was both confident and intensely aware of its own existence. This last is demonstrated by the use of its self-adopted label, the Aufklaurung or Enlightenment.

At first sight the Enlightenment thinkers are an extraordinarily diverse collection of individuals. What could people as different as Voltaire, Diderot, Smith, and Helvetius, to name just four, have in common? Indeed, it is impossible to construct any kind of list of political, social, or philosophical ideas which were shared by all of the movement's leading thinkers. Quite apart from the divide between the Scots and the Continentals, even the latter were divided on a wide range of issues. Many shared Voltaire's view that the best and most progressive form of government was by an 'enlightened despot' guided by wise advisers (i.e. people like Voltaire!); others were classical republicans (e.g. Rousseau) or supported a limited parliamentary government on the English model (e.g. Montesquieu); some favoured *laissez-faire* while others (e.g. Mably and Morelly) were proto-socialists; many were deists but an influential minority were outright atheists while some were Christians, albeit lax ones. It would be wrong to conclude, however, that the movement was incoherent with its figures having nothing in common. Underneath the apparent diversity were shared attitudes and methods, more significant than the varied conclusions they produced. What we can discern are, first, a shared *mentalité* or mind set and, second, a discourse, a set of discursive rules which united the seemingly disparate views and arguments through a shared mode of expression and vocabulary.

Among the Continentals this underlying unity has seven main elements. First, automatism, the notion of the world or human society as a self-regulating machine or device. For some this led to the idea that institutions and societies could be designed while others concluded that the 'machine', being self-regulating, was also self-developing and should be left alone. In argument this led to the use of analogies with physics, particularly mechanics, as well as the biological sciences.

Second, there was a tremendous faith in the power of reason and a lauding of reason as the only source of true knowledge. There was a corresponding hostility to tradition, castigated as superstition, and to all forms of belief and argument which relied upon prescription or reference to historical precedent.

Third, the idea of progress, a view of the cosmos, humanity, and society as constantly improving and, despite setbacks, moving through time towards the ultimate good. Assertions and proposals were commonly justified by appeals to teleological (i.e. goal-directed) or evolutionary metaphors. Thus there was a justification of changes in political or judicial practice on the grounds that what had been appropriate for an earlier age was unsuitable for the present or future, with any innovation representing an improvement, a move towards a final goal. This often produced an intense hostility to the past, which was regarded as backward and inferior.

Fourth, the idea of humaneness, the argument that brutality, cruelty, and wickedness were not inevitable features of human nature but were caused by mistaken beliefs and bad organization of society. This could imply that human beings were naturally good but the majority saw humans at birth as a *tabula rasa* with no inherent predilection to either good or evil. Fifth was optimism which found its classic expression in Condorcet. Even though Voltaire satirized this attitude in *Candide* he shared the generally upbeat outlook of the movement.

In sixth place was methodological individualism. Most analysis assumed that the autonomous, self-motivating individual was the basic component of society and defined essential selfhood or identity in asocial terms. Hence the tremendous popularity of the Robinson Crusoe myth in which identity is ultimately self-created, surviving total exclusion from human society for many years. This individualism rested on the assumption that there were no inherent or fundamental differences between different classes of humans or people from separate historical epochs. Few went as far as Helvetius who argued that all men were so alike as to be essentially indistinguishable, but Hume's assertion that 'men are much the same in all times and places' articulated a general view. This made cultural and other differences epiphenomena, not part of the true or essential nature of people but simply a mark or imprint made on a common human nature by social and historical conditions. Lastly, there was the rejection of revelation as a source of truth which meant animosity to organized religion, its rituals, and beliefs and the adoption of a critical approach to all institutions and received beliefs.

The shared assumptions of the Scottish branch show important deviations from the list above. The Scots thinkers, including such figures as Smith, Hume, Reid, and Ferguson, were a much more coherent group than the

Continentals since Scotland was simply a more intimate and focused environment with a distinctly provincial and local rather than transnational outlook. They produced certain distinctive and important ideas. The most significant was the insight that most institutions and social structures were the unintended consequences of human action, in Ferguson's words 'the result of human action but not of human design'. Smith's account of the 'invisible hand' of the market was only one application of this principle. Equally famous was Hume's account of the contingent and unintended emergence of the British constitution in the seventeenth century.

Second, the Scottish thinkers shared the Continentals' belief in progress but construed it differently. Smith developed an evolutionary model of historic social and economic development with societies defined as passing through successive stages, but the teleological emphasis of the Continentals was absent. This process of development was not seen retrospectively as inevitable or necessary but rather as a fortunate, unintended accident. As Smith and Ferguson pointed out, many societies had remained at one stage instead of developing. Consequently, the Scots were more reluctant to criticize existing institutions by measuring them against an ahistorical standard of virtue or progress. Hume in particular eschewed the notion that there was one best way of organizing affairs which could be used or applied in all places. Instead they tended to advocate more limited, piecemeal reforms within existing institutions, so continuing the slow, unplanned process of development.

The Scots made two main contributions to Enlightenment political thought. First, they developed the notion of civil society as an entity distinct from, and independent of, the state. Civil society consisted of the totality of private and voluntary social relations while the state was the totality of public and political relations, the *res publica*. This was a longstanding distinction, but the Scottish Enlightenment elaborated it not least through the invention of the discipline of political economy, the systematic study of the workings of civil society. In contrast to most thinkers of that time, the Scots did not see the public sphere as the superior domain and most of them were critical of the widely held belief that the development of private civil relations at the expense of public political ones was regrettable and a sign of decadence. Hume argued this very strongly; Ferguson tended to the opposite, more conventional view.

Second, the Scots originated the notion of 'manners' or 'opinions' as the key political force. This was initiated by Hume who pointed out that in every society the balance of physical power lay overwhelmingly on the side of the governed. States therefore depended for their existence not on force but on opinion, i.e. the beliefs and mental outlook of the subjects. Moreover, Hume argued, the style and nature of government depended not upon laws or constitutions but on the style of manners, i.e. general notions of acceptable and proper behaviour. Where manners were rude and uncivilized, violent and severe rule would be the norm. As manners and opinion became more refined so government would become more gentle and humane. This would happen regardless of the structure of the state. The great enemy of civilized and restrained behaviour and government was 'enthusiasm' i.e. fervent or fanatical adherence to beliefs. This produced a violent, aggressive form of politics where compromise was impossible and led to a jaundiced view of the status quo as corrupt and requiring radical restructuring. This Hume rejected as both naïve and dangerous.

The impact of the Enlightenment on later western thought cannot be overestimated. All subsequent political and social philosophy is either a continuation and development of its main themes or else a reaction against them. In either case it sets the frame within which all later discussion is located. Only in the present century has the overall world-view of the Enlightenment been questioned with the rise of 'post modernism'. Until recently socialist thought has largely ignored the Enlightenment, either taking it for granted or else dismissing it as 'bourgeois ideology'. This argument sees the Enlightenment as the ideological superstructure of an emergent capitalist social system with its thinkers producing ideas and theories which served the interests of the 'rising capitalist class'. Conservatives and liberals, however, have always been acutely aware of their relation to the Enlightenment and have sharply differing views of it and its ideas.

Conservatism from Burke onwards is often defined as a 'counter Enlightenment', a reaction against the main ideas and principles of the Enlightenment and a critique of both its assumptions and its practical consequences. Whether Burke and others saw themselves in this way is debatable; Burke himself can be seen as a member of the Scottish part of the movement, reacting against its Continental wing. In practice, however, the arguments of Burke and others were developed into a powerful critique of the philosophy of the Enlightenment and other conservatives such as De Maistre were avowedly hostile. Most conservative thought thus takes a jaundiced view of the Enlightenment. Its ideas are criticized on several grounds: as being overly rationalistic with an exaggerated and unjustified confidence in the capacity of abstract reason; for their optimism, seen as foolish and dangerous in its disregard of the human potential for evil; for an excessive individualism which ignores the true, social nature of human identity; and above all, for their hostility towards tradition and prejudice.

Also longstanding is the conservative critique of the actual effects of the Enlightenment. It has been blamed, initially by Burke, for causing the French Revolution. More generally, conservatives have argued that the methodology of the Enlightenment disenchants the human world by criticizing and undermining social myths and rituals which, while not capable of being justified in rational terms, are none the less necessary for the effective functioning and survival of human society. This destabilizes society and politics as practices and institutions increasingly lack legitimacy.

Despite all this, many conservatives admire or follow particular Enlightenment thinkers and ideas. In Britain and America in particular, many, while critical of the Continental wing, are ardent supporters of the Scottish one and its ideas. Hayek in particular has argued many times that the Continental Enlightenment was guilty of what he calls 'constructivist rationalism' but that the Scottish Enlightenment produced major breakthroughs in our understanding of human society and the way social institutions utilize dispersed and tacit knowledge, which no one knows in full. He has defined himself several times as a Whig, placing his ideas in an intellectual tradition which goes back to Burke, Hume, Ferguson, and Smith. In Britain one can discern a Whig tradition, including such figures as Lecky, Maine, and Bagehot, which descends via the Edinburgh Reviewers from the Scottish Enlightenment. On the Continent Constant, De Staël, and De Tocqueville are in the same line of descent. The Utilitarian English liberals such as Bentham, the philosophic radicals, and the two Mills derive rather from the Continentals, as did the more radical French and German liberals. Contemporary classical liberals therefore tend to look more favourably on the Enlightenment as a whole although there is almost universal rejection of some of its figures, especially Rousseau.

SD

Further reading

Chitnis, A.C., *The Scottish Enlightenment*, London, Croom Helm, 1976.
Gay, P., *The Enlightenment: An Interpretation*, New York, Knopf, 1966.
Gay, P., *The Science of Freedom*, New York, Knopf, 1969.
Hampson, N., *The Enlightenment*, Harmondsworth, Penguin, 1970.
Palmer, R.R., *The Age of the Democratic Revolution*, Princeton, NJ, Princeton University Press, 1959 (2nd edition 1964).

ENTREPRENEURSHIP

The function of the enterpriser – or more usually and for some reason unknown the, in French, *entrepreneur* – is to identify and to arrange for the taking of economic opportunities. An economic opportunity is here defined as a possibility of producing some sort of good or service for which people will be willing to pay a price higher than the costs of production by an amount sufficiently great to make taking the initiative of launching this fresh enterprise seem worthwhile. This function may, of course, be fulfilled either by an individual or by some co-operating set of individuals. And how much and what percentage is worthwhile must necessarily depend upon the character and circumstances of the particular entrepreneur, whether that particular entrepreneur be an individual or a collective.

Goods or services which can thus be sold in a given market for a worthwhile profit over and above all their costs of production and supply either will or will not be already abundantly available in that market. If they are, then there will be an incentive to establish a fresh enterprise (or for some existing firm to branch out into this, to them, new line) only if and in so far as it is believed that the costs of production and supply by this fresh venture will be so substantially less than the costs incurred by the existing competition that that fresh enterprise will be able to reduce prices by enough to win a sufficient market share. If they are not, then the establishment of the fresh enterprise (or the branching out of the already existing firm into a new line) will result in desired and previously unavailable products becoming available and being freely bought. In either case the fulfilment of the entrepreneurial function results in economic growth.

The greatest of all the comparative advantages claimed by competitive and pluralistic capitalism over all its rivals, socialist and non-socialist, is that it both provides by far the strongest incentives to enterprise and opens to by far the largest proportion of the population the possibility of becoming entrepreneurs. (This possibility will of course be actually realized only by those, always relatively very few, who succeed in first identifying some economic opportunity and are then able to proceed to exercise the necessary attributes of character and fortune effectively.) So the words of Dr Goh Keng Swee, Minister of Finance in what, perhaps perversely, describes itself as a socialist government, are very much to the point. They were copied down from a plaque erected in the central market-place of Singapore, one of the two economically dynamic city states of the Pacific rim: 'A society which wishes for economic growth should nurse the creative talent which its enterprising members possess, and should encourage the development of such talent to its full stature.'

It has often been remarked that the most eloquent tribute ever paid to the incomparable effectiveness of capitalist social arrangements as means for achieving economic growth was that of the *Communist Manifesto*. Yet it is rather rare to notice that neither Marx nor Engels, either there or elsewhere, either asks or attempts to give an answer to a question which, to anyone proposing to revolutionize these arrangements, ought to have appeared crucial: namely, 'What was the secret, and how shall we ensure that, under our proposed alternative arrangements, that secret is not lost?'

That most eloquent and never too-often-repeated tribute reads:

> The bourgeoisie, during its rule of scarce one hundred years, has created more massive and more colossal productive forces than have all the preceding generations together. Subjection of Nature's forces to

man, machinery, application of chemistry to industry and agriculture, steam-navigation, railways, electric telegraphs, clearing of whole continents for cultivation, canalisation of rivers, whole populations conjured out of the ground – what earlier century had even a presentiment that such productive forces slumbered in the lap of social labour?

'Well,' we ought to ask, 'what were these forces, how were they awakened and activated, and how are they to be kept awake and active?' The authors immediately proceed to tell us that

The bourgeoisie cannot exist without constantly revolutionising the instruments of production, and thereby the relations of production, and with them the whole relations of society. . . . Constant revolutionising of production, uninterrupted disturbance of all social conditions, everlasting uncertainty and agitation distinguish the bourgeois epoch from all earlier ones.

But neither here nor later does either of these authors attempt to answer their crucial question.

But now, why does this constant revolutionizing of production – what Schumpeter was later to describe as a 'gale of creative destruction – present itself always and to every individual bourgeois as a compelling need? To this question the first, preparatory response must be that it does not. For there are in fact plenty of firms, not protected by monopoly privileges, which nevertheless continue to stay in business for long periods without even trying to effect any revolutions in their methods of production. (Can anyone, for instance, point to any reference in the Marx–Engels correspondence to any such revolution effected in the Manchester mill of that mini-multinational, Ermen & Engels, during all the long years of the managerial involvement of Friedrich Engels?) This supposedly ever compelling felt need will in fact be felt only when and in so far as there is a perceived threat of formidable competition.

The importance of this first response is as a reminder that all economic innovation involves an exercise of a kind of creativity which cannot be either precisely predicted or guaranteed to occur. Someone has actually to think up what would in fact be a better, more efficient way of doing whatever it may be. Or else, more fundamentally, someone has to invent a new product to be produced or a fresh service which might be provided. After that someone – perhaps, yet not necessarily, someone else again, but very necessarily someone who is in, or can get into, a position to realize that creative idea – someone has to become both persuaded that it is a winner and persuaded actually to put it into effect.

And the greatest comparative advantage of pluralist and competitive capitalism as against more centralized and collectivist systems of ownership and control is not only that the incentives to enterprise are both substantial and widely spread, but also that it is legally and politically possible for almost anyone to take up the role of entrepreneur. For besides manageable attributes of character, the fortune required is not a fortune but luck. And, just so long as the ownership of capital is widely spread, there will be plenty of persons with money to invest who could be persuaded to back a would-be entrepreneur who is pressing some idea which promises to become generously profitable.

AF

Further reading

Gilder, G., *The Spirit of Enterprise*, New York and Harmondsworth, Simon & Schuster and Penguin, 1984 and 1986.
Hayek, F.A., *The Fatal Conceit*, Chicago, IL, and London, Chicago University Press and Routledge & Kegan Paul, 1989.
Kirzner, I., *Competition and Entrepreneurship*, Chicago, IL, Chicago University Press, 1973.
Schumpeter, J.A., *Capitalism, Socialism and Democracy*, New York and London, Harper and Allen & Unwin, 1942.

ENVIRONMENT

In modern political discourse, 'environment' is a word which stands for a whole bundle of issues including such matters as economic growth and its costs, the problems incidental upon rising population, pollution, and the preservation of the natural world, and the management of finite natural resources. In recent years these have become the central themes of 'green politics', a political movement which sees the only real political issue today to be the supposed destruction of the natural environment by modern industrialism. In recent years concern over environmental degradation and the greenhouse effect has led to a rise in support for 'green' parties and has put environmental issues on the political agenda in many countries.

The 'green' movement is conventionally placed on the left but this is simplistic and misleading. Green movements contain a wide range of political views from eco-feudalists to anarcho-communists. What unites them is the view that modern industrial society, whether socialist or capitalist, is not viable in the long, or even medium, term. This is because it requires an ever-increasing consumption of finite natural resources and also because its consequences include damage to the planetary eco-system so severe that, if unchecked, it will cause a general ecological catastrophe and the collapse of human society. A range of measures are proposed to deal with this, some limited and concrete such as the virtual elimination of the private car, others more sweeping such as the end of conventionally defined economic growth.

The response of conservatives and classical liberals to the rise of green movements and their agendas has been mixed. One common response has been to criticize sharply both the programme and analysis of green movements. Their programme, calling for reduction in consumption and energy use, a cessation of economic growth, major changes in personal lifestyles and even, in the extreme version, the end of industrialism, has been attacked on several grounds.

In the first place, the detailed policy proposals of the greens would lead in practice to a totalitarian state because of the need to regulate and control many aspects of people's private lives. Measures such as restrictions on the use of cars would drastically limit the choice and self-determination of individuals. Second, green movements, or parts of them, are marked by a strident irrationalism and hostility to science and reason, despite the immense benefits these have brought to ordinary people. Instead there is a cult of mysticism and primitivism which has alarming similarities to much fascist doctrine. The most serious objection is that the practical effect of environmental policies would be to condemn the overwhelming majority of the world's population to a life of drudgery and poverty since economic growth is the only way they can hope to improve their condition. Green ideas are condemned as being the self-indulgent fantasies of well-off middle-class westerners. Even worse are the ideas of fundamentalist greens that industrialism *per se* should be eliminated. This would lead directly to the death of some three-quarters of the world's present population. Such people are accused of being motivated by hatred of human beings rather than love of animals or the environment.

The greens' basic analysis has also been attacked. Authors such as Simon argue that natural resources are much more plentiful than most green analyses allow and that the earth is capable of supporting far more than its present population without significant environmental damage. The computer models used by such organizations as the Club of Rome are criticized as faulty and self-fulfilling since the initial parameters and assumptions inevitably produced the desired output. This was a classic case of GIGO (garbage in, garbage out).

A more moderate response, mainly from classical liberals, has been to accept the reality of severe environmental damage such as deforestation, species loss, and widespread soil erosion, but then to argue that this is preventable, indeed only preventable, through the use of market mechanisms. This line of argument, developed most thoroughly by Stroup, has several strands. The problem of overpopulation or, to be more precise, over-rapid population growth, is seen to have a simple twofold solution: prosperity and the emancipation of women. Empirical evidence and the theoretical models of economists such as Becker show that as incomes rise, so the need for children as labour and insurance for old age declines while the cost of children (particularly the opportunity cost) rises sharply. The consequence of economic growth is therefore a decline in the birth-rate. The demands of a market economy for labour lead to increased female participation in the labour market, greater female autonomy, and less willingness on the part of women to put up with a life of constant pregnancy.

The second main strand is to argue that markets, prices, and property rights provide the only mechanism which can prevent over-use of finite resources. In the case of finite energy and mineral reserves the combination of property rights and market prices has two effects. As the resource becomes more scarce its price will rise. This will discourage consumption and encourage the search for alternatives. It will also make formerly non-viable sources competitive. Thus renewable energy resources become viable once costs have gone above a critical level. The effect of a price system is also to encourage long-term conservation of resources as this will yield a higher return on capital and guarantee that the conserver will enjoy it. When this is also linked to heritable property rights the market will solve the problem of transgenerational rights, i.e. how to prevent the present generation from using up all of the stock of any good rather than preserving it for future generations.

This relates to the best-known element in the argument, of property rights as a solution to 'the commons problem'. Economic theory predicts that where there is free access to a resource due to incomplete or non-existent property rights then the resource will be overconsumed. The classic statement of this in Hardin's article concerns the case of common grazing land. It is in the general interest that the land be not overgrazed. However, if one individual grazes two goats rather than one the benefit (twice as much milk, meat, and hide) accrues only to that individual and is considerable. The cost (too much grazing) is shared by everyone so one individual's part is miniscule. Therefore all have an incentive to maximize their own use of the resource and it is overconsumed or destroyed. This process is happening today in tropical rainforests. Appeals for restraint are useless in this situation because each actor cannot know for certain that every other actor will also show restraint. If one does and the others do not the individual loses out: consequently no one shows restraint. This is an instance of the wider problems of a 'prisoner's dilemma'. The only solution which has worked is to establish complete property rights in the resource which include the vital power to exclude others from use of it. A contemporary example of this is the case of the African elephant: in eastern Africa it is being hunted to extinction but in Zimbabwe, where local communities have been given property rights to herds, the numbers are increasing.

The third strand of this argument is to apply public choice analysis to conservation issues. This suggests that where resources are allocated through the political process a number of factors will lead to worse problems of pollution and overconsumption than if the resources in question are allocated by the market. Among the factors producing this outcome are the uncertainty of political grants which lead people to maximize short-term gains, the short time horizon of politics generally which leads politicians to pursue policies that will maximize short-term gains rather than long-term sustainable use, and above all the tendency of politics to favour organized special interest groups. This has led in the United States to a disastrous water use policy by which almost every western river has been dammed and water diverted to the politically powerful farmers of southern California. This analysis is borne out by the empirical fact that, while there are environmental problems in western mixed economies, these are nothing compared to the disasters that have occurred in the Soviet Union and its satellites.

This market environmentalism also generates specific policy proposals on several questions. The problem of traffic congestion is seen as due to the fact that road space is free at point of use: the solution is some form of road pricing. Nuclear power is demonstrably not the system that any economically rational actor would use in present circumstances because of the massive downstream costs (waste disposal and the problem of defunct stations) and the prohibitive cost of insurance against the risks involved. This demonstrates another element of the market case, that markets can calculate both the hazards of any activity and the possible trade-off benefits: if the benefits of nuclear power were sufficient the potential insurance costs would be acceptable. As it is, they are not.

The above arguments have been mainly put by classical liberals. Some people, mainly conservatives, go further and accept a substantial part of the green case. Stephen Clark is a classical liberal who has argued the case both for animal rights and for acceptance of the 'Gaia hypothesis', i.e. that the ecosphere is in some sense a single entity. In general, though, he argues the case described above. Some conservatives go further. Waldegrave, a practising politician, has argued both that conventional economic growth may not be sustainable and that conservatism as an ideology has a natural fit or affinity with environmentalism. This is plausible as much traditional conservative argument, such as Burke's stress that each generation has a contract with both future and past, lends itself to an environmental gloss. Many other conservative thinkers such as Southey, Weaver, and Kirk have argued a case against economic growth as the main end of politics. There is also interest in J.S. Mill's concept of the steady state or evenly rotating economy as providing the basis for an economic model of a free and environmentally sound economic system. There is a tradition of conservative thought, hostile to urbanism and industry, sceptical of progress and of science, which has been submerged by economic liberalism but could well come to the fore as other issues than that of whether one is for or against socialism play a greater part in politics.

SD

Further reading

Hardin, G., 'The tragedy of the commons', *Science* 1968, 162: 1243–8.
Hardin, G. and J. Baden, *Managing the Commons*, San Francisco, CA, W.H. Freeman, 1977.
Simon, J., *The Ultimate Resource*, Princeton, NJ, and Oxford, Princeton University Press and Martin Robertson, 1981.
Stroup, R. and J. Baden, *Bureaucracy Versus the Environment*, Ann Arbor, MI, University of Michigan Press, 1981.

EQUALITY

Since the eighteenth century only the most hardy of conservatives have been prepared to argue against any kind of equality. All liberals and most conservatives favour equality in one sense of the term. Yet the idea of equality is at the heart of the debate between conservatives and classical liberals on the one hand and socialists and revisionist liberals on the other. The reason for this is that the word 'equality' is used in political argument to mean two different though related things which conservatives and classical liberals argue are distinct while the other side see them as inextricably intertwined.

The form of equality which all liberals and most conservatives favour is equality of status or legal equality. According to this all responsible adults should be equal before the law. They should all be treated in the same way and have the same legal rights and responsibilities. The political system should not be based upon a structured inequality of status; rather every voter or citizen should have the same standing and rights as any other one. The demand for this type of equality was a basic element of liberalism throughout the nineteenth century. Its existence is now so taken for granted that we forget how revolutionary and unprecedented in European history is this state of affairs.

For almost all political theorists of the medieval and early modern periods it was a basic assumption that there must be a hierarchy in social and political life, with people at different levels of the hierarchy having different political and legal status. The laws of most kingdoms explicitly distinguished between people of different rank or degree; there was not one law for all. It was thought that anything else would be monstrous and unnatural as the entire cosmos was seen as organized on a hierarchical basis with close correspondences between the natural and the human hierarchies. Since all this was divinely created, to challenge the hierarchy was a form of blasphemy. The removal of hierarchy or its subversion would lead to chaos. This view is found in many literary works of the period, particularly those of Shakespeare who produced the classic statement of it in the speech of Ulysses in *Troilus and Cressida*.

In practice medieval and early modern societies were organized on the basis of the threefold division into the clergy (those who prayed), the aristocracy (those who fought), and the third estate (those who worked). This social division was reflected in law and in the organization of the political system. It was sustained by the fundamental division in society between gentlemen and commoners, with political participation reserved in theory for gentlemen. So the achievement of equality of status and equality before the law by liberals during the nineteenth century was a profound revolution in social and political organization. Many nineteenth-century continental conservatives such as Moeser and De Maistre opposed it but modern conservatives, apart from a few eccentrics, are reconciled to it, while many now see the liberal doctrine of legal equality as a vital part of their own view of the world.

Most classical liberals have argued that equality in this sense is all that is needed in a free society. Attempts to go beyond it and realize some other kind of equality by, for example, redistributive taxation or some form of positive discrimination for certain groups, will in fact subvert equality before the law because such actions violate the essential principle that the law treat all alike. However, socialists and revisionist liberals such as Hobhouse and Dewey have argued that legal equality by itself is not enough. For the equality and rights of individuals to be truly meaningful there has to be a degree of equality of condition – meaning in practice equality of wealth. This, they argue, requires redistribution of the social product by the state since the market left to itself produces gross inequality in this regard. The more radical socialists, though not the revisionist liberals, go further and say that the market must be eliminated before meaningful equality in any sense can be attained.

Socialists and revisionist liberals have a battery of arguments to support this position. First, they argue that in a society with marked inequality of wealth, those with relatively little are unable to participate in the life of society and to exercise the legal equality which they undoubtedly possess. Legal equality is not realizable without effective agency, the capacity to use it. Moreover the poor in such a society are in a position of dependency, if not on the state then on private individuals or coporations, and are unable to realize themselves in the way liberals would have them do. They are not truly autonomous. Second, the existence of private concentrations of wealth leads to an unequal distribution of power which can threaten liberty as much as the state does. The paradigmatic case of this was Bolivia before the 1956 revolution when over half of the GNP (in this case tin) was controlled by one man. Most important for many socialists is the thesis that inequality of condition violates a principle of social justice or fairness. The principle cited varies from one author to another, however, with little agreement on what it may be. For some it depends upon a notion of desert, others depend upon an entitlement theory which focuses upon the process by which inequality is created, while for Marxists it is a corollary of the labour theory of value. For many, perhaps the majority, the notion of social justice is simply a rationalization of a gut feeling that things are just not fair.

The arguments and positions of revisionist liberals and socialists are therefore not uniform. Some argue simply that there must be a limit to inequality, in particular that there should be a threshold or minimum below which no one should fall relative to the rest of society. This threshold will inevitably be raised as society becomes richer and expectations higher and it will also be culturally influenced: thus a television was not a necessity of life in the 1950s but can be argued to be one today. Some classical liberals and conservatives accept this minimal egalitarianism but often with the proviso that the threshold be defined in terms of some objective quality such as the 'physical efficiency' criterion used by Rowntree.

Most egalitarians, however, go further. A common position is to argue for an equality of opportunity or 'starting gate equality'. All should start on an equal footing but any inequality which arises thereafter is allowable. This leads to far more radical conclusions than one might at first suppose. For example, it implies the complete abolition of inheritance. The problem in fact is that to arrive at equality of opportunity is exceedingly difficult given the immense influence of family circumstances, not all of which can be equalized without drastic interference with personal liberty and family life.

A slightly different and apparently more radical form of egalitarianism is to argue that there should so far as possible be an equality of end-state. This means that the end result of market outcomes should be adjusted so that the differential between top and bottom of the income range is minimized. The most elegant formulation of this thesis is that given by Rawls who argues that end-states should be equalized to the point where any further equalization would harm rather than help the least well off. The most radical egalitarian position is to demand full equality of outcome. Quite apart from the difficulty of realizing this state the very notion of equality becomes hard to define in such a rigorous way because of the subjective nature of value. If two people each have a television but one hates it and never uses it, in what sense are they equal?

Conservatives and classical liberals have responded to this challenge in a variety of ways. One of the simplest is to reject the thesis of social justice and to argue that in a free economy the distribution of goods is just because it is governed by desert. Wealth will go to the able, hard-working, and industrious while the poor, apart from the special case of the infirm, will be the idle, thriftless, and indigent. In support of this thesis it is pointed out that few people remain poor if they stay married, complete school, and hold down a first job for at least a year. This means that there are two kinds of poor, the deserving (a small group) and the undeserving (the great majority). It also implies that there are deserving and undeserving rich but with the proportions reversed.

Rather different is the position of Hayek who argues that any concept of distributive justice is meaningless. He thus rejects both the left-wing concept of social justice and the traditional notion of desert. For Hayek justice is a concept which can only apply to deliberate intentional actions. Since the distribution of wealth is the unintended outcome of a multitude of actions it cannot be described as just or unjust. The gaining of wealth is so much a matter of chance that it is impossible to define any distribution as just or unjust in terms of desert. Because value is essentially subjective it is impossible to say what equality means since we are talking of equality not of needs, once basic physical minima are met, but of wants. Moreover, it is impossible to know what should be done to achieve any given end-state because the action taken will have unforeseeable consequences. Hayek's powerful argument is very influential but has been criticized both from the left by writers such as Plant and from the right by Kristol.

A different position again is that of writers such as Nozick who argue that one can specify a just end-state and that an end-state, even if sharply unequal, will be just if the distribution was arrived at in a way which did not violate anyone's rights. This entitlement theory of social justice is philosophically very powerful but suffers from the disadvantage of being almost wholly detached from the real world since the requirement of just entitlement is virtually impossible to establish.

Most conservatives and classical liberals, even if they accept one of the philosophical arguments given above, argue against the egalitarians primarily on consequentialist grounds. That is, they argue that even if equality were possible the attempt to achieve it would have disastrous consequences, undersirable even for the egalitarians. First, any attempt to realize equality of condition will involve severe and growing infringement of personal liberty. Second, the kind of actions needed will undermine the prime liberal value of the rule of law because that principle requires that the law should treat all alike and make no distinction between persons and groups. In a redistributive state, groups and people must be treated in different ways to bring about the desired equality of condition. Consequently the rule of law will be replaced by administration of arbitrary, politically inspired rules. The most practical argument is the economic one, that actions taken to bring about equality will, if successful, destroy the incentive to work. Even if unsuccessful their effect will be to so disrupt and distort the signals given by the market to producers and consumers that the productivity of work and capital will be drastically reduced. The end result will be that all will be worse off, not least the poor. Furthermore, the political effect of redistribution will be to turn politics into a desperate struggle to control the state so as to ensure that the redistribution is in one's own favour. In such a Hobbesian war of all against all it is the disadvantaged who will lose out.

A rather different range of arguments are put by those classical liberals (not conservatives) who accept that some degree of equality of condition is desirable but reject the means proposed by the revisionist liberals and socialists for achieving it. One position is to argue that an unfettered market economy is the best means of realizing equality.

This argument has a positive and a negative component. On the positive side it is asserted that the natural tendency of a market economy is towards equality and a more rapid circulation of capital, i.e. even if people become rich they do not stay rich and concentrations of wealth and poverty are evanescent rather than structural. The existence of marked inequality and of longstanding concentrations of wealth is explained as the consequence of state intervention as the state is used by the already rich to defend their position through tax breaks, subsidies, patents, and monopolies, and institutions such as limited liability which favour them. A specialized version of this argument is the Georgist one which sees the inequality of market economies as being the consequence of the private ownership of land leading to the creaming off of wealth in rents and land values which accrue as unearned increment to a class of parasitic landlords.

The negative part of the argument consists of the application of public choice theory to questions of distribution. It is argued that the logic of politics and the vote motive mean that in practice state intervention to promote equality of condition will never realize its ostensible aim but will in fact work to the benefit of privileged groups. This has been summed up as Director's Law, that redistribution is always from the top and bottom to the middle, never from top to bottom. Politically determined distribution of goods as opposed to market distribution will always favour groups with political clout such as farmers rather than the majority of the population.

Classical liberals who take the above line differ over how equality should be achieved. Some argue simply for a minimal state and a *laissez-faire* economy. However, if this means the abolition of institutions such as limited liability and wage labour with everyone being self-employed, then the economy and society envisaged are very different from what goes under the name of capitalism today. Others argue for some kind of measure to give everyone a certain amount of property. This argument, associated with Belloc and Chesterton, was popular before the First World War and has resurfaced in a modified form in proposals for a 'capital grant' put forward by Peacock and others.

Arguments about equality are the most powerful and effective weapon available to revisionist liberals and socialists in their debate with conservatives and classical liberals. As the above indicates, classical liberals are much more defensive on this score than conservatives. This is because the existence of deep inequality of condition *is* a problem for classical liberals even if they decide that for consequentialist or other reasons nothing can be done about it. If private property and the market are defended on the grounds that they promote autonomy, then it is hard to resist the arguments given above, that inequality poses a threat to autonomy and makes the promise of freedom in a market society less than meaningful for many.

For conservatives, by contrast, there is no such difficulty since for them freedom is not the primary political good. For conservatives the state of inequality is natural and, within wide limits, desirable. Conservatives have always argued for the need for an elite to provide social, cultural, and political leadership and have argued like Melbourne that 'there's no damned merit in it'. The existence of a hierarchy is both inevitable and desirable since for conservatives it is an important source of social stability and cohesion.

At the same time, while scoring points with some of their arguments, the revisionist liberals and socialists have had to take on board much of the negative argument of the conservatives and classical liberals. They are now much more aware of the difficulties of using the state to redistribute wealth and that in practice there has to be a complex trade-off between the values of equality and liberty which limits the scope of egalitarianism. The sharp and fundamental division on this question which existed twenty years ago is now much less clear.

SD

Further reading

Flew, A., *The Politics of Procrustes*, Buffalo, NY, and London, Prometheus and Temple Smith, 1981.
Gray, J., *Hayek on Liberty*, Oxford, Blackwell, 1986.
Hayek, F.A., *Law, Legislation and Liberty*, London, Routledge & Kegan Paul, 1982.
Plant, R., *Equality, Markets and State*, London, Fabian Society, 1985.
Rawls, J., *A Theory of Justice*, Oxford, Oxford University Press, 1972.

F

FAMILY

The term 'family' has two distinct meanings: (i) a system of kinship arrangements among people related by blood and marriage and living (for some part of their lives) in a common household; (ii) blood relations as such, conceived as linking generations through the inclusion of individuals through either maternity or paternity.

Clearly, the family is the most ubiquitous social institution known in history. It comes in various forms, but at the heart of every form are parenthood and durable sexual relations. In the West, in particular, and in trading societies in general, the conventional husband–wife–child form of the family has been dominant. Less close ties of kinship are often reflected in co-operative relations for economic purposes, as in the extended family typical of agrarian societies.

Conservatives are generally concerned to uphold the family as a social institution common to all classes and integral to social and political order. For Burke, the family, not the individual, is the basic unit of social order, expressing the fact that human fulfilment depends on participation in customs and institutions and respect for norms and laws which convey to the individual a sense of unity with his closest fellows. Where some conservatives have seen the family as an institution grounded in natural law, much of conservative thought has regarded the family as providing a form of primary social bond that is reinforced by, and constitutes the basis of, the inheritance of values, knowledge, discipline, and skills, and also of property.

Plato notoriously advocated collective nurture, education, and ownership. Aristotle, in his answer to Plato in the *Politics*, laid down a defence of marriage, the family, and the household based on a connection between the relations of domestic love and those of private property. Hegel went beyond this by regarding the family as a necessary part of individual development, from the level of undifferentiated union with others to those of civil society and of the state. His theory of the family is just one stage in the unfolding or actualization of Right. For Hegel, marriage is the distinctive and appropriate relationship between the sexes. It involves the mutual renunciation of independence, of 'selfish isolation', and the consequent awareness of mutual unity. Through their membership in a family, individuals cease to be 'independent persons' and come to recognize themselves as first and foremost members of some larger entity. Hegel insists that the family, like the state, is not contractual in nature; family bonds arise not out of consent, but are based in piety, i.e. in a natural and involuntary form of allegiance.

Marxist thought derives its call for 'the abolition of the family' voiced in the *Communist Manifesto* from ideas contained in Engels's *The Origin of the Family*. Anticipating the ideas of modern feminism, Engels argued that the bourgeois family rested on a material foundation of inequality between husband and wife, the latter producing (legitimate) heirs for the transmission of property in return for mere board and lodging. As an institution dependent on capitalist relations of production, the (bourgeois) family will collapse together with the institutions of private property and of the state. On the basis of such ideas, much of contemporary Marxist thought has concentrated on characterizing the family as a (purely accidental) social institution and as an ideology. Such attempts have at times coalesced with psychoanalytic doctrines of suppression centring on the idea that individuals become inevitably crippled by growing up in a family environment which requires from them conformity to a source of authority outside themselves. The radical critique of the family along these lines finds some backing in Rousseau's view that education should not be left to the family but rather be made the task of the state.

Liberal thought is in principle consistent with a view of the family as arising from a contract among its members (such was the view propounded by both Hobbes and Kant). This view finds its most pronounced expression in the claim of modern economists that the family, like any other producing unit, makes use of a long-term marriage contract to reduce the (transaction) costs and greater risks that a solitary existence would involve for all family members. Not only can spouses produce certain goods (such as children, prestige, status, sex, and companionship) not otherwise readily duplicated; families operating as a single household can, on account of the economies of scale involved, also produce many goods more efficiently than can several single-person households.

Economic explanations of this kind, however, which centre on the costs and benefits of family life, invariably neglect the non-rational aspects of spouse selection and of family bonds, many of which are not readily reducible to economic benefits. The lack of appreciation of much of human nature expressed by such attempts is, for instance, reflected by the attacks of classical liberalism on the inheritance of property.

Conservatives, on the other hand, generally reject the idea of family ties as contractual, or family obligations as in any way arising from a free relinquishing of autonomy. The family is an autonomous form of social organization, desirable as an instrument for the transmission of morals, tastes, knowledge, and property which is singularly apt for the launching of the individual in life. But it is also the most important generator of social cohesion, and the place where the quality of the next generation is to a large extent determined. The family is also the focus of one of the most powerful of human incentives – the urge to found a dynasty, to leave one's descendants in a more favourable situation. Much of the motivation behind entrepreneurship comes from the desire to have a durable and substantial legacy to pass on to one's offspring. This is the one central respect in which the existence of families modifies the principles of individualism.

Intimacy and communality are virtues in a small social group such as the family, monastery, club, and small village community. To transfer to the state or other large-scale organization the kind of communality that fits the small group, is, from the conservative point of view, to invite regimentation, sterile uniformity, and repressive collectivism. The support and protection of the family will therefore be central to the conservative outlook, and changes in the law which are calculated to loosen or abolish the ties of family life will consequently be resented. This institution and the energies it engenders is, from the conservative point of view, to be fostered, not harassed.

WG

Further reading

Aristotle, *Politics*, trans. E. Barker, Oxford, Clarendon, 1948.
Becker, G.S., *A Treatise on the Family*, Cambridge, MA, Harvard University Press, 1981.
Hegel, G.W.F., *Philosophy of Right*, trans. T.M. Knox, Oxford, Oxford University Press, 1942.
Mount, F., *The Subversive Family*, London, Jonathan Cape, 1982.
Scruton, R., *The Meaning of Conservatism*, London, Macmillan, 2nd edition, 1984.

FEDERALISM

Federalism is a political system in which sovereignty is divided between central and local government rather than being located in one place. The United States, Canada, Australia, and West Germany are all federal states. Strictly speaking a distinction should be made between federal states which are unitary entities with divided sovereignty and confederations such as Switzerland where sovereign entities, in that instance the cantons, devolve part of their sovereign power to a central administration while retaining ultimate power themselves, most crucially the right to withdraw or secede from the arrangement. In practice the term 'federalism' is used to refer to both situations with distinctions being made between varying degrees of federalism. Federalism is to be contrasted with the unitary state where there is no division of sovereignty. The United Kingdom is one such: all power rests with 'the Crown in Parliament' (in reality a majority of the House of Commons) and all other authority, e.g. that of local government, is delegated. Parliament may legislate as it pleases to amend, restrict, or control the exercise of the powers of local government. By contrast, in a federal state such as Australia or the United States the scope of the power and activity of central and local government is defined by a constitutional law, and legislation passed by one side which infringes the prerogatives of the other can be declared invalid.

Federalism first arose towards the end of the eighteenth century as a reaction against the centralizing tendencies of absolute monarchies in the latter phase of the *ancien régime*. Most of the Enlightenment *philosophes* supported centralization as a progressive measure which would remove reactionary and obscurantist provincialism. The French Revolution proved to be strongly centralist and exported the model of a centralized unitary state to other parts of Europe such as Switzerland where the Helvetic Republic set up in 1798 replaced the cantons. Federalism thus came to be associated with resistance to the revolution and support for old traditional decentralized forms of government. However, not all of the radicals were centralizers; there was another tendency, typified by the Girondins in France, which favoured a radical decentralization of sovereignty. Federalism was developed as a constitutional theory after 1815 by a number of writers, the most important in Europe being Proudhon and the Spanish libertarian Pi y Margall. In the United States the most significant figure was Calhoun. The central doctrine was that political power should be exercised at as local and small scale a level as possible with only the most minimal functions being reserved for central government. Power and sovereignty should flow upwards from the locality to the centre not the other way round. This would inevitably mean a wide variation in laws, practices, and ways of life between the various parts of a federal state, and implied that any political measure which affected all of the constituent parts of a federal state, or which derogated the specific interests of certain parts, must be supported by more than a simple arithmetical majority to be valid. This was essentially the argument put forward by Calhoun in his doctrine of the 'concurrent majority'.

In most countries conservatives and classical liberals are strong advocates of federalism. The main exception is Britain where the dominance of the doctrine of absolute parliamentary sovereignty is such that only minor parties and individuals support moves to a federal state. Contemporary conservatives and classical liberals have a variety of arguments in favour of federalism. Most important is the argument that the division of political power limits the damage that any one authority or political body can do. A socialist administration in a district or part of a federal state can only affect the lives of those people directly under it. In a unitary state, if the wrong people gain control of the central legislature and government there is no limit to the scope of their misdeeds. Federalism in practice works, therefore, to limit the scope of politics since national administration will only be concerned with a limited range of matters while at the local level governments which, because of the limited size of their tax base, lack the redistributive and spending potential of larger, national, governments will not be such an attractive target for pressure groups. Another argument is that federal systems will help to protect a diversity of local customs, communities, and lifestyles. Also, power is more widely distributed, instead of being concentrated in one place or institution, so again minimizing the dangers of power being seized by dangerous people. Some exponents of the public choice theory have argued that the problems which exist in the political decision-making process are minimized at a small-scale, localized level because then the relative costs and benefits of any measure are more clearly apparent and the scope for 'log-rolling' is correspondingly less. Yet another argument is that a federal state is less likely to be warlike or to pursue an interventionist foreign policy because only very pressing matters in that area will agitate all of the units of such a state.

There are, however, some conservatives and classical liberals, in Britain and elsewhere, who take a very different view. One argument put by some is that in reality sovereignty cannot be divided as in any political system there must be an ultimate source of authority. If an attempt is made to divide political power there will be acute tension, even outright conflict, until the location of the ultimate power is settled one way or another. Another argument is that localized government can be more dangerous to individual liberty than the national variety and that central government must have the power to intervene and override local administration so as to protect individuals. However, the main actual counter-argument, though often not explicitly stated, reflects the contemporary political situation and expediency rather than abstract principle. It is that the argument for the limiting capacity of federalism is all well and good when the main problem is the attempts of central government to expand the state, but that today when the state has been expanded and the aim of conservatives and classical liberals is to reduce its role a federal system would be used primarily to block attempts by central government to reduce the scale of state action.

In the twentieth century the tendency in most federal states has been to expand the powers of the centre at the expense of the locality. The only major exception is Canada. This may reflect technological change or the decline of local patriotism or may be a consequence of the workings of a mass democracy. However, there are signs that this trend is being reversed in several countries, and if so the federalist component of conservative and classical liberal thought which has had little prominence of late may once again come to the fore.

SD

Further reading

Dicey, A.V., *An Introduction to the Study of the Law of the Constitution*, London, Macmillan, 1959.
Proudhon, P.-J., *The Idea of Federalism*, Toronto, Toronto University Press, 1982.
Wright, B.F. (ed.), *The Federalist Papers* , Cambridge, MA, Harvard University Press, 1961.

FEMINISM

'Feminism' is a term which refers both to a body of ideas and to an active political and intellectual movement based on the application of those ideas to contemporary society. Feminism is highly variegated, both as a movement and as theory and cannot be fitted easily into any simple political spectrum. Contemporary feminism is usually seen as being on the left and as having affinities to socialism, but the reality is much more complex. Historically, feminism has been as closely linked to classical liberalism as to socialism. The central belief which all forms of feminism share, whatever their other differences, is that women as persons are of equal value to men. This means that the personhood or identity of a woman is as complete and fully possessed of rights as that of a man. The polemical assertion of all types of feminism is that this equal worth of women and men is denied by existing laws, social arrangements, and attitudes. These are charged with denying women complete and autonomous identity – a woman is defined in terms of her relationship to a man and is not seen as a complete and separate person. Feminists are particularly critical of three ideas: the existing concept of femininity, which sees women as emotional, illogical, and passive; the 'angel in the house' model of domesticity which sees women as finding self-realization only or primarily through motherhood and caring in the household; and the idea of 'separate spheres' which divides life into a masculine sphere of public affairs, politics, and power and a feminine one of private life, domesticity, and caring.

Historically, feminism is a product of the Enlightenment. There were 'proto-feminists' before then but they laboured under the handicap of arguing within a traditional Christian world-view. Since then there have been three main schools of feminist thought, individualist, socialist, and radical. The first argues that women are denied freedom and autonomy as individuals because of their sex by a combination of laws and social structures which deny them choice and self-realization. This was the dominant form of feminism in nineteenth-century Britain and America.

The major works in the tradition are those of J.S. Mill and Wollstonecraft. Feminists of this school have often advocated an economy of total *laissez-faire* as the necessary environment for female emancipation. Socialist feminism in contrast argues that the peculiar subjection of women is an inherent part of capitalism and that the replacement of that system by socialism is a necessary condition of their liberation. Radical feminism is more recent, only emerging in the 1950s and 1960s with the works of writers such as Millett, De Beauvoir, and Firestone. The assertion here is that all women are oppressed by men through the basic social structure of patriarchy; their subordination is thus collective since they are dominated as a class.

Feminism's relationship to all other ideologies is problematic. Although many feminists are socialists, feminism poses severe problems for socialist analysis. In particular, the idea of sexual divisions and domination cuts across the class analysis which is the core of most socialist thought. Also, feminists argue that economic change is not enough because patterns of belief are autonomous. This conflicts with the Marxist idea that ideas and beliefs are ultimately determined by the organization of production. Finally, it is not easy to reconcile the feminist insistence on self-discovery, freedom of lifestyle, and autonomy with collectivism. Much contemporary conservative thought is profoundly antipathetic to feminism, seeing it as hostile to the family, as collectivist in philosophy because it defines the identity and interests of women in collective terms, and as subversive of social stability. There are also sharp disagreements on particular issues such as abortion and the rights and moral standing of homosexuals. Classical liberals are generally more discriminating, making a distinction between the different varieties of feminism. The debate here is more about means than ends, with liberals arguing that the state and collectivism are not helpful in the search for women's emancipation. The crucial issue for liberals, conservatives, and feminists is the nature and role of the traditional family. For conservatives and many liberals it is the basic building-block of society, an entity in itself; for most feminists and strictly individualist liberals it is an arrangement between individuals, a means to an end rather than an end in itself. This divide between feminism and conservatism seems likely to widen, given the increased prominence of 'family issues' in contemporary politics.

SD

Further reading

Charvet, J., *Feminism*, London, Dent, 1982.
Elshtain, J.B., *Public Man, Private Woman*, Princeton, NJ, Princeton University Press, 1981.
Richards, J.R., *The Sceptical Feminist*, London, Routledge & Kegan Paul, 1980.
Rossi, A.S. (ed.), *J S Mill & Harriet Taylor: Essays on Sex Equality*, Chicago, IL,

Chicago University Press, 1970.
Wollstonecraft, M., *A Vindication of the Rights of Woman*, Harmondsworth, Penguin, 1975.

FREEDOM

The idea of freedom is an important one for all schools of political thought but a vital one for liberalism. For liberals, as the etymology of the word 'liberal' suggests, are those who 'put freedom first' and see freedom as the primary political good. For liberals other goods, such as prosperity, are of value only in so far as they contribute to freedom. It is this commitment to freedom as the primary political value which is the distinctive mark of the genus liberal, as opposed to other political philosophies, including conservatism. The divisions and disagreements among liberals, and particularly those between the classical and revisionist varieties, are primarily due to differing notions of what freedom is and how it may be established.

This confusion arises because the concept of freedom is not a simple one and also because, as Berlin's classic work *Four Essays on Liberty* pointed out, there are two separate and different concepts of freedom which generate very different prescriptions for public policy. Broadly speaking, revisionist liberals and social democrats adhere to one of these definitions, classical liberals to the other. Problems arise because the same word is used for both concepts and its has therefore become customary to distinguish them by speaking of positive and negative liberty. We also need to recognize yet another notion of freedom, that of political liberty which is, and has been, influential in non-liberal political movements.

The words liberty and freedom have been used in western political writing since the high Middle Ages, but originally freedoms or liberties meant specific rights or entitlements, usually given or recognized by the king, which were held by specified groups such as urban communities, the aristocracy or clergy as a whole, or specific persons or corporations. These were the 'liberties' which English monarchs vowed to uphold in their coronation oaths. The idea of freedom as a general condition, shared equally among all citizens in a free society, only begins to appear in the sixteenth and seventeenth centuries, in the works of writers such as Hobbes, Locke, and Sidney. It was during the eighteenth century that British and Continental thinkers firmed up these ideas into the concept of what is now generally, following Berlin, called negative freedom.

Negative liberty, as defined by liberals such as Constant, Berlin, and Hayek, is so called because it is in some sense a negative condition, consisting of the absence of restraint and coercion. It is *freedom from* rather than *freedom to*. Negative liberty is linked to individualism in that the concept implies the existence of a personal, private sphere of untrammelled action in which individuals can do as they wish and are not inhibited from doing so by a force external to themselves. As Berlin puts it,

I am normally said to be free to the degree to which no man or body of men interferes with my activity. Political liberty in this sense is simply the area within which a man can act unobstructed by others. If I am prevented by others from doing what I could otherwise do, I am to that degree unfree.

A crucial point in this is that negative liberty cannot be infringed by the unintended consequences of human action such as customs, the distribution of wealth, and unplanned social structures.

Liberals recognize two qualifications to negative liberty. It must be equal, that is the freedom enjoyed by one person must be the same as that enjoyed by every other one. Classical liberals argue that it is only negative freedom which can be universalized in this way since it is feasible to remove all restraints on human action equally from all individuals. Equality of freedom also implies that the freedom of one individual should not infringe the freedom of others since if that were the case one person would have more freedom than another.

This leads to the second qualification, that freedom must be exercised under law. There must be a body of neutral rules which regulate clashes between the private spheres of individuals. This proviso can cause difficulty to liberals. J.S. Mill attempted to specify when law was necessary with his Liberty Principle, that law could only restrain the free action of an individual when their action harmed someone else. This is vitiated by the intractable ambiguity of the concept of harm. Others argue for a procedural test. Hayek, for instance, argues that to be bound by law is not to be coerced, and one is therefore free in the negative sense, when laws are general rules which bind all equally and in the same way. This is not coercion since, for Hayek, coercion means being subject to the arbitrary, because unknowable, will of another person or persons. Many liberals say this is not enough since, for example, in Hayek's own view conscription is not an infringement of negative liberty if it is conducted in a way which does not discriminate between individual cases. The overwhelming majority of liberals would dissent very strongly from that view and therefore argue that there has to be some body of absolute freedoms, a sphere of negative liberty which cannot be limited by law, no matter if that law is neutral.

There is also another definition of freedom, in terms of agency, that is of capacity or ability to act even in the absence of restraint. This derives from the idea of autonomy, of freedom as self-realization, which originates in Continental idealist metaphysics. The idea of autonomy exists in two forms, one narrowly, the other broadly, defined. The first can be traced back to Kant, possibly to Spinoza, the other to Hegel.

In the Kantian idea of autonomy, to be autonomous is to be a self-governing agent, to rule oneself and decide for oneself rather than being ruled by others. This derives from two key elements in Kant's thought: that we should always treat human beings as ends in themselves, not as means; and that all rules must be capable of universalization so that we would wish them to apply in our own case as much as any other. In this way of thinking someone who is free to act, i.e. negatively free, may still not be a free person if their action is restricted by fear, delusion, social pressure, or other impersonal constraints. This does not mean that one can only realize one's self in conditions of zero restraint, only that restraint can be internalized as well as external. This addresses one of the most serious criticisms of the negative concept of freedom, that it defines coercion too narrowly to mean primarily coercion by the state. The insight of Kantian argument is that power and coercion can take many forms other than overt political power. This more extended, yet still limited, concept of freedom was very influential in Germany as, for example, in Schiller and Humboldt. Through the latter it profoundly influenced J.S. Mill.

Many classical liberals still see this definition of freedom as dangerous. It can be used to justify paternalist interference with personal lifestyles on the grounds that some habits or ways of life (e.g. that of a habitual drunkard) render the individual incapable of acting as a free agent. It also raises very difficult issues of parental power and the rights of children: what view should a liberal take of parents who bring up their children in a religious environment that limits the Kantian autonomy of women, for example? More conservative oriented liberals such as Hayek also criticize it on the grounds that it leads (as in Mill and Humboldt) to a hostility to tradition when tradition is a necessary feature of a free society since the alternative to it is rationalist construction.

The more extended version of freedom as autonomy is the fully fledged notion of positive liberty. Here freedom is taken to be not just the absence of restraint but the capacity to act. If freedom means self-realization then, in this conception, to be free means that one must have the means to achieve that realization. This means, first, that negative freedom is seen as not enough by itself; one has to be *able* to perform the act one is free to do. This is the view summarized in such remarks as 'a hungry man is not free' or 'a poor man is not free to buy a Rolls-Royce'. Second, it means that freedom is a positive state or condition brought about by access to resources. Hence revisionist liberals from T.H. Green onwards have argued that extensions of state intervention and some forms of interference with freedom of contract can lead to an increase in total aggregate freedom. The most extreme form of the Hegelian idea of positive freedom is that found in writers such as Stirner and many neo-Marxists, not to mention Marx himself. Here freedom means unrestricted self-realization, with all social and other restraints defined as oppression. As Minogue has pointed out, this leads to a paranoid vision of the world where even the most free society is seen as embodying a system of concealed domination.

Classical liberals have been severely critical of all forms of this notion of positive freedom. In the first place, there is a confusion of thought between being *free* to do something and being *able* to do it. Second, this way of thinking makes freedom equivalent to power and it is not possible to distribute power equally. Liberals agree that it would be better in some cases if all were able to do things as well as being free to do them , but they argue, first, that the attempt to achieve that will destroy negative freedom and, second, that much positive freedom argument assumes that all desires are fundamentally similar and capable of being made possible of realization for all people at once. This is theoretically impossible, because some objects of desire cannot be held or enjoyed equally by their very nature (e.g. positional goods), while in other cases it is practically impossible for everyone to be able to do something they are free to do – even if they all wanted to. So, for example, while everyone is free to have a Rolls-Royce it is not feasible for everyone to be able to do so. This brings out the intimate connection between positive liberty and equality and suggests the way that positive liberty can be used to justify considerable restriction of negative liberty.

These issues were shown very clearly in an example given by the great Victorian judge, Lord Bramwell. When Bramwell said, 'Every Englishman is free to dine at the Ritz', a remark which has been the object of ridicule from leftists ever since, he was not making the kind of fatuous and naïve comment which so often brings the English judiciary into well-deserved disrepute. He knew full well that many people, while free to dine at the Ritz, were unable to do so and he wished to draw this narrow but vital distinction. In a society enjoying negative freedom the only reason why someone could not do this would be that they lacked the wherewithal. To give everyone the means to do so would make the good in question no longer desirable and would involve distributing resources by political criteria rather than market ones. In societies where access to resources is determined by politics, *both* negative and positive liberty are diminished. In South Africa until very recently no black person, however wealthy, could dine at their equivalent of the Ritz because access was determined by politically defined racial categories, while in Leninist states enjoyment of such pleasures is dependent upon possession of a Party card.

Liberals argue, in other words, that negative liberty is the primary good. Many socialists argue that a poor man who enjoys negative liberty is worse off than if he trades his negative freedom for the positive freedoms provided by state welfare. Thus a Cuban living under Castro's vile regime is better off, even more 'free', than a slum-dweller in Costa Rica. Liberals deny this directly: to be poor but free is still better than to be well off but enslaved. (Not that these last two ever coincide in reality!) Even if a criterion of autonomy is used, a poor person who enjoys negative liberty is still freer than a rich person who does not because they still have more choice, even if their capacity to make use of it is limited, and free choice is essential if one is to act as an autonomous agent. The crucial argument between classical and revisionist liberals, as well as social democrats, is over how far negative and positive definitions of liberty are compatible.

There is no disagreement among liberals over the third common definition of freedom, which regards it as participation in political life. This is the kind of view which leads its proponents to argue that former colonial populations are now more free than when under colonial rule, even if under the thumb of tyrants, because they are 'self-governing'. This is to confuse political procedure with freedom. It also means that one is not free unless one participates in a process of public choice regardless of whether one wishes to or not. Liberals of all varieties have been hostile to this idea and have recognized that any political process can lead to a loss of liberty. The classic critique of this concept of freedom was produced by Constant. He pointed out that 'ancient' liberty (i.e. freedom as participation) led to a situation where the public sphere was all and there was no liberty for the private domain of lifestyle, opinion, and belief because everything had been politicized.

As the above suggests, concepts of freedom, particularly when taken to be the prime political good, generate detailed agendas. Broadly speaking, the positive theory leads to the agenda of social democracy, of the need to use the public authority to enable individuals to actualize their freedoms. The more limited conception of autonomy generates a political programme which, while far more limited than the social democratic, still gives an enabling role to the state. The strictly negativist view leads, if taken seriously, and not combined with a conservative view of politics, to the minimalist state, although this is also compatible with a limited notion of autonomy, as in the case of Humboldt.

The question of freedom is of great interest to liberals because it is, as said, their definitive goal. This is not the case with other political philosophies, several of which do not give freedom such an elevated place. Some socialists, such as Arblaster, freely admit that they place it below other values such as equality or improvements in physical conditions. From a religious political perspective the main goal is to please God: freedom may be instrumental to this end but is not a good in and of itself. Most significantly for this work, conservatives do not in general see freedom as the *summum bonum*. Although most modern conservatives regard freedom, defined negatively, as *a* good, they will subordinate it to others, particularly order and tradition. This reflects the standard conservative view that without order no other political good is possible so that freedom is a secondary, consequential good. Conservatives are also suspicious of the moral relativism which they detect in much theorizing of liberty: why should people be free to pursue ends if those ends are bad? (Bad, that is, in the sense of violating a traditional or religious code, not in the sense which liberals would accept of diminishing another's freedom.) This reflects either the belief that there is a single standard of virtue which the state should promote or else the belief that no society can survive if there is not a consensus on moral values. Arguments of this sort have led conservatives like Cowling to assert that there is now not too little freedom but too much.

SD

Further reading

Benn, S.I. and W.L. Weinstein, 'Being free to act and being a free man', *Mind* 1971, LXXX: 194–211.
Berlin, I., *Four Essays on Liberty*, Oxford, Oxford University Press, 1969.
Brittan, S., *Capitalism and the Permissive Society*, London, Macmillan, 1973.
Cranston, M., *Freedom: A New Analysis*, London, Longman, 1953.

FRENCH CONSERVATISM

In France since 1789 the basic political division has been that between left and right, terms far more precise and meaningful than in other countries, with the right defined as those who were opposed to the Revolution and its values. In France more than anywhere else conservatism consists of what one historian, Alfred Cobban, calls 'a revolt against the eighteenth century'. Some confusion arises because as time passed and the prospect of restoring the *ancien régime* slid into the realms of fantasy so the location of the right in politics moved steadily to the left. A constitutional monarchist, a centrist in 1815, would have been on the extreme right by 1915. This process, known to the French as the *glissade à gauche* (slide to the left) happened throughout Europe in the nineteenth century but was particularly important in France. French conservatism as theory was both a critique of the Revolution and Enlightenment and an attempt to arrest the *glissade* by keeping right positions intellectually and politically respectable.

French conservatism is very different from the Anglo-Saxon variety both in style and content. It is more abstract and logical, far more uncompromising and extreme. It has for much of its history an intransigent, fundamentalist quality not found in conservatism in Britain or most of the United States. French conservatism has a strongly clerical character, being intimately associated with ultramontanist Catholicism. French conservatives have been more fundamentally alienated from and hostile to modernity as such and have consequently been much less friendly to democracy and capitalism – indeed some have been sharply critical of market economics. In practical terms French conservatives have since at least 1830 been alienated from the state and its institutions, regarding them as illegitimate. Consequently French conservatism became in its penultimate phase a revolutionary doctrine.

The collapse of the *ancien régime* in 1789–91 produced several politicians who sought to defend the old ways in the constituent assembly, the most important being Maury. However, a comprehensive intellectual response to the Revolution and its events only appeared later in the works of Bonald and De Maistre. For them the revolution was something unprecedented in history, a threat not just to France but to the whole structure of civilization. Consequently their hostility to the Revolution and its ideals was so fundamental that it led to a profound critique of modernity in general and of what they saw as its main features – democracy, secularism and the cult of reason, the open society based on personal rights, and the competitive market economy.

Democracy is attacked, particularly by De Maistre, as inherently non-sensical. Power is always in the hands of a few rather than the many and never held by all. In any society there are always rulers and ruled and to suggest otherwise is foolishness. Power must be absolute in its own sphere, otherwise the right of private judgement is set above it and the consequence of that can only be chaos. True order is only possible if there is one final authority – in secular matters the state, in spiritual ones the Pope.

Secularism and the Enlightenment cult of reason are criticized on the grounds that a stable social and political order are only possible if there is an underlying consensus on spiritual values. The corrosive scepticism engendered by the Enlightenment and the corresponding loss of certainty occasioned by the secular world-view create an anomic, valueless world which is without meaning and where nothing has any true value. The lack of consensus divides society into warring groups who do not even talk a common moral language and makes possible the ruthless amoralism of Robespierre or Marat since it is no longer possible to pass judgement. Where nothing is forbidden everything is permitted.

The competitive market economy, Bonald and De Maistre argue, destroys stable social relationships and communities and produces an atomized social order where purportedly free individuals are at the mercy of impersonal economic forces. The creation of an economy driven by the search for profit elevates greed and destroys the aristocratic virtues of honour and chivalry.

Most serious is their attack on the notion of an open society based on personal rights. True flourishing and fulfilment of individuals is only possible, they argue, in an organic society where everyone has a place and role and consequently a clear identity. To insist upon personal rights is to split society up into a mass of *déraciné* individuals, each one cut off from the historic roots which are the true source of identity and therefore a stunted, undeveloped person. The result can only be the demise of civilization and the rise of a new barbarism.

This kind of conservatism is clearly different from the more moderate and pluralistic conservatism of Burke. However, the distinction should not be exaggerated: Burke and his French counterparts shared many beliefs but Bonald and De Maistre may have been more clear-minded about their implications. The vile state of modernity is contrasted with an idealized version of the past, for Bonald the *ancien régime*, for others the Middle Ages, while De Maistre located it between the Fall and the Flood. He was, perhaps paradoxically, realistic because for others the problem was that of explaining how such a good and divinely ordained social order had been subverted. Some blamed Protestantism, others Freemasonry, yet others the Jews.

This intransigent philosophy went along with an equally rigid political position and after 1814 its exponents, the ultras, sought to restore the old order in full. They had their opportunity in 1828 under Charles X, but his policies soon led to the 1830 coup and the establishment of the July monarchy. However, a substantial body of French conservative opinion remained unreconciled to the established state and continued to burnish their arguments. In this they were supported by the Catholic Church, particularly under Pius IX whose Syllabus of Errors condemned just about every single liberal doctrine. There were more moderate conservatives as well such as Chateaubriand and the early Lamennais, but in many ways they shared the basic analysis of the ultras while taking a more realistic and historical approach to their application in the modern world.

However, after 1848 the mainstream of French conservatism took a more moderate turn, under the influence of the historical approach pioneered by Bourget and Brunetière. Brunetière developed the concept of genre and used it as the basis for a basically historical and anti-individualist account of the evolution of national cultures and identities. Bourget made other conservatives more aware of the values of pluralism and the existence in society of a wide range of intermediate traditional institutions. These ideas were extended and applied by scholars such as Taine and Le Play. The general thrust, however, was anti-modern and opposed to individualism.

As the nineteenth century came to a close the two streams of French conservatism were united in a movement which between 1880 and 1910 bid fair to dominate the cultural and intellectual life of France. There were several brilliant intellectuals involved, notably La Tour du Pin, Barrès and Le Bon, but the central figure was Maurras. These intellectuals introduced new ideas to French conservatism and sought to apply the principles of Bonald and De Maistre to the modern world. La Tour du Pin developed the concept of corporatism, the idea that society should be reorganized into corporate bodies based on the medieval guilds. Le Bon founded the discipline of mass psychology and extended the critique of democracy. Maurras produced a blueprint for reviving the *ancien régime* in the conditions of modern times. There were major concessions made to modernity. Thus Maurras identified truth not with religious revelation as De Maistre had done but with a body of objective truth established by study. However, he argued that religious belief should be maintained as it was necessary for social stability. He was in fact one of the first of those atheists who think everyone else should be a Catholic.

This conservative movement, centred latterly on Maurras's journal *Action Française*, acquired great intellectual influence but had little impact on politics. French conservatives were utterly opposed to the Third Republic, which they despised as corrupt and the outcome of a humiliating defeat. They remained steadfastly opposed to democracy, but two other elements now came to the forefront, a militant nationalism and a virulent anti-semitism. For Maurras and his circle the Jew typified all that was wrong with modernity. He was rootless and cosmopolitan, lacking a clear identity; he was committed to commerce rather than manly or honourable pursuits, and he was the representative of secular idealism (*sic*).

This led to the disastrous defeat of French conservatism in the Dreyfus Affair. The actual case of Dreyfus and the issue of his wrongful conviction became the occasion for a struggle, often violent, between right and left. French society was deeply and passionately divided but the outcome was a total victory for the left. The long-term consequence was the exclusion of conservatives from political life until they made the fatal choice of collaboration with Nazi Germany. It may seem deeply paradoxical that a movement holding intense nationalist ideas of France's greatness should collaborate with their country's enemies, but in another sense it was inevitable in 1940, given the marginalization of French conservatives. The intransigent nature of French conservatism and its profound opposition to modernity also meant that by 1900 it had become a movement calling for the overthrow of the status quo and its replacement by a radically different social order, in short a revolutionary movement. This made it much easier for men like Maurras to co-operate with other revolutionaries like the Nazis.

The Vichy state can be seen in fact as a revolutionary conservative regime, seeking under the conditions of war to undo the Revolution of 1789. The consequence, however, was that in 1945 French conservatism was totally discredited. There was a right in France under the Fourth and Fifth Republics but it lacked any clear ideology beyond nationalism and a defence of the economic status quo. In the case of De Gaulle, style and rhetoric were vastly more important than content or ideas. There were individual conservative thinkers, notably Ellul, who expressed in several works a deeply pessimistic view of the condition of modern man. He, however, never became the centre of a school, mainly because the basis of his thought (Calvinism) was too marginal in the context of France.

Two developments can be seen in recent years, however. On the one hand there has been a revival of traditional French conservatism. Maurras is once again taken seriously and the philosophy he espoused has been taken up by the so-called *nouvelle droite* based on the GRECE (Groupement de Recherche et d'Études pour la Civilisation Européenne). The tradition of ultramontanism survives and flourishes in the circle around Lefebvre. On the other hand there are signs that the divisions in French society over the Revolution and its legacy are at last healed and that a more recognizably Anglo-Saxon type of conservatism is emerging, combining social conservatism with economic liberalism. The complete collapse of Marxism in France has left an enormous vacuum in intellectual life and one cannot yet say what will fill it.

SD

Further reading

Lively, J. (ed.), *The Works of Joseph de Maistre*, London, Allen & Unwin, 1965.
Nisbet, R., *Conservatism*, Milton Keynes, Open University Press, 1986.
O'Sullivan, N., *Conservatism*, London, Dent, 1976.
Weber, E., *Action Française: Royalism and Reaction in Twentieth Century France*, Stanford, CA, Stanford University Press, 1962.

FRENCH LIBERALISM

As with conservatism, the history and nature of liberalism in France were determined by later generations' reactions to the cataclysmic events of 1789–94. French liberals were defined as being on the 'left', i.e. they were part of that body of French society which held that the Revolution had been inevitable and in some sense necessary. In any discussion of French liberalism it is vital to distinguish liberals and their percursors from their deadly enemies, the Jacobins and their spiritual heirs such as Gambetta. The critique of Jacobinism and of its sage, Rousseau, was a central element of French liberal thought. Accounts which see the Jacobins and their heirs as being merely radical liberals on the English model misunderstand both ideologies.

French liberalism had its own features which serve to distinguish it from both the British and German varieties. Unlike their English counterparts, French liberals inhabited a society where the most basic principles of liberalism were contested. They had not become part of a consensus as in England. Consequently liberals were much more aware of what separated them from both conservatives and socialists. French liberal thought is more abstract and rigorous than the English equivalent, with a more astringent quality. As compared to the Germans, French liberals espoused a more limited and negative view of personality and identity, rejecting the romantic notion of the self which had such a profound influence on all varieties of German political thinking. Another element of great importance for French liberalism was secularism with virulent anti-clericalism a common feature. This reflected the anti-liberalism of the Catholic Church and, not surprisingly, many French liberals were deists or Huguenots. There were Catholic liberals such as the later Lamennais but they were a minority among both liberals and Catholics.

Liberalism as a political and intellectual movement did not exist in France before 1814. However, both before and during the Revolution there were individuals and movements which articulated ideas that would later be called liberal. In this protean stage French liberalism can be seen as a set of originally unco-ordinated attacks on the central features of the *ancien régime*.

The French Enlightenment produced a series of criticisms of the clericalist policy of the *ancien régime* and corresponding arguments in favour of religious toleration. Because of the great importance of religion as a public doctrine these had a wider relevance and importance than might be realized today. Writers such as Voltaire were well aware that religious toleration necessarily implied freedom of speech and expression, freedom of association, and much greater freedom of personal lifestyle than the old order in theory allowed. Voltaire argued that it was possible to have a functioning and stable social order without there being a shared system of moral values. All that was needed was for people to be tolerant and to mind their own business. Toleration did not imply approval, as Voltaire made clear in his famous remark about free speech.

Simultaneously other thinkers produced a trenchant critique of the economic basis of the *ancien régime*. These were the physiocrats, particularly Turgot and Quesnay, who argued that the web of restraint and regulation which existed only served to hamper a natural economic order which could produce far greater prosperity if the state ceased to interfere and left people to their own devices. They rebutted the argument of the regime's apologists, that this would cause social unrest and disorder and so undermine social stability, by arguing that it was in fact the interventions of the state at the behest of self-interested groups which were the cause of disorder. There was, according to the physiocrats, a natural harmony of interests in society which would lead people left to themselves to co-operate spontaneously. Conflict arose when one group saw the opportunity to gain at the expense of others by using the state. During the early phases of the Revolution some of the physiocrats such as Dupont de Nemours had considerable influence and their ideas were shared by most of the left in the constituent and national assemblies. The party which most consistently favoured this programme were the Girondins. However, following the Jacobin seizure of power and under the pressure of war, the convention moved away from these doctrines with the passage of such measures as the law of the maximum, a form of price control.

The best known of these proto-liberal arguments are those which attacked the governmental system of the *ancien régime*. Montesquieu produced the seminal work of this tendency in 1748, the *De l'Esprit des lois*. At one level this was a scathing indictment of the French absolute state, calling for a strict separation of powers and the establishment of an English-style constitutional monarchy. Montesquieu argued that government must never be arbitrary, but lawful, limited, and restrained by law, and that the state must be constitutional, that is bound by a set of rules which delimited the form and nature of government. However, he also argued that the constitution of any particular state was a product of historical evolution and that it was neither possible nor desirable to reconstruct government in accordance with some abstract theory. Others were more exercised by the inherent problems of a state with a constant tendency to expansion and sought ways of limiting and dividing state power on the American model. This reached its apogee in the Girondins, who advocated a constitution based upon a minimal state and a radical decentralization of power away from Paris.

The other proto-liberal argument was against the social order and hierarchy. Traditional deference to the aristocracy and division of society into three estates was attacked by authors such as Sieyes. They argued that the aristocracy were a parasitic class who produced nothing and subsisted on the labour of others. The complex system of social gradations which marked eighteenth-century France was condemned as unjust and lacking any rational foundation.

Later French liberals inherited the following arguments from their precursors. First, a commitment to personal liberty, defined as non-interference in belief and the pursuit of private ends, and support for what would now be called an open society. Second, a policy of strict economic freedom which they were not afraid to call *laissez-faire*. Third, a doctrine of limited government, and lastly a theory of class or social structure. These separate arguments were put together to form a coherent philosophy during the restoration period.

The most important contribution in this regard was made by De Staël and her lover Constant. They made a distinction between personal and political liberty. In the ancient world, argued Constant, liberty meant full participation in public life. This also meant that there was no private sphere of independent personal life, instead everything was subject to political choice and argument. This was the model which Rousseau and the Jacobins had followed. Personal liberty, which Constant saw as modern, consisted of 'the right of each person to seek his opinion, to choose his own opinion and to follow it, to dispose of his property, even to misuse it, to come and go without obtaining permission and without rendering an account of his motives and movements'. De Staël and Constant argued that when political liberty was paramount, personal liberty was destroyed. Therefore the defence of personal liberty required that not just government but the scope of politics be limited to a narrowly defined range of public matters which affected all equally and in the same way. It was the attempt to politicize private matters in the pursuit of virtue which had led to the terror and to the despotism of Napoleon as people sought relief from politics in the rule of a tyrant. This concern was the cause of the hostility to democracy shared by most liberals after 1814. They feared that the extension of the franchise would inevitably lead to an extension of the sphere of politics.

The 1820s also saw a great development of political economy. Writers such as Say and Bastiat developed a much more rigorous body of principles. As compared to the English classical economists, they were far more purist in their commitment to non-interventionism. A truly revolutionary form of political economy was developed on the basis of Say's ideas by Dunoyer and Charles Comte. Their writings contained an integrated model of historical development which combined history, political science, and economics. This line of thought reached its apogee in Molinari who argued that the more developed society became the smaller the sphere of politics and the less the need of the state until eventually an anarchist social order would appear.

These thinkers also developed the most misunderstood element of French classical liberalism, its theory of class. For Comte and Dunoyer and others such as Thierry there was a fundamental division in society between those who gained wealth through production, the industrial class, and parasitic groups such as aristocrats who obtained wealth through the manipulation of state power. Modern historians have interpreted the writings of French classical liberals on this subject as a selfish and narrow defence of the bourgeoisie. Their argument was in fact radical, amounting to a fundamental critique of traditional social structure and government. Their ideal was a one-class society in which all but the feckless would be bourgeoisie with rank based on achievement and a circulation of the elite. Guizot's exhortation 'enrich yourselves' was not a call to economic selfishness but a shorthand statement of what French liberals saw as the primary need in modern society, the acquiring of property by the masses. For such writers as Dunoyer and Thierry, government was essentially a machine which served the interests of the already wealthy at the expense of the rest of society and supported a parasitic elite.

After 1814 most liberals supported a constitutional monarchy and in 1830 they supported the replacement of Charles X by Louis-Philippe. There were divisions between moderates such as Guizot and Ruyer-Collard and more radical figures like Lafitte and Destutt de Tracy but in practice the only deep division was that between the theorists such as Say and Constant and the politicians such as Guizot.

The other major liberal thinker during this period was De Tocqueville. His main contributions were to invent a sociology of politics and to provide a new theory of democracy. He argued that in every epoch the form and content of politics was determined by the type of social structure which existed with pure ideas having a circumscribed impact. He believed that the nature of the modern world was to move in the direction of democracy, that democratic politics were natural and inevitable in modern society where local, hierarchical social structures had broken down because of greater mobility and economic development. He was therefore critical of the obdurate resistance to democracy of other liberals such as Guizot, regarding it as a futile attempt to obstruct an inevitable movement. However, he did not regard this process as an unmixed blessing. The consequence of democracy was a passion for equality which could threaten liberty, coupled with a withdrawal of many from active participation in social life to the purely private. He also thought that the democratic society could be more uniform and less tolerant of variation. Like J. S. Mill he feared the tyranny of public opinion even though it would be mild. His other contribution was to make French liberals more aware of the limits of reason. He argued that social processes were in a real sense impossible to understand by pure reason and that it was neither possible nor desirable to have an a priori justification for all social institutions. In this he was close to an English Whig thinker like Burke or Bagehot.

French liberalism before 1848 had a paradoxical character. As a body of theory it was far more radical and thoroughgoing than its English counterpart. Yet as a political movement it was much more cautious, even timorous, particularly on the question of the franchise. This paradox derived from the fundamental weakness of French liberalism: it was the creed of a minority. The majority supported either ultramontanist catholicism or jacobinism, both vehemently anti-liberal. Hence the disaster which struck French liberalism in 1848 with the revolution of that year followed by the establishment of the imperial regime of Napoleon III in 1852. Under the empire some liberals, such as Thiers, collaborated with the regime, seeking to defend liberal values from within, while the more purist, such as Simon, remained in opposition. The early phase of the Second Empire was a dark period for French liberalism, confronted by a despotism at once more popular and more effective than the *ancien régime*. After 1860, during the so-called 'liberal empire', liberal policies and ideas had more influence, particularly in the field of trade with the passage of the Anglo-French commercial treaty of 1860.

Following the sudden collapse of the empire in 1870 and the failure of the royalists due to the obduracy of their candidate, the Comte de Chambord, French liberalism in one sense came into its own. The Third Republic was a more liberal state than any since 1791, and although there was no one liberal party, liberals of various types played an important part in most of the governments. However, this was also the period when liberalism in France lost its intellectual cutting edge and influence. The official liberalism of the politicians became ever more cautious and conservative, except on the vexed question of secularism. Intellectually there were further developments during this period, associated particularly with the names of Faguet and Leroy-Beaulieu. The former produced a penetrating critique of the dangers of economic egalitarianism and proposed the principle of 'practical fraternity' or mutual aid as the best means for overcoming the disadvantages of the poor. Leroy-Beaulieu, an admirer yet also a critic of Spencer, developed a comparison between the *modus operandi* of state and commercial enterprise which led him to conclusions very similar to those of the modern public choice school. Politics, he argued, worked in a different yet similar way from commerce. The state could be compared to a joint stock company in so far as both were associations of individuals for the realization of common ends, but the stockholders were in a fundamentally different position since they were subject to the restraints of the market. Politicians and voters by contrast faced no such limitations and so in practice politics was much less efficient as a means of realizing shared goals and tended constantly to corruption.

However, despite these contributions French liberalism became more *étatiste* after 1870 and lost much of the intellectual ground to socialism and the renascent conservatism of Maurras and Barrès. This was part of the general drift to statism in Europe at that time and was very largely due to the impact of nationalism and imperialism on French politics. Also, as the republic was identified with liberalism, so the ideology suffered from association with the involvement of liberal politicians in the many scandals of that period. During the Dreyfus Affair liberals were firmly on the Dreyfusard side, but it was the socialists who benefited most from the outcome. During the first half of the twentieth century French liberalism suffered a total collapse both as an intellectual and as a political force. There were isolated individuals such as Alain but the movement had ceased to exist in any real sense.

This situation continued after the Second World War, prompting Hayek to remark that France was 'the most hopeless country' for the cause of classical liberalism. There were outstanding liberal intellectuals such as De Jouvenal and Aron but they suffered the prophets' fate of being more honoured abroad. In the years since 1968, however, the collapse of Marxism in France has led to a sudden revival of classical liberalism, led by figures such as Lepage, and the word 'liberalism' has become respectable in intellectual circles once more, having been a term of abuse for most of this century. This has as yet had little impact on everyday politics but this reflects rather the fragmented and unstable nature of the French party system than any lack of interest on the part of individual politicians.

SD

Further reading

Bramstead, E.K. and K.J. Melhuish (eds), *Western Liberalism*, London, Longman, 1978.
Fontana, B. (ed.), *Constant, Political Writings*, Cambridge, Cambridge University Press, 1989.
Halévy, E., *The Era of Tyrannies*, New York, New York University Press, 1966.

De Ruggiero, G., *The History of European Liberalism*, Gloucester, MA, Peter Smith, 1927.

Schapiro, J.S., *Liberalism and the Challenge of Fascism*, New York, McGraw-Hill, 1949.

G

GERMAN CONSERVATISM

In one sense German conservatism did not exist until some time in the 1860s. Before then there were German-speaking conservatives, but most of them wished to maintain the old order which meant supporting the old German states and opposing the unification of Germany. Only with the rise of Bismarck did German conservatives come to see a single German state as the force that would preserve the old order.

German conservatism came into being at the start of the nineteenth century as a conscious reaction to the Enlightenment and to the French Revolution which had had such a devastating impact on the old Holy Roman Empire. Conservatism in this part of Europe was profoundly influenced by the cultural response to the Enlightenment which we call romanticism. Romantic notions of the self and identity and the anti-rationalism of the movement had a particularly powerful impact on the development of conservatism in the German-speaking lands.

Initially, however, German-speaking conservatism was apparently not too different from that of Britain or France. The founding father of German conservatism, who deserves comparison with Burke, was Mueller. Like Burke an intellectual rather than a member of the old elite, he nevertheless produced a powerful defence of the old order. The centre-piece of Mueller's thought was a sceptical view of the power of reason and a defence of the value of tradition. This was linked in his thought, as in Burke's, to an organic conception of society. For Mueller the individual human being was an incomplete and crippled entity. True fulfilment could only be found through participation in a comprehensive social whole since only that gave the individual life real meaning. This meant that Mueller, like other early conservatives such as Novalis, was an ardent advocate of the Middle Ages as opposed to modernity. In the Middle Ages society, politics, and life had been an organic whole; the distinction between public and private had not existed. The other great figure in the early phase of conservatism was Haller. He, like Mueller, was opposed to the idea of the

113

modern unitary state and contrasted it unfavourably with the organic state of the *ancien régime*, which meant in the German context small, localized political units. He was more moderate than Mueller and Novalis and closer to Burke.

In the above we can already see what became the dominant ideas of German conservatism. The first of these is idealism, derived from the epistemology of Kant. For Kant there is an objective world which human beings, however, do not directly experience: instead they interpret it through mental categories. German conservatives went further and argued that there was no distinction between subject and object, between physical and mental. In fact the external world is entirely the product of the mental world of ideas. Ideas exist, objects do not. The second idea is that of the romantic conception of the self. This has it that each self or person has a unique quality which can only be realized in conditions of absolute freedom. This could lead to a form of ultra-individualist anarchism as it did in Stirner, but for conservatives a third notion qualified romanticism. This was the belief that the whole was greater, more real, than the part because a better approximation of the ideal. So true fulfilment of the individual could only come from complete subordination to the whole, to the organic state. True freedom meant the merging of an alienated and isolated self in an organic whole. Hence also the state or nation has an existence independent of its constituent parts and is more real than any of them. The fourth idea was the contribution of Hegel, a curious mixture of the historical and ahistorical. Because state and nation exist at the level of the ideal rather than the material they exist antecedent to any concrete institution or culture. For Burke and most other conservatives the nation is an historical entity, the product of a complex evolution. For most German conservatives the German nation had always existed, but only at the level of idea. However, the process of history sees the gradual realization of the ideal, a process by which the material is made to coincide with the ideal.

Early German conservatives were not conventionally nationalistic. Indeed, Novalis and Haller combined a stress on the importance of cultural diversity and organic communitarianism with support for a form of cosmopolitanism. Most supported the rule of the traditional aristocratic and princely class and many were great admirers of what they believed to be the British constitution. However, during the first half of the nineteenth century German conservatives came to make the fateful equation of the organic state with the nation. So gradually German conservatism moved in a distinct and idiosyncratic direction. The writings of the early conservatives use idealist philosophy to defend the *ancien régime* against the threat of liberal cosmopolitanism. They did this by identifying the old order with the organic state which could realize true freedom. Hegel, for example, thought that the ideal had been realized and history brought to a full stop in the Prussian state created after the battle of Jena in 1806. Gradually, however, conservatives came to argue that the true organic state could only be realized in a German national state.

This was linked to another notion which derived from the combination of historical and philosophical idealism. History became a process through which the consciousness of peoples was created and intensified through struggle. This meant there was no one best form of government. Instead each nation would instinctively create those institutions which were suited to the stage of consciousness which it had reached. The Germans were, of course, the most advanced.

The writer who first gave German conservatism its distinctive cast was Fichte. He developed what became the essential model for later German conservatives, the idea of the closed commercial state. This was a self-sufficient entity, engaging in the minimum of trade and organized on the basis of a place for everyone but everyone in a place. In practical terms this was developed into the system of 'national political economy' by List, who favoured liberal political institutions himself but advocated a policy of managed trade and protectionism. During the first half of the century there were conservatives such as Gierke and Savigny who can be seen as still belonging to a more moderate Burkean tradition, but gradually the line of argument begun by Fichte became dominant.

Three crucial political events contributed to this. The first was the failure of the 1848 revolutions in Germany. This led many conservatives who had opposed the ideas of nationalism on the grounds that they were liberal to the conclusion that their fears were groundless. The second was the rise of Bismarck, who held out the prospect of realizing traditional German conservative ideals in a paradoxically modern state dominated by Prussia – one where liberalism would pose no threat. The third was the crushing defeat of Austria at Sadowa in 1866. Austrian conservatives from Metternich onwards had been concerned more to conserve what they could of the old order than to realize the ideas of such as Fichte. This more limited conservative political agenda was obliterated by the Prussian victory of that year.

The person who more than anyone else amended German conservatism from the 1860s onwards so as to fit the world Bismarck made was Treitschke. He introduced the idea that the dominant feature of history was struggle and that in history it was force and power which determined success in that struggle. He also explicitly argued that the state, in Machiavellian mode, was superior to and not bound by codes of morality. To subject state policy to moral judgement was, he thought, sentimental foolishness which could only result in disaster for the citizens. A statesman has no right to subordinate the interests of the state to the demands of his private conscience.

The outcome of Bismarck's politics and the intellectual thrust of men like Treitschke was the political culture of imperial Germany, dominated by what one critic has called reactionary modernism. That is, a state which combined a highly conservative social system with a modern economy and used the techniques of modernity for reactionary ends. A crucial element in this was the *Sozialpolitik*, the social security system introduced by Bismarck which drew on the conservative conception of the organic state for its justification. It is important to realize just how influential this model was in the years before 1914, not least in Britain where, during the so-called 'national efficiency' debate, Germany was held up as a model by people right across the political spectrum.

The defeat of imperial Germany in the First World War was thus in a very real sense a defeat of German conservatism as well. During the Weimar republic conservative opinion, articulated through the Nationalist Party of Hugenberg, was opposed to the state. This led conservative political and military leaders in Germany to their catastrophic delusion that they could use Hitler for ends of their own. In reality, of course, the reverse happened. This led, however, to the most tragic and moving episode in the history of German conservatism, its participation in the German resistance and the 20 July plot. It is seldom realized that most of the actual resistance to Hitler from within Germany came from (often aristocratic) conservatives. To some extent this derived from the German conservative tradition: Hitler and the Nazis were seen as violating and destroying the German nation, defined in the traditional romantic fashion. But it also involved a rejection of the political amoralism of Treitschke and an insistence instead that political processes must be subjected to moral judgement. This could have led to a revival of traditional German conservatism in a post-war Germany, but almost all of the figures who might have led such a resurgence were killed in the savage aftermath of the 20 July plot.

In 1945 conservatism in Germany, as in France, seemed utterly discredited. Certainly the old school of conservatism was dead and those who might have led a renewal were mostly literally dead. However, what did emerge in Germany in the post-war years was a form of liberal conservatism which combined classical liberal economics with a more conservative social theory. The most distinguished exponent of this was Roepke. In a series of works he sought to combine insights drawn from classical economics with a pessimistic analysis of modern mass society which could have come straight from the older tradition of Novalis and Haller. In politics it was a form of moderate conservatism which dominated until the 1970s. It may be that German conservatism has returned to its roots.

SD

Further reading

Nisbet, R. *Conservatism*, Milton Keynes, Open University Press, 1986.
O'Sullivan, N. *Conservatism*, London, Dent, 1976.

GERMAN LIBERALISM

German liberalism arose from two separate roots. On the one hand, there was the German Enlightenment, especially the thought of Kant. He was himself a proto-liberal, as his political writings clearly demonstrate. He was responsible for one key concept of German liberalism, that of the *Rechtstaat*, and he contributed the vital philosophical underpinning with his argument that human beings as free moral agents must always be, and treat others as, an end in themselves.

The other source was the impact upon Germany of the tumultuous events of 1789–1815. German liberals wished to take on board some aspects of the French Revolution and see them applied in Germany, such as its anti-clericalism and the removal of artistocratic rule, but they also sought to define how and where they differed from it. This twofold intellectual process led to the emergence of German liberalism in the years between 1815 and 1848.

One part of the reaction to the French Revolution which deeply influenced German liberalism was the romantic notion of the self. This is more commonly associated with conservatism, but in Germany it also produced a strongly libertarian doctrine. This was the concept of *Bildung*, a term with no exact English equivalent, which best translates as self-realization. In this, each person is possessed of a unique personality and one's life work consists of the realization of the potential of that personality. The self is seen both as something which is found or uncovered and as a work of art, created through free choice and expression. The classic application of this idea to politics was the work of Humboldt, written in 1792–3 but only published in 1851 under the title *The Sphere and Duties of the State*. This text, which inspired much of J.S. Mill's *On Liberty*, was a more strict and rigorous presentation of the same theme. Its argument was that the flourishing and development of the individual required the maximum of freedom and self-determination, which in turn meant a minimal state and upholding individual rights against the claims of custom and community pressure. The state for Humboldt was strictly an enabling institution with only one real function, to protect the rights (defined in negative terms) of individuals. This idea and other liberal principles also found expression in the literary works of Schiller and Goethe.

This might suggest that German classical liberals supported a strict definition of minimal statism. In fact, their attitude was more ambivalent. Many supported state action in the educational field because they saw it as the only alternative to the domination of education by the Catholic Church. Humboldt himself had, as a Prussian civil servant, been responsible for a major reconstruction of a state education system. Again, although most liberals followed the lead of Prince Smith and supported free trade, it was a liberal, List, who produced a powerful justification of protectionism for infant industries. Most serious was their ambivalence over the concept of the nation and its relation to the state.

In the first half of the nineteenth century a liberal movement grew up in Germany, in the face of often severe repression. Among its leaders were such figures as Rotteck, Welcker, and Dahlmann. They argued the classical liberal case for constitutional government, individual liberty, freedom of conscience, free trade and free movement of labour, and, above all, the rule of law. This was the key concept of the *Rechtstaat*, the state founded on law where all were bound equally by general impersonal laws which served no sectional interest. It is important to realize that the *ancien régime* in Germany was more repressive than elsewhere in Europe. German princely states regulated their subjects' lives to a greater extent than anywhere else except Sweden. The small size of many states made this easier. So the demands listed above were more radical than if made in England or France. The classical expression of this view was in the monumental *Staatslexikon*.

German liberals soon revealed their ambivalence on nationalism. Most argued that liberty could only be realized in a democratic national state. Rotteck, however, argued that it was liberty which was the main end and national unity the means. If national unity could only be realized in a despotic state he would rather live in a liberal Baden. Others reversed this priority or saw the two as so inextricably connected that the distinction made by Rotteck was not feasible. We can see in this debate the origin of later arguments which would split German liberalism and bring it to the brink of destruction.

German liberalism reached a peak of influence and support in the middle decades of the century. In 1848 it seemed for a short time that they would achieve their ideal of a liberal united Germany. However, the revolutions were crushed and the ineffectuality of the liberals at the Frankfurt Assembly did their cause great harm. In the years after 1850 liberals faced challenges from both socialists on the left and the conservatives led by Bismarck. They had particular difficulties dealing with the social problem posed by the appearance of a large proletariat. If the end of life was autonomy and self-realization then it was hard to resist the arguments of socialists like Lassalle that this was an impossible ideal for a labourer who lacked true economic independence. Some liberals such as Sonneman and Naumann reacted by developing a revisionist liberalism similar to that of the British new liberals.

A different response was that of the radical classical liberal Schulze-Delitzsch. He advocated a programme of collective self-help or mutual aid. Through this, the individual worker would gain independence by merging his assets with those of others in a strictly voluntary, non-state association. Schulze-Delitzsch put these ideas into practice and assisted the creation of a large number of voluntary associations or *Genossenschaften*. These provided the whole range of functions taken up by the welfare state and were highly successful: between 1864 and 1874 their number doubled, their membership tripled and their capital increased eightfold. Schulze-Delitzsch was hostile to both large corporations and wage labour. His ideal was a mutualistic society of small entrepreneurs where virtually everyone was self-employed.

Following the rise of Bismarck a split developed in the ranks of German liberals. This came to a head in 1867 when the liberal party split between the national liberals who supported Bismarck's policy and the classical liberals led by Richter who opposed him. Richter, a great classical liberal of immense integrity, carried on an increasingly lonely fight against both the domestic and foreign policies of imperial Germany. He was also an important critic of socialism, giving a grim picture of a future socialist society in his dystopia *Picture of the Socialist Future*. Gradually, as the years went by, classical liberalism lost ground in Germany.

The Weimar republic was in some sense a liberal state and the DDP (German Democratic Party) was one of the founding parties of the state. However, study of the Declaration of Rights and Duties, which formed part of the constitution, reveals the extent to which German liberalism had become socialized. The DDP never recovered from the hyperinflation of the early 1920s which wiped out much of its natural support. By 1933 German liberalism had effectively ceased to exist as a political force. There were intellectuals left such as Swartschild but most of them fled into exile on Hitler's accession.

While in exile many of these intellectuals thought deeply about what had happened to their country and the nature of totalitarianism. The result was an extraordinary resurgence of classical liberalism in Germany after 1945. Some of those involved, such as Roepke (actually Swiss), are hard to place ideologically, and he is best classified as a conservative or maybe Whig. Others, however, were clearly classical liberals. Among the most important were Rustow, the author of a monumental work of philosophical history, and Eucken. German liberals played a major part in the formation of the Mont Pelerin society and disseminated their ideas within German intellectual circles through the journal *Ordo*. Although the titular German liberal party remained electorally weak, the classical liberals had great influence on the economic policy of Erhardt and so were in no small part responsible for the 'economic miracle' of the 1950s. There was also a revival of social liberalism in Germany at this time, with figures such as Dahrendorf making important contributions to that tradition of liberal thought. Paradoxically, as classical liberalism has gained ground elsewhere in the West since 1970 it has lost it in Germany. However, it would seem that German liberals have finally achieved something close to their ideal of a democratic *Rechtstaat*, and so they may be forgiven for resting on their laurels.

SD

Further reading

Bramsted, E.K. and K.J. Melhuish, *Western Liberalism*, London, Longman, 1978.
Humboldt, W. von, *The Limits of State Action*, Cambridge, Cambridge University Press, 1969.
Sheehan, J.J., *German Liberalism in the Nineteenth Century*, Chicago, IL, Chicago University Press, 1978.

H

HISTORY

History as a discipline is not simply the study of or recounting of past events. It can only exist in cultures which have a historic sense, i.e. a realization that things have not always been as they are now and that the present is the product of a long process of change and development. Awareness of change through time in institutions, beliefs, and lifestyles is necessary for history as a discipline to exist. Otherwise there can only be chronicle and antiquarianism. In medieval Europe this historical sense did not exist, so that authors, with no sense of anachronism, could portray Troy as a typical medieval town and the heroes of the Trojan War as knights errant. History has an important part to play in all modern political philosophies as one of its main purposes is to explain how the present came to emerge from the past. It is therefore essential to any account of the nature of the present which would be comprehensive and complete that it contain an element of historical analysis. For some political philosophies, including, notably, Marxism, an account of history is the core of the entire philosophy.

History, moreover, cannot be the simple accumulation of empirical fact. All historical investigation requires and employs a theory or model. This is needed simply to make sense of and to organize the mass of new facts which confronts the historian. If the theory or model is not explicit and consciously worked out, then the historian will carry over unexamined and unconscious assumptions into their work. Historical models and theories come in many forms. Some are limited, only giving an account or explanation of a particular event, e.g. the French Revolution. Others are larger in scale and more abstract, e.g. a theory of the nature and causes of revolutions in general. The most large-scale and ambitious are those which seek to explain the nature of the discipline and the course of history as a whole. These macro-theories or philosophies of history come in many varieties and are not politically neutral since they have to contain positions on matters such as the nature of political power, the role and origin of the state, and the importance of economic change and development, to give just three examples. So it is not only political philosophy which needs a theory of history: history itself needs to engage with the concerns and subject matter of political thought, as well as other disciplines.

It should not be surprising, then, that conservatism and classical liberalism are informed by particular historical perspectives nor that much historiography can be identified as liberal or conservative. However, this kind of statement does indeed provoke comment. It is frequently assumed that the only overtly theoretical approach to history on the market is Marxism, and this had indeed been the case until recently in both Britain and the United States. This abandoning of historical theory to the enemy is a mid-twentieth-century phenomenon only. Before then classical liberalism in particular was identified with several elaborate and sophisticated theories of history.

The best known of these was Whig history. The term 'Whig history' means in general an approach to history which sees the past simply as a process leading up to a consummation in the present or recent past, the achievement of which is seen as the purpose of all that has gone before. This pejorative sense, derived from the work of Butterfield, has obscured its other meaning of a school and theory of history which Butterfield himself espoused. Whig history in this sense is an account of political and social development derived from a reading of English history but applied to the history of Europe in general. According to this, the central fact of history is the gradual emergence of free societies, initially in north-west Europe and especially in Britain and the Netherlands. History is therefore in essence the story of liberty, what it is, how it came to be established, and what its preconditions are. There is a pattern of progress in history but, contrary to misrepresentation by critics, the Whig historians did not see this as an inevitable process. They rather, from Hume to Macaulay to Motley, emphasized how precarious the history of freedom had been and how often the growth of freedom had suffered setbacks.

This history of freedom had four main elements: the appearance of a concept of the independent person or self; the growth of personal liberty with the development of open societies which would tolerate a variety of beliefs and lifestyles; the emergence of political freedom, i.e. of free representative institutions; and not least the rise of the rule of law, of politics where power was limited by general rules which bound all equally. Certain events were seen as crucial to this process; the fall of the Roman Empire and the growth of law and representative institutions during the Middle Ages; the Reformation and the slow emergence of religious toleration, but above all the successful revolt of the Dutch against Philip II in the sixteenth century and the defeat of the Stuarts in seventeenth-century Britain, culminating in the Glorious Revolution of 1688. This was a theory of history which gave pride of place to politics and ideas. The growth of liberty was explained primarily in terms of these factors rather than of economic and social development (although these were not ignored – see, for instance, Halévy's *England in 1815*).

The other main feature of Whig history was its moralism. This is usually identified with Acton but it can be found in most Whig historians. Whig history was moralistic in two ways; the historians argued that one of the main purposes of history was moral instruction, that one could learn moral as well as other lessons from the past. They also held that the historian had a duty to pass moral judgement on the subjects of his research. This was the point that Acton emphasized many times.

Whig history was not the only liberal theory of justice, however. In France there was a more radical form of this doctrine practised and articulated by a whole school of writers of whom the most important was Thierry. This was not simply a national split: Guizot was a classic Whig historian while Thorold Rogers belongs firmly in the same camp as the French radicals. The French argued that most conventional history was the study of the deeds of masters and oppressors. The state and the sphere of politics were thought of as the instrument by which a parasitic class enriched itself at the expense of society. History as a discipline, therefore, had to concern itself rather with the apolitical, the history of civil society and free association and the manifold forms of popular resistance to power. This school put much more emphasis on economic history, seeing the emergence of free markets, and particularly free labour markets, in the fourteenth and fifteenth centuries as the turning point in European history. As with the Whig historians, however, the national history of England was seen as being of crucial importance and certain events in particular got close attention, especially the Civil War, the Glorious Revolution, and the Norman Conquest.

The third liberal theory of history was that which derived from the Scottish Enlightenment and can best be described as a school of historical sociology. Although it looked back to Smith, Ferguson, Millar, and Kames its main exponents were Buckle and Robertson. These historians adopted a materialistic theory of history in which the development of the whole of society rather than simply its political aspects was studied and explained in terms of material forces such as climate, geography, and population. Buckle and Robertson argued that the development of free societies was a historical contingency brought about by a combination of physical circumstances, economic changes including technological innovations such as printing, developments in the areas of ideas and belief and the spontaneous and unintended growth of important social institutions and practises such as contract law. Sheer chance and natural disaster had also played a major part, with great emphasis given to the Black Death of 1353 because of its role in undermining the feudal economy.

All of these theories shared one central premise: that the most important subject for the historian was the history of freedom and that the study of the past should be organized around this fact. They differed over the theories of the causation of this growth of freedom and over what area of the past record to concentrate on. All had a markedly different view of the past from that provided by Marxism, which sees the history of the world as the history of class struggle and the growth of freedom as simply one aspect of the rise of the capitalist class. For Marxist historians the freedoms celebrated by the liberal historians are limited and partial. There are yet other liberal theories of history, such as Croce's liberal Hegelianism, but none was as influential as the three outlined above. However, the theoretical approach to liberal historiography went into sharp decline just before and after the Great War. Until recently there were liberal historians in the sense that there were individual historians who were liberals, but there was not a functioning liberal theory of history. This was just one component of the 'failure of nerve' on the part of twentieth-century liberal intellectuals.

There are also distinctive conservative approaches to the discipline of history which have found expression in many distinguished works. The notion of a conservative theory of history may seem strange, given the hostility of many conservatives to abstract theory, but, as stated earlier, all history makes use of theory at some level: the rejection of structural and teleological theories itself implies a theory of a different kind. We can distinguish two main schools of conservative historiography.

One, primarily British, is broadly empirical and sceptical in outlook. Its exponents, from Bury to Elton and Clark, have stressed the autonomy and paramount importance of politics. Political history is therefore given pride of place over social or economic history, although these are not ignored or regarded as unimportant. Another central argument is the rejection of any element of teleology; instead there is a stress upon the importance of contingent events and the role of key individuals. Consequently, structural explanations for historical events are rejected in favour of ones which concentrate upon immediate causes. Thus present-day accounts of the English Civil War deny that one needs go back to 1600 to explain the outbreak of war in 1642 in terms of structural economic change; 1640 is far enough. Another consequence of this approach is a stress upon narrative as the most appropriate form for the writing of history as opposed to analytical or descriptive accounts, even though, paradoxically, several leading lights of this school have indeed produced large analytical works.

These conservative historians also eschew both the elaborate theorizing of the Whigs and Marxists and the attempt to derive universal lessons or rules from history. Instead they follow Oakeshott in arguing that history is a subject which should be studied for its own sake, with a subject matter radically separated from the present, a silent mistress in Oakeshott's phrase. Another element in this approach is the stress upon continuity in the past rather than change. For historians such as Clark and Elton modern historiography in a frantic search for change, revolution, and radicals in the past has overlooked the undoubted truth that historically things have stayed the same more than they have changed, that revolutions are rare events and unknown in the modern sense before 1789, and that most people in most times are conservatives who are satisfied with or actively support the status quo. One important application of this general principle in contemporary conservative historiography is to stress the importance of religion and elites as subjects for historical study. Elites should be studied more than powerless groups such as women and the lower classes, Elton argues, because they *were* simply more important: they had power so what they did mattered. Religion is emphasized on the grounds that to ignore it is to impose modern secular attitudes onto the more typical human experience in which religion is a matter of great or critical significance and religious institutions are as important as secular ones. Lastly, most conservative historians argue that the nation is the proper unit for historical study and research. Consequently they reject the contemporary trend towards trans-national or world history.

Very different is the other conservative theory of history, that of Hegel. For Hegel there is indeed a pattern or order to history, that of the development through time of *Geist* or spirit. *Geist* means not the spirit of individual human beings but rather the common spirit or essence of human groups and societies and ultimately the entire human species. History is the study of the process of development of the spirit and its relations with the material world. History as subject is therefore profoundly teleological and progressive, two notions which are anathema to the British conservatives described above. In Hegel's own writings the end of history was something which looked suspiciously like the Prussian state, but his method could be used in a variety of ways. One disciple, of course, was Marx who kept the structure but made the basis of history material forces rather than ideas or spirit. In Germany in particular there were historians who kept closer to Hegel's original theme and produced a school of conservative Hegelians. For them the main phenomenon of history was the nation, defined as a spirit entity, and its gradual development to self-awareness.

Since 1960 the discipline of history has developed and moved in many new directions. The response to this from conservatives and classical liberals has been mixed, to say the least. Some, such as Himmelfarb, have strongly criticized the 'new history', and called for a return to traditional historical practice. Many conservative historians belong to the 'revisionist' school of historiography which over the last decade has sought to refute most of the accepted wisdom of post-war historians, most notably in the field of British history. On the other hand, some liberal historians have argued in support of the 'new history', seeing it (correctly) as a revival of the radical liberal historiography of Thierry and Thorold Rogers. Recently, self-aware (as opposed to unthinking) Whig history has begun to revive.

History is one area where the tensions and divisions between conservative and classical liberal are clearest. Both reject the economic reductionism of classical Marxism and the conspiracy theories of neo-Marxists, not to mention the nihilism of Foucault. However, on the other side there are deep disagreements: over the nature and practice of the discipline, the pattern, if any, of historical development, and the interpretation of individual historical events.

SD

Further reading

Clark, J.C.D., *English Society 1688–1832*, Cambridge, Cambridge University Press, 1985.
Fears, R. (ed.), *Lord Acton: Essays and Writings* (3 vols), Indianapolis, IN, Liberty Press, 1988/9.
Hall, J.A., *Powers and Liberties*, Harmondsworth, Penguin, 1986.

HUMAN NATURE

Classical liberalism and conservatism exemplify sharply contrasting views of human nature. Indeed, it could be said that the differences between the two political philosophies resolve into differences in beliefs about the powers, limitations, and prospects of human beings. On the view of the classical liberal, in order to flourish human nature needs to be emancipated from a multiplicity of social, cultural, and religious hindrances. Among the most noteworthy of these are restrictions on free trade, class structure and national boundaries, and religious dogmatism. The fact that such hindrances have grown up as a result of human activity, and therefore show human nature at work, is only partly recognized by the liberal.

One way in which it is recognized is through the need for vigilance. The emancipation of human nature can only take place where the tendency of people to make exceptions in their own cases, e.g. through class or professional privilege, or by placing restraints on trade, is actively curbed, as it is when the conditions for individual freedom are optimized. So while the liberal view of human nature is optimistic, it is not perfectionist.

In theory at least men and women, according to liberalism, behave in an amoral fashion. It is the 'naturalness' of self-regard which provides the sole acceptable and all-powerful motive of human action. By each pursuing his or her own interests co-operative ventures are begun, to the mutual advantage of each. The only acceptable constraint upon such freedom is the prudential one that contracts entered into – in trade and in marriage, for example – ought not to be broken unilaterally. This is one reason why liberals, in common with conservatives, stress the importance of the rule of law. Such rule preserves the framework of objectivity and predictability in which human beings, and the associations which they voluntarily enter into, can retain their identity and flourish.

Beyond the obligation to keep contracts, which the rule of law is meant to reinforce, there are no other moral demands, certainly none imposed by the public interest, or by a categorical imperative, or by the command of God. Rather, it is held that the fear of possible disadvantage is held to be the only necessary constraint upon conduct; apart, that is, from those co-operative efforts needed to preserve the integrity of a society through defence and the judiciary. It is held that many if not all criminal offences have their source in market imperfections. There would be no 'drug problem' if all manner of drugs were freely available; a plentiful supply would reduce the drugs' value and the incentive for anyone to act criminally to maintain the flow of illicit drugs.

So at the heart of liberalism there is something of a paradox; human beings, although of supreme value, and certainly of supreme political importance, are to be viewed in a somewhat abstract fashion. They form a currency which is interchangeable within states and among nations. And so differences of race, or national culture, are discounted, as are differences in sex. Liberals were prominent in the movement to 'emancipate' women, and to extend the suffrage to them. The historic Christian ideal of a woman's subjection to a man in marriage is totally rejected. Liberals are strong advocates of feminism and its implications; e.g. the liberalization of abortion laws, the provision of easier divorce, and equal opportunities at work.

The liberal's chosen means of emancipation from the various forces, such as 'anti-feminism', that hold human nature in thrall are invariably gradualist; e.g. through nations adopting wise constitutions, through the extension of the franchise, the growth in popular education, improvements in health and hygiene, and the dissemination of culture. Behind the advocacy of such changes lies a view of human history – the Whig view of history as mankind's slow but sure progress to enlightenment.

As a concession to remaining non-liberal elements in society the liberal draws a contrast between matters which are private, and therefore of no concern to anyone except members of the private circle, and those which are public, and which may offend or outrage others. But this *is* a concession; in theory, in a liberal society, mutual tolerance should permit each individual to lead that style of life, in both its private and public aspects, that he or she thinks fit. The only acceptable censorship is self-censorship. In practice, however, what liberals have regarded as tolerable behaviour has been heavily conditioned by Christian values. Thus although liberals are, in the abstract, in favour of toleration, in fact few Western liberals would find the reintroduction of blood-sacrifice or witchcraft tolerable.

Diverse though the factors leading to mankind's progress to enlighten-ment are, the liberal draws the line at centralist or statist solutions to political problems. Progress is not achieved through imposition from the centre (except for defence and the judiciary, and for the provision of goods and services having 'neighbourhood effects'), but by individual commercial and cultural enterprise. And so classical liberals have little time for 'social justice', not because they oppose human equality, but because they are distrustful of any state mechanism designed to ensure such justice.

The central liberal virtues are those of individual rights, and in particular the right to be free from constraint and restraint of any kind, so-called 'negative freedom'. Coupled with this has often been a sceptical, critical questioning of established ways of doing things. Thus liberalism is rationalistic in a way in which conservatism could never be.

In conservatism the taxonomy of views of human nature is somewhat more complex than in classical liberalism. Conservative views stress the importance for politics of human limitations, and the constraints that these place upon planning; not only state planning, but any attempts to provide general prescriptions for human betterment such as those favoured by the liberal.

One principal trait of human nature highlighted by conservatives is its liability to act corruptly; not only selfishly, but wickedly; to abuse power, to lie and cheat and steal. The conservative antidote to this is to diffuse political power through a system of checks and balances, particularly in government. At such a point the day-to-day political policies of the conservative and the classical liberal may coincide, for both may seek the diffusion of power away from the centre. But their reasons for seeking this diffusion are fundamentally very different: the liberal because it maximizes individual opportunity; the conservative because it minimizes the multiplier effect that the concentration of power has upon human corruption in the growth of tryanny and arbitrary power.

While the conservative seeks the diffusion of power as a check on tyranny and dictatorship, these two political conditions are themselves corruptions, the betrayal of the duties and responsibilities of those who, by breeding and social position, are called to rule. So the diffusion of power sought by the conservative is the diffusion of centralized power; *local* authorities, expressed historically through squirearchy and patriarchy and in more recent times through professional associations, for example, are acceptable because limited and face-to-face.

Pauline and Augustinian emphases in Christianity harmonize with the conservative outlook which stresses human corruption. But not all Christians favour conservatism; those from a perfectionist or Anabaptist tradition tend to support radical, leftist political philosophies. An important Christian influence upon liberalism has been the 'Nonconformist conscience' of the Victorian and Edwardian eras, which combined an emphasis upon the free market with a heavy moralism in matters of individual conduct.

For conservatives of a more Aristotelian bent 'human nature' is part of a wider natural order, an order of natural law embracing a moral order of human relationships in which human beings can flourish. The political emphasis falls upon *order*, and even upon hierarchy, a system in which people know their places in society, excesses of disorder are avoided or curbed, and through which individual lives gain intelligibility for those who live them.

From time to time an explicitly Christian emphasis has overlaid such a view, as in the political writings of Aquinas and Hooker, who used Aristotelian ideas as the base for the construction of a view of the social order as a 'divine society'. Sometimes an emphasis upon the need to retain or restore Christian moral values has become the dominant or single issue of a conservative movement. It would be understood as such by the members of the so-called 'Moral Majority' in the United States.

For the Aristotelian conservative what is 'unnatural', and therefore immoral, is radical change; the extreme case is the violent overthrow of the existing order. Where that order is identified with an overarching national or racial interest such conservatism approaches fascism. What is unnatural for Christian conservatism is political and social behaviour which flouts the law of God or, more narrowly, which causes men and women to sin.

There are, besides those types of conservatism already mentioned, more secular versions, based neither upon the corruptibility of human nature, nor on the idea of natural order, but on necessary limitations upon human knowledge. Hume's conservatism was built upon his scepticism. Because none of us can ever know anything, and particulary because we can know little about the course of future events, it is prudent to rely upon habits, including engrained political modes of behaviour which have grown up imperceptibly as the result of past regularities. So, in one of those paradoxes with which political philosophy abounds, Hume's radical scepticism led him to political conservatism; to a suspicion of abstract theorizing, and to a reliance upon tacitly held social and political conventions.

For other conservatives it is not so much that human beings know nothing, but that they can never know sufficient to plan an economy to satisfy the manifold needs and wants of human beings in society. And so socialist, centralist planning is futile for epistemological rather than for ideological reasons. The only way in which knowledge of what men and women need can be transmitted is not from the capacious brain or computer of a central planner, but by means of the manifold transactions of the market, as buyers and sellers continuously adjust their supply of or demand for goods and services in the light of others' demands and supplies. The essentially impersonal transactions of the market-place become the economic basis of all other social institutions within the state. Limitations upon knowledge in this sense is the controlling factor in the economic conservatism of Hayek.

Finally, conservatism has been justified as a consequence of human weakness. It is claimed that human beings form themselves into societies, and in particular they willingly submit to the authority of a sovereign, and the rule of law, because they fear the consequences of not doing so. The classic exponent of such conservatism is Hobbes, who held that the dominant political motive was a particular kind of self-interest, the fear of death. Because, in a state of anarchy, each human being fears for his life, he willingly yields up unreserved obedience to a protector, the sovereign, in exchange for preservation and security. Hobbes is an outstanding case of a thinker who derives the whole of his political theory from a characteristic view of human nature.

Conservatives in general have a more developed sense of the social side of human nature than have liberals. Because of their individualism liberals have a strong tendency to see every grouping of human beings as being a matter of contracts freely entered into by individuals who are otherwise autonomous and self-sufficient. This is too abstract and unreal a view for most conservatives, who regard individual human beings as being history- and culture-laden. Far from every responsibility being the result of a free contract, many human responsibilities are unsought, e.g. obligations to family and nation. It is partly for this reason that conservatives maintain that people gain full humanity – freedom, rationality, and personal fulfilment – only in society with others.

For the conservative, 'human nature' is itself an unhelpful abstraction. On the conservative view both the politician and the political theorist have to reckon not with human nature but with people with varying human natures who understand their lives from the vantage point of their own place in culture and history. Although there are underlying parameters of what is intelligible and acceptable that are common to all human beings, and therefore there is some reason to endorse the idea of natural law, one ought none the less not to expect a German to behave as a Brazilian, nor people in the seventeenth century to value exactly those matters valued by those living in the twentieth century.

At one extreme such an emphasis can verge upon pluralism; at the other, the Hegelian extreme, what the social nature of people implies is an organic view of society in which no human action is intelligible that is not the product of such a society. Thus, in polar opposition to liberalism, this view asserts that the individual is the product of society and throughout his life is borne along by it.

Typical conservative virtues are loyalty and deference to established forms and ways of doing things; the valuing of the particular and even the eccentric; the liberty not so much of the individual as of the family and of the innumerable voluntary groupings which creativity and social diversity produce. Such liberty as is linked to the idea of service and vocation; and respect for established, i.e. *de facto*, tried and tested authority.

Neither the liberal nor the conservative favours the 'politicization' of human nature and therefore of all important human activities. Each maintains an important place for human activities which carry no political significance, though their reasons for providing this place are characteristically different.

The liberal's approach is conditioned by the belief that the state should be minimalist in character, the ring-holder within which human creativity and inventiveness can flourish. The conservative stresses the non-political character of human life through stress upon the importance of the multiplicity of contingent, accidental factors, the multifariousness of traditions and ways of thinking which arise unplanned and certainly uncoordinated. The conservative, more than the liberal, stresses the importance for human beings of pursuing interests for their own sake, and not because a utilitarian or pragmatic justification can be provided for them.

PH

Further reading

Friedman, M. and R. Friedman, *Free to Choose*, New York, Harcourt, Brace, Jovanovich, 1980.

Passmore, J.A., *The Perfectibility of Man*, New York, Scribners, 1970.

Quinton, A.M., *The Politics of Imperfection*, London, Faber, 1978.

Stevenson, C.L., *Seven Theories of Human Nature*, Oxford, Oxford University Press, 1974.

I

IDEOLOGY

Ideology is one of the most difficult and complex concepts in political science and philosophy. Difficulties arise because the term 'ideology' has a series of related yet separate meanings. Most notably it can be used as either a pejorative and critical term or as a neutral, technical one. Confusion often arises because the word can be used in these two senses by the same author, even in the same text or passage. There is also a distinction to be made between the popular usage of the term and its usage in academic and technical writings. In popular usage an ideology is a body of abstract political beliefs which are adhered to even in the face of contrary evidence. A holder of an ideology, an ideologue, is a person so committed to certain theoretical beliefs as to be beyond the reach of common sense and reason. This use of the term is common in Anglo-Saxon countries, although it originated in France. In academic argument, 'ideology' loosely defined means a complex system of attitudes, ideas, and beliefs which gives, or purports to give, a comprehensive account and explanation of the human and natural world. In its most vague and imprecise formulations this comes close to the more general concept of *Weltanschauung* or world picture, i.e. the general concept or notion of the nature and form of the world which cultures, societies, or even individuals may have as part of their mental furniture. Properly used, ideology should refer to more abstract and complex systems of ideas. The pejorative usage of ideology derives from the thesis that most systematic theories and explanations of the world are not truly objective but rather articulate the interests of a particular class or group and serve to obscure reality rather than to explain it. Ideology in this sense is a type of obfuscation or mystification.

The word 'ideology' was first invented in 1796 by the French author Destutt de Tracy. He intended it to mean the systematic study of knowledge, beliefs, and ideas. However, the word soon acquired a very different meaning; it came to refer not to the study of beliefs but to the

132

object of study, the beliefs themselves. It soon became a pejorative term and was first used in its popular sense by no less a person than Napoleon, who described opponents of his regime such as De Staël as ideologues, i.e. impractical theoreticians. However, the major development of the concept came with Marx and Engels, most notably in Marx's *The German Ideology*. In classical Marxism a distinction is made between the 'base', which consists of the material mode of production and its social relations, and the 'superstructure' which is everything else, including ideas and beliefs. In any class society, systematic theories and explanations of the world will be produced which claim to be objective. In reality the account of the world which they give serves the interests and justifies the actions of a particular class. This is usually the ruling class which controls 'the means of intellectual, as well as physical, production'. These theories are ideologies: they serve the ruling class by preventing the subordinate class from realizing the reality of its position. Ideologies both produce and are the product of a 'false consciousness', i.e. a mistaken understanding of society and one's position in it. Because they articulate the interests of a class one can speak of 'aristocratic' or 'bourgeois' ideology. As class conflict proceeds the 'rising class' produces its own ideology which undercuts that of the ruling class: it is therefore 'progressive'. Once the rising class is established as the new ruling class its ideology will become 'conservative'. In classical Marxism ideology is distinguished from science which gives a true account of the world. Marx claimed his own theory was not ideological but scientific, hence the term 'scientific socialism'. (See also Engels's funerary eulogy of Marx.) Marxists have consistently claimed that their own theses are objective whereas their opponents' ideas, being ideological, are tendentious and self-serving.

Faced with the failure of workers in the western democracies to develop a revolutionary class consciousness a succession of thinkers, starting with Gramsci, have extended the concept of ideology, effectively standing Marx on his head. They argue that in advanced capitalist societies the position of the bourgeoisie depends upon consent derived from their ideological domination rather than from state repression. This ideological control, or 'hegemony', is exercised through the institutions of civil society rather than the state. Consequently revolution cannot be realized through a Leninist-type coup (a 'war of movement') but only by a slow cultural transformation (a 'war of position') brought about by 'organic intellectuals'. This thesis implies, first, that class consciousness is not, as Marx supposed, an automatic product of relations of production but a cultural phenomenon. A class can exist without having a fully developed class consciousness: if so, it will fail to act as a class. Moreover, ideologies (the superstructure) can influence and shape the development of the process of production (the base). The concept of ideology is expanded to include virtually all beliefs as well as everyday lifestyles. For these thinkers the freedoms of liberal democracies are spurious: everyday life is in fact a system of hidden or concealed domination and oppression. People are slaves without knowing it. In its extreme forms this owes more to Stirner or Nietzsche than Marx.

Non-Marxists also use the term 'ideology' but in a different way. Some retain the pejorative notion of a set of ideas which serves the interests of, and mobilizes, a group while rejecting the Marxist element of class analysis. Any group with a common interest can have an ideology in this sense. Many follow the usage found in Mannheim's sociology of knowledge. Here ideologies are systems of ideas which seek to provide an explanation of the world as it is but which, unlike scientific theories, contain an explicit normative element as well, so providing guidance on how one *ought* to act. This usage is neutral rather than pejorative: all ideologies are necessarily partial and biased accounts of the world but they are necessary in the absence of generally accepted traditions in order to provide normative arguments and to create coherent syntheses of many different kinds of knowledge. Moreover, they need not derive simply from a group interest. Again, this use denies the Marxist identification of ideology with class.

Others, including not a few conservatives and classical liberals, have used the word in a critical sense to refer to systems of ideas which are so organized as to be incapable of disproof by empirical evidence. In this usage, derived from Popper, Marxism is ironically the classic case of an ideology! In Popper's thought ideology is again contrasted with science but is not seen as the expression of a group interest. It is rather the term for a specific type of explanation of the world. For many conservative thinkers, such as Gilmour, conservatism is the one political doctrine which eschews ideology, being based on empirical observation and concern with actual historical conditions rather than abstract principles and definitions. This view implies that there can be no such thing as a conservative ideology. In this usage ideology is virtually identified with theory *per se*. This line was also followed by the very influential school of thought which at the end of the 1950s argued that, as social problems were now largely solved, there was 'an end of ideology'.

Until recently most conservatives and classical liberals had ignored the whole question of ideology. This partly reflected the atheoretical approach of Anglo-Saxon academics who used the word only in a very vague or loose sense. More recently the entire Marxist theory of ideology has been strongly criticized, most notably in the work by Minogue. Conservative and classical liberal criticism of the Marxist conception of ideology has four elements.

First, the classical form is reductionist, having ideas exist only as a consequence or epiphenomenon of material factors. This is contradicted by the demonstrable historical autonomy of ideas and the tremendous power and impact of beliefs. Ironically Marxism itself is the best example of this! Attempts to use the classical Marxist theory of ideology lead to all sorts of contortions, such as attempts to show that religious beliefs, e.g. in early modern Europe, are really expressions of class interests. It also makes it very difficult to explain feminism since it cannot be easily linked to a class: some purist sects are reduced to defining it as a 'bourgeois deviation'. The modern western variety of Marxism escapes this trap but only by abandoning several key Marxist ideas, particularly its materialism. Neo-Marxist works commonly contain the claim that 'in the last analysis' base determines superstructure, but this is only window dressing.

Second, the western Marxist notion of the pervasiveness of ideological domination creates several difficulties. If ideology is so pervasive, then how were people like Marx and Gramsci able to escape it? There is an underlying elitism: people are fools and dupes except for a small elect (intellectuals, of course) who have seen the light. If the proletariat are such fools then how can they perform the historic function presribed for them by Marxism? If escape from ideology is impossible (as Foucault argues) then truth and moral judgement are impossible and illusory. This can only lead to nihilism.

Third, writers like Minogue have criticized the fundamental assumption of much Marxist theorizing of ideology, that the apparent and obvious facts of everyday life are only a surface of a deeper structure where real truth can be found while the obvious and overt is misleading and false. This is an assumption which by its very nature can never be disproved as all information can be interpreted in a way that supports the thesis of concealed domination. The assumption itself, as well as violating Occam's Razor, is essentially a religious one derived, as many have argued, from the heresy of Gnosticism which holds, first, that true knowledge is to be found by looking beyond the overt and, second, that the world is wholly corrupt and the work of a diabolic power. Finally, most Marxist critical theory derives from a wholly unreasonable concept of freedom wherein freedom is taken to be the unrestricted exercise of the will and of self-realization. Since in any actual historical situation there are rules, conventions, and traditions (defined as ideologies) which prevent this 'freedom' it is argued that people are not truly free. However, as thinkers from Aristotle on have argued, such asocial and ahistorical 'freedom' is possible only for gods and beasts, not for actual human beings. Moreover, this kind of argument serves to undermine respect for real, actually existing freedom.

SD

Further reading

Bell, D., *The End of Ideology*, London and New York, Macmillan, 1960.
Merquior, J.G., *Western Marxism*, London, Paladin, 1986
Minogue, K., *Alien Powers: The Pure Theory of Ideology*, London, Weidenfeld & Nicolson, 1985.

INDIVIDUALISM

'Individualism' has a great variety of meanings in social and political philosophy. Three important types can be distinguished: (1) ontological individualism, (2) methodological individualism, and (3) moral and political individualism. These three are often confused by highly reputable liberal and conservative philosophers, e.g. Sir Karl Popper. It should be noted that the establishment of the case for methodological individualism as a valid form of explanation in social science does not logically establish the case for political individualism (or liberalism).

1   Ontological individualism is the uncontroversial metaphysical doctrine that social reality consists, ultimately, only of persons who act and choose. Collectivities, such as a social class, a state, or a group, cannot act. It is more easily understood in contrast to ontological collectivism, which does suppose that such collectivities have a reality independent of the actions of persons. That organic entities have an independent existence was held by, for example, Hegel in his theory of the state and Durkheim in his theory of society. It was not, however, the view of Marx; despite the fact that he was a methodological collectivist.

It is true that all methodological individualists are also ontological individualists, but is not necessarily true that all ontological individualists are methodological individualists.

2   A methodological individualist holds that the only genuinely scientific propositions in social science are those that are logically reducible to the actions, dispositions, and volitions of individuals. This does not exclude the possibility that there are meaningful propositions about collectivities; it only assumes that such propositions must be logical or mental reconstructions out of the actions of individuals. Thus market theory does refer to a collective phenomenon, the regularized and more or less repetitive behaviour of an aggregative social and economic institution, but the market system itself is not an observable institution. Methodological collectivists assume that the collective entity itself displays regularities rather than derive aggregate theoretical propositions from individual action. Hayek calls this collectivist doctrine the error of 'conceptual realism'.

If we refer to the history of a country we must always be able to write out (logically at least) that history as a series of individual actions and events. The state does not have a biography as a person clearly does. Methodological individualists claim that some words that refer to aggregate phenomena, such as the market, are theoretically useful, others are not. The concept of 'class', which dominates modern sociology, is thought to be useless precisely because no predictions can be derived from theories of class. The concept of 'class' is, in fact, a 'fiction'.

The paradigm case of a methodological individualist explanation is micro-economics. The propositions in this refer entirely to the consumption, saving, and investment patterns of individual transactors. Some economists maintain that the entire corpus of economic theory can be constructed out of the axiom of individual rational choice under scarcity. Nevertheless, macro-economists maintain that there are regularities (albeit of a statistical kind) between economic aggregates, such as the rate of interest, the level of employment, and the money supply, which cannot be reduced to individualistic propositions. This does not entail ontological collectivism, i.e. the claim that such aggregates 'act', but only that economics contains some irreducible propositions.

3 Political individualism is the normative theory that individuals should be left, as far as is possible, to determine their own futures in economic and moral matters. It puts a prohibition on the delivery of collective goods, except for the provision of those essential public goods and services that cannot be priced by the market. In moral conduct, the individualist believes that coercive law should not be used to prohibit behaviour which does not harm others, even if the action itself is intrinsically undesirable.

Political individualism can have a natural rights or a utilitarian foundation. The natural rights foundation is that, because of their rationality or their common humanity, all men have the right to equal liberty. Historically the clearest expression of this moral axiom is in Locke and Spencer. In the contemporary world, Nozick's *Anarchy, State, and Utopia* is the most sophisticated justification of the free market and the minimal state in individualist terms. Here the foundation of moral individualism is the Kantian imperative, i.e. that it is immoral to use individuals as a means to advance the ends of others. This would be to violate their autonomy and integrity. The objection to using persons on behalf of a collective entity called 'society' is that this entity cannot have an end or a purpose apart from the ends and purposes of its constituent members – individuals.

Individualism does not limit personal liberties to 'civil' liberties, freedom of expression, association, etc. It also includes the right to acquire (by legitimate methods) personal property. To tax persons for purposes other than the financing of genuine public services is to violate their rights. The right to welfare, for an individualist, cannot be a genuine universal right because to satisfy it for some entails the abrogation of the rights of others.

The major twentieth-century utilitarian political individualists are the economists Mises, Hayek, and Friedman. For some utilitarian political individualists the objection to a natural rights foundation for individualism derives from their ethical subjectivism. This is the doctrine that all evaluative expressions, such as 'good', 'bad', 'justice', and 'injustice', do not refer to anything empirically verifiable but are expressions of personal judgement. However, it is presupposed that there is a considerable amount of agreement about the ends of individual and social life and that the familiar economic and political individualist institutions are demonstrably the most efficient means for their realization.

In Mises, economic theory predicts with apodictic certainty that individualistic economic orders are superior in the generation of prosperity and happiness than planned systems. In Friedman's individualism, its virtues are justified by reference to the observable defects in numerous types of economic intervention. Friedman makes the important point that civil liberties (such as freedom of expression) would be useless without individual ownership of private property. In Hayek, the justification for individual liberty rests upon a theory of the progress of human knowledge. Without an open society and individual freedom, new experiments in economics and social forms would be impossible. The utilitarian advantage of individual liberty stems, then, from the incurable ignorance that characterizes the human condition.

Although utilitarian individualists believe that 'society' in some sense is better off under conditions of individual freedom, they reject the idea that some collective welfare function can be derived from individual preferences. This is, of course, not because of a belief in natural rights but because of the impossibility of scientifically measuring and comparing individual utilities.

Traditional conservatives, while not hostile to individualism, certainly reject its extreme versions, on both methodological and political grounds. Society, they claim, cannot be understood entirely in terms of individual volitions: for this is to ignore a host of historical and institutional factors that influence human conduct. Political individualism is similarly deficient: to reduce the bulk of social activity to individual transactions, subject only to the cash nexus, is to overlook those crucial institutions, such as the family, the church, and the state, which cannot be analysed in this way.

NB

Further reading

Hayek, F.A., *Individualism and Economic Order*, London, Routledge & Kegan Paul, 1940.
Hayek, F.A., *The Counter-Revolution of Science: Studies in the Abuse of Reason*, Glencoe, IL, The Free Press, 1952.
Lukes, S., *Individualism*, Oxford, Blackwell, 1973.
Popper, K.R., *The Poverty of Historicism*, London, Routledge & Kegan Paul, 1957.
Rothbard, M., *Individualism and the Philosophy of Social Sciences*, San Fransisco, CA, Cato Institute, 1979.

INTELLIGENTSIA

The word 'intellectual' first began to be employed as a noun in the middle or late nineteenth century. In its plural form it is a synonym for the originally Russian 'intelligentsia', which in imperial Russia from the 1860s onwards designated that section of the university educated youth who were 'critically thinking personalities' (Pisarev's phrase) or 'nihilists' (Turgenev's term), those who questioned all traditional values in the name of reason and progress. In France it was used, pejoratively or proudly, of and by the Dreyfusards.

These movements tended to associate the intelligentsia with the left, although in both these cases it should be understood as an extremely broad left, incorporating not only socialists of every stripe but also classical liberals and, in Russia, constitutional democrats (the KDs or Kadets). This association was strengthened, and the understanding of leftism tightly narrowed, by what was to prove a very effectively suggestive passage in the *Communist Manifesto*: 'when the class struggle nears the decisive hour . . . a small section of the ruling class cuts itself adrift and joins the revolutionary class, the class that holds the future in its hands'. This 'portion of the bourgeoisie which goes over to the proletariat' is in particular a portion of the bourgeois ideologists, who have 'raised themselves to the level of comprehending theoretically the historical movement as a whole'.

This is a most memorable passage, which must not be allowed to pass without a mention of the fact that the first successful revolution made in the name of, and supposedly in the interests of, a proletariat was – like so many of its successors – actually led and dominated by a group including almost no one with any real claim to be or even ever to have been a proletarian. Marx and Engels would surely have had to rate the Bolshevik leadership 'bourgeois ideologists, who [had] raised themselves to the level of comprehending theoretically the historical movement as a whole.' So the hands which actually held the future were not, after all, proletarian.

Observations of this sort have led some of the friends and some of the enemies of such a revolution to maintain that the truly revolutionary class is not a progressively prospering proletariat but the alienated intelligentsia. Revolution apart, however, it would be a mistake to overlook the possibility that individual and class interests may be involved not only in the opposition to but also in the promotion of Procrustean redistribution and the expansion of the welfare state machine. For if equality is to be state enforced, then there have to be, as well as the equalized proles, directing and controlling equalizers.

There is no doubt but that, both in the United States and in most of the other countries of democratic capitalism, the intellectuals – the academic and media establishment, and the 'knowledge class' as a whole – today stand considerably further to the left (or, in US idiom, are more liberal) than the population as a whole. Their generally adversarial attitudes towards the institutions and cultures of these countries, and their at most half-hearted opposition to external and totalitarian enemies, go far to prove the foresight of Schumpeter: 'Capitalism stands its trial before judges who have the sentence of death in their pockets. They are going to pass it, whatever the defense they may hear; the only success victorious defense can possibly produce is a change in the indictment.'

But, unless we implicitly define the word 'intellectual' as requiring such leftward leanings – as indeed is sometimes done – it has to be recognized that at other times or in other places many persons who would have to be so accounted cherished quite contrary commitments. Between the wars, for instance, whatever may have been true of the majority, some of the most prominent must be rated as having been on the right: Maurras, Bernanos, Mauriac, Stefan George, Pirandello, Yeats, and Eliot, for instance. The very title of Benda's *La Trahison des clercs*, first published in 1927 – a title best translated as *Betrayal by the Intellectuals* – should serve as a salutary reminder of the many centuries when literacy was confined almost exclusively to the clergy, and when the manuscripts recording and constituting the cultural achievements of ancient civilizations were preserved and reproduced only in monasteries.

AF

Further reading

Ashford, N., 'Is there a new class?' *The World & I* 1988, 3 (6): 661–74.
Benda, J., *The Treason of the Intellectuals*, Boston, MA, Beacon, 1955.
Feuer, L., *Marxism and the Intellectuals*, New York, Doubleday Anchor, 1969.
Schumpeter, J.S., *Capitalism, Socialism and Democracy*, New York and London, Harper and Allen & Unwin, 1942, Ch.13.
Stigler, G., *The Intellectual and the Marketplace*, Cambridge, MA, and London, Harvard University Press, enlarged edition 1984, Ch.18.

INVISIBLE HAND

Adam Smith uses the phrase 'an invisible hand' in at least two passages of his published writings. In *The Wealth of Nations* he states that each individual was 'led by an invisible hand to promote an end which was no part of his intention', while in his *Theory of Moral Sentiments* he claims that

The rich only select from the heap what is most precious and agreeable. They consume little more than the poor, and in spite of their natural selfishness and rapacity . . . they divide with the poor the produce of all their improvements. They are led by an invisible hand to make nearly the same distribution of the necessaries of life which would have been made, had the earth been divided into equal portions among all its inhabitants.

The basic thought is that in acting selfishly the rich, in fact, and by an almost inevitable process, benefit the poor. They do this because in seeking the gratification of their desires they need the co-operation of others, and in order to gain that co-operation, they need to reward the others. In language used more recently by sociologists, while the 'manifest function' of the transaction between buyer and seller is to satisfy the desires of the buyer, the 'latent function' is to provide work and wealth for the seller. The invisibility of the hand is due to the dislocation between what the rich intend and what they in fact effect by their actions.

The invisible hand doctrine provides one of the main moral defences of classical liberal economics. For the individualism of liberalism is open to the charge that it sanctions selfishness, not only in the sense that people do what they want to do, but also that they do what they want to do even when it is at the expense of others. But if it can be shown that individual selfishness can be for the general good, or better, that it must be for the general good, then an acceptable utilitarian defence of selfishness will have been found. Trading is not a zero-sum game; all traders may profit by their trade, a fact systematically misunderstood by socialists who equate profit-making with exploitation. It is noteworthy, however, that Smith restricts his claim about unintentional redistribution to 'necessaries'.

On another interpretation, however, Smith's invisible hand illustrates the amorality of the market. For the market brings together buyer and seller in spite of, or in indifference to, whatever may be the moral relations betweem them. Buyer and seller may have no common interests other than their interest in the market; nevertheless, according to Smith, this is sufficient for them to co-operate freely, and anonymously, as each fulfils his or her aims; the rich obtain gratification, the poor obtain employment.

The invisible hand doctrine illustrates vividly the basic thesis of economic liberalism, that economic relations are individualistic and not collective; that people come together *qua* buyer and seller and for no other reason; that economic relations are anonymous and paramount. Thus the idea of a just wage, for example, has no application in the world of the invisible hand. The 'just wage' is simply the wage that buyer and seller, freely bargaining together, agree.

In one important sense of 'natural' the world of the invisible hand is a natural order. If left to himself each man will, by a natural process, and despite his intentions, not only attain an end which was to his own best advantage, but one which also furthered the common good. This is part of the natural order not in the sense that it obeys the natural law as Aquinas or Hooker understood this, but because it is part of a natural mechanism of human interaction, a mechanism which each member in society participates in willy-nilly. Smith even went so far as to say that individual and societal advantage coincide to a greater degree when and because it is unintended than if it is planned.

The world of the invisible hand is a natural order so long as it is not interfered with from the outside, notably by government. For Smith does not doubt that, given the chance, people will seek privilege for themselves, and an escape from the rigours of the market. (As the above quotation from the *Theory of Moral Sentiments* shows, its author has an unflattering view of human nature.) But they will succeed only with the support of a government which permits or encourages monopolies and other restraints of trade.

One straight political consequence of this is that government ought to be minimal; to defend against foreign aggression, to provide for a sytem of internal justice, and to provide an infrastructure of public works which the market cannot provide because they are unprofitable.

It is a short step from Smith's invisible hand to the Hayekian emphasis that the markets are unrivalled transmitters of economic information. For in bringing buyer and seller together the markets provide constantly changing signals as to what is buyable and therefore sellable, and produceable and therefore buyable, indicating supremely well the vagaries of style and taste as well as more substantively based changes in the scales of human preferences.

The conservative will enter a number of caveats against Smith's position while broadly welcoming its central thrust that government should adopt a minimal economic role. The caveats are mainly two. The first is that Smith's doctrine of the invisible hand, and what it entails, is ahistorical in character. Smith treats the natural order, quite consistently, as applying to all nations at all times. But this takes no account of national temperament or character, the distinctivenesses and particularities of national institutions and different traditions' ways of working and organizing. In the second place he, in common with all individualists, neglects the importance of the state and of other social institutions in rendering intelligible the motives and goals of men and women within them.

PH

Further reading

Barry, N., *The Invisible Hand in Economics and Politics*, London, Institute of Economic Affairs, 1988.

Hayek, F.A., *Law, Legislation and Liberty*, London, Routledge & Kegan Paul, 1982.

Nozick, R., *Anarchy, State, and Utopia*, Oxford and New York, Blackwell and Basic Books, 1974.

Smith, A., *The Wealth of Nations*, 2 vols, Indianapolis, IN, Liberty Press, 1981.

Smith, A., *Theory of Moral Sentiments*, Indianapolis, IN, Liberty Press, 1976.

J

JUSTICE

1 Justice, without prefix or suffix. In *The Republic*, traditionally sub-titled 'Concerning Justice', the first suggestion is that it is 'to render to everyone their due'. This would, presumably, have been accepted by most of Plato's contemporaries as at least on the right lines, if perhaps not completely adequate. But 'Socrates', speaking for Plato, is concerned to promote a preferred alternative; a persuasive redefinition epitomizing the foundation principles of his first utopia. So his interlocutors are here scripted to admit as a more than sufficient refutation what are instead and in truth *reductiones ad absurdum* of two characteristically Socratic assumptions covertly conjoined with that first suggestion.

That that does in fact embrace the heart of the matter becomes clear once we attend to the subsequent story. For *suum cuique tribuere* (to render to each their own, their due) is for all the Roman jurists the key phrase. In Ulpian the just man is also redundantly required *honeste vivere* (to live honourably) and *neminem laedere* (to harm no one). But in the *Insistutes* of Justinian these accretions are omitted. The mark of the just person is *constans et perpetua voluntas jus suum cuique tribuere* (a constant and perpetual will to render to each their own, their due).

'Their own, their due' is to be construed as their deserts and entitlements. These two terms are not equivalent. You may be entitled to something which you have in no way deserved; while all deserts presuppose a necessarily undeserved entitlement to the capacities and potentialities which have to be appropriately exercised – or deliberately not exercised – if you are to acquire any deserts at all. It would, too, be at best odd to speak of someone being *entitled* to severe punishment, however richly that unwelcome treatment might have been deserved.

Because people necessarily have a right to whatever is truly their own, their due, justice is both a minimal virtue and one the mandates of which one may properly be compelled to obey. Thus, taking this as an obvious and incontestable truth, Smith observed:

143

> Mere justice is . . . but a negative virtue, and only hinders us from hurting our neighbour. The man who barely abstains from violating either the person, or the estate, or the reputation of his neighbours, has surely little positive merit. He fulfills, however, all the rules of what is peculiarly called justice, and does everything which his equals can with propriety force him to do, or which they can punish him for not doing.

J.S. Mill says much the same thing: 'When we think a person is bound in justice to do a thing, it is an ordinary form of language to say that he ought to be compelled to do it.' This is, of course, the reason why, from Plato onwards, people eager to impose their own personal political and social ideals have laboured to present these as ideals of justice.

The institutions thus recommended in *The Republic* were in the last degree inegalitarian. But in our own day such ideals almost always demand, or at any rate are presented as demanding, a universal, although perhaps more or less qualified, equality of condition. Nevertheless their protagonists – not unfairly described by opponents as Procrusteans – still argue or assume that what they are proposing is the enforcement of the imperatives of (social) justice.

Aristotle asserted: 'If injustice is inequality, justice is equality – a view which commends itself to all without proof.' He, however, proceeds at once to argue: 'If the persons are not equal, they will not have equal shares.' It would, for instance, be grotesque to maintain that criminal justice requires that persons convicted be not discriminated against, but treated in exactly the same way as the innocent.

The truth, as the Victorian conservative Fitzjames Stephen was to insist is

> that the only shape in which equality is really connected with justice is this – justice presupposes general rules. . . If these general rules are to be maintained at all, it is obvious that they must be applied equally to every case which satisfies their terms.

The rules of justice, like all rules, require not that all cases, but only that all relevantly like cases, be treated in the same way. Given this purely formal agreement there still can be and often is substantial disagreement about what is and is not to be allowed to be relevant.

2   Social Justice. The first occurrrence noticed by the revisers of the *Oxford English Dictionary* of what has since become the cant expression 'social justice' is in Chapter V of *Utilitarianism*. By not indicating what he had it in mind to exclude through the insertion of this qualification, J.S. Mill set an example which continues to be very widely followed. Yet if we are going to distinguish non-social from social virtues, as Hume distinguished the natural from what he unhappily labelled the

artificial, then justice surely has to count as the fundamental and paradigm social specimen?

Rawls advertises his enormous book as containing *A Theory of Justice*. Inside, however, it soon emerges that what he is actually offering is 'a theory of social justice'. Although he is as reluctant as other users of that expression to specify what other, non-social sorts he is thus excluding from attention, he does explain the function of the principles actually proposed: 'they provide a way of assigning rights and duties in the basic institutions of society, and they define the appropriate distribution of the benefits and burdens of social cooperation'.

Like so many others Rawls, in presenting what he calls principles of social justice, is propounding and commending his personal ideal of a good and fair society. But, *pace* Rawls, actual justice cannot properly be identified with his or anyone else's ideal of fairness. Social justice so contrued is no more a kind of justice than Bombay duck is a kind of duck or People's Democracy is a kind of democracy.

In this same understanding *The Republic* must itself be rated the first treatise on social justice. But, whereas Plato tried hard, if not in the end successfully, to relate his own preferred persuasive redefinition to the ordinary meaning of (the Greek word translated as) 'justice', Rawls continues never to discuss, nor even to quote, any version of that traditional definition. Instead he congratulates himself on making an assumption which, allegedly, 'allows us to leave questions of meaning and definition aside and to get on with the task of developing a substantive theory of justice'.

The question whether such 'social justice' is correctly called justice is by no means merely verbal. For it is only and precisely in so far as the equalizing redistributions said to be mandated by social justice are, in the traditional sense, just, that Procrusteans can have an adequate answer to the conservative challenge: 'By what right is your Chancellor Robin Hood seizing property from those who have earned or otherwise become entitled to it and transferring this property to others who, even though it may well be through no fault of their own, have not?' It was in this conservative spirit that Hayek, who pretends not to be a conservative, asserted that ' "Social justice" is a socialist euphemism used to describe any condition which the user would like to bring about by flouting the principles of justice'.

The most brilliant liberal critique of Rawls, indeed quite simply the most brilliant critique, is that of Nozick. But he, too, fails to quote the traditional definition, and hence is misled to refer to his own offering as 'The Entitlement Theory'. This is as if someone were to try to distinguish their account of chastity as 'The Sexual Restraint Theory'. Curiously, too, and in a way which separates him sharply from any Burkean conservative, Nozick finds no room for prescription; the just acquisition of property and other rights through long possession, and the sheer effluxion of time.

Some of those who speak of social justice take this expression to be equivalent to 'distributive justice'. But Aristotle, who first distinguished distributive from corrective justice, certainly did not assume, as many of our contemporaries do, that everything is up for (re)distributive grabs. He did not, that is to say, assume that all wealth – apparently including those services which are someone's actions – has been, is, and will be – in Nozick's happily memorable phrase – 'manna from heaven'; which falls into the hands of would-be (re)distributors unpreempted by any legitimate prior claims to possession.

Those who, whether they recognize it or not, do make this assumption are thereby committed to the contrary claim that what they like to call 'the nation's wealth' already is, as the realization of their socialist ideals would make it, collective property, rather than a fictitious theoretical accumulation of all the present assets of all the individual citizens of that nation.

To upset this assumption it is both necessary and sufficient to bring home to our – on their own stated principles – often conspicuously underdeprived Procrusteans that, if the enforcement of equality is to be *just*, as opposed to merely desirable upon some different ground, then that can only be because those who at present enjoy a more than equal share of 'the nation's wealth' are in possession of – are, that is to say, 'stealing by keeping' – some of the property of people worse off than themselves.

AF

Further reading

Aristotle, *Nicomachean Ethics*, Book V.

Flew, A.G.N., *The Politics of Procrustes*, London and Buffalo, NY, Temple Smith and Prometheus, 1981, Chs 1–6.

Hayek, F.A., *Law, Legislation and Liberty*, London, Routledge & Kegan Paul, 1982, Chs 8 and 9.

Nozick, R., *Anarchy, State and Utopia*, New York and Oxford, Basic Books and Blackwell, 1974, Ch. 7.

Rawls, J., *A Theory of Justice*, Cambridge, MA, and Oxford, Harvard University Press and Clarendon, 1971 and 1972.

L

LAISSEZ-FAIRE

The term *laissez-faire*,though of course French, is currently much more common in English. It designates an unrestricted system of capitalism, in which the role of the state is at most confined to police, justice, and defence. This system is favoured by contemporary libertarians, e.g. the American economist Rothbard and his followers.

Advocates of *laissez-faire* are not necessarily libertarians. Mises, an Austrian economist, is the most notable twentieth-century advocate of *laissez-faire*. In works including *Socialism* and *Human Action* he opposed all government regulation of the economy. He did so not on grounds of natural rights, but because he held that all government regulation would, from the point of view of its own advocates, fail in its intended purpose. Minimum wage laws will produce unemployment, and price controls will lead to shortages. Since interventionist measures are self-defeating, either they will be abandoned entirely or further interventions will be undertaken in a futile effort to counter the ill-effects of the first interferences with the market. The eventual result will be socialism. This in turn, Mises contended, could be proved incapable of working efficiently. Thus, on Mises's view, the most important social choice was prosperity or economic chaos. If one elected the first, *laissez-faire* capitalism was necessary.

Some advocates of *laissez-faire* oppose Mises's utilitarian grounding for the system. Rothbard, a student of Mises and the founder of modern libertarianism, has argued for *laissez-faire* on the basis of natural rights. Among these are 'self-ownership', i.e. the right of each person to own his or her own body and the rights of individual property acquisition, control, and transfer. The Harvard philosopher Nozick adopted a similar view in his influential *Anarchy, State, and Utopia*, and the novelist Rand supported capitalism on the basis of her own ethical system.

Space limits do not permit discussion of the nineteenth-century advocates of *laissez-faire*. Among the most important of them were Spencer and Bastiat.

The term, in addition to its strict meaning, also refers to the advocacy of capitalism. Deviations from complete reliance on the market do not in the wider sense prevent the application of the term. This usage encompasses a much wider range of positions than the libertarian view just sketched. First, many economists, e.g. Milton Friedman, Buchanan, and Tullock, believe that the free market better serves to allocate resources than alternative systems. These economists do not, however, oppose government intervention in the economy under all circumstances. Friedman, for example supports a governmental monetary system operating by fixed rules and also defends a 'negative income tax', i.e. cash subsidies to the poor.

DG

Further reading

Bastiat, F., *The Law*, Irvington-on-Hudson, NY, Foundation for Economic Education, 1981.
Mises, L.von, *Human Action*, New Haven, CT, Yale University Press, 1949.
Nozick, R., *Anarchy, State and Utopia*, Oxford and New York, Blackwell and Basic Books, 1974.
Rothbard, M., *Man, Economy and State*, Princeton, NJ, Van Nostrand, 1965.
Rothbard, M., *Power and Market*, Kansas City, MO, Sheed, Andrews, & McMeel, 1977.

LANGUAGE

Language is a matter of conservative concern in three ways: first, a particular language is often a main uniting and differentiating principle of the nation; second, language is the essential instrumentability of tradition; and third, the origin and development of the natural languages has provided a model of and for the properly conservative development and reform of institutions.

The revival and extension of Hebrew as the common language of the state of Israel constitutes the most remarkable case of simultaneous unification and differentiation. The attempt to establish Erse in the Republic of Ireland certainly differentiates. But it erects yet another obstacle against the incorporation of all the populations of geographical Ireland into a single nation state. English, which was the original and only possible uniting language of the Indian National Congress before independence, might still unite but cannot differentiate India as an established nation state.

Julian Huxley once reviewed the biological peculiarities of our species. First came the far-extended period between birth and maturity, the incomparable capacity for learning, and the consequent predominance of learned as opposed to instinctual behaviour. This unrivalled capacity for learning, he argued, together with its instrument and expression, developed language, provides our species with a serviceable substitute for the genetic inheritance of acquired characteristics.

It is language, and language alone, which makes possible a continuity of national tradition; while particular languages are essential to particular traditions. Famously, Burke presented his vision of society as

> a partnership in every virtue, and in all perfection. As the ends of such a partnership cannot be obtained in many generations, it becomes a partnership not only between those who are living, but between those who are living, those who are dead and those who are to be born.

Without language, and that the particular language common to all the partners, 'the whole chain and continuity in the commonwealth would be broken. No one generation could link with the other. Men would become little better than the flies of summer'.

To appreciate the importance of the origin and development of the natural languages as a model we must turn to Hume, whom many nowadays consider to have anticipated Burke in establishing the modern conservative intellectual tradition. Hume's solution to the problems of actual origins is hard-headed and profound. Where his less enlightened and less truly sociological opponents tell tales referring back to deliberate foresight and contractual agreement, Hume argues that the fundamental social institutions could not have originated from this sort of planning. What is possible is that recognitions of common interest will lead to the regulation of conduct in ways which are not, and often could not be, derived from prior contracts:

> two men, who pull the oars of a boat, do it by an agreement or convention, tho' they have never given promises to each other. Nor is the rule concerning the stability of possession the less deriv'd from human conventions, that it arises gradually, and acquired force by a slow progression. . . In like manner are languages gradually establish'd by human conventions without any promise. In like manner do gold and silver become the common measures of exchange.

To the philosopher that penultimate illustration is the most impressive. To think that the natural languages, formations whose richness and subtleties it is so hard even faithfully to delineate, not merely may but must be progressively evolved rather than comprehensively planned; by-products of the actions and interactions of people who were themselves incapable of designing, whether individually or collectively, anything of comparable complexity. In what language, after all, would the committee charged with the task of designing the first language have conducted its deliberations?

Wittgenstein once said: 'Language is a part of the human organism, and no less complicated than it.' From J.L. Austin we may learn: that the vocabulary already available here in colloquial English is vastly rich and subtle; and that – contrary to what has been so often said – Austin himself always insisted that even these rich and too-often unexploited resources might sometimes need supplementation or correction. In his awareness that, although reform is often necessary, it should always be grounded in a comprehensive and sympathetic understanding of both the weaknesses and the strengths of what is to be reformed, Austin was, of course, truly conservative.

In his *Dialogues Concerning Natural Religion* Hume scripted Philo to say:

> If we survey a ship, what an exalted idea we must form of the ingenuity of the carpenter, who framed so complicated, useful and beautific a machine? And what surprise must we entertain, when we find him a stupid mechanic, who imitated others, and copied an art, which, through a long succession of ages, after multiplied trials, mistakes, corrections, deliberations, and controversies, had been gradually improving.

Certainly the natural languages must be, as was argued also by the other Scottish founding fathers of social science, products of still continuing processes of this kind. It has been well said that the history of every language is a history of corruptions; in the sense that every change must involve some deviation from what was previously established as correct usage. Presumably it was ever so. Presumably the whole growth of language has, from the beginning, been a series of unplanned lapses and intended initiatives; some of which have, through the passage of time, become accepted usages.

Later, this particular case of the partly observed and the partly inferred generation, through the not intentionally and collectively co-ordinated initiatives and responses of various persons or groups of persons, most of whom cannot have been directly acquainted with one another, of what may suggest brilliant individual or collective design was to become one of Darwin's models for his account of the origin of the species by natural selection. (Natural selection is, of course, no more conscious selection than Smith's invisible hand was a guiding hand.)

The contemplation of unintended results of intended action in general, and of the production of the natural languages in particular, should teach us how fallacious it is to argue that, if something is the product or result of human agency, then it must always be in practice possible radically to redesign and reshape that product or that result in such a way that it shall the better accommodate the wishes of the persons concerned. It may be, or then again it may not. Every case needs to be examined separately, and argued on its individual merits.

Descartes was, therefore, quite simply wrong when he made his characteristic claim that there is, typically, 'less perfection in works composed of several portions, and carried out by the hands of various masters'. So too, and consequently, is the entire tradition of what Hayek has labelled 'constructivistic rationalism'.

That tradition resonates to the cry of Cabet, an early French socialist: 'Nothing is impossible for a government which really wills the good of its people.' But nowhere and by no Providence is it guaranteed that good intentions will produce all and only their intended good effects. To the disappointed it should nevertheless be some consolation to contemplate the other side of this coin. For intentions less than perfectly disinterested and universally benevolent are perhaps the more common; and these too, in this universe, are equally liable to produce consequences additional and even contrary to those intended.

AF

Further reading

Austin, J.L., *Philosophical Papers*, Oxford, Clarendon Press, 1961.
Hayek, F.A., *New Studies in Philosophy, Politics, Economics and the History of Ideas*, Chicago, IL, and London, Chicago University Press and Routledge & Kegan Paul, 1967, Chs 15–16.
Hayek, F.A., *Studies in Philosophy, Politics and Economics*, Chicago, IL, and London, Chicago University Press and Routledge & Kegan Paul, 1967, Chs 5–7.
Sampson, G., *Liberty and Language*, Oxford and New York, Oxford University Press, 1979.

LAW

The idea of law has been a crucial one for conservatives and classical liberals from Montesquieu onwards. Law is a body of rules, whether enacted or customary, which govern the relations among the members of a community and between individuals and institutions and which are recognized as having a binding and enforceable quality. A major concern of all political theory is to establish precisely what it is that distinguishes law from other kinds of rule and what the source of law is. This is a difficult question, complicated by the general recognition of most thinkers that there are various types of law which may have different origins.

The dominant theory of law among modern lawyers is the positivist theory formulated by the nineteenth-century English utilitarian philosopher Austin. According to this, laws are artificial rules invented or created by human beings through a conscious act of will. Clearly not all rules are laws: the rules of a private club do not come into this category even though they are consciously formulated. Austin's second proviso, therefore, is that laws have a public character and are the rules laid down by those with legitimate political power, i.e. the legislators. This theory has great advantages over its rivals, particularly for lawyers. It is clear and straightforward with the great benefit of simplicity – laws are simply positive legislation and all other issues are dismissed as otiose.

However, the positive theory of law has been subjected to vehement criticism by conservatives and classical liberals, among others. The theory is circular and self-proving, i.e. true by definition. It implies that any rule, no matter how arbitrary or bizarre, is law if promulgated by a political authority. Most serious is the objection that it makes power the only source of law so that without political rule there can be no law. This is both objectionable and historically inaccurate. Indeed, another objection to the theory is its radically ahistorical nature.

A quite different theory is that of natural law. Rather confusingly this exists in two distinct forms. The first is the rationalist theory of natural law found in writers such as Hobbes and Pufendorf. Here the idea is that the natural order of things, the inherent nature of human beings and the world they inhabit (which is usually, though not always, seen as divinely created), contains principles or rules which can be discovered by the use of a reasoning capacity common to all people. This kind of law is inherent in the nature of the world and human beings and is in some sense internal to all humans, 'writ by God in the heart of man' as one seventeenth-century writer put it. Laws of this kind are common to all people of all times and places.

The other form of natural law theory is a variant of the notion of spontaneous order. It can be found in the writings of thinkers such as Hume and those of seventeenth-century English common lawyers such as Coke and Hale. For them laws and legal institutions are the product of a historical process which is unplanned and undirected, not the result of ratiocination, and which varies from one part of the world to another, being influenced by such factors as geography, climate and culture. The system of law is an unplanned harmony, the consequence and result of many individual decisions and cases, and embodies not some natural reason but rather the tacit knowledge and wisdom of the people and the past. However, there is still a residual element of naturalism arising from the assumption, most explicit in Hume, that there is a basic human nature shared by all people in all times and places. Certain features of law such as the prohibition of theft will therefore occur in all legal systems since they derive from that nature and without them a stable social order would be impossible. This is often linked by lawyers to the idea of equity or natural justice, principles which are inherently and necessarily true and are instinctively perceived as such by all persons capable of moral judgement.

This more limited form of natural law is very close to the third major school of legal theory, the historical school founded by figures such as Savigny and Gierke and, later, Maine. Their account of law is similar to that of the minimal natural lawyers but with two crucial differences. They are more fundamentally historicist, and there is an element of evolutionism. This is most marked in Maine, who constructed an elaborate theory of the historical evolution of law relating the domination of different types of law to various stages of economic and social development. For him the main movement in the history of law was from status to contract. The historical school were concerned primarily to put the history of law on a firm empirical basis and to move away from the 'natural history' approach of the eighteenth century which had emphasized theoretical models. For them law was a historical phenomenon, it was what had been law in the past and in contemporary societies. Because a legal form or principle has existed in one time and place does not mean that it is universally applicable or the outcome of a general principle. The major contemporary exponent of this argument is Oakeshott who sees 'nomocracy' (his term for the rule of law) as a peculiar outgrowth of the history of western Europe, not necessarily valid elsewhere. The major contribution of the school was a great increase in knowledge and understanding of law in the past and the creation of the discipline of comparative legal studies.

Most theorists who reject strict legal positivism accept that in any historical legal system there may be a variety of different types of law. Thus Montesquieu recognized nine, including civil, canon, natural, and divine law. It is generally accepted that at any given time the law will consist of a mixture of historically evolved or common law and legislative or positive law.

Rejection of the simple positivist position, however, raises serious issues, of great importance for conservatives and classical liberals. If law can come from somewhere other than the state does it represent a superior authority to that of the state? If a conflict arises between the positive law of the state and natural law, however defined, which takes precedence? In other words, can a refusal to obey the laws of the state be justified by appeal to a higher law? If law can derive from other sources than political authority, is it possible to have a completely non-statist legal system? Given that in modern societies there are a great number of rules which are laws by traditional definition, are there criteria by which we may discern those which are true laws and those which are merely administrative orders or regulation?

Conservatives have a fairly clear and consistent position with regard to the first three questions. They have always argued that, in the modern world at least, law cannot ultimately exist in the absence of political authority. That is because the crucial criterion that laws be recognized and enforceable can only be met in a just and proper way if there is one institution with a monopoly of force. So the laws apparently generated outwith the state are only effective while there is a state which can be appealed to to enforce them. The alternative is that laws can be enforced by anyone with sufficient power, which means vigilantism, mob rule, and chaos. Similarly they argue that there must be a final legislative authority which can decide or determine what the law is, otherwise there will never by agreement on hard cases. It follows from all this that one cannot appeal to a higher authority to justify refusal to obey a law or a court. This does not necessarily mean that the state is above the law, only that it is the highest source of law and that there is no authority higher than that of actually existing law, whether statute or common.

This position can be derived from either a historical or natural law perspective (as in Hobbes). Classical liberals are more divided. Standing on the same two bases, some broadly agree with the conservative position but others arrive at quite different destinations. Following the classical maxim *Lex injusta non est lex* (an unjust law is no law), some argue that legislation which violates reason and the law of nature is not a true law and can, or even should, be defied. In this tradition the purpose of laws is to protect the natural rights of property and person, so legislation which violates these is not true law. This argument has been used many times by radical classical liberals, the best-known case being the defiance of pro-slavery legislation such as the Fugitive Slave Act by American abolitionists. The problem with this position is that there is no clear agreement in practice on the content of the rights or laws of nature. Some critics, such as Gray, have gone so far as to argue that the concept is simply vacuous, impossible of definition.

Another radical conclusion is that of authors, such as Leoni, who argue that a state is not necessary to maintain and create law. The conservative position outlined above is criticized on the grounds that it ignores the many examples in history of what are technically called acephalic legal orders, i.e. legal systems which do not involve a state or monopoly legislature. The best known of these is the law merchant of medieval Europe, but there are many other examples, from Ireland to Iceland to Africa. Leoni makes a distinction between law, which he sees in historical terms, and legislation which is created by political rulers. Law is created by societies to serve their own needs and in particular to provide security. Legislation is unnecessary and almost always sectional, designed to serve a special interest.

What both of these positions assert is that law, however defined, is superior to the state and overrides sovereignty whether popular or otherwise. This position can only be sustained if there is held to be a source of law other than the state, whether located in 'nature' or the historical process. The conservatives' reply is to argue that in any case there must be some body or persons who declare what the law is, and it or they will really be the state by another name. What both sides agree, however (apart from some extreme conservatives of the De Maistre or Pobedonostev variety), is that the free society must be marked by the rule of law. There must be a government of laws and not of men. This involves an answer to the last question put earlier, and several thinkers have produced arguments concerning the procedural forms which must be followed if a legal system is to qualify as part of the rule of law.

Although the rule of law is a vital concept for conservatives and classical liberals there is a surprisingly wide range of views as to what the term means. For some it is almost the same as constitutionalism, the idea that in any free society there must be some fundamental law which governs relations between state and citizen and is not the subject of partisan debate. In particular it must place limits on or define the sphere of government action.

A different though related conception of the rule of law is that which sees it as embodied in the *Rechtstaat*. This idea, associated with German thinkers such as Rotteck, is also found in the works of English writers, notably Dicey. For these writers the rule of law means that rulers and their agents are subject to the law as much as anyone else, and to the same law. The citizen is thus not subject to another person's will since both citizen and ruler are ruled by the same law. This means that the state and its agents cannot do as they like, behave in an arbitrary, self-willed fashion: they must obey the law and can be held to account if they fail to do so.

A slightly different and very influential model of the *rechtstaat* is that proposed by Hayek. As well as the above, Hayek adds the proviso that true laws must pass a Kantian test of universalizability, that is they must be general abstract rules which apply to all equally and without discrimination between groups and individuals. The problem with both of these last two models of the rule of law for classical liberals can be easily put. They both prescribe only that the state should be ruled by law but say nothing as to the content of that law. For Dicey the rule of law was compatible with the unlimited sovereignty of parliament. The laws made by parliament could by highly illiberal and oppressive but so long as they bound the government as well as the citizens the rule of law was not threatened. Similarly in Hayek's model, as Hamowy and Raz amongst others have argued, there are many possible laws which, while universal, could be strongly repressive. In short, the rule of law is not enough, it is only a necessary condition of a free society, not a sufficient one. For that to be the case it must be linked to some definite theory of rights which will enable the observer to decide whether a given law is proper or not. One could imagine, they argue, a *Rechstaat* which was oppressive, even a communist one.

In reply to this Gray has argued that this misunderstands the nature of the universalizability proposed and that Hayek's conception of the rule of law proscribes certain types of content as well as form. Universalizability means the application of the Kantian categorical imperative, i.e. 'the possibility of willing that the rules should be applied to all instances that correspond to the conditions stated in it'. Hayek adds that this means that in any system of rules no one rule may conflict with any other, i.e. the system must be compossible. Gray argues that this implies three stages of universalizability: it implies consistency between similar cases; the principles of impartiality, i.e. that one must assume that the rule will apply to oneself as well as anyone else; and that the rules be morally neutral, i.e. make no distinction between different conceptions of the good life. These rule out a whole range of interventionist policies, including moral interventionism. Gray argues that to apply the principle of universalizability to the domain of law leaves a system with a liberal content as the only one which satisfies these requirements. A socialist *rechtstaat* is thus a chimaera.

The concept of law is thus one of vital importance for conservatives and classical liberals, but also hedged about with thorns of argument. However, whenever reduced to doubt by the seeming difficulty of establishing a firm basis for their concept of law and the rule of law, their faith is restored by the terrible spectacle of truly lawless polities such as fascist and communist states. The theory may be abstruse, but the empirical argument for law as a necessary component of a free society and its absence or subversion as the greatest of threats seems obvious and undeniable.

SD

Further reading

Gray, J., 'F.A. Hayek and the Rebirth of Classical Liberalism', *Literature of Liberty*, Winter 1982: 19–67.
Hayek, F.A., *The Constitution of Liberty*, London, Routledge & Kegan Paul, 1960.
Leoni, B., *Freedom and the Law*, Princeton, NJ, Van Nostrand, 1961.

LEGITIMACY

A power is exercised illegitimately if there is no right to its exercise; otherwise it is exercised legitimately. About the legitimacy of governments we may ask questions of two sorts: one is whether they are truly legitimate – a question of ultimate justification; the other – a question of political sociology – is how as a matter of fact they come to be, whether rightly or wrongly, perceived as legitimate.

Ordinarily untheoretical people rarely raise questions about the legitimacy of their governments, save either in periods of deep and widespread dissatisfaction or when the state is afflicted with some sort of succession crisis. Except in such abnormally troubled times the main principle both urged and accepted in justification is that of prescription: regimes become acceptably legitimized by virtue of their long and uncontested establishment. The same principle appears to work retrospectively also. For, if monarchs who were in their own days judged to be usurpers succeed in establishing dynasties, then this achievement will be generally accepted as having conferred posthumous legitimation. And much the same seems to apply when the original usurpation of sovereignty was achieved – in Hobbesian terms – not by 'one man' but by 'an assembly of men'.

In the seventeenth century there were two main rival doctrines: that of the Divine Right of Kings, which traced the source of royal authority back to the alleged biblical beginnings of earthly monarchy; and that of an original contract, which must necessarily be voided if an actual present ruler breaks its terms. The first doctrine, as presented by Filmer, is criticized in the first of Locke's *Two Treatises of Civil Government*; while the second treatise expounds and advocates the second doctrine. Both treatises were originally published in the year after the House of Commons had, in order to legitimate the Glorious Revolution:

> Resolved that King James II, having endeavoured to subvert the constitution of his kingdom by breaking the original contract between King and Parliament, and by the advice of Jesuits and other wicked persons having violated the fundamental laws; and having withdrawn himself out of his kingdom, has abdicated the government; and that the throne is thereby vacant.

Hobbes, a contemporary of Locke and perhaps the most formidable of all England's political thinkers, would have had no patience with either of these popular doctrines. For him effective sovereign power was its own sufficient justification, on earth as it is in heaven. But Hobbes in his own time had no political influence. Later Hume, and others who welcomed the gains of the Glorious Revolution, rejected the attempt to legitimize the resulting regime by reference to an allegedly actual and historical contract supposedly made in the unrecorded past. Much more influential was Locke's insistence upon consent:

> And thus that, which begins and actually constitutes any political society, is nothing but the consent of any number of freemen capable of a majority to unite and incorporate into such a society. And this is that, and only that, which did, or could give beginning to any lawful government in the world.

For all subsequent seekers for some master principle of legitimization – including, most recently, Rawls – any social contracts admitted have become hypothetical rather than historical. But the idea that 'the consent of any number of freemen capable of a majority' is somehow necessary to 'give beginning to any lawful government in the world' is one which, at least and if only in words, appears to be ever more widely accepted. For, while it is only in a small minority of the states members of the United Nations that any incumbent administration ever has been or ever could be removed as the result of a general election, most of the actual rules of the rest seem to find it necessary to conduct, more or less regularly, sheerly fraudulent or otherwise effectively choiceless electoral charades. And how is the persistence of these seemingly unintelligible and pointless procedures to be explained, save as the hypocritical tribute which despotic and dictatorial vice pays to consensual and democratic virtue?

Before the establishment of the first Marxist–Leninist regimes it was usual for professing Marxists to proclaim that it is the necessarily distorting and deceptive function of ideology to (appear to) legitimize various forms of class rule; and hence that ideology was one of all the bad things for which there would – come the Revolution – no longer be either need or place. But once so many such single-party despotisms became both long and firmly established, their masters apparently felt a continuing need to legitimize themselves by appealing to the doctrines of Marxism–Leninism itself; which system was originally supposed not to be an ideology at all, in this sense, but simply scientific socialism.

But immediately after the Bolshevik October coup Lenin was, characteristically, franker and more direct. For, he tells us, the ruling elite, where what is curiously called a 'dictatorship of the proletariat' is in place, may sometimes consist, in effect, of a single person: 'The will of a class, may sometimes by carried out by a dictator.' And the 'scientific definition' of the meaning of the word 'dictatorship' is, once again in Lenin's own words, 'power which is not limited by any laws, not bound by any rules, and based directly on force'.

It is of course possible to challenge the legitimacy of some of the additional operations of some particular government without thereby and at the same time challenging its authority to fulfil the more fundamental functions of all government. In the twentieth century the vast expansion of the welfare and redistributivist activities of so many states certainly encourages such questions.

The main response has been to urge that all these additional activities accord with the imperative mandates of (social) justice; with a gloss, usually unappended, to the effect that everyone has always allowed the legitimacy of employing state power in order to secure (without prefix or suffix) justice. Against that the usual counterclaims are: first, that much of the actual redistribution is from heavy general taxation to sets of often above average well-off rent seekers; and second, that the call to supply welfare services to those unable to provide for themselves is a call not for justice but for charity, and hence is not properly to be financed by moneys forcibly collected.

AF

Further reading

Hayek, F.A., *The Constitution of Liberty*, Chicago, IL, and London, Chicago University Press and Routledge & Kegan Paul, 1960.
Locke, J., *Two Treatises of Government* (1690).
Nozick, R., *Anarchy, State, and Utopia*, New York and Oxford, Basic Books and Blackwell, 1974, Ch. 7.
Rawls, J., *A Theory of Justice*, Cambridge, MA, and Oxford, Harvard University Press and Clarendon Press, 1971 and 1972.

LIBERALISM

This is perhaps the most ambiguous word in the political vocabulary. It describes a position of focal point in political philosophy and also the ideological equipment of a number of political parties in the Western world. Only perhaps in the nineteenth century did liberal political parties espouse policies directly derived from the political philosophy of liberalism.

What is worse, although all contemporary political theories of liberalism claim a common source in their belief in the value of individual liberty, there is such a variety of liberalisms that its current usage has a somewhat limited descriptive value. For analytical convenience it is useful to distinguish between American liberalism and European liberalism in political theory. The latter has much more in common with the classical liberal tradition.

First, let us consider American liberalism. There is no one writer who has presented a complete political economy of American liberalism: the doctrine has to be culled from a variety of economic (mainly Keynesian), philosophical, and political sources. Perhaps the jurisprudence of Dworkin represents its most coherent form. The economists Arrow, Samuelson, and Galbraith in differing ways espouse its main economic tenets; although Galbraith's political economy is the least orthodox of the three.

American liberals are not hostile to the market and individualism; it is rather that they demand constant corrections of its apparently random processes by a benevolent state if the traditional value of freedom can be realized. The experience of the Great Depression was the major causal factor in the growth of American liberalism, for this seemed to confirm the theory that the market was not self-correcting. Hence American liberal economists are unanimous in their approval of government demand management for the creation of full employment. Furthermore, the market is thought to create poverty and inequality which are, they claim, destructive of personal liberty. Hence they argue that state action is essential in all welfare areas, including pensions, unemployment insurance, and medicine.

America has had special problems with deprived minorities, especially blacks, and it is argued that state action to correct past wrongs to them and to create equal (in some cases, superior) opportunities for them is fully consistent with liberalism. Dworkin has been the most sophisticated advocate of the view that such 'affirmative action' programmes are fully consonant with a general liberal philosophy that protects individual rights. Nevertheless, most European liberals maintain that so many areas are now open to state action that American liberalism is scarcely distinguishable from non-Marxist socialism.

European liberalism is perhaps better known as classical liberalism. It is not an active political movement, in the way that socialism often is, but is a way of looking at the political economic world that dates back at least to Smith. Liberals may find themselves supporting policies from different parties if those policies conform to individualist values. In the twentieth century, conservative parties have embraced liberalism, though not with great enthusiasm. However, during the heyday of the German social market economy, the post-1958 Social Democrats were perhaps more committed liberals than the Christian Democrats.

Liberalism began in eighteenth-century Europe with the discovery that there are ordering mechanisms in society which maintain stability (or a kind of equilibrium) without central control. A society did not need dictatorship, but through general laws and market arrangments individuals could act freely without chaos ensuing. Although the intellectual legacy of the Enlightenment was not all favourable to liberalism, its important effect was to make social reality amenable to a rational explanation: it need no longer be enveloped in mysticism and superstition.

The basic tenets of liberalism were formulated in this period. They may be summarized as follows. The individual is the source of his own moral values; the process of trade and exchange between individuals has both efficiency and freedom-enhancing properties; the market is a spontaneous order for the allocation of resources; exchange between nations will not only maximize wealth through the international division of labour, but also tends to reduce war and political tension; and public policy should be limited to the few common concerns of individuals. Liberals have traditionally made a distinction between the range of government and the question of who is to do the governing; logically, if government is limited by constitutional rules then the form that it takes is of secondary importance. Nevertheless, liberals in the nineteenth century were prominent in the demand for universal suffrage and democracy; to them equal voting rights in politics seemed a natural counterpart to choice in the market as well as a protection against aristocratic privilege. Only later did the fear emerge that majoritarian democracy might threaten individual liberty.

Perhaps the most spectacular example of liberalism at work in the nineteenth century was the long struggle to secure the repeal of the Corn Laws in Britain, achieved, ironically, by a conservative government in

1846. By severely restricting the import of cheap foreign grain, government was obviously violating a fundamental principle of liberal political economy. Also, the preservation of those laws was only possible because of the undue influence of the landowning aristocracy on politics. Classical liberalism on this issue was seen to be a common creed (in the interests of employers and employees alike), opposed only by sinister interests. To this day the agricultural question divides liberals and conservatives. In the nineteenth century, free trade was the major liberal issue: many continental writers, especially the French political economist Bastiat, contributed to its intellectual popularity. As liberalism developed as a political creed it was seen to rest somewhat uneasily on two separate philosophical foundations, utilitarianism and natural rights.

The utilitarian foundation is itself complex; comprising indirect and direct variants. The indirect variety originates with Hume and Smith and suggests that social utility emerges accidentally from self-interested individuals engaged in exchange under general rules of just conduct. This is especially important in relation to law, for indirect utilitarianism pre-supposes that the spontaneously developing common law is superior to statute. Direct utilitarian classical liberals, such as Bentham, regarded the common law as inherently conservative and that the conditions for an individualist order must be created by legislation. Thus, although on some economic issues Bentham was more *laissez-faire* than Smith, his general rationalist belief that reason can improve on spontaneity has led many contemporary liberals to question his individualist credentials. This doubt is compounded by the belief of direct utilitarians that a social utility function for a whole community can rationally be devised and imposed on a community.

Natural rights liberals justify individual liberty on the ground that state intervention, because it is rights-violating, is immoral irrespective of any consequentialist considerations. The origin of this is essentially the natural law tradition: the political philosophy of Locke is the prime source. Although in Locke's political philosophy government is legitimate, it is so only when it is based on consent. However, a major source of non-utilitarian liberalism is Kant's ethics. In this doctrine the only acceptable rational ethic is that system of values which can be willed by the autonomous moral agent as a universal law. This, coupled with the Kantian injunction to treat each individual as an end and never as a means, is a major philosophical foundation of a liberal individualist morality.

The more recent classical liberals have elaborated on those themes. The primary source for the utilitarian justification for liberalism is economics, in particular the Austrian and Chicago Schools. The natural rights version, especially when expounded by writers such as Nozick, tend to slip into libertarianism.

The two Austrian economists who have written at length on politics are Mises and Hayek. For Mises, liberalism was little more than applied economics. For him a priori reasoning could demonstrate that the co-ordinating properties of the market were the only means to efficiency and social happiness. With regard to ethics, Mises was a crude positivist. He thought that value judgements were expressions of feeling for which no rational justification could be given. However, he assumed that there was a considerable amount of agreement about social ends and that socialists were simply mistaken about the means to achieve them. Although many classical liberals adopt this positivism, with regard to ends, it is clearly inadequate for an ethical individualism.

Hayek's classical liberalism is more complex. Although he rejects conventional utilitarianism on the ground that it involves the rationalist fallacy that the consequences of human action can be calculated, his liberalism would appear to be of an indirect consequentialist kind. This is because he believes that progress and the accumulation of knowledge are only possible in open societies and free markets. His most significant contribution to the liberal theory of government action is to assess its limits, not by reference to social utility, or on theory of rights, but by its conformity to the standards set by the rule of law. He argues that most government intervention, because it proceeds by arbitrary decree and necessitates treating equals unequally, fails this test. It is this that underlies his rejection of policies of social justice. Such policies disrupt the efficiency properties of the market by sanctioning methods of payment that depart from the marginal productivity criterion: furthermore, they involve breaches of the rule of law.

In America, the Chicago School of economics has done most to popularize a kind of empirical liberalism. Throughout the heyday of Keynesian macro-economics, Chicago economists stressed the importance of the self-regulating properties of the market and the malign effects of government's discretion in the control of money. Chicago liberalism is heavily quantitative and positivist (with the exception of Knight). It tends to eschew any ethical individualism and prefers to make the case for a free order rest on the observable effects of *dirigiste* social and economic policies. A good example is Milton Friedman's empirical studies of American monetary history: those indicate the harm caused by govern-ment discretion in this area.

Of particular significance is the recent work, in the Chicago tradition, critical of those typically 'American liberal' policies that aim at improving the condition of minorities through direct government action. Sowell has done extensive work to show that the market is the least discrimin-atory of all institutional arrangements: competition itself simply makes it costly for employers to persists with discriminatory practices based on race or sex.

The traditional liberal values of individualism, a stable currency, and the 'nightwatchman' state suffered a serious decline in the decades following the end of the Second World War. A notable exception to the prevailing orthodoxy, in both theoretical and practical terms, was the German 'social market economy'. The economists and philosophers Eucken, Rustow, Muller-Armack, Bohm, and Roepke reconstructed, in a series of theoretical works, the traditional values of liberalism, and for the period from 1950 to the late 1960s government policy in the Federal Republic was largely guided by them. However, in this doctrine the 'social' element, i.e. the positive commitment of the state to the establishment of welfare and other conditions of well-being, was much more prominent than in other versions of liberalism.

NB

Further reading

Barry, N.P., *On Classical Liberalism and Libertarianism*, London, Macmillan, 1986.
Gray, J.N., *Liberalism*, Milton Keynes, Open University Press, 1986.
Haakonsen, K. (ed.), *Traditions of Liberalism*, Sydney, Centre for Independent Studies, 1988.
Hayek, F.A., *The Constitution of Liberty*, London, Routledge & Kegan Paul, 1960.
Mises, L. von, *Liberalism*, Kansas, MO, Sheed, Andrews, & McMeel, 1978.

LIBERTARIANISM

Libertarianism as a political doctrine must be distinguished from the philosophical theory about the freedom of the will, a doctrine which is opposed to determinism. Libertarianism has become a descriptive term for the individualist political doctrine in recent years largely because the nineteenth-century word 'liberalism' has been used by semi-collectivist creeds, especially in America.

It is difficult to distinguish precisely between the tradition of classical liberalism in, say, Smith, the two Mills through to Hayek and Milton Friedman and the contemporary libertarianism of Nozick, David Friedman, and Rothbard. All writers in both traditions share some common ideological commitments, including a belief in the efficiency and freedom-enhancing properties of the market economy, private property, the rule of law, and the sovereignty of the individual. However, these ideas are carried to extremes by libertarians (in some cases, to the claim that the state itself should be abolished). A further contrast between classical liberals and libertarians might be made by reference to the philosophical foundations of these respective individualist political doctrines. The former tend to be utilitarian or consequentialist: individualistic economic and social institutions are valued because of the discernible benefit they bring to the anonymous public. The latter tend to hold to a theory of individual natural rights and therefore state intervention is to be condemned because of its rights-violating properties irrespective of any consequentialist considerations. However, this is not a conclusive distinction since there are individualists whom one would call libertarians yet who do not accept the doctrine of natural rights.

All versions of libertarianism stress that any legitimate social order must respect the sovereignty of the individual. They do not locate personal freedom in the context of an ongoing set of rules and procedures, as some classical liberals and all conservatives do, but rather evaluate a given political order in accordance with how far it meets with the demands of liberty. Libertarians are rationalists in the political sense that the human mind is deemed to be capable of constructing a social order in which tradition and its 'immanent wisdom' has no necessary priority.

Definitionally, liberty is interpreted in the 'negative' sense, i.e. a person is free to the extent that his choices and actions are not impeded by laws and institutions of human origin. Thus there is no suggestion that personal liberty should be defined in terms of the moral quality of the ends pursued, or in terms of their issuing from a special 'rational will'. Indeed, the concept of the person that informs libertarian thought is a rather uncomplicated one that bears close similarity to the utility-maximizing agent of neo-classical economics.

In the normative sense, a person's freedom should be maximized so far as is consistent with a similar liberty for others. The principle frequently alluded to is Spencer's 'equal liberty' principle. The major objection to government activity is that this inevitably grants to political officials a liberty to act (e.g. to tax and conscript) which is not available to others. This approach to the limits of liberty is favoured rather than John Stuart Mill's principle, that permits state intervention with other-regarding acts but not with purely self-regarding acts, on the ground that the ambiguity surrounding 'other-regarding' could permit a much greater extent of coercive law than would be sanctioned by libertarianism.

Libertarianism, then, proposes 'voluntarism': that any voluntary, uncoerced exchange between individuals is permissible. Thus although libertarianism is associated with *laissez-faire* economics and capitalism it does not logically exclude socialism: a collectivized system of ownership would be legitimate if it were a product of uncoerced agreement. The equal liberty principle renders illegitimate laws against 'victimless' crimes, such as the consumption of, and trade in, addictive drugs. Whatever harm these cause to the addict, there can be no reason for forbidding their manufacture and consumption since such a prohibition would be the violation of an equal liberty. Libertarianism is then resolutely opposed to any form of paternalism by the state. This renders all form of compulsory state welfare illegitimate.

The concept most germane to libertarianism is 'self-ownership'. This simply means that as persons are the owners of their bodies and minds, all state intervention that interferes with this is a form of slavery. From self-ownership derives the justification of private property. From Locke, libertarians have argued that property may be legitimately acquired by the application of labour to previously unowned objects, by gift and transfer, and by voluntary exchange. The possession of legitimate property gives owners a right to use it in any way they choose subject only to the proviso that they must not infringe the equal liberties of others. Some libertarians argue that there can, conceptually, be no such thing as 'public' ownership: their rigorous individualism implies that, since the 'public' is not a person, it cannot act and therefore cannot 'own'. Cases of alleged public ownership are in reality cases of private ownership of property by political and administrative officials.

The property principle plays a crucial role in political argument for libertarians, for some, especially Rothbard, maintain that all the traditional disputes in political theory can be settled by the determination of ownership. For example, the liberty to protest and demonstrate is often thought to conflict with the claims of public order, and therefore some political resolution is required. However, Rothbard maintains that if streets and public places were under genuine private ownership then the owners could prohibit or permit a demonstration as they saw fit. If they forbade it, this would not count as a deprivation of liberty. In this libertarianism all claims to liberty are, in effect, reducible to claims to property. It is maintained by critics that this approach could diminish the claims to liberty to vanishing point, since the person who has no property (except, of course, the property in his own person) has, in effect, no liberty.

Not all libertarians are natural rights theorists. Milton Friedman has produced some extreme anti-statist proposals but they are justified entirely by the utilitarian calculus. In the case of victimless crimes, for example, he would argue that, whatever the moral rights and wrongs, the observable consequences (usually to do with increases in crime) of prohibition are worse than the acts themselves.

Libertarians believe that it is legitimate only to enforce the rules of justice between individuals: these are entirely to do with procedural rules covering crime, tort, contract, and property. Egalitarianism is not only conceptually incoherent but its political imposition violates individual rights. Although all libertarians believe in the necessity for legal rules some, anarcho-capitalists, believe that these can be enforced by private agencies without a monopoly state. However most, including Nozick, believe in the necessity of a minimal 'nightwatchman' state.

Conservatives regard libertarianism as an unacceptable doctrine – mainly because its rationalistic individualism presupposes that established order can be dispensed with in pursuit of a *laissez-faire* utopia. The immediate introduction of libertarianism would disrupt a whole host of 'legitimate' expectations which tradition had sanctioned; these would include many state welfare claims. Indeed, the greatest intellectual problem for libertarians is the explanation of the transition from a semi-collectivist to a free society.

NB

Further reading

Barry, N.P., *On Classical Liberalism and Libertarianism*, London, Macmillan, 1986.
Hospers, J., *Libertarianism*, Los Angeles, CA, Nash, 1971.
Nozick, R., *Anarchy, State, and Utopia*, Oxford and New York, Blackwell and Basic Books, 1974.
Rothbard, M., *The Ethics of Liberty*, Atlantic Highlands NJ, Humanities Press, 1982.

M

MANCHESTER SCHOOL

Name given by contemporaries to a tendency within nineteenth-century English liberalism, so called because its leading figures were connected with the city of Manchester. Used more generally to refer to the *laissez-faire* form of classical liberalism. Some historians have argued that the Manchester School, as an organized movement, did not exist, but this is contradicted by the clear evidence of contemporary accounts from both members and opponents. There is more room for debate as to who the members were, but most would agree that the main figures were Cobden and Bright. Bastiat may be counted as a fellow traveller while Hirst consciously saw himself as a successor or follower of the earlier school.

The Manchester School as a movement came into being with the formation in 1838 of the Anti-Corn Law league, the purpose of the league being to bring about the complete and immediate repeal of the Corn Laws. These banned the importation of grain into Britain unless the price of grain should pass a set level. Their effect was therefore to raise the price of bread, the staple food of the poor, and to prevent other countries from selling low-cost grain to Britain. This meant that the other countries could not afford to buy British manufactured goods, so depressing demand in Britain as well. The Corn Laws were regarded by both sides to the argument as the keystone of the system of protectionism so their repeal was the main event in the move towards free trade. The campaign against the Corn Laws, which acquired the quality of a moral crusade, was ultimately successful when in 1846 Peel introduced a Bill for their repeal. This introduced a policy of free trade which was followed by Britain until 1931.

There is much debate as to whether there ever was a coherent body of ideas shared by the members of the school other than that of the need to repeal the Corn Laws. Certainly, there was a wide variety of views and opinions among them. However, historians have concluded that there was no shared set of beliefs only by subjecting the opinions of the people

167

concerned to the kind of scrutiny which, if applied to any political movement, would dissolve it into an aggregate of associated individuals. In reality there were several related ideas which together formed the 'doctrine' of the Manchester School.

The fundamental ideas were twofold. First, a distinction between civil society – which was natural, arising out of the free association of individuals, and peaceful, not involving force – and the state which was artificial and based on relations of power and force. Second was the notion of personal responsibility, linked in most cases to strongly held Christian beliefs. For Cobden and his colleagues, people had been put on earth by God and given the gift of free will (which made them responsible for their actions) while being put under an obligation to work and strive to improve and better themselves and the world. These led in practice to three main political 'planks'.

In the first place was free trade, the ideal state being one where all people, everywhere, were free to trade and exchange goods with no obstacles of any kind put in their way. Free trade was argued for on the classical, Ricardian, grounds that it would lead to the most efficient use of resources, but this economic argument took second place to political and moral ones. Protection was seen as a policy which served the interests of a particular class at the expense of the whole community. This class was identified in general terms as the ruling class which controlled the institutions of the state, and more precisely as the landed aristocracy. There was thus a connection between the move to free trade and political reform. Moreover, free trade was presented as the most certain way to promote peace. As the economies of the nations became more interdependent and the peoples of the world came to relate to each other through the peaceful medium of trade, so the occasion and possibility of war would diminish. Cobden looked forward to a future in which the territorial state would have been dissolved away by trade with people living in small, self-governing communities, all open to trade and peaceful relations, none with the capacity or desire to make war.

Closely linked to free trade was the idea of freedom of contract by which there should be no statutory limitation placed on agreements freely entered into between consenting individuals who had the capacity of judgement. This again was defended on moral grounds. The physical and moral development of societies and individuals could only happen through free contract and exchange. Only by free, uncoerced actions could people realize their moral responsibilities, to make the most of themselves and their talents and so improve the world. Coercive and paternalistic legislation undermined the direct responsibility of all persons for their actions and so demoralized them. The corollary of all this was hostility to state action with demands for close control of state spending and a policy of retrenchment, i.e. reductions in the role of the state and the size of its budget.

The element of 'Manchesterism' which has received least attention is its pacifism. Yet for Cobden and Bright this was the primary political value. Hostility to spending on armaments, to colonies, secret treaties, and an aggressive foreign policy were constant themes in the political careers of the school's members. Cobden and Bright both lost their seats over their opposition to the Crimean War. War, colonialism, and imperialism were all seen as further consequences of the domination of an autonomous and natural civil society by a parasitic class, hence Bright's description of British foreign policy as 'an enormous system of outdoor relief for the aristocratic classes'.

None of the school's members was an intellectual. Consequently their ideas were not expressed with any great degree of sophistication. Historically, however, they were closer to the views of many liberals than were theorists such as J.S. Mill. The historical significance of the school is debatable. Much recent historiography has argued, first, that the ideas of the Manchester School were politically marginal, with little direct influence on the policies of Whig or Liberal governments, and second, that the school's major achievement, the repeal of the Corn Laws, would have happened anyway. The first argument has some force, but underestimates the ideological impact of the school on nineteenth-century English liberal thought and culture. The second is very weak and is not supported by the evidence of other countries. Moreover, it again ignores the ideological impact of the school which in this area was massive; for many years after 1846 it was political suicide for a British politician to stand on a protectionist platform.

Finally, the Manchester School came to have a mythical or stereotypical status. For some, Cobden and Bright became hero-figures and the Anti-Corn Law campaign one of the great moral events of modern history. More often 'Manchesterism' was portrayed by critics of liberalism as the stereotype of *laissez-faire*, a harsh unfeeling ideology, concerned only with money and trade. This 'black image' appears many times in nineteenth-century writings, not least in Germany. Indeed, the image or notion of the Manchester School held by others has been as important a historical force as the school itself.

SD

Further reading

Grampp, W.D., *The Manchester School of Economics*, Stanford, CA, Stanford University Press, 1960.

Greenleaf, W.E.H., *The British Political Tradition*, Vol. II, *The Ideological Heritage*, London, Methuen, 1983.

Hirst, F.W., *Free Trade and Other Fundamental Doctrines of the Manchester School*, New York, Kelley, 1903.

MARKET

The market is a social institution that is developed spontaneously by individuals as a mechanism for the efficient satisfaction of their desires. Although markets are normally associated with the exchange of goods and services according to their relative prices, this is not an exclusive feature of them. There can, for example, be markets in ideas or values; and there are clearly markets for votes in democratic political systems. Wherever there are scarce resources and individuals are allowed, by law and custom, to compete for them, orderly markets will develop. However, it is an important truism that the market is but one of the ways in which men may organize themselves for the production of goods and services and for the allocation of scarce resources. Central command and altruism are the major alternatives. Proponents of the market order claim that central command is both inefficient and destructive of personal liberty, and that altruism, the reciprocal satisfaction of people's needs without coercion or monetary incentive, makes impossible demands on human nature.

The market mechanism is not necessarily identified with capitalism; this is more to do with the social economic system of private ownership of resources. The market is a means for determining and satisfying individual wants and is logically consistent with a variety of systems of ownership. Some collectivists (market socialists) believe that it works more efficiently without private ownership. Nevertheless, most theorists maintain that a market can only advance efficiency and personal liberty within a regime of private property.

The market mechanism is, in essence, a signalling device to transmit to individuals in a decentralized process information about tastes, productive techniques, resources, and so on. It operates through prices. If the price of a good rises this indicates that it is in short supply and thus factors of production will be automatically drawn into the activity. The prices of all goods and factors of production (wages to labour, interest on capital, and rent to land) are all determined ultimately by conditions of supply and demand. In a functioning market the price mechanism is an impersonal system (Smith's 'invisible hand') which ensures, albeit imperfectly, the allocation of necessarily scarce resources to the production of wanted goods and services. Competition between producers will tend to drive down prices to costs of production. This may be called its 'efficiency' or 'welfare' property.

Since this property emerges as an unintended consequence (Hayek's phrase) of individual activity, a better term than market economics might be catallactics. Catallactics is the science of decentralized exchange: it is concerned not with the efficiency of an overall economy as such but with the regularities that can be predicted to occur when individuals are left free to exchange their labour and property in the advancement of personal goals. The world of catallactics is the world of micro-economics, small firms and individual traders, rather than macro-economics, which is concerned with the behaviour of the whole economy.

The discovery that an order does emerge from the transactions of decentralized agents was first made in a comprehensible form by the Spanish Jesuits of the sixteenth and seventeenth centuries. But its most sophisticated expression came in Smith's *The Wealth of Nations*. Smith showed that prosperity was maintained not through accumulating stocks of gold through protection but by increasing the flows of tradable goods and services. The market encouraged specialization and the division of labour. People's natural propensity to 'truck, barter, and exchange' within a system of 'natural liberty' was much more effective in wealth creation than the deliberate intentions of government. Smith stressed the fact that intervention could not increase the quantity of industry in an economy, 'it can only divert a part of it into a direction which it might otherwise not have gone'. Smith also emphasized another feature of the market: it is an impersonal system that in no way favours the merchants as a class. In fact, they were assiduous evaders of the market's disciplines.

There was nothing in Smith's theory that implied that the market was in some kind of 'equilibrium', i.e. the perfect co-ordination of all economic plans. At most there is the suggestion that there is a tendency for the price mechanism to ensure a process towards this.

The association between equilibrium theory and market economics came with the 'marginalist revolution' in economic theory in the 1870s; especially in the work of Walras. After this, market economists became obsessively concerned with the description (usually mathematical) of the imaginary state of 'perfect competition – general equilibrium'. Here all prices are correct, there are no welfare losses due to monopoly, all resources are allocated efficiently, and there is no incentive for any one transactor to initiate change.

It was this model of economic society that market socialists (the two most sophisticated writers were Lange and Lerner) used to recommend a form of economy whose output did reflect individual choice but which did not contain the familiar capitalist features of entrepreneurship and private property. Since real world markets were characterized by many imperfections, such as monopoly and supra-normal profits (i.e. income over and above that required to keep a factor of production in operation), it was thought that the state could replicate the outcomes of a perfectly competitive market. Although conventional markets would remain for consumer goods and labour, efficiency and rules would replace the profit motive, salaried managers would replace entrepreneurs, and collective ownership of the means of production would replace capital markets.

It was from a critique of equilibrium socialist models that the modern theory of the market emerges. In the work of Mises and Hayek, especially, the argument is that a market must be seen as a process rather than an equilibrium, and that such a process cannot work without the profit motive and entrepreneurship.

In market process theory an exchange system is, in a sense, always in disequilibrium. The market is a 'discovery procedure' by which restless individuals continously seek new ways of satisfying wants. In the real world perfect competition is a delusion since there are always price discrepancies to be corrected; in fact, a more accurate description of the process would be 'rivalrous competition'. The market is a self-correcting mechanism and it is superior to the correcting mechanism of the state for two major reasons. First, the dispersed knowledge (i.e. of consumer tastes, productive techniques) that exists in economic society is better co-ordinated by the price system than by central command, and second, without the possibility of entrepreneurial profit there would be little to motivate market transactors. Entrepreneurs, and their mental alertness to profitable opportunities, are therefore essential agents in this process. Even monopolies may not be harmful in a market process: they rarely arise spontaneously and where they do they are constantly being threatened by rivalrous competition.

Market theorists do not claim that all wanted goods and services can be generated by the market. There are public goods, such as law and order, defence and clean air, which for technical reasons cannot be priced by the market, and those have to be delivered collectively. Smith had a considerable list of activities, including building roads and bridges, which he thought would be better performed by the state. However, contemporary market theorists have been fertile in the invention of schemes for subjecting more economic activities to the market. One example is the problem of pollution. It is now argued that this and other 'external bads' could be internalized without state action if the legal system and property rights structure enabled individuals to sue for damages.

The conservative attitude to the market is ambiguous. On the one hand, it is admired for its efficiency and liberty-enhancing properties: a completely collectivized economy is anathema to all traditions of conservatism. But on the other, conservatives have always distrusted the 'economism' that appears in much of the more extreme market philosophies. To a conservative, a stable society presupposes the existence of rules and conventions that cannot be explained in transactional terms. A society is held together by the less tangible bonds of affection and loyalty. Furthermore, for the traditional conservative, the state is more than an artifice for the production of public goods: it is the primary institutional representative of a society's law and morality. It is this that justifies, for example, a more extensive extra-market welfare system than would be acceptable to pure market theorists.

NB

Further reading

Barry, N.P., *The Invisible Hand in Economics and Politics*, London, Institute of Economic Affairs, 1988.

Buchanan, J., *Liberty, Market and State: Political Economy in the 1980s*, Brighton, Harvester, 1986.

Hayek, F.A., *Individualism and Economic Order*, London, Routledge & Kegan Paul, 1948.

Kirzner, I., *Competition and Entrepreneurship*, Chicago, IL, University of Chicago Press, 1973.

Smith, A., *An Inquiry into the Nature and Causes of the Wealth of Nations*, ed. R.H. Campbell and A.S. Skinner, Oxford, Clarendon Press, 1976.

MARXISM

Marx and his collaborator Engels elaborated a comprehensive doctrine of economics, history, politics, and (to a lesser extent) philosophy. The prime focus of the system consists of the analysis of capitalism, culminating in the advocacy of socialist revolution by the proletariat.

The philosophical basis of Marxism is militant atheism and materialism. Only matter possesses the power to act, and mind does not exist apart from matter. This principle at once rules out the existence of God and the Absolute Idea of Hegel. Matter develops by a dialectical process, characterized by conflict and transformation rather than purely quantitative change.

Marx himself did not write extensively on philosophy after his criticism of Hegel's system, and much of his 'dialectics' stems from Engels. The key elements of Marxism lie in its views of history and economics. According to Marxism, the forces of production, i.e. the tools people use in producing material goods, have a constant tendency to expand. The level of development of the forces at a particular historical time determines the type of economic system that a society institutes. The function of a society's economic system, or 'relations of production', is to develop the forces of production to the greatest extent possible at the time. Only one kind of economic system can do this for each level of the forces' growth, and it is for this reason that the forces are held to 'determine' the relations. As the forces continue to develop, the relations that exist cease to develop them best. Accordingly a new system of relations will arise by means of the forcible overthrow of the earlier relations.

The relations of production of a society determine its principal characteristics. These include the legal and political system, and the dominant religion, philosophy, and social thought. The ideas and non-economic institutions prevalent in a society form its 'superstructure', which in Marx's view reflects the interests of the dominant class. The system of productive relations divides people into large groups, according to the role these groups play in the productive process. In particular, one social group or class is responsible for 'doing the work' while another directs the process of production. The members of the latter rule the labourers and live by extracting wealth from them: they are the dominant class whose interests largely determine the society's superstructure.

The major economic systems are characterized by the relations between the ruling class and the labourers. The main social systems are primitive communism, slavery, feudalism, and capitalism; opinions differ over whether oriental despotism is also a distinct system. Whether the stages must occur in a fixed order is a controversial point of interpretation. There is no doubt, however, that in the Marxist view socialism will replace capitalism. In this system, no ruling class exists. All the other systems, except for primitive communism, are characterized by class antagonism.

The bulk of Marx's work was devoted to the analysis of capitalism. As in previous social systems, capitalism has a ruling class, the capitalists or bourgeoisie, and an exploited class, the proletariat. Unlike in previous systems, labourers are not legally compelled to work for the dominant class. Slaves and serfs were physically forced to labour; proletarians are not. Nevertheless, Marx maintains that the exigencies of the economic system leave labourers no choice except to work for a capitalist. The capitalists own the means of production. Since workers have nothing to sell but their labour, unless they secure capitalist employment they will starve. Further, the capitalists' monopoly of the means of production is protected by the force of the state against revolutionary overthrow. The state is the 'executive committee of the ruling class'.

How does exploitation enter the picture? The Marxist account rests on an entire system of economics, elaborated on at vast length by Marx in the three volumes of *Das Kapital*. (Only the initial volume, published in 1867, appeared during Marx's life.) Marxist economics begins with an explanation of commodity exchange. The exchange value of a good consists of the labour required to produce it. 'Labour' here means 'abstract labour', i.e. not skills of a particular kind needed to make something, but units of bare labour. The labour that determines a good's value must be 'socially necessary' – roughly, the average amount needed to produce a good of a particular kind.

According to the labour theory of value, an exchange is an equality. If one bushel of corn is exchanged for half an ounce of silver, then equal amounts of socially necessary labour are required to produce the respective amounts of corn and silver.

The labour theory creates a paradox in the analysis of capitalism. The capitalist system cannot operate unless capitalists make profits. To obtain a profit, one must sell for more than one buys. If, however, all goods exchange at their value, how is profit possible?

Marx found the answer to his paradox in the purchase of labour. Since labour is a commodity, it must by the labour theory exchange according to its labour value, i.e. the socially necessary time required to produce it. More simply put, the value of labour is what it costs to produce the labourers. This consists of the labour value of the goods required to maintain them at the level of subsistence. In return for their purchase, the capitalist gains the workers' labour power, i.e. whatever they can produce during a period of work. The value of this exceeds the value of labour: workers can produce more than it costs to produce them. Here then lies the solution to the paradox. Although labour exchanges for its value, purchasing it enables the capitalist to gain a profit. Marxists term the gain the 'surplus value', and the process by which the surplus or gain is extracted is called 'exploitation'. Surplus value is the source not only of profit but of interest on money and rent as well.

The labour theory of value faces a severe problem. Goods in a capitalist economy do not in fact exchange according to their labour values. A great part of *Das Kapital* consists of attempts to derive prices of production from labour values. Marx thought that if he could show how labour prices are 'transformed' into prices of production, he could solve the difficulty for his theory.

In the Marxist view, the constant struggle of capitalists to extract surplus value will result in control of the capitalist system, in its most highly developed form, by large monopolies. Along with this, the market constantly expands until its scope is worldwide. These facts ensure that the depressions which plague the system will worsen, at some point in the future enabling the proletariat to overthrow capitalism.

Marx spent little time discussing the state of affairs that would replace capitalism. The workers would smash the existing machinery of state and replace it with a 'dictatorship of the proletariat'. This would forcibly suppress all resistance to the new order by the former ruling class. Marx expected this resistance to be of great strength and coping with it necessitated a policy of revolutionary terrorism.

The new socialist regime would abolish money and production for exchange on the market. Instead, a centrally planned economy would bring about a vast expansion of the forces of production. Labour would become less specialized, and people would have much greater leisure time. A 'higher stage' of socialism would extend these developments even further. A general abundance would then prevail.

Not all of those who accept the label 'Marxist' defend the entire body of doctrine just presented. Many contemporary Marxists attempt to do without the labour theory of value. The insistence on revolutionary change and historical inevitability have proved sticking points for many, beginning with the German revisionists headed by Bernstein and continuing to the present with various groups of 'social democrats'. The Soviet regime and its Eastern European satellites have stressed adherence to all of the standard Marxist doctrines. Lenin, the leader of the Bolshevik Revolution of 1917, placed strong emphasis on the need for armed revolution. In the Leninist view, a tightly centralized 'vanguard party' acted as the supposed agent of the workers both in the overthrow of capitalism and in the conduct of the successor regime.

Both conservatives and classical liberals have strongly combated Marxism. The most extensive criticism of it stems from classical liberal economists.

Boehm-Bawerk, a Professor of Economics at the University of Vienna during the late nineteenth and early twentieth centuries, criticized the labour theory of value with such effectiveness that few later economists outside the Soviet camp have tried to revive it. Boehm-Bawerk stressed the failure of Marx's efforts to show that labour values could be transformed into prices of production. Also, Marx's assertion that equal abstract labour time underlies an exchange of commodities is arbitrary. Why *must* an exchange be regarded as an equality of some common element? Even granting the existence of a common element, is labour the only possible example of one? Many contemporary Marxists, recognizing the invalidity of the labour theory, have dropped it. No replacement for it that supports the view that capitalists exploit labour has won general acceptance. This poses a severe problem for Marxists who wish to eliminate the labour theory, since without exploitation of labour one does not have a recognizably Marxist view at all.

Mises, a student of Boehm-Bawerk, argued forcefully that a centrally planned economic system cannot engage in economic calculation. Without markets, a central planning board cannot determine the most efficient production methods to use. Far from being more productive than capitalism, as Marx thought, a socialist economy could not operate at all. Proponents of this argument think that existing socialist regimes function either by reliance on the prices of capitalist societies or by refraining from total state direction.

Critics of Marxism have not confined themselves to raising technical difficulties in economic theory. Both liberals and conservatives have emphasized that the totalitarian nature of Soviet Russia is 'no accident', but the foreseeable result of the attempt to subject all persons and social insitutions to an omnipotent state.

A system whose chief devotees have engaged in mass murder and the imprisonment of millions in labour camps hardly has much to recommend it; and conservative and classical liberal writers have been at the forefront of those attempting to bring these atrocities to public notice.

Although conservatives and classical liberals agree very closely in their condemnation of Marxism, the conservatives have tended to place greater emphasis on the militantly atheist nature of Marxism which has led to massive religious persecution in the communist countries, as well as compulsory indoctrination in atheism. Conservatives also argue that social differences, including traditional class hierarchies, are essential to civilization. The Marxist assault on these is in their view a compelling reason for opposition to it.

DG

Further reading

Carew Hunt, R.N., *The Theory and Practice of Communism*, Harmondsworth, Penguin, 1963.
Conway, D., *A Farewell to Marx*, Harmondsworth, Penguin, 1987.
Kolakowski, L., *Main Currents of Marxism*, Oxford, Oxford University Press, 1978.
Mises, L. von, *Socialism*, Indianapolis, IN, Liberty Press, 1981 (1st edition 1922).
Popper, K., *The Open Society and its Enemies*, Vol. II, London, Routledge, 1945.
Sowell, T., *Marxism*, London and Boston, MA, Allen & Unwin, 1985.

MORALITY

In a sense little can be said about the views on morality or virtue held by liberals. It is not that the members of this category lack strong sentiments or convictions about the nature of praiseworthy conduct or moral obligation, but rather that they are likely to hold a great diversity of opinions, the only common denominator being that individual freedom comes first and that no one may be coerced into conformity with a particular moral code. For liberals the government may only insist that individuals refrain from violence and theft, and honour all freely entered contracts to the full. Beyond that point, morality is a private and personal matter and it is up to each individual to choose and follow his or her own ethical code. Most liberals would probably add that parents have an enforceable duty to care for their young and dependent children whose very existence in a world of freely available contraception and abortion is the result of decisions which have implied responsibilities. Other liberals have been known to argue that liberty implies considered choice and the possibility of changing one's mind. Accordingly for them a liberal state could prohibit activities such as suicide and suicide pacts, voluntary contracts of slavery, consensual maiming or injury, or the sale of addictive drugs. Individuals could no doubt, if they wished, still make monastic or marriage vows for life but these irreversible contracts would be essentially unenforceable.

Although liberals would, as indicated, tend to disagree about what constitutes a virtuous individual, it seems likely that in a liberal society the self-reliant would be the most admired and the values of achievement, ambition, perseverance, tolerance, and independence more highly regarded than others.

Conservatives are likely to view the liberals' idea of a society based largely on varied and unpredictable patterns of contractual agreement as inherently unstable. For them, some kind and degree of common shared morality is a necessary component of a cohesive society, and stability and continuity are to be valued for their own sake. For the conservative, the citizens of a society are not in a position each to devise his or her own morality but of necessity must accept the particular customs and traditions of their community, and indeed the formal and informal regulations of their profession or calling and the sentiments of their kin. Should this detailed and many layered structure of rules break down due, for instance, to rapid social change or excessive mobility, then an undesirable state of anomie will ensue. The individual, far from feeling free, will feel lost when faced with too many choices, too few rules, and no customary limits to his or her appetites or expectations.

Although conservatives are apt to see the contents of their own particular moral code as possessing some absolute validity or at least marked superiority over those of others, they are also aware that it is in many ways arbitrary and even inconsistent, yet they remain undisturbed by this for the moral code is an end in and of itself. In its crude form the conservative argument that a shared obedience to common rules and a shared abhorrence of deviance have the vital function of maintaining social cohesion is dangerously close to being circular. Social moralities do change and yet the societies in which this occurs do not necessarily collapse into chaos and disorder or even into decadence and debility. None the less, the continued survival of particular recognizable societies or peoples does seem to be empirically related to the possession of a strong moral law which enables its members to survive major challenges to their collective identity. The Jews and the Parsees have thus been able to withstand long periods of exile that would have caused peoples with a less tenacious code to fade away. For the liberal, for whom the individual is the sole important unit, this would hardly matter, but for the conservative, with a commitment to the maintenance of a social order that in very many senses endures beyond the individual, the preservation of a distinct collective identity is one of the key functions of morality.

For similar reasons, the conservative is likely to prize such virtues as duty, loyalty, obedience, and honour, all of which serve the needs of an enduring, ordered, traditional hierarchy. The other side of such a morality is the exercise of the benevolent and paternalistic virtues which offer each individual a degree of security and welfare as a recognition of his or her loyalty and a mark of citizenship. Indeed, the conservative may even go further and justify the enacting of prohibitions whose intention is to save individuals from the consequences of their own errors or indulgence. Where the liberal will argue that the result of shielding men from the effects of folly is to fill the world with fools, the conservative is likely to see the world as already full of fools whom it is our duty to protect.

What is notably absent from the moral thinking of both liberals and conservatives is the Procrustean obsession with equality of their socialist opponents which is a perennial source of legitimation of plans to control human conduct in oppressive detail, not in order to make individual men and women virtuous but to make them equal. Both liberals and conservatives may under particular circumstances seek to moderate the degree of inequality in their society, whether from charitable motives or as an incentive to opportunity and competition, but they see the pursuit of equality for its own sake as meaningless, destructive, and restrictive of human freedom. Indeed, they are likely to agree that the zealous envy that provides the motive force for so much moralizing socialist rhetoric is one of the worst of vices and should be shunned by the virtuous citizen.

CD

Further reading

Davies, C., 'Sexual taboos and social boundaries', *American Journal of Sociology* 1982, 87 (5): 1032–63.
Devlin, P., *The Enforcement of Morals*, London, Oxford University Press, 1965.
Hart, H.L.A., *Law, Liberty and Morality*, London, Oxford University Press, 1963.
Mitchell, B., *Law, Morality and Religion in a Secular Society*, London, Oxford University Press, 1967.
Schoeck, H., *Envy: A Theory of Social Behaviour*, Indianapolis, IN, Liberty Press, 1969.

N

NATIONALISM

There is a vision of mankind as divided naturally into non-overlapping groups, called nations, each nation enjoying its own single government, legal system, army, and church, each occupying a fixed and clearly delineated and continuous territory. The vision sees all persons living within each such territory as speaking a common language, reading the same newspapers, sharing a common history, racial origin, culture, and traditions, and it sees all of them as feeling loyalty towards, and as identifying themselves with, their nation for the very reason that these things are shared. This reason may be more or less explicitly formulated and more or less in correspondence with the facts. Were the vision to be realized in full – Iceland is the best example – then there would obtain a one-to-one correspondence between nations, states, languages, cultures, races, and territories. Nations, as constituted by the vision, must not be too large: they must embrace no mixtures of, for example, languages or cultures. But neither must they be too small: if necessary they must expand to accommodate all those who share a given language, culture, historical or racial origin.

The vision is – of course, according to which candidate national group one takes as one's starting point – to different degrees remote from reality. Yet it can none the less play an important political role. And however groundless the vision in a given case, it can unleash real and powerful forces which can be channelled both in positive and in negative directions.

Nationalism itself, now, is a rather loosely connected family of views which come to prominence wherever members of a group strive to realize or to preserve aspects of the vision, in many cases against a real or imagined external threat. Nationalism is therefore coeval with national consciousness, i.e. with a consciousness, dispersed throughout a given territory, of the supposed fact that these traditions, customs, etc., are in fact shared by all those who happen to be living within this territory.

The extent to which a national consciousness of this sort can become established depends upon the existence of an effective means of communication of a sort which will allow the dissemination and exchange of ideas across the entirety of a given territory. The church had long possessed a virtual monopoly of such means of communication and was thereby able to bring about a certain sort of supra-national consciousness which enabled it to serve at least to some degree as a check on other, more local political and military ambitions. With the rise of mass-production newspapers, however, and of the railway, all the speakers of a given language in a given territory began for the first time to be brought together into a single whole, and to be set apart as a whole from the speakers of other languages in other territories. The rise of the modern nationalist idea and of nationalism itself as an effective political force is therefore virtually simultaneous with these technical developments, which brought about also a decline in the importance of the church.

German philosophers, especially, contributed to the fixing of the idea, as they saw the separate political entities which made up the patchwork of separate German-speaking states as no longer constituting the most natural or effective or rational unit of political organization. The possibility of a realization of the vision and of the creation of a German nation to match that of the English and the French gave great impetus to the nationalist idea. Multinational empires such as that of the Habsburgs began to seem anachronistic and were successively brought down, in part by nationalist agitations among their constituent groups, despite the fact that, as subsequent history has shown, many of these groups did not themselves come close to promising a viable realization of the nationalistic vision.

The conservative, now, is likely to see many of the moments constitutive of the nationalistic vision – religious and linguistic unity, common traditions, shared loyalties, a feeling of common identity, etc. – as well as their associated images and symbols as important sources of value in their own right. Conservative nationalism is a political attitude which can arise wherever the vision is realized locally to a high degree, and it is an attitude which will tend to make itself felt in a forceful way to the extent that the vision is threatened by either internal or external forces.

Conservative nationalism is tied intriniscally to the vision itself; it is a nationalism of a type which depends exclusively on the formal characteristics of a nation as such, as embodied within the vision. Liberal nationalism, on the other hand, is a type of nationalism which depends strictly upon a specific sort of realization of the vision. It can come to expression as a political attitude only where the vision is realized to a high degree among the members of a group which as a group embraces or puts a high value on the political and economic practices otherwise characteristic of liberalism as such. Liberal nationalism can accordingly come to expression only where these liberal practices have come to form part and parcel of the customs and traditions which constitute the relevant national identity. It will tend to become forcefully expressed wherever liberal practices are threatened by internal or external forces: appeals to national identity can then form part of the effort to defend these practices and therefore also liberalism itself.

Liberalism, then, in contrast to conservatism, has little to do with nationalism as such, except as a potential instrument of its own furtherance, and the liberal is accordingly unlikely to place a high value on those movements which are characteristic of national identity. An intrinsic connection between liberalism and nationalism could be established only if it could be proved either that a liberal political and economic order would be particularly conducive to the realization or preservation of the vision in some given locality, or that the vision itself is conducive to liberalism. Both alternatives are, however, ruled out, above all by the fact that liberalism tends to encourage phenomena – such as the free movement of peoples – which are detrimental to the national idea.

The different political attitudes within the wider family of nationalisms reflect the different ways in which the vision may, in a given locality, fail to be realized completely. It may be, first of all, that a given candidate national grouping lacks a corresponding state, a state of its own, with true political power. The term 'nationalism' is nowadays perhaps most closely associated with the strivings to bring about a correspondence between nation and state, strivings which will almost certainly always be with us, given that the vision is so unevenly realized throughout the world. (Consider Serbian, Ukrainian, Palestinian, and Kurdish nationalism.) It may be that what would otherwise be natural national groupings are mixed together within a given territory, or that their territories overlap, and again, 'nationalism' will then be employed to denote the strivings to bring about a state of affairs which will seem more ordered from one or other perspective. It may be that a given putative national grouping has no clearly delineated or continous (or militarily defensible) territory and seeks to expand or fill in the gaps in its territory to the point where such boundaries would be reached, or to create *Lebensraum*, even at the expense of surrounding groups. In the period before the nationalist vision took hold in its modern form, this process was often extended by sheer military momentum beyond the stage where a given group had reached what might count as natural borders. Imperialism, in this sense, preceded nationalism, and lost much of its attraction, and justification, with the growth in importance of the nationalist vision.

A putative national grouping may constitute a realization of the vision in all respects save that of, say, a shared religion, or language, or race, and it may then seem important to particular sub-groups within the larger group to strive to bring about by force a homogeneity of the relevant sort: to 'purify' the body of the state. Such phenomena are again nowadays particularly characteristic of non-developed areas of the world. The extent to which the nationalist vision is able to give rise to forceful measures of this sort in the developed west seems to be declining, and is largely confined to incidental instances where particular groups can utilize national feeling in such a way as to bring about measures designed to penalize particular deviations from the prevailing norm for their own economic benefit.

Given that the spectrum of nationalities is full of interpenetrations, ambiguities, twilight zones, it must follow that the vision of a 'just' or 'natural' or even 'rational' order of nation states can be realized at best only locally, to a limited degree, and even then perhaps only for relatively limited periods of historical time. The very idea of a unitary nation state must thereby involve a factor of arbitrariness, a dimension of unintelligibility. For the more mystical conservative this unintelligibility can constitute a positive virtue. For the theoretical conservative or classical liberal, however, mindful of the havoc that has been so often wrought in human affairs by the nationalistic idea, the unrealizability of the vision ought to imply the need to consider more seriously other, alternative forms of political order. Federalism, pluralism (the existence of distinct and mutually competing levels of political competence), absentee government (of the sort that has for some time been enjoyed by Hong Kong), even imperialism, are forms of political order that have received little serious consideration from political philosophers, who have been blinded, in effect, by the exceptional purity of the nationalistic vision. Yet what political philosophers have put together they can also tear asunder, and it seems at least possible that such philosophers might one day succeed in assembling a sufficiently forceful justification of other kinds of order. Until then, it seems, it will be the proponents of the nationalistic ideology who will continue to dictate the terms within which contemporary political problems are conceived, whether in Ireland, in India, in the Lebanon, or in South Africa.

BS

Further reading

Acton, Lord, 'Nationality', in *Essays on the History of Liberty*, ed. J. Rufus Fears, Indianapolis, IN, Liberty Classics, 1985, 409–34.

Grassl, W. and B. Smith, 'Politics of national diversity', *Salisbury Review* 1987, 533–7; reprinted in R. Scruton (ed.), *Conservative Thoughts*, London, Claridge Press, 1988, 101–14.

Kedourie, E., *Nationalism*, London, Hutchinson, 3rd edition 1966.

Minogue, K., *Nationalism*, Harmondsworth, Penguin, 1970.

NEO-CONSERVATISM

Loosely used to describe the revival of conservatism in recent years, 'neo-conservatism' has also been used, more helpfully, to describe particular intellectual schools of conservatism in the United States and the United Kingdom.

1   In the United States, neo-conservatives are a group of former left-liberal intellectuals who became more conservative as a response to the New Left of the 1960s, the left-liberal view of America as morally corrupt in Vietnam, and the failures of government programmes. Kristol published critiques of social programmes in his journal *Public Interest*, while Podhoretz's *Commentary* discussed the nature of totalitarian communism and the decline of liberal anti-communism. Leading neo-conservatives include sociologists Glazer, Bell, and Lipset and political scientists Kirkpatrick, Wilson, and Moynihan.

Neo-conservatives became increasingly sceptical about the ability of government to solve or even ameliorate the problems that it addressed. Indeed, government seems to be ruled by 'a law of unintended consequences': that the unintended effects of government are more important and usually more damaging than the intended and positive consequences. The failure of government is explained by: unintended consequences; the limits of knowledge; conflicting goals; the weakening of traditional institutions such as the family; the existence of vested interests in an expanding state; 'the New Class'; and utopianism. Neo-conservatives fear that the combination of excessive expectations and government failure could threaten liberal democratic societies.

They advocate: the creation of a consensus on moral and political values; the use of a corrected market for the promotion of social goals; the revival of community structures; the restoration of a pluralist political system; and the vigorous defence of American values in international affairs.

The neo-conservatives in America have been most significant in contributing to the climate of scepticism towards government and the reassertion of American self-confidence in foreign affairs.

2   In the United Kingdom, 'neo-conservatism' has been used to describe the revival of traditionalist conservatism which distinguishes itself from both the interventionism of post-war conservatism, as represented by Macmillan and Heath, and the liberal conservatism of Thatcher. This group is sometimes known as the Peterhouse School, after the Cambridge college whence several have come, or the Salisbury Group after the journal, *Salisbury Review*, which is their main platform. Members of the group include Scruton, editor of the *Review*, Cowling, Worsthorne, Norman, Vincent, and Casey.

The British neo-conservatives insist that order is the main concern of conservatism. They reject interventionist conservatism because of its tendency to compromise with the left rather than to oppose it, and liberal conservatism because of its excessive concern with liberty at the expense of order. There must be a common moral order if men are to live peacefully together and it is the role of government to promote and enforce that moral order. The search by neo-conservatives for the means to maintain the civil order leads them to emphasize themes of immutable human nature, authority, hierarchy, allegiance, duty, national identity, family, and social bonds. The British neo-conservatives believe that they are articulating popular beliefs and assumptions which most people do not or are unable to articulate.

NA

Further reading

1

Ashford, N., 'The neo-conservatives', *Government and Opposition* Summer 1981, 16 (3): 353–69.
Kristol, I., *Reflections of a Neo-conservative*, New York, Basic Books, 1983.
Podhoretz, N., *Breaking Ranks*, New York, Harper & Row, 1979.

2

Cowling, M. (ed.), *Conservative Essays*, London, Cassell, 1978.
Scruton, R., *The Meaning of Conservatism*, London, Macmillan, 2nd edition 1984.
Scruton, R. (ed.), *Conservative Thoughts*, London, Claridge Press, 1988.

NEO-LIBERALISM

1 'Neo-liberalism is the revival and development of classical liberal ideas such as the importance of the individual, the limited role of the state, and the value of the free market. It is a consequentialist or utilitarian approach to social problems, examining the consequences of social actions by the standard of the degree to which the goals of individuals will be advanced. It argues that the consequences of allowing individuals the freedom to pursue their own interests, subject to the prevention of force and fraud, will usually be far more beneficial than government action.

Classical liberalism went into decline at around the end of the nineteenth century, and the term 'liberal' became frequently used to describe an interventionist or social liberalism, particularly in the United States and the United Kingdom. Because of this, neo-liberals are sometimes described as libertarians, but this term is more usefully applied to those such as Rand and Nozick who base their defence of liberty on a concept of rights. The explanation for that decline is a subject for much debate, but includes the rise of social liberal and socialist ideas; cultural, economic, and techno-logical change; and deficiencies in classical liberal thought. After a period in the wilderness, the revival of neo-liberal ideas began after the Second World War, focused on the Mont Pelerin Society of intellectuals founded by Hayek in 1946.

Neo-liberalism can be summarized as the belief that government intervention usually does not work and that markets usually do. The failure of government to achieve its goals, 'government failure', is predictable and confirmed by experience, despite the expenditure of considerable resources. The market, the voluntary exchange of goods and services, will usually satisfy the wants of individuals more effectively than government, within the constraints of limited resources. The existence of 'market failure' can frequently be located in the creation of obstacles by government, e.g. on entry into a market, or the failure of government to carry out its proper functions, e.g. the protection of property rights in the environment.

Despite agreement on these two principles, there are significant differences between the three major neo-liberal schools, Chicago, Austrian and Public Choice. The Chicago School explains government failure by the lack of incentives in the public sector to satisfy consumers, and the superiority of the market to the existence of incentives to satisfy consumers of profit and the avoidance of bankruptcy. The Austrians explain government failure as due to the lack of knowledge available to political decision-makers and the much richer but widely dispersed knowledge in the market which is conveyed through prices. The Public Choice School explains government failure as a result of the perverse effects of the normal pursuit of self-interest in the political realm in contrast to the invisible hand in the economic realm.

2   'Neo-liberalism' has been used in the United States to refer to a group of politicians and intellectuals associated with the Democrat Party, who accept that government intervention has been too extensive in the past and greater use should be made of the market. They are part of left-liberalism rather than the revival of classical liberalism, but are less hostile to the market than most left-liberals. Their ideas are: vigorous economic growth achieved through an industrial policy involving the co-operation of government, business, and labour to obtain greater international competitiveness; support for innovation and technology; investment in education and training; national service; 'military reform' so that defence can be achieved more effectively and cheaply; and the use of markets in social reform. Those identified with the movement include academics Reich and Thurow, Peters, editor of the *Washington Monthly*, contributors to the *New Republic*, Senator Bradley, and 1988 presidential candidates Gore, Hart, and Babbitt. Most conservatives and classical liberals are sceptical that this group offers any distinctive intellectual contribution and believe that it should be seen primarily as a political response by some Democrats to electoral defeat.

NA

Further reading

1
Barry, N., *On Classical Liberalism and Libertarianism*, London, Macmillan, 1986.
Barry, N., *The New Right*, London, Croom Helm, 1987.
Gray, J., *Liberalism*, Milton Keynes, Open University Press, 1986.

2
Rothenberg, R., *The Neoliberals*, New York, Simon & Schuster, 1984.

THE NEW RIGHT

The 'new right' is a term with two distinct meanings: it refers to the entire collection of conservative and neo-liberal movements which have grown up in Europe and North America since about 1960, and to just one of them, the populist New Right of the United States. Here 'new right' is the wider term, 'New Right' the more precise one.

The term 'new right' is used by left-wing and socialist commentators as a portmanteau label for the many anti-socialist movements in politics and philosophy which have become prominent in recent years. This assumes that the various movements so put together are ideologically akin in some fundamental sense so that it is proper to consider them as a single object. This is simply not true and reflects the difficulty many commentators have had in coming to terms with movements which do not fit into the conventional 'left/right' spectrum. In practical politics this categorization makes more sense in so far as the varied components of the new right have co-operated on the basis of a shared, though largely negative, agenda. In fact the movements lumped together under the heading 'the new right' are disparate and have little in common other than a hostility to socialism. The primacy of economic debate in contemporary politics has highlighted this common ground and obscured the many and profound divisions on other issues. Some of the more recent commentary has shown awareness of this.

The various components of the new right first appeared in Western Europe and North America from 1960 onwards. They were both a response to the growing intellectual crisis of socialism (as in a different way was the new left) and a reformulation of other ideologies, notably classical liberalism. Since then the various tendencies have grown in influence and intellectual strength, partly because of the concurrent revival of political philosophy. The various tendencies can be divided into two broad groups – one neo-liberal, the other neo-conservative – each containing many particular groups. Among the many separate groups several main schools or movements can be identified. First, in France the most prominent is the Nouvelle Droite, its central institution being the GRECE which now functions as a think tank for the fascistic National Front. This movement is effectively a revival of the French tradition of radical reaction formerly expressed in the Action Française of Maurras. Similar groups are found elsewhere in Europe, e.g. in Austria and Belgium.

Second, in both Britain and the United States there is a movement of traditionalist conservatism, represented by such figures as Scruton and Kirk and journals such as the *Salisbury Review* in Britain and *Modern Age* in the United States. This school emphasizes traditional Tory interests such as tradition, hierarchy, and order and is as hostile to liberalism as to socialism. It is less interested in economic than moral and social issues. Third, there are some, especially among politicians, who combine economic liberalism with social and moral conservatism but this stand lacks the focus of the traditionalists. More influential intellectually are the fourth school of neo-liberals of whom the most important are Hayek and Milton Friedman. They argue for both economic and personal or moral freedom. The general thrust is much more individualistic with little stress on the nation as community – a central theme for the first two groups.

The most extreme or fundamentalist liberals form the fifth tendency, the libertarians. These are especially strong in the United States where there is an active Libertarian Party. The crucial emphasis here is on the need to reduce the state to its minimum function of protecting rights, or even to abolish it.

Finally there are three groups which are entirely American. The most intellectually formidable are the 'neo-conservatives' such as Kristol and Podhoretz. A more apt label for these would be 'chastened liberals'. The Moral Majority is the name usually used to describe the many Protestant fundamentalist groups which have appeared in the United States since the early 1970s. The New Right proper is a populist movement in American politics, linked to, but distinct from, the Moral Majority, its major figures being active political organizers such as Viguerie. Both of these movements are mainly interested in issues of public and private morality. It is impossible to draw up any list of positions and views held by all of these groups. Some are moral authoritarians, others libertarian, some argue for an active state, others for a minimal one. Their only common feature is anti-socialism, but their criticisms of socialism start from widely separated initial positions.

SD

Further reading

Barry, N., *On Classical Liberalism and Libertarianism*, London, Macmillan, 1986.
Barry, N., *The New Right*, London, Croom Helm, 1987.
Bosanquet, N., *After the New Right*, London, Heinemann, 1983.
Green, D., *The New Right*, Brighton, Wheatsheaf, 1987.

King, D., *The New Right*, London, Macmillan, 1987.
Seldon, A. (ed.), *The New Right Enlightenment*, Sevenoaks, Economic and Literary Books, 1985.
Viguerie, R., *The New Right: We're Ready to Lead*, Fall Church, VA, Viguerie, 1980.

O

OBJECTIVISM

Opponents of capitalism often claim that this system takes insufficient account of the needy. Defenders, e.g. Milton Friedman and other members of the Chicago School, counter by adducing the benefits of capitalism for the poor and the deficiencies of competing systems. Ayn Rand, a philosopher and novelist who founded Objectivism, adopted a more radical view. She denied any obligation to assist the needy as a class. Each person possesses certain natural rights, which include freedom from aggression and the liberty to acquire property. For each person, his or her own life as a rational being ought to rank as the highest good, and one's pursuit of this good faces no limitation from positive obligations unless one has voluntarily contracted with someone to perform some service. In the absence of agreement, one's only obligations to others are to observe their negative rights.

As one might expect, Rand favoured a state with only minimal functions: its only duties are defence against aggression, the enforcement of rights, and the settlement of contractual disputes. The state has no power to tax: it raises money through selling its services. It can, however, forbid competition from rival protective agencies within its territory.

Rand's ethical system, developed principally in her novels *The Fountainhead* and *Atlas Shrugged*, stresses individual virtue in a fashion reminiscent of Aristotle, by whom she was greatly influenced. Ethics rests not on absolute obligation but rather concerns each person's development of himself or herself as a rational being. She believes that individuals will find it in their interests to support a society of *laissez-faire* capitalism. Unless a social institution is in one's long-term interests, there is no moral obligation to support it. Rand, although the author of a volume entitled *The Virtue of Selfishness*, does not support 'selfishness' as understood in ordinary language: she places high value on friendship and romantic relationships. She holds distinctive views of these based on her value theory. Her views are not confined to ethics and politics. She strongly supports atheism and holds a realist position according to which we directly perceive the world. Our knowledge does not consist of representations of an unknowable reality, as in her view Kant taught. Kant's doctrines in both epistemology and ethics are in her opinion pernicious. As a militant atheist, she looks on religious teachings as a principal rival to her ethical system.

DG

Further reading

Rand, A., *Atlas Shrugged*, New York, Random House, 1957.
Rand, A., *The Virtue of Selfishness*, New York, New American Library, 1965.
Rand, A., *The Fountainhead*, New York, New American Library, 1968.
Rand, A., *Philosophy: Who Needs It*, New York, Bobbs-Merrill, 1982.
Uyl, D. den and D. Rasmussen (eds), *The Philosophic Thought of Ayn Rand*, Chicago, IL, Illinois University Press, 1986.

ORDER

According to the dictionary, order is a condition of social harmony, the absence of tumult, insurrection, or threats to life and property. It also implies, as well as a state of social peace, the existence of a multitude of rules and institutions which make it possible for large numbers of people to live peaceably together in a complex social order. More specifically one can speak of order in both the human and natural world when there is a degree of regularity and predictability. Order in this sense is the opposite of chaos or randomness, although in recent years this simple antinomy has been undermined. The question of what precisely order is and whence it comes has divided thinkers since the later eighteenth century.

In the pre-modern period the concept of order was central to most political thought but it was conceived of rather differently than is the case today. Order meant the absence of conflict and above all a stable hierarchical structure. This order existed in both the social and the natural world and there were close and meaningful correspondences between the one and the other. Thus in *Richard II* Shakespeare could compare Richard in one passage to the sun, a lion, and an eagle, confident that his audience would know that these all corresponded in their own sphere to Richard's kingly status in the human world. Nor was this a matter of poetic conceit as arguments from correspondence and analogy were commonplace at that time. This order was seen as divinely ordained and its development in human life was seen as the working out of divine providence. A purely human or natural order was inconceivable as all order was the product of divine will without which there could only be chaos. In the human world order meant reverence for established authority, particularly the patriarchal power of fathers, lords, magistrates, kings, and priests. It also meant support for the traditional division of society into three orders.

Disorder, injustice, and evil were explained as only apparent or else as a part of divine providence which is inscrutable to humans, known only to God. This is theodicy, the argument that ultimately all is for the best.

This image of an orderly world was transformed by the scientific revolution and especially by the work of Newton. Classical mechanics painted a picture of a deterministic, mechanical universe which ran according to fixed, predictable laws. This led some like Laplace to argue that in theory the entire history of the universe could be recreated from one single event. God survived, but only as the cosmic watchmaker who had created the world, built laws into it, and set it going. Some, notably Diderot, drew more unsettling conclusions, arguing that God was no longer necessary and that chance rather than providence ruled human affairs making them radically indeterminate.

In response to this intellectual revolution, eighteenth-century thinkers began to explore the patterns of order which existed in both the human and natural worlds. In the hands of such as Butler this led to a natural theology, the argument being that study by reason of human and natural life and their order led inevitably to a belief in God. However, when used by more secular observers it led to a fundamentally new perception and understanding of order. It became clear to many eighteenth-century thinkers that while order could be found in the human world, in politics, law, and economics it had no obvious or proximate cause once divine providence was rejected. Instead it seemed that in these areas pattern and order arose spontaneously. Not, that is, automatically but unintentionally, out of free interaction and decisions made by people. People, moreover, who were acting on partial and tacit knowledge rather than the all encompassing knowledge of God. There were orders in human affairs which were, in the famous phrase, 'the product of human action but not of human design'.

This argument was first developed at length by Mandeville in his *Fable of the Bees*, published in 1705. He argued that paradoxically the pursuit of selfish, egoistical ends by individuals promoted the general good and produced an unintended moral and commercial order. Hayek has argued that the specific case put by Mandeville is a clear example of the wider case that institutions can evolve as the unintended consequence of self-regarding actions. In other words, that an aggregate of individual actions can produce a structured whole which no one had intended or designed. Viner and others have argued that this was not Mandeville's intended argument, but this was indeed how it was read by some of his contemporaries. The idea of a spontaneous order was fully developed and applied to the whole range of human institutions by the thinkers of the Scottish Englightenment. Smith, Ferguson, and Millar in particular used this notion to explain a wide range of human institutions and practices and their ideas were built on during the nineteenth century by thinkers such as Savigny, Buckle, and Maine.

Several areas of human life were identified by these writers as spontaneous orders. These included economic life and exchange, language, law and legal systems, social and class structures, political systems, the course of history in general, and, most controversially, customs and morals. Thus the anti-rationalist explanation of human social organization had a major impact on most disciplines during the nineteenth century. Some of its exponents argued that the existence of spontaneous orders in human affairs showed how little they were governed by reason and drew the conservative moral that one should therefore leave well alone and not subject traditional institutions to rationalist criticism. Savigny shows this response quite clearly. Others, such as Buckle, believed that although orders might arise without intent this did not mean that they were necessarily good or should not be subject to rational criticism. This reveals a disagreement on this topic which continues to the present day.

As well as the theory of spontaneous order, the eighteenth and nineteenth centuries produced another concept of order, diametrically opposed to it. This way of thinking derived from scientism, the application of a mistaken notion of the methods of science and the nature of scientific knowledge to all aspects of life. This approach was based on three assumptions. First, that through reason it is possible to understand everything about a particular area of study, at least in theory. Put another way, that there exists a body of definitive concrete knowledge on any subject which can be discovered by reason and is superior to tradition or evolved practice. Second, that through reason one can design an order which is superior to one that has emerged spontaneously without design. Indeed, order is defined in this way of thinking as only being possible where there is design and intent. Anything else is chaos. Third, that no social institution or practice is defensible unless it can be justified by an appeal to reason. This approach came to enjoy great prestige because of the high standing of science and scientific knowledge. It was in many ways the application of a Newtonian world-view to other disciplines and areas of study.

Gradually this second concept of order came to dominate intellectual life during the last third of the nineteenth century and achieved almost complete domination of several disciplines during the present century. This was particularly true of economics and the social sciences. The point, of course, is that both of these conceptions of order have consequences for political argument and public policy. The second one can be used to justify interventionist and activist policy by the state on the grounds that humans should use their knowledge and reason to plan social life rather than leave everything to chance. It can also lie behind attempts through social policy to reshape traditional social custom and practice to bring it into line with rational standards. The spontaneous model of order implies that the state should not intervene in economic and social life since it lacks the necessary knowledge and that progress means leaving the unintended consequences of human action to work themselves out.

This would appear to imply that there is a straightforward split with interventionists and planners on one side, conservatives and classical liberals on the other. However, things are not that simple. Some classical liberals, such as Mises, argue their case on the basis of an abstract model of human motivation. Mises also thought that it was essential to base policy on rational analysis rather than tradition because such a perspective would inevitably show that the best means of realizing most ends was a minimal state. On the other side some socialists, particularly in Germany, used a mystical notion of spontaneous order to justify their programme.

However, it is true that since 1945 the theory of spontaneous order has been mostly associated with conservatism and classical liberalism. This is primarily due to the impact of Hayek. He has made major contributions to the theory, most notably through his extension of Hume's insight that unintentional co-ordination leading to a spontaneous order is needed to enable the knowledge scattered throughout society to be used to best effect. Hayek argues that there are two types of order, which he calls *cosmos* and *taxis*. The first is a spontaneous order, the second an intentional or planned one. The paradigmatic instance of the first is a system of market exchange or catalaxy. The state is, or can be, the most obvious example of the second. In modern conservative and classical liberal writing this notion of spontaneous order is used to justify a sharp reduction in state intervention on the grounds that it interferes with the more effecient and rational process of markets and other examples of *cosmos*. Thus the traditional socialist attack on the anarchy (meaning chaos) of unplanned orders is turned on its head. It is in fact the attempt to plan a social order, futile because of people's inevitable lack of knowledge, which produces chaos and disorder. This argument can lead in some writers to an anarchist position and many now quote Proudhon's dictum that 'liberty is the mother not the daughter of order'.

However, despite the immense contribution which Hayek and others have made to our understanding of social processes which is now universally recognized, the concept of spontaneous order is still problematic for many conservatives and classical liberals, especially the latter, and particularly where Hayek's version of the concept is concerned. Conservatives find this whole tradition of thought most congenial as it clearly fits in well with the conservative desire to defend established institutions, moral codes, and ways of life. They no longer have to try and find rationalist justifications such as utility for existing practices. However, some conservatives, especially those who argue from a Christian perspective, are unhappy about the implied moral relativism of much spontaneous order theory. Others dislike the subversive potential of the argument and resist the notion that all order can be explained as the outcome of unplanned action.

Some at least, they argue, is unnatural, the consequence of political power.

However, most conservatives find this argument highly congenial. It is classical liberals who are less happy with spontaneous order theory, and particularly with Hayek's version. This divide between the two ideologies has not been so apparent because most modern political argument is about economics. Here the implications are that the state should not intervene and the market should co-ordinate economic activity, principles which both conservatives and classical liberals can agree on. When the model is applied to areas such as law and moral codes, many classical liberals draw back.

The reason for this is another element of Hayek's thought, its evolutionism. His argument is that social and political orders evolve through a process of natural selection and the 'best' ones will survive. In a recent work, *The Fatal Conceit*, he seems to make the criterion of what is best the capacity to support more population. This sort of argument has many problems. It means that traditional institutions cannot be subjected to criticism on rationalist or a priori grounds such as violation of rights. All one can do is to try a different practice and see if it passes the evolutionary test. Strictly applied this means that the British were wrong to abolish suttee in India, for example. This exemplifies the wider objection that there is no guarantee that spontaneous evolution will lead to liberal institutions; indeed, the evidence of history suggests the reverse is the case and that the liberal west is the outcome of a fluke. In Hayek's version the theory of spontaneous order comes close to Pope's argument that 'whatever is, is good'. Most classical liberals would say that there has to be a role for reason to criticize and reform traditional social institutions whether these are spontaneous orders or not.

However, in spite of these criticisms the notion that order can arise out of chaos is gaining ground in all disciplines and looks set to become one of the central ideas of future scholarship. Yet the main reason for this is the slow but massive impact of the twentieth-century revolution in science and mathematics. The old mechanistic world of Newton has been overthrown by quantum mechanics and relativity theory. The idea of definitive all-embracing knowledge has been destroyed by the Goedel theorem and the uncertainty principle. In many areas scientists find that entropy and random processes generate order and structure but in a way that cannot be predicted. This has already been applied to human institutions by the disciplines of information theory and systems analysis. Gradually, as these often abstruse concepts are popularized and taken on board by other disciplines, so the world-view of intellectuals changes. Increasingly the universe is seen as orderly, but in a chaotic way, with order the outcome of random processes and with the world at a very basic level unpredictable and impossible of final description. That this often involves a misunderstanding of what the scientists are saying is a separate issue. Just as the

Newtonian revolution led many intellectuals to adhere to one concept of order and knowledge, which had one sort of political impact, so the scientific revolution of this century is bringing the other concept of order and its attendant agendas to the fore.

SD

Further reading

Barry, N., *Hayek's Economic and Social Philosophy*, London, Macmillan, 1979.
Barry, N., 'The tradition of spontaneous order', *Literature of Liberty* Summer 1982: 7–58.
Bateson, G., 'Conscious purpose versus nature', in *Steps to an Ecology of Mind*, New York, Random House, 1972.
Hayek, F.A., *The Fatal Conceit*, London, Routledge, 1989.

ORGANIC SOCIETY

The philosophical contention that society as such is an organism goes back to Plato and Aristotle. Since the Romantic period, however, many aesthetes and literati have used the term 'organic society' to denote a specific, idealized kind of society against which modern civilization is to be judged. For them the 'organic society' is local, rural, and traditional rather than cosmopolitan, urban and mobile. Its central feature is that in it *all* human relations, including and especially the economic and political, are in some sense personal. This distinguishes it from both 'market' and totalitarian societies, which are rejected, along with industrialism, as 'mechanical'.

Kant defined an organism as a whole of which 'every part is reciprocally both means and end'. In the philosophical sense, an 'organic' society is one in which individuals (the parts) are not only indispensable to society (the whole), but are also regarded, in turn, as its Aristotelian *telos* (goal, purpose, consummation). In a 'mechanical' society, by contrast, either individuals exist to fulfil a 'social' function wholly external to themselves (collectivism), or, conversely, society exists purely to satisfy their egoistic needs and desires (individualism). The organicist contends that neither 'society' nor 'the individual' should mechanically 'determine' the other, since the two are mutual correlatives.

Seen in this light, a collectivist society is a mere monolith or ant-heap, while an individualist society is not only aesthetically and morally unpleasing, but also cannot command the allegiance necessary for its survival. Individualism, Plato observed of Athenian democracy, will always tend to collapse, first into anarchy, and then into collectivism (tyranny).

Organicists emphasize the value of spontaneity – i.e. of non-mechanical organization, change, and development – in social arrangements. However, they see individuals' spontaneity as an expression of their social essence, and hence as primarily altruistic. Thus they regard its more egoistic manifestations as 'unnatural' or even as coerced, for all that formal coercion may be relatively lacking. Indeed, where their eastern counterparts have criticized collectivism, post-Romantic western champions of the organic society have overwhelmingly concentrated their fire on *laissez-faire*. They have done so on account of the materialism and 'alienation' (of society and the individual from each other and from their respective 'true' natures) which *laissez-faire* is supposed to foster, and have reaffirmed the freedom, autonomy, and spiritual wholeness which it is similarly alleged to repress or deny.

The accusation is of course paradoxical, and smacks of Berlin's 'positive freedom'. But the implication is serious, to the effect that, as in modern theories of collective choice, the unforeseen aggregate outcome of 'free' individual choices may be a social system, or a cultural climate, which either the choosers do not desire, or, even if they do, is not objectively desirable.

As a cultural rallying-cry, 'the organic society' has united people and movements as politically diverse as Coleridge and Cobbett, Ruskin and Morris, Hardy and Lawrence, Yeats and Rilke, F. R. Leavis and E. P. Thompson, the New Left and the Old Right, Eastern European dissidents, and the recently emergent 'Greens'. Many observers see this striking concurrence of opinion as evidence that something is indeed wrong with the modern world. Others, however, regard 'the organic society' at best as utopian nostalgia, and at worst as a feudal–authoritarian reaction to sponaneous socio-economic development. The latter, they would say, liberates precisely *because* it depersonalizes all relationships except those which the parties involved have expressly decided shall be personal. ('Contract', in Maine's terminology, has superseded 'status'.) Durkheim, indeed, applied the term 'organic society', not to some self-conscious, traditional, close-knit order, but to its opposite, the infinitely complex, unfolding world of modern urban capitalism, governed by Adam Smith's 'invisible hand'.

RG

Further reading

Aristotle, *Politics*, ed. and trans. E. Barker, New York, Oxford University Press, 1978, Book I ('The politics of the household').

Gellner, E., 'Hegel's last secrets', *Encounter*, April 1976; reprinted as 'The absolute in braces', in E. Gellner, *Spectacles and Predicaments*, Cambridge, Cambridge University Press, 1979.

Grant, R. A. D., 'The state as end: the organic tradition', in G.H.R. Parkinson (ed.), *An Encyclopaedia of Philosophy*, London, Routledge, 1988, 693–703.

Leavis, F. R., and D. Thompson, *Culture and Environment*, London, Chatto & Windus, 1962, especially chapters on 'The organic community' and bibliography.

P

PEACE

Peace is not simply the absence of war but a positive condition, a state of affairs in which war is impossible. This necessarily implies that war is not an inevitable part of the human condition but has specific causes the removal of which would then lead to a state of general peace. The notion of peace has been a central one for western political philosophy from the Middle Ages onwards and the twin questions of whether peace is possible and, if so, how it may be brought about are important for all ideologies. In more recent times this question has become prominent because of the threat of nuclear war and the rise in most western societies of an organized 'peace movement'. The current attitudes of most conservatives and classical liberals are strongly influenced by contemporary political disputes and the partisan identification of 'peace theory' with the political left. This obscures a more complex history.

Until at least 1914 classical liberals believed that peace was both possible and realizable. The idea of peace was a vitally important one for most liberal thinkers and politicians. For some such as Cobden it was the core of their philosophy. For liberals of that time, as the world developed so it moved towards peace: war was backward, peace progressive. This development towards peace had economic, political, and intellectual components. In the field of economics they argued that as the world economy became ever more closely integrated and the international division of labour more advanced, so it became increasingly difficult for states to wage war. Moreover, they held that the social and economic order of commercial society was naturally conducive to peace which served the self-interest of a commercial ruling class. By contrast, an aristocratic class benefited from war and its political effects. So, as societies moved from the 'military' model of rule through a strong state to the 'commercial' one of a limited state, peace came nearer.

In the field of ideas the classical liberals argued that, as free trade and free movement of people brought the peoples of the world into closer contact, so the prejudices and beliefs which led to popular support for war would decline. Patriotism in particular was seen as a backward notion set to decline – most classical liberals were strong cosmopolitans. On the global scale they anticipated the demise of national sovereignty and the replacement of the nation state by a regime of small-scale localized administration. In the interim they looked to the government of inter-national relations by a system of international law and the settlement of disputes by arbitration, together with generally agreed disarmament. In practical terms all this implied a programme consisting of complete free trade; economic development; international law and collective security; and the demise of the nationalism.

This vision was wrecked by the events of the twentieth century, not least those of 1914–18. In particular, liberals had to come to terms with the enthusiastic popular response to the outbreak of war and the massive support it enjoyed. Like the socialists, they had underestimated the power of nationalism, the dominant ideology of modern times. Some however, more farsighted, had warned of the rising flood of jingoism in the thirty years before 1914. They also, like socialists, have had to accept that politics, and particularly geopolitics, is autonomous and not determined by economic forces and structures. Today most liberals are much chastened and advocate measures simply to avoid war through deterrence – not the same thing as peace. The most important exponent of this 'chastened liberalism' was Aron. Others adhere to the classic liberal arguments but assert that the world is in a phase of regression. If peace can only be achieved by the effective demise of the state then it is at most a possibility.

Conservative thought faces different problems. Most conservatives have argued that peace is only an aspiration given the nature of humans and the human condition, something to be striven for but not attained. The best that can be hoped for is to avoid war through diplomacy and firm defence. Conservatives in general do not share the classical liberal antipathy to nationalism, seeing the nation as the prime historic community. They are therefore hostile to moves towards a reduction of national independence. This way of thinking has the advantage of being more directly addressed to present circumstances. Both conservatives and 'chastened liberals' such as Aron have argued that to maintain peace in the limited sense is a difficult task enough with efforts to eliminate war at best a distraction, at worst destabilizing and positively dangerous.

SD

Further reading

Aron, R., *Peace and War*, London, Weidenfeld & Nicolson, 1966.
Aron, R., *Clausewitz: Philosopher of War*, London, Routledge & Kegan Paul, 1983.
Hobson, J. A., *Richard Cobden, The International Man*, Brighton, Harvester, 1968.
Taylor, A. J. P., *The Troublemakers*, London, Panther, 1969.

POLITICS

The question was once set in an Oxford philosophy examination: ' "Power politics" – what other sorts of politics are there?' Certainly all politics must be concerned in some way with power. But, equally certainly, those conflicts of interest between states which are resolved wholly or mainly by appeals to force or the threat of force are not the sole sort. For there are also the paradigmatically peaceful internal politics of long-established democracies, where the only appeal to force is usually tacit, and to the lawful force sustaining orderly procedures and preventing intimidatory intrusions. There are, no doubt, such similarly non-violent politics even in the Vatican.

Etymologically the word 'politics' derives from the classical Greek *polis*. This referred to a city state, where anyone who was not interested in the affairs – the policies or politics – of his city was put down as an *idiotees*; or, as we would say, an idiot! Most of what are offered as definitions here are, or are intended as, wise sayings rather than as explications of the meaning of the word. Such are, for instance, Lord Butler's 'the art of the possible' or Isaac (not Benjamin) d'Israeli's 'the art of governing mankind through deceiving them' or even Adolf Hitler's 'the art of carrying out the life struggle of a nation for its earthly existence'.

Perhaps a modestly satisfactory interim definition would be that the word 'politics' refers to all the various ways in which the senses of the policy decisions of organizations may be determined; save when these determinations are made by single individuals. It has to be extended to organizations in general and not just government organizations in particular because everyone wants to speak, indeed insists on speaking, about the politics of all manner of non-government organizations – of the politics which determines how these organizations are internally governed and how their external decisions are made. The exception clause regarding individuals has to go in because politics cannot arise until and unless several people are involved in determining an outcome. That outcome may itself be only influence and not the operative decision. For there may be politics in the court or the council of an autocrat, where the outcome of these politics is only to determine who gets the ear of, or what advice is given to, the despot; who may or may not then choose to act accordingly.

One narrower definition, which makes the objects of the concept somewhat more appealing, was provided in a book conformably entitled *In Defence of Politics*. This makes politics

> the activity by which differing interests within a given unit of rule are conciliated by giving them a share in power in proportion to their importance to the welfare and survival of the whole community. And . . . a political system is that type of government where politics proves successful in ensuring reasonable stability and order.

The adjective 'political' is usually but not always limited in its reference to the politics of government, in the sense in which governmental may be contrasted with non-governmental organizations. It is in this understanding that issues are said to have become political or to have been politicized. Both liberals and conservatives are, if perhaps for rather different reasons, concerned to limit the sphere of politics, in this understanding of 'politics'. For liberals this is a matter primarily and definitionally of wanting to limit the scope and activities of government. For conservatives the emphasis may be rather more on the positive values of the family and of private life in general.

Both socialists and even – in the contemporary understanding – social democrats are in effect, if not always in conscious intention, committed to an enormous expansion of the sphere of the political. (The expression 'social democrat' in its present employment requires such qualification, since both the original model Marxist party in Germany and Lenin's party in the old Russian empire called themselves Social-Democratic.) Socialists are definitionally so committed, since in any socialist economy all economic management must be ultimately if not immediately governmental. Social democrats – even those most aware of the merits of plural ownership and the competitive employment of the means of production – must necessarily, through their commitments to heavily redistributive taxation and other 'incomes policies', make government the ultimate arbiter of who gets how much, thus politicizing all questions of what otherwise it would be misleading to call wealth distribution.

The adjective 'political' is being employed with a similarly limited extension when political offences and offenders are distinguished from the ordinarily criminal. Two criteria have been suggested for making this distinction: (i) whether the facts alleged amount to a recognized crime, discounting political motivation; or (ii) where there actually was political motivation. If the second of these is used, then the 'political offender' asking for asylum can get away with anything, including the most murderous terrorism. Guided by the first the courts in country A will refuse to extradite to country B any offenders whose offences would not have been crimes at all under its own more liberal laws.

The term 'politics' is also employed to designate a set of academic disciplines. Here the most fundamental distinction is between what is broadly describable as political science and what, with an equally broad embrace, we may call political philosophy. Political science is thus a comparative and explanatory study of actual political arrangements and activities. Political philosophy in the present comprehensive understanding considers possible justifications for possible and actual alternative political arrangements.

Aristotle was the undisputed founder of the discipline of political science. For besides composing his own *Politics* he both established and directed the first major research project – studies of the constitutions of over 150 Greek city states. But the first classic of political philosophy, at any rate in the Western tradition, has to be *The Republic* of Plato. Those, however, who think of philosophy as essentially and exclusively a kind of conceptual enquiry should be warned that few of the acknowledged classics of political philosophy – *The Republic* of Plato, the *Leviathan* of Hobbes, Locke's *Two Treatises of Government*, Rousseau's *Social Contract*, for instance – contain much, if any, such philosophical analysis.

AF

Further reading

Crick, B., *In Defence of Politics*, Chicago, IL, Chicago University Press, 2nd edition 1972.
Scruton, R., *A Dictionary of Political Thought*, New York and London, Hill & Wang and Macmillan, 1982.

POWER

Power is thought by some political scientists to be the key explanatory concept in social theory: politics is said to be about the possession or distribution of power in the sense of the ability to make decisions that affect the community as a whole. The emphasis on power implies that law and morality do not operate as strong constraints on political action. Their apparent autonomy is always compromised by the necessary exercise of power in political relationships. Hence the expression *Realpolitik* – which purports to describe the realities of political life.

The theorist credited with the first formulation of this view is Machiavelli. In *The Prince* he describes the mechanics of power and prescribes the means by which it may be maintained or exercised. This is in direct contrast to the medieval world-view which envisaged politics in terms of authority, ultimately derived from natural law. For Machiavelli, traditional law and morality exist to the extent that they are useful aids and instruments to those who possess and wish to maintain power.

Power (unlike most formulations of authority) is a sociological concept, in principle capable of measurement and observation. Propositions about power in society necessitate that power exists: it would be incoherent to suggest that some person or group was in power without specifying evidence of that power. Again this contrasts with authority: it would make sense to describe a person or group as being in authority even though that authority was ineffective. Although power is always about the ability to get things done, it does not, of course, follow from this that power may not be legitimate. In some social affairs power is exercised illegitimately, but political science is largely concerned with the explanation of such things as 'prime ministerial power' and 'presidential power' where legitimacy is not at issue: what is crucial is the success in politics of those who occupy certain roles. Power, although it is often backed by force, is not the same thing as force. The direct application of force normally indicates the absence of power.

Power is often thought to be exercised against the will of another, or against that person's interests. Power exists when A gets B to do X when he would rather do Y. This is a feature of both liberal and Marxist theories of power. In liberal theory it is supposed that freedom and autonomy are features of voluntary exchange relations (although these are not confined to narrow economic exchanges). In contrast, the exercise of political power, since it reduces the range of choice, must be opposed to individual well-being. Marxists see economic exchange relationships, under a capitalist regime, as destructive of autonomy since private ownership is itself a system of economic power. In their very different ways, both schools envisage the possibility of spontaneous social co-ordination, with power reduced to the absolute minimum, if not eliminated.

In contrast, some political theorists, e.g. Arendt, do not contrast power and autonomy but view power as a resource to be used for the well-being of the community. It is the absence of political power which is the danger: this is a feature of anomic, mass societies and it makes them vulnerable to totalitarianism.

The difficulty with power in the social sciences is in locating what are the facts that enable one person to determine the actions of another. The threat of sanctions is one obvious way, but clearly most instances of power in society are not explicable in this way. There is a cluster of concepts, which include, in addition to power, influence and persuasion, that describe similar phenomena. This makes it difficult to isolate causal factors in power relationships. A frequent objection to liberalism is that the market is said to be a system of power rather than voluntary exchange.

Economic or market power exists when one agent can determine the actions of another without threats. In a market this could occur with the emergence of a natural monopoly. Monopolists, through their control of vital resources, can reduce their output and raise prices so as to secure abnormal profits. They may be said to have the power to determine the actions of consumers because there is no alternative supply of the wanted good. The exemplar case is that of the sole owner of a water-hole in the desert. Such cases of natural monopoly are extremely rare in real-world markets, although there are degrees of market power.

Critics of capitalism, such as Galbraith, maintain that economic power exists even in competitive markets. This is because of the alleged inter-dependence of supply and demand. It is claimed that producers do not passively respond to demands of consumers but actively promote wants in individuals (wants they would not otherwise have) through advertising and other techniques of persuasion. Here people appear not to be in conflict, but power is nevertheless said to be exercised. There is little evidence produced for this and, more importantly, it is difficult to see how a theory could distinguish between willing and 'coerced' consumer behaviour.

In political science there is perhaps an even greater difficulty in the identification and measurement of power. It has been suggested that power is an 'essentially contested concept' in that there is no agreed criterion for its application and that its usage is determined by evaluative and more general philosophical considerations. If this is so, then a 'positive science' of power is an illusion and power is just as philosophical a notion as authority.

There have been in recent decades, however, a number of purported theories of power. The discipline of sociology tends to produce theories of the concentration of power in democratic societies while political science claims that it is diffused.

Mills argued, in *The Power Elite*, that despite the federal and decentralized formal structure of American government, in reality a cohesive body drawn from the business, political, and military world determined major political decisions. However, Mills produced only evidence for some sociological similarities in this group; he did not show that it was decisive over a given range of decisions. It was for this reason that the pluralist political scientist Dahl claimed that 'power elite' theories were unscientific.

In a number of studies, followers of Dahl claimed that power, in cases of conflict over defined issues, was not exercised by one group but by a plurality of groups. Power was diffused in liberal democratic societies because citizens exercised autonomous choices through political participation. Liberals and conservatives argue that the case for democracy and limited government is that here power is diffused.

Other writers, however, have claimed that power is not only observable in conflict issues but also may be unobservable; e.g. the fact that some areas are excluded from the political agenda indicates that power is exercised in the absence of a visible conflict of interests. The neo-Marxist theory of power, held by Lukes, depends upon a distinction between real and apparent interests. Thus, power may be exercised over people, even when their wants are fully satisfied, by free economic and political processes, since these wants are determined by social and institutional forces over which individuals have no control. Democratic choices are, then, not real choices. Again, it is difficult to see how this theory could be tested.

The plethora of theories about power suggests that, despite the claim that it is in principle susceptible to measurement, there is little agreement as to what power is. Also, many of the attempts to show that power exists in some non-observable form, as when wants are said to be predetermined, are attempts to distort some obvious facts of liberal-democratic society, such as choice in voting and competition between parties.

It is, however, a chimaera (pursued none the less by extreme individualists) to suppose that power can be replaced completely by exchange in free societies. The necessity for political decisions means that power will always exist. The conventional liberal-conservative view is that power can be controlled by constitutions and rules. Acton's dictum that 'power tends to corrupt and absolute power tends to corrupt absolutely' is still a potent reminder of the need for the diffusion of power: hence the importance for liberal-conservatives of the doctrine of the 'separation of powers' and the theory of checks and balances. It is the doubt about what constitutes the 'good' that leads them to deny the grant of absolute power to those who would implement it. Although conservatives have a less hostile attitude towards political power than liberals, they still believe that it should be used for the preservation of an existing social order rather than the enforcement of an imaginary utopia.

NB

Further reading

Blau, P., *Exchange and Power in Social Life*, New York, Wiley, 1964.
Dahl, R., *Who Governs?*, Yale, CONN, Yale University Press, 1961.
Joueval, B. de, *Power*, London, Allen & Unwin, 1952.
Rothbard, M., *Power and Market*, Kansas, MO, Sheed, Andrews & McMeel, 1970.

PREJUDICE

Prejudice is belief, whether correct or incorrect, which is held without reasoned support. In a wider sense, it is a term of abuse for all strongly held, erroneous, or alien convictions.

According to some conservative thinkers in the anti-rationalist, evolutionary tradition – such as Hume and Burke – human beings participate in the accumulated experience of their innumerable ancestors and intuitively use this experience as a guide for their own outlooks and decisions. Only a small part of this knowledge, however, is ever made conscious and explicit; the greater part remains embedded in instinct, custom, common usage, and prejudice. Often men may not realize the meaning of their immemorial prejudices and customs; but they may be confident that the 'wisdom of the species' has endowed them with a significance beneficial to the social whole. Prejudice is prejudgement, the answer supplied by intuition and ancestral consensus of opinion when the individual lacks either time or knowledge to arrive at a decision based upon evidence or reason. It is thus distinct from bigotry and superstition, although prejudice may sometimes degenerate into these.

Burke's defence of prejudice and custom was taken up by social scientists like Hayek, who see social behaviour as being shaped and guided to a large extent by undesigned rules and conventions of whose significance and workings we are often unaware. Social rules must be regarded as vehicles of inarticulate knowledge, knowledge of a kind that is indispensable to social order. Once society comes to be pervaded by the attitude that all behaviour (particularly in the moral sphere) is made contingent upon sufficient evidence and proper reasoning, then, Hayek argues, much of the common stock of tacit knowledge is inevitably lost and a measure of social chaos must ensue.

The affection for prejudice, customs, and conventions typical of many conservatives stands in stark contrast to the attack against 'superstitions' that was a principal concern of Enlightenment liberalism. In support of their view conservatives can adduce evidence from the advancement and success of much of modern science, which was often guided by non-rational considerations. Not only must the 'context of discovery' of a presumed scientific fact be distinguished from its 'context of justification'; it has been shown that the framework within which scientists work typically relies on assumptions and prejudices which are themselves not open to scientific proof. For this reason, many modern philosophers of science reject the extension of the concept of prejudice to all beliefs which are not demonstrably true and recognize the role of non-rational considerations in the advancement of knowledge.

WG

Further reading

Acton, H.B., 'Prejudice', *Revue internationale de philosophie* 1952, 21.
Burke, E., *Reflections on the Revolution in France*, Harmondsworth, Penguin, 1976.
Hayek, F.A., *The Constitution of Liberty*, London, Routledge, 1960.
Popper, K., *Conjectures and Refutations*, London, Routledge, 1963.

PROGRESS

The movement or development of an entity or institution through time, in the direction of a particular end-state so that certain elements or qualities are enhanced while others are diminished as the end-state is more closely approximated. For this to be progress the change has to be for the better: the concept is thus not morally neutral. In western political thought progress occurs not only in institutions but crucially in entire societies and ultimately the whole human species. The elements which western thought has commonly identified as those which are increased through progress are knowledge, virtue, and freedom. The concept necessarily involves the notion of a *telos* or goal, since unless there is some idea of the goal towards which society/humanity is moving it is impossible to decide if any particular change is progressive.

The history of the idea of progress, as recounted by Bury and others, can be traced back to classical antiquity. At that time, however, notions of progress were overlaid by the notion that history centred on a pattern of cyclical change, of growth followed by decay. The idea of linear progress was contributed by Christian thinkers, most notably St Augustine in his *City of God*. Christian theology also introduced the notion of automaticity, that the movement of mankind to greater knowledge, etc., was a necessary consequence of the way God had made the world and so a part of the plan of divine providence. However, this was heavily qualified by the contrary doctrine that the Fall had inaugurated an age of decay and decline which would only end with the Second Coming. This Christian model was secularized, and the caveats regarding the fallen nature of men discarded, during the Enlightenment, which saw the production of the classic statement of the doctrine of progress, Condorcet's *Sketch for an historical picture of the progress of the human mind*. Since then it has been a central part of most Western political thought, with much argument centred on the questions of how to define it and how to account for it. In recent times the notion has taken some hard knocks but it is still of great significance as an often unexamined assumption.

Progress plays an important part in classical liberal thought, which has an elaborate and sophisticated account of its nature and cause. This was initially formed in the Scottish Enlightenment and found its definitive expression in the writings of Smith, Hume, and Ferguson. Smith in particular produced a sophisticated account of the progression of societies through a series of stages of development. These were hunter-gathering, pastoral, ancient, feudal, and commercial. The progressive movement involved the following changes: first, from a partial to a more developed division of labour; second, from lower to higher productivity and wealth; third, from a state where social relations were few and simple to one where they were many and complex; from a condition where most behaviour and manners were rude and barbarous to one where they were increasingly civil and refined; from self-sufficiency and limited contact with others to a dependence upon trade and interdependency between communities and, lastly, from a situation where government while small was unlimited and based on force to one where although much larger it was bound by laws. Hume added that this went along with a movement towards greater humanity and virtue.

Smith and the others were quite clear that this progress had not affected all communities since some had remained at an earlier stage. This was explained in terms of contingent events which promoted or discouraged progress. Ferguson developed the idea that it was material pressures such as population which forced communities either to progress or to decline. These early thinkers were not persuaded that progress was inevitable. Gibbon's account of the Roman Empire was an account of the reversal of progress, and the Scots all speculated as to whether this relapse from civilization to barbarism could be repeated.

In the nineteenth century this scheme was elaborated by various authors. The Manchester School added the idea that progress included a move towards the peaceful settlement of disputes and the demise of war. Buckle and, later, Robertson produced sophisticated models of historical progress. The main elaborations, however, came from Maine and Spencer. Maine argued that in 'primitive' societies human relations were based on status, with individuals relating to each other in terms of their relative position in a social hierarchy. Progress involved movement away from this to relations based on contract, which was far more egalitarian, and led to an increase in voluntaristic social organization since the way people related to each other was less determined, shaped more by personal choice. He also refined the ideas of the progressive changes in the nature of law and the state. Spencer argued that progress consisted of a movement from 'military' societies to 'industrial' ones. In the former, society was organized on a hierarchical basis with a large state which served the interests of a ruling class, with warfare and force the most effective route to wealth. In the latter there is legal and social (though not economic) equality, and the increasing complexity of society and social relations means that the state becomes ever more redundant. Production becomes the main source of wealth. By the middle of the nineteenth century, liberals saw progress as inevitable. This confidence was shattered by the events of the twentieth century and had been waning before then. There has been a reversion to the contingent view of progress put forward by the Scottish Enlightenment.

This can be seen in the most impressive contemporary liberal theory of progress, that of Hayek. He argues that progress is made possible by the spontaneous emergence of traditions and customary practices which enable large social groups to function by helping them to utilize the knowledge scattered among their members. Societies with 'good' traditions will survive and prosper, those which lack them will disappear. Unfortunately, Hayek argues, these customary practices run counter to the instincts formed over nearly a million years of existence in hunter-gatherer bands so there is a constant tendency to reject them for the reactionary proposals of socialism. Hence progress is not inevitable and could well go into reverse.

This is similar to, yet different from, the notion of progress found in Marx. The same idea of stages is found (primitive communism, slavery, feudalism, capitalism, socialism, communism). However, for Marx progress is inevitable, brought about by the class conflict which is both cause and effect of the 'contradictions' of a mode of production. The great problem for Marx was the obvious existence of societies which had not progressed in his terms, such as India. His solution was the 'Asiatic mode of production', a sort of side track to the main line of historical development. This, however, leaves Marxists with a dilemma. If they accept the

Asiatic mode then the movement from slavery to feudalism to capitalism was not inevitable but rather a fluke, so Marxism is not a universal theory. If they throw out the Asiatic mode then they must admit that large parts of the world have not progressed so Marxism loses its doctrine of inevitability.

In marked contrast to all of this, conservatives have always been sceptical of the very idea of progress. Some, like De Maistre, have rejected it as hubris. Most have argued that the kind of pattern of development found in classical liberal models is an illusion, that the reality is more messy. Also, many conservatives reject the idea that there is some potentially universal model of progress, preferring to emphasize the peculiarity and distinctiveness of each society's historical experience. This means that for conservatives there is no standard of progress by which one can measure different societies as either progressive, stationary, or regressive. This approach means that they are much better equipped to deal with the disillusionment brought on by the terrible events of the last ninety years, but also that much conservative thought balks at giving moral judgement on actual societies past and present.

SD

Further reading

Barraclough, J. (ed.), *Condorcet, Sketch for a Historical Picture of the Progress of the Human Mind*, Westport, CT, Hyperion Press, 1955.
Bury, J.B., *The Idea of Progress, its Origins and Historical Development*, New York, Dover, 1955.
Hall, J.A., *Powers and Liberties*, Harmondsworth, Penguin, 1986.
Nisbet, R.A., *The History of the Idea of Progress*, London, Heinemann, 1980.

PROPERTY

The institution of property implies that all wanted objects are *owned* by some person, family, social grouping, or public authority. Since scarcity is an ineradicable feature of the human condition, all societies have developed rules and conventions for legitimate entitlement to wanted objects. Thus, analytically, property rules are not necessarily exhausted by private ownership. There are some things, e.g. the air and parts of the sea, where there are no formal rules governing their use, but even here modern conditions and progress are producing the feature of scarcity making limitations on free use inevitable. While some wanted objects, including land and animal and vegetable resources, have at some times in history, been held in 'common', i.e. with no formal restrictions on use, the absence of ownership rules means that such resources will be rapidly depleted to the detriment of everybody. This is known as the 'tragedy of the commons'.

Property does not just mean an ownership system covering tangible assets, e.g. land, houses, and movable goods; it refers to a 'bundle of rights' to use things in certain ways. Most obviously, these include the right to sell one's labour in a market, the right to dispose of one's property, the right to inherit, and the collective right of a community not to have its immediate environment damaged by others. The modern economic theory of property rights has been significantly expanded to solve the problem of 'negative externalities' without state intervention. In those cases where individual property owners accidentally cause harm to the environment, the complete specification of property rights would permit other individuals to sue for damages at common law.

Private and public ownership of resources represent theoretically two extremes rarely realized in practice. The polar case of private ownership would be where there was completely unrestricted use by an individual of that to which that individual had a legitimate title. It would not only envisage the private ownership of roads and land, and prohibit all taxation and government, but also permit persons to sell themselves into slavery. Complete public ownership would entail the abolition of all private titles and would imply, theoretically, that the clothes one wore would be rented from the state. All societies can be located somewhere between these extremes: no property rules allow completely unrestricted use and communal societies permit private ownership of personal goods.

Liberals and conservatives have historically stressed the importance of private property but have done so in differing ways. Liberals have opposed taxation, nationalization, and other attenuations of property rights from the standpoint of the rights of individual ownership. Conservatives have favoured private property, not from an individualistic position, but from a standpoint that stresses its social utility: a view that sanctions some public regulation of private property.

The main questions that concern the classical liberal view of property are the criteria of legitimate ownership. The classic text is Locke's *Second Treatise on Government*: there he claimed that 'every man has a property in his own person. This nobody has any right to but himself. The labour of his body and the *work* of his hands, we may say, are properly his'. Thus claims to property derive from the sovereignty individuals have over themselves. Exchange of property titles creates further property rights so that the capitalist system derives entirely from individual ownership. The worker is entitled to the marginal product of his labour: but not, of course, the whole product of a co-operative enterprise since part of this will be income earned by the capital invested. In this, the individualist position contrasts sharply with Marxism: the latter attributes value solely to the labourer and denies that capital itself is productive. Many liberals argue that the return on capital is justified as a reward for 'waiting', i.e. abstinence from consumption.

Reward for labour is not the only entitlement to property. Gifts and bequests are legitimate, not on the grounds of the worthiness of the beneficiary, but because donors can do what they like with that which is rightfully theirs.

The justification of the acquisition of original property titles is also Lockean. If a person 'mixes' his labour with a previously unowned object, e.g. land, he is entitled to it. Although there may be few genuinely unowned natural resources (in the Lockean sense) in the contemporary world, liberals argue that a private property system still allows for much greater liberty than all known alternatives. However, the fact that land is in fixed supply, and therefore generates 'economic rent' for the lucky owner, has led some liberals to recommend some restrictions on individual land ownership. Spencer, in his early writings, suggested that land should be communally owned.

The liberal justification of private property is not only based on a natural rights argument. It is also argued that individualistic ownership leads to greater economic prosperity since private owners will make more efficient use of property than state controllers. This is partly because of the incentive structure of a private property system and partly because the flow of 'tacit' knowledge, on which economic progress depends, is greater in it. Public officials do not know how to use property efficiently. These two reasons have influenced many liberals, including J. S. Mill, to oppose progressive taxation because this prevents new entrants into the market acquiring sufficient property for their personal independence.

For liberals, property is indissolubly bound up with liberty. The presence of private property holdings is an essential element in the freedom from state control of individual lives. In a socialist system formal guarantees of civil liberties are ineffective if private means for making use of them are not available. In a market economy even individuals with little in the way of tangible goods still have freedom in their own persons to make the best of their life. Although some liberals, such as Nozick, have recognized that, logically, a free market could restrict liberty if vital resources fall, legitimately, into a few hands, it is argued that open competition and the price system make this unlikely.

Although conservatives believe in the importance of private property on some of the above grounds, there are crucial differences. Traditionally, they have rejected the 'individualizing' of property and prefer to derive property from ancient and feudal law. Thus they have favoured primogeniture, the system by which landed estates are passed on to the eldest son, since this preserves the integrity of the aristocracy. They do not favour that fragmentation of property which is regarded so highly by liberal individualists. There is an essential link between property and family in the conservative ideal of an organic society. Hence it is argued that private property should be vested in the church, guilds, and the aristocracy rather than possessed exclusively by atomistic individuals: though this is a traditionalist rather than a modernist conservative argument.

Since the conservative sees property as an indispensable element in social order, rather than as primarily a means to liberty, that person would not permit unrestricted use of private property. Thus public regulation of private property, to protect a heritage and tradition, would be permissible.

Even though the modern conservative accepts the capitalist property system, its expansion must always be checked and validated by the permanent interests of society. Like socialists, some conservatives fear that large-scale accumulation of assets by private business corporations can be a threat to ordered liberty. Since landed property has a social value beyond that which is revealed in economic exchange, conservatives are prepared to use the law to preserve its integrity. This may mean the prevention of business expansion in rural areas and the exemption of landowners from general taxation. Also, conservatives believe that monuments and other symbols of the national heritage should be protected from the normal exchange process in property titles.

NB

Further reading

Becker, L., *Property Rights*, London, Routledge & Kegan Paul, 1977.
Blumenfeld, S. (ed.), *Property in a Humane Economy*, La Salle, IL, Open Court, 1974.
Furubotn, E. and S. Pejovich, *The Economics of Property Rights*, Cambridge, MA, Ballinger, 1974.
Ryan, A.J., *Property and Political Theory*, Oxford, Blackwell, 1984.

PROTESTANTISM

Protestantism is a type of Christianity which appears in the sixteenth century with the Reformation and the division of the medieval church. The main theologian of Protestantism was the Frenchman Calvin who formulated the central doctrine of predestination. According to this, salvation comes only from the free gift of divine grace; moreover, God has decreed from before the Creation who is to receive this. There are two kinds of people – the elect, chosen for salvation, and the reprobate, doomed to eternal damnation. One's status as elect or reprobate is fixed and immutable. The question is how to know if you are elect? Calvin's answer was that the elect would have an inward conviction or faith. There would also be outward signs, such as a moral and upright life. Unfortunately there was always the possibility of error – you might only think you were elect. Relapse into sin (e.g. sinful thoughts, especially carnal ones) was a sign that you could well be reprobate. This led in practice to an emphasis upon introspection and self-analysis and, arguably, the creation of a strongly 'inner directed' and self-aware personality.

The attitudes of conservatives and liberals to Protestantism are mixed to say the least and depend upon the interpretation of its historical significance held by the individuals concerned. It is an undoubted fact that in Britain and America there is a close historical connection between Protestantism and liberal individualism, while Roman Catholicism was until recently associated throughout Europe with conservatism. There is also the controversial argument associated with Weber of the connection between Protestantism and the 'spirit of capitalism'. According to this, protestantism promoted a philosophy of life and morality which was especially congenial to the emergence of what Weber called the 'capitalist spirit'. In particular it encouraged self-control, personal responsibility, acquisitive individualism, 'deferred gratification', and what is often called 'the Protestant work ethic', i.e. the idea of work as a moral duty and essential feature of the good life. This thesis has been severely criticized but is still influential, especially with modern American neo-conservatives, who argue that capitalism depends upon the kind of morality described by Weber and fear the consequences of the (perceived) decline of the 'protestant work ethic' and its replacement by an 'ethic of hedonism'.

In England from the seventeenth century onwards there has been an intimate connection between liberalism and extreme Protestantism, so much so that nineteenth-century liberal politics was largely the politics of Non-conformity. This led to a school of history in which the histories of liberty and Protestantism were seen as almost identical. Historical Protestant figures such as Cromwell and Milton were prominent in the liberal pantheon. Overseas, the sixteenth-century Dutch Revolt was presented by historians such as Motley as both a struggle against the Catholic tyranny of Spain and a positive fight for freedom. In this way of thinking Protestantism had been both a positive force for liberty and the source of much of the liberal ideology. A similar tradition existed in the United States, with the recalling of the Protestant foundations of New England and the central part of Protestant theology in the development of liberal ideas in the colonial and revolutionary period. Again, particular Protestant figures, such as Williams and Penn, were part of the patriotic pantheon. All this, while often true enough, overlooked the often repressive and intolerant practice of Protestantism and the stultifying effect on personal development of much of its theology. The counter-tradition, strong on the continent, but found among Anglo-Saxons as well, saw Protestantism as a disruptive and subversive force which had played a major part in the destruction of stable community and authority and the atomization of society. This view of Protestantism's historical significance is still strong amongst traditionalist conservatives in both Europe and America. This perhaps reflects the strong association of this school of conservatism with Roman Catholicism and, in the English context, High Anglicanism.

SD

Further reading

Kossman, E.H. and A.F. Mellink (eds), *Texts Concerning the Revolt of the Netherlands*, Cambridge, Cambridge University Press, 1974.
Laski, H.J. (ed.), *A Defence of Liberty Against Tyrants*, London, Bell, 1924 (1574).
Tawney, R.H., *Religion and the Rise of Capitalism*, London, John Murray, 1926.
Woodhouse, A.S.P., *Puritanism and Liberty*, London, Dent, 1974.

PUBLIC CHOICE

Public Choice is a theory of politics, sometimes called 'the economics of politics', which explains and predicts political behaviour on the assumption that political actors are rational 'utility maximizers', seeking to promote their own self-interest. This view of man, which has been fruitful in explaining economic behaviour, is applied to politics, in contrast to theories which see politics as the pursuit of the public interest. The conclusion of most Public Choice writers is that government is much larger than people desire because the preferences of politicians, bureaucrats, and interest groups are satisfied instead. The leaders of the Public Choice school are Buchanan and Tullock, who founded the Centre for the Study of Public Choice and the academic journal *Public Choice*.

Buchanan and Tullock present a contract theory of the state according to which the state exists to protect individual rights and to provide public goods in return for obedience. Such decisions will be accepted even when they are not unanimous providing that rights are protected, but when the state goes beyond that to the transfer of resources, the legitimacy of the state is questioned and disobedience grows. This contract between individuals and state is not a historical description but a standard by which to measure the role of government which has gone far beyond the limited government of the contract. Public Choice explains why government has grown by the behaviour of politicians, bureaucrats, and interest groups.

Politicians are perceived as vote maximizers, eager to retain office. In order to win votes, politicians use competitive vote-buying, promising voters benefits without regard to costs. One example is the political business cycle, when governments increase the budget deficit or the money supply before an election, to boost employment and create an impression of prosperity, aware that the negative consequences will not occur until after the election.

The self-interest of bureaucrats is 'size maximization' or empire-building, because the status, salary, power, and desire for a quiet life are increased with the size of the agency or 'bureau'. Bureaucrats are in a strong position to obtain their goals because of their strategic location, their control of information, their low costs of organization, and their ability to co-operate with interest groups. Bureaucrats are usually monopoly suppliers of their services to politicians, and the politicians with responsibility for the oversight of bureaucrats often represent groups with a high demand for the service, so there is an oversupply of the service and a lack of incentives to be efficient. Niskanen, who has developed a Public Choice model of bureaucracy, has argued that the budget and outputs of bureaucracies are up to twice that which the voters would demand if they were aware of the costs.

Interest groups are the third source of over-government. Small and homogeneous groups, like manufacturers or workers in the same industry, will be easier to organize than large and diverse groups, such as taxpayers and consumers. These organized groups are distributional coalitions, attempting to redistribute income and wealth in their favour by the use of government power. They are likely to be successful because they are the direct beneficiaries, while the costs are dispersed widely, so there is little incentive to organize against them. Examples are the influence of farmers over subsidies and industries over protection. Olson has used this problem of 'concentrated benefits and dispersed costs' to explain the rise and decline of nations, as stable societies accumulate more interest groups over time, who concentrate on the distribution rather than the production of the economic pie. The destruction of these groups in the Second World War helps to explain the economic miracles of Japan and West Germany.

Although conservatives feel that it exaggerates the self-interested and rational side of man, Public Choice is now widely used by conservatives to explain the growth of government and why it has been so difficult to reduce it. Public Choice has been influential in the movement for a balanced budget amendment of the US constitution and the political strategy behind privatization in the United Kingdom.

NA

Further reading

Buchanan, J. *et al.*, *The Economics of Politics*, London, Institute of Economic Affairs, 1978.

Buchanan, J. and G. Tullock, *The Calculus of Consent*, Ann Arbor, MI, University of Michigan Press, 1962.

Niskanen, W., *Bureaucracy and Representative Government*, Chicago, IL, Aldine, 1971.

Olson, M., *The Rise and Decline of Nations*, New Haven, CT, and London, Yale University Press, 1982.

Tullock, G., *The Vote Motive*, London, Institute of Economic Affairs, 1976.

PUBLIC GOODS

The effectiveness both of the extended market order and of its essential institution of private, pluralist, or, as Hayek would have us say, several (as opposed to common or collective) property, depends upon the fact that in most cases potential producers of wanted goods and services can reasonably expect to be able, if and when they have once produced these goods or services, to restrict their provision thereof to those particular persons who are prepared to pay for that individual provision. Public or collective goods are, in economics, defined as those goods and services the provision of which cannot be so restricted – either because non-payers cannot be excluded from enjoying the goods if they are provided at all; and/or because it is not possible to determine effectively how large a share each actual beneficiary has enjoyed. Among the stock examples of such public goods are streets and street lighting, police protection, such navigational aids as market buoys or marine lighthouses, and national defence.

The first two points to notice are: that in the present context possibility and impossibility are sometimes a matter of degree or of greater or lesser costs; and that technological changes may from time to time shift some particular sort of good or service from one category to the other, and then later perhaps back again. Before the invention of radio-telephony providers of concerts and other entertainments could fairly easily arrange to charge all and only those coming during performances within earshot and/or within sight of their stages. Afterwards the only possible, and notoriously less than perfectly efficient, way of charging those receiving broadcasts of such performances became some sort of state enforced licensing of the possession and operation of radio receivers – as in the United Kingdom. The same before the development of cable technology, and of devices for scrambling and unscrambling, used to be true of television transmissions.

It is not possible for providers to continue their provision indefinitely unless at least their costs of production are somehow refunded. Since we cannot, if payment is voluntary, reasonably expect all, or even perhaps many, of those to whom such public or collective goods are supplied to pay their fair share, it becomes necessary, if these goods and services are to be provided sufficiently or at all, to call in some level of government. For government, enjoying as it does a legal monopoly on forcible extortion, is able either to compel everyone to pay the costs directly or itself to fund the provision in some way or other – normally out of tax monies collected under the threat of force.

The final sentence of the previous paragraph is, as it needs to be, carefully phrased. For it is too often taken for granted both that any good or service supplied by any public body has to be supplied without charging at the point of supply, and that all public goods, if they are to be supplied at all, must necessarily be supplied by some directly or indirectly government owned and operated producer. As an argument this is no better than the contention that 'He who drives fat oxen must himself be fat'. Presumably the reason why both assumptions are nevertheless still widely cherished is that the two examples of public goods most commonly cited are, on the one hand, national defence and, on the other, police protection and the criminal justice system as a whole.

But what is true of these two paradigm cases is not true of all public goods. Furthermore, it is wrong to insist upon applying these same assumptions to all the goods and services which particular governments may from time to time decide ought to be available to, and perhaps ought to be compulsorily consumed, either by absolutely all their subjects or else by all members of particular sets of those subjects. All First and Second World governments long ago decided that at least a minimum of medical and educational services must somehow be made available to all, and almost all have made exposure to some measure of those educational services compulsory. ('Consumption' hardly seems the right word here: the brutes – all animals, that is, other than the human – are not the only creatures which may be led to the water but cannot be made to drink!)

It is, however, possible in both these most important cases, as well as in many others, to achieve these comprehensive ends by making use of three different sorts of providers, whether separately or in combination. In the case of medical services the example of Britain – which in 1948 established the National Health Service (NHS), which has since become the second largest, if not the largest, single employer outside the former socialist bloc – has been followed in only one other First World country, Italy. And even in Britain there is a small but growing independent sector as well as, most recently, an attempt to improve efficiency by introducing market discipline into parts of the NHS. The possible alternatives or complements to such state provision are provision by for-profit and non-profit organizations, with various tax-funded arrangements to ensure that services are equally available to all those who could not otherwise afford to pay.

Whatever might be said about educational programmes broadcast on radio or television, there appears to be little room for a public good justification for any tax-funded state support for the supply of educational services – at least in the present, economists' understanding of the term 'public good'. But it is commonly argued even by liberals that such support, especially in order to ensure some universal minimum standard of achievement, is necessary in the public interest; inasmuch as and in so far as, besides being good for the educated, such education also has indirect, neighbourhood effects on others. It thus becomes a public or collective good in a different sense.

None of this, however, even begins to warrant the establishment of a state education monopoly, even at the primary or secondary level. Faced with such systems the liberal is bound to recall J.S. Mill's warning:

> A general state education is a mere contrivance for moulding people to be exactly like one another: and as the mould in which it casts them is that which pleases the predominant power in the government, whether this be a monarch, a priesthood, an aristocracy, or the majority of the existing generation; in proportion as it is efficient and successful, it establishes a despotism over the mind, leading by natural tendency to one over the body.

For a liberal the ideal here must surely be an independent education for all: an educational system, that is, in which every school, however it may be owned and run, has to attract customers who have a choice of some other school; a system in which the teachers are, because the fees follow the pupils, truly independent professionals. To ensure that no child is deprived of education by reason of parental poverty the liberal will advocate a tax-funded voucher system: the sort of scheme first suggested by the radical Paine, urged by J.S. Mill in the work cited above, and in our own time merely revised and named by Friedman.

In so far as taxes are extracted to finance not 'redistributive' handouts to favoured sets among the citizenry but only the provision of public goods, there is a ready reply to the libertarian contention that taxation is theft. Certainly it is true that direct taxes on income or capital do constitute extortions under the threat of force of property which was, presumably, justly acquired. But in the present case such taxing may reasonably be considered as the extraction, under the threat of force, of payment of a debt due for services actually rendered.

AF

Further reading

Cowen, T. (ed.), *The Theory of Market Failure: A Critical Examination*, Fairfax, VA, George Mason University Press, 1988.

Hayek, F.A., *Law, Legislation and Liberty*, Chicago, IL, and London, Chicago University Press and Routledge & Kegan Paul, 1982, Ch. 14.

Mill, J.S., *On Liberty*, many editions, 1859.

Seldon, A., *Charge*, London, Temple Smith, 1977.

R

RACE

The first distinction needed is between race and culture. For it is by confounding these two concepts that many people conclude, invalidly: that multiracial societies have to be multicultural; and that an education embracing some study of British history, of the Hebrew Bible, and of Greco-Roman civilization cannot be accounted multicultural. Such nowadays common confusions are preposterous. For it is heredity which determines race, and necessarily. But cultures are products only of interactions between environments and the choices of individuals. Certainly, whereas individuals may socialize themselves out of one culture and into another, always providing that the other is not defined as racially exclusive, they cannot choose their race.

The prime sources for the doctrine that culture, and especially national culture, is conditioned or even perhaps wholly determined by race were Gobineau and H.S. Chamberlain. This in its most notorious and catastrophic form was the fundamental misguiding doctrine of Hitler's National Socialist German Workers' Party. That entire tradition should be dismissed out of hand, if only because of the amount of interbreeding which has occurred between members of whatever varieties are to be distinguished within what quite certainly is a single species. But, equally certainly, this is not to assent to the 1965 proclamation of the US Department of Labor: 'Intelligence potential is distributed among Negro infants in the same proportion and pattern as Icelanders or Chinese, or any other group. . . . There is absolutely no question of any genetic differential.'

It is in the last degree unlikely that this claim is correct. Indeed the strength and persistence of the opposition to scientific investigations here must suggest that these opponents are themselves less than completely confident of what open-minded enquiry would reveal. However what is most important for us is to appreciate the unimportance of the disputed questions. For if there are differences in the distribution of different particular genes within the gene pools of these different sets, then all that will follow is that there must be differences *on average* between the

219

members of these different sets; that the members of one are *on average* more this and less that than the members of another. From statements about the average characteristics of the members of some set, however, nothing can be validly deduced about the actual characteristics of any particular member of that set.

But racism – in the only sense in which that much abused term of abuse refers to a sort of action to be unreservedly condemned as self-evidently wrong – is a matter of advantaging or disadvantaging someone for no other or better reason than that he or she happens to be a member of one particular racial set and not another. Such behaviour is obviously wrong, because obviously unjust. For, while there are very few, if any, cases in which racial set membership is properly relevant, justice essentially requires the treating alike of all (but only) relevantly like cases.

It is nowadays often taken for granted that the rejection of racism demands denial that there are – even on average – any substantial, hereditarily determined and occupationally relevant differences between the memberships of different racial sets. But any usage of the term 'racism' demanding such a denial should be put down as altogether unacceptable and obnoxious. For it makes racism, in the most literal sense, a heresy. Heretics are anathematized not for what they do or fail to do but simply for holding what are alleged to be false beliefs. If this is what racism is to be, then we are left with no warrant for denouncing the racist as wicked. Of what moral fault is the heretic supposed to be guilty – always, of course, providing that that person's convictions, however mistaken, result from honest and open-minded enquiry?

Far more dangerous and disruptive is the concept of institutionalized racism. Under this it is stipulated that, in a racially mixed society, everything causing the members of some racial minority to be, relative to their representation in the population as a whole, underrepresented in any sort of desirable position or occupation, must be put down as racism; but now as institutionalized racism. By thus redefining 'racism' in terms of social consequences rather than of individual intentions, these redefiners remove the original grounds for moral condemnation without even attempting to provide any substitute.

By accepting that racism so redefined remains an abomination, we become, most paradoxically, committed to institutionalizing racism, as previously understood. For, if anything causing these disfavoured under-representations has to be repudiated, and unless they are in fact wholly or mainly due to hostile racial discrimination, then we find ourselves committed to introducing all manner of paradigmatically racist practices. It may start only with 'affirmative action', to seek out more well-qualified candidates. But – unless the underrepresentations really have been largely if not entirely due to hostile discrimination – it soon moves on to preferential hiring, 'positive discrimination', and mandatory quotas.

However commendably colour-blind it may actually be, any system of testing or selection resulting in underrepresentations in desirable occupations (or overrepresentations in undesirable positions) then has to be replaced by some substitute under which skin pigmentation becomes a decisive determinant of success or failure. Some or all of these practices have been and are officially and more or less strongly promoted in the United Kingdom, the United States, Australia, Malaysia, and elsewhere – including the Republic of South Africa.

The most effective nutshell refutation of the assumption that any considerable overrepresentations or underrepresentations have to be due to positive or negative racial discrimination is to point out: that, whereas only 3 per cent of the population of the United States are Jews, 27 per cent of America's Nobel Prize winners have been Jewish Americans; and that, whereas not more than 13 per cent of the population of that country is black, blacks provide over half of all America's professional basketball players. Even the most doctrinally infatuated 'anti-racists' must, surely, be hard put to bring themselves either to accuse the classically Nordic committee selecting Nobel Prize winners of pro-Semitic prejudice; or to contend that the predominantly white managements in the intensely competitive business of professional sport are pro-black bigots.

Anyone, however, who is more deeply interested in and concerned about the problems of assimilating and integrating racial and other minorities and of providing equality of opportunity for people of different races, sexes, or national origins has to turn to the by now abundant writings of Sowell, a Harlem-raised, Chicago-trained, black American economist.

Sowell's *Ethnic America* is a study of the track records of all the main sets of Americans, by origins: the Irish, Germans, Jews, and Italians from Europe; the blacks from Africa; and so on. Sowell deploys overwhelming evidence of spectacular differences between these track records; differences which simply cannot be explained by anything other than what were, in the broadest sense, the cultural differences between the members of the different sets in question. Often these – unlike the set of blacks – were sets the members of which could not easily be distinguished as such by outsiders.

AF

Further reading

Flew, A.G.N., *Sociology, Equality and Education*, London, Macmillan, 1976, Ch. 5.
Sowell, T., *Ethnic America*, New York, Basic Books, 1981.
Sowell, T., *Markets and Minorities*, New York, Basic Books, 1981.
Sowell, T., *The Economics and Politics of Race*, New York, William Morrow, 1983.
Williams, W., *The State Against Blacks*, New York, McGraw-Hill, 1982.

REASON

In philosophy the concept of reason is normally contrasted with experience as the source of our knowledge of the external world. Rationalists maintain that an understanding of existence is by means of mental categories that are prior to all experience and that therefore knowledge is a complete deductive system. Empiricists say that reason is limited to the manipulation of analytic truths (as in formal logic and mathematics) and the classification of empirical data: knowledge is acquired by observation and experience and is therefore never certain. This has ethical and political implications. Rationalists argue that appropriate moral and political systems can be demonstrated objectively while anti-rationalists hold that normative judgements that are not in some way grounded in particular political traditions are utopian; their implementation will necessitate authoritarianism and, possibly, totalitarianism. Conservatives are always anti-rationalist: many classical liberals are also sceptical of the claims of an unaided reason but there is a rationalistic wing of individualism (libertarianism) which is as critical of tradition as are socialist utopians.

In Marxist and socialist thought, the strong rationalistic element that they display makes them revolutionary doctrines. This is because all received traditions of economic and social organization, especially market systems and common law rules, are criticized according to abstract rational plans of a more humane and socially just order. Marxism in theory is a scientific account of the development of social systems in accordance with changes in the economic mode of production; so that the demise of capitalism and its replacement by socialism (and ultimately communism) is a historical prediction rather than a product of human reason. However, in practice communist orders have been imposed in countries which, in Marxist terms, were not yet ready for fully fledged collectivism. Hence Marxist critiques of capitalism tend to be conducted in rationalist terms rather than in terms of the 'inevitable' collapse of market and private property systems.

More humanistic Marxists and orthodox socialists use reason overtly to condemn traditional political and economic systems. Socialist economists believe that the market does not contain adequate co-ordinating mechanisms and that, in the absence of state direction and control, it will produce periodic unemployment and the under-utilization of resources. The role of reason here is crucial because it is assumed that reason is a human faculty that can take a synoptic view of the economic universe and thence design an economy so that the perfect co-ordination of individual action is achieved without the trial and error of the market. In ethics, the socialist rationalist presupposes that income can be distributed to individuals according to merit, need, and desert rather than by the apparently random processes of the market and the accident of inheritance.

The anti-rationalist conservative tradition begins with Hume. He argued that reason is, and could only be, the 'slave of passion'. By this he meant that reason is inert: it cannot motivate us to action nor provide any foundation for moral and political values. As he put it, somewhat dramatically, it is not against reason 'to prefer the destruction of the world to the scratching of my finger'. He opposed, therefore, all attempts to found property, law, and justice on abstract principles of natural law. Nevertheless, there are reasons to prefer some moral and political principles over others. Although morals are derived from the passions, experience shows that men tend to approve of those laws and institutions that have utilitarian value. Thus rules of justice and property will develop spontaneously as conventions: they will survive, not because reason determines that they are 'efficient', but because they are consistent with more or less permanent features of the human condition, such as scarcity, limited altruism, and a natural tendency in people to prefer the present over the future. Thus although such rules are 'artificial' they are natural to the extent that imperfect men cannot do without them.

In a not dissimilar manner, Smith and Burke claimed that tradition and experience were better guides to the conduct of human nature than an unaided reason. In *The Theory of Moral Sentiments*, Smith attacked the 'men of system' who thought that a human society could be arranged as if it were like the pieces on a chess board: they neglected the fact that individuals moved and acted independently of rational plans. Burke attributed the French Revolution to the malign influence of abstract ideas. In his view 'prejudice' had its 'reason' which was derived from tradition and incapable of being expressed in ideological form. Hence, men's 'rights' were prescriptive; derived from a particular mode of political behaviour rather than deduced from an alleged universal entity, 'man'.

Although this anti-rationalist conservatism is of a broad utilitarian kind, it should not be confused with the utilitarianism of Bentham and his successors. These do presuppose that reason can prescribe a utility function (the 'general happiness') for society as a whole; and existing laws and institutions are to be evaluated in accordance with this. Since the common law had developed spontaneously, it was unlikely to meet the standards set by a rationally designed legal order and was, to that extent, condemnable. The anti-rationalist argument, however, is that the human mind is incapable of designing such a perfect order. In the absence of that knowledge which would be required for such a legal code, traditional rules and practices provide more reliable guides to conduct and therefore have an indirect utilitarian justification.

In the twentieth century, the conservative philosopher Oakeshott and the classical liberal Hayek have continued the anti-rationalist tradition. Oakeshott attacks the Cartesian legacy in European thought that pre-supposes that the mind can be drained of all prejudice so that reason can prescribe political forms independently of experience. Oakeshott argues that this is a delusion: all prescriptive political philosophies are 'abridgements' of existing practices and traditions. The political error in the rationalist attitude lies in the fact that it emphasizes 'technical knowledge' (i.e. knowledge that can be articulated in codes and manuals) rather than 'practical knowledge' (knowledge that is derived from experience of political life and cannot be precisely expressed).

In Hayek's liberalism, anti-rationalism takes the form of a critique of all attempts to plan and design a human society as if it were an 'object' or mechanical entity. Rationalism derives from a misunderstanding of the nature of the market. A market is an exchange process through which individuals make better use of necessarily dispersed information than could a central planner. In his later political writings Hayek argues that appropriate rules and institutions will emerge through a process of natural selection. Evolution will determine social and political forms. In this view, 'survival' is the test for the validity of an institution rather than its conformity to the standard of abstract reason; and societies prosper to the extent that they 'imitate' successful practices. Although much of Hayek's work (especially *The Constitution of Liberty*) is in the tradition of 'critical rationalism', i.e. institutions are appraised in the light of their contribution to human progress and freedom, some critics have argued that the stress he places on social evolution has an unfortunate disabling effect on the role of reason in human affairs.

A clearer exposition of critical rationalism is perhaps to be found in the political philosophy of Popper. Although he has produced devastating critiques of all varieties of collectivist rationalism (Platonism, Hegelianism, Marxism, and utopian engineering), he retains a faith in reason. Piecemeal social engineering and the rational design of small-scale social institutions remain as important elements in his liberal–conservatism. For him the model of the scientific community, characterized by the method of seeking truth by conjecture and refutation, is the standard at which a rational politics should aim.

There is, however, a much more rationalistic type of classical liberalism, associated with the followers of Mises. Here the model of a free enterprise society based on the universally true principles of subjectivist economics is held to be appropriate for all circumstances. The knowledge of the co-ordinating mechanisms of the market, the explanation of money, the role of prices, and the theory of production and distribution are held to be prior to all experience. Social institutions have value to the extent that they aid the operation of the free market. Since tradition and the results of evolutionary processes have no intrinsic value, this rationalistic liberalism would license the rejection of all institutions that appear to impede the operation of a complete *laissez-faire* economy. It contrasts with a crucially important feature of 'critical rationalism', namely, the argument that revolutionary change is to be distrusted because the human mind cannot predict all the consequences of institutional innovation.

NB

Further reading

Hayek, F.A., *The Counter-Revolution of Science: Studies in the Abuse of Reason*, Glencoe, IL, The Free Press, 1952.
Hume, D., *Essays Moral, Political and Literary*, ed. E. Miller, Indianapolis, IN, Liberty Classics, 1985.
Oakeshott, M., *Rationalism in Politics and Other Essays*, London, Methuen, 1962.
Popper, K.R., *The Open Society and its Enemies*, London, Routledge & Kegan Paul, 1945.
Smith, A., *The Theory of Moral Sentiments*, Indianapolis, IN, Liberty Classics, 1976.

RELIGION

Although Christianity does not formally entail a conservative attitude in politics, it strongly supports it, for the following reasons. Like conservatism, Christianity stresses the flawed character of human nature: selfishness and lust for power on the one hand, weakness and liability to be overcome on the other. Christianity has a stake in the past, as does conservatism, for the truth about what has happened ought to be preserved and handed on. Christianity stresses the importance of intermediate institutions between the state and the individual, notably the church and the family. Their existence diffuses power and stimulates individual initiative. Finally, both stress the centrality of personal responsibility.

The Christians' attitude to the law is an important theological and political crux. It is clear from the New Testament that Christians have a fundamental obligation to obey the 'powers that be', e.g. Caesar, whose rule is ordained by God. But there are limits to such obedience. In particular, a Christian ought not to obey a law which forces him or others to sin.

Conservatives of whatever religious stripe would find natural political allies in such Christians. However, as is well known, the political attitudes of individual Christians and whole churches have ranged from pietistic withdrawal from society (as in the case of the Mennonites) to an espousing of revolutionary socialism in the name of Christ (as in the case of liberation theology) to support for persecuting policies and connivance at dictatorship. Behind such atypical positions have usually been either an optimistic view of human nature, leading to the belief that the kingdom of God can be established on earth, or cynical political calculation.

Turning from doctrine to institutions, the Christian church has sometimes been part of a social elite, part of an establishment in a formal legal as well as in a sociological sense. Some versions of Christianity have seen a formal church–state link as important and natural, others have seen it as compromising and worldly, and have advocated a sectarian approach. Such an approach is not synonymous with political radicalism, however, as can be seen from the vigorous church life in the United States and in the history of orthodox Dissent in England. Indeed the history of Dissent, at least until the era of the 'Nonconformist conscience', can be taken as a model of the way in which a disadvantaged minority may argue and lobby for the removal of those disabilities within the framework of the rule of law.

Difficult problems can arise in the area of religion and national identity – a tension between respect for that identity and either political or religious imperatives. This tension can be illustrated from both the political and social problems raised by the presence of important racial and religious minorities in otherwise fairly homogeneous nations, and by the religious imperative to evangelize while at the same time respecting cultural and social identities.

The position of classical liberalism *vis-à-vis* religion is more ambivalent. Historically speaking, in England liberalism has been the product of Protestant dissent. But onto it has been welded a view of human nature and human capabilities having much in common with the Enlightenment. On this view the basic political problem is the existence of social barriers to freedom of expression. Such political liberalism has found in religious liberalism a natural bedfellow. In so far as liberalism upholds the rule of law, and supports institutional independence, it has the general support of Christians; the line must be drawn at the progressivism of liberalism, even though such a view can often be traced to millenial ideas arising from within the Christian tradition. The extent to which religion, and in particular Calvinism, is a crucial factor in the rise of modern capitalism is a matter of continuing debate.

Just as the political allegiances of Christians in the modern world are very varied (partly due to the varied political arrangements in which they find themselves), so it is equally difficult to generalize about the other 'major religions'. The Jews have frequently benefited from the freedoms of capitalism, yet Jews such as Marx and Marcuse have been in the vanguard of socialism. This is perhaps due to the fact that historical capitalism has been an outgrowth of conservative Christian conditions with which Jews have found it difficult to ally themselves intellectually.

While other-worldliness is a marked feature of both Buddhism and Hinduism these religions nevertheless have a considerable political impact, yet one which it is difficult to classify in Western political terms. Hinduism, for example, is vitally concerned to uphold the caste system, and its attitude to the natural world makes it either indifferent or antagonistic to the development of science and its application in technology, whether or not these applications are made on commercial grounds.

There are similarly divergent, even contradictory, emphases in Islam. On the one hand there is a fatalistic tendency and a theocratic emphasis which is at odds with individual liberty, responsibility, and entrepreneurship. On the other hand many Muslims are willing to fund capitalistic ventures through oil revenues, to import technology and the appropriate infrastructure, and, at the individual level, to take advantage of trading opportunities in establishing shops and other businesses.

The respective attitudes of the classical liberal and of the conservative to these diverse phenomena will themselves differ. The liberal will find many of these political standards falling short of his or her ideals, and will work for change. The conservative will be more ambivalent, less willing to disturb national and regional cultures in the interests of progress, while nevertheless believing that often the degree of personal liberty and cultural opportunity people in such circumstances enjoy falls below that which he or she enjoys and regards as tolerable.

PH

Further reading

Block, W., G. Brennan, and K. Elzinga (eds), *Morality of the Market: Religious and Economic Perspectives*, Vancouver, Fraser Institute, 1985.
Eliot, T.S., *The Idea of a Christian Society*, London, Faber & Faber, 1954.
Norman, E., *Christianity and the World Order*, Oxford, Oxford University Press, 1979.
Novak, M., *The Spirit of Democratic Capitalism*, New York, Simon & Schuster, 1982.
Sombert, W., *The Jews and Modern Capitalism*, London, T. Fisher Unwin, 1913.

REPUBLICANISM

Republicanism is a political philosophy based on a reading of classical history which has influenced both classical liberalism and conservatism and provided a critique of them. Classical republicanism, or civic humanism as it is sometimes called, was a political philosophy which appeared in northern Italian city states in the fourteenth and fifteenth centuries. This was a time of great interest in the life and ideals of classical antiquity. The Italian philosophers and historians were particularly interested in the accounts given by classical authors such as Sallust, Tacitus, and Livy of the rise, decline, and fall of the Roman Republic which they saw as paralleling their own historical experience. This interest found its classic expression in Machiavelli's *Discourses upon Livy* and in this and other texts the doctrine of republicanism was formulated.

The starting point was the belief that the highest form of life was that of republican liberty. A republic was a state in which all adult citizens participated in public affairs, the *res publica*. This was to be contrasted with monarchy where only one person participated, and with oligarchy where it was confined to a small minority. Central to this was the argument that public life was superior to private affairs and that true freedom and fulfilment could only be achieved through participation in the public life of the community. This state of republican liberty, however, was fragile and delicate. It depended for its existence upon *virtu*. This meant roughly, public-spiritedness – being prepared to sacrifice one's personal interests to the public good – as well as virtue in the wider sense of honesty, moral uprightness, and probity. This was seen as exemplified in actions such as that of Brutus the Elder in sentencing his own sons to death for treason. This quality found its most complete and perfect expression in the act of dying for one's country. It was thought that the appropriate type of army for a republic was therefore a militia, enrolment in which was a civic duty, as opposed to either a conscript or mercenary army. The great destroyer of *virtu* was 'luxury', i.e. an excessive concern with worldly goods. Trade was seen as promoting this and hence as demoralizing, especially as when compared to the inherently virtuous activity of agriculture.

The Italian city states all became either oligarchies or princely despotisms by 1500, with Venice the only possible exception. The philosophy of republicanism, however, survived and became more sophisticated as its theorists sought to explain the failure of republics to sustain themselves by producing a theory of the necessary conditions for republican liberty. The most important work in this tradition for later history was Harrington's *Oceans*, published in England in 1656. In this work Harrington argued that an active and virtuous citizenry required a wide distribution of property, especially in land, so that no one would be utterly dependent for their livelihood upon the whim of another since all would be economically independent. His followers also argued that stable republics would have a 'mixed' constitution, i.e. one which combined elements of the three forms of government, monarchy, oligarchy, and democracy.

This philosophy was very influential in the intellectual life of eighteenth-century Europe. There are certain motifs, themes, and arguments which derive from classical republicanism and which recur many times in the political literature of the time. These are the advocacy of a citizens' militia as opposed to a standing army; of the need to maintain a balanced or mixed constitution in the face of an alleged growth of executive power and corruption; of laws and reforms to check the concentration of landed wealth and create a class of independent small proprietors; of direct participatory democracy as the highest form of politics and the key to the good life; and of vehement demands for the restoration of civic virtue, seen as threatened by the growth of trade and 'luxury'. The literature and art of the time are replete with motifs drawn from Greco-Roman history which often put over a republican message. Republican ideas were influential in both the Scottish and Continental Enlightenments. Rousseau was almost entirely a product of this tradition. In the French Revolution many of the leading figures were classical republicans, including Robespierre and Saint-Just. Many of the American founding fathers were strongly influenced by these ideas, particularly among the Virginians.

Classical republicanism has therefore had a marked influence upon liberalism. However, the relationship is ambiguous. Many liberals have explicitly rejected republican ideals. One of the earliest to do so was Constant, who compared ancient and modern ideas of liberty to the former's disadvantage. He argued that the classical definition of liberty was participation in the decision-making process while the modern definition was the absence of forcible restraints. Classical republicanism has also provided the basis for many sharp critiques of liberalism, mainly on the grounds that it lacks a definition of the good life and fails to promote virtue. Republicans also argue that liberalism promotes a selfish private-minded attitude which undermines civic responsibility and that this leaves liberal democracies vulnerable when challenged militarily by despotic regimes.

Republicanism as a political philosophy has been revived and recon-stituted in recent years, in the work of writers such as Arendt and Sandel. Much contemporary socialist writing is actually articulating a republican 'line'. The main response to this from classical liberals has been, first, to reiterate the criticisms made by people such as Constant and, second, to point out that while long on diagnosis the 'neo-republicans' are short on prescription. They offer an extended critique of liberal capitalist democracy but make no concrete suggestions as to what should replace it. This suggests that while it may remain influential in the academy, republicanism will have little influence on politics.

SD

Further reading

Fink, Z.S., *The Classical Republicans*, Evanston, IL, Northwestern University Press, 1945.

Pocock, J.G.A., *The Machiavellian Moment*, Princeton, NJ, Princeton University Press, 1975.

Sandel, M., *Liberalism and the Limits of Justice*, Cambridge, Cambridge University Press, 1982.

REVOLUTION

Although often used loosely to mean simply a big change, the term 'revolution' has a more specific meaning in political and historical thought. Broadly, it refers to change or attempted change in the social, political, and economic order which is fundamental, abrupt, and violent. Revolution is to be contrasted with evolutionary or piecemeal change which is limited, peaceful, and builds on the past rather than attempting a decisive rupture.

Revolutions are radical in the strict sense of going to the root or origin of political and economic systems but are not necessarily radical in the popular sense of 'left wing'. Today a revolution may be 'right wing' in conventional terminology if it seeks to replace a socialist or interventionist system with a market led one.

In fact, revolution, as defined above, is a modern phenomenon both in theory and practice. Before 1789, although European history was full of political upheavals and violence, there were no revolutions or revolutionaries. Rather, there were rebels and rebellions. In a rebellion violence is used to attain political ends such as a change in policy or the location of power, but there is no desire or intention to alter the system. Indeed, historically many rebels have taken up arms to defend established institutions against innovations, e.g. by a reforming monarch. (Of course the result of rebellion may be to bring about change but that falls into the category of unintended consequences and such change is inevitably limited rather than total.)

Before the nineteenth century, 'revolution' was used in its literal sense of rotation, and when applied to political events described a process by which affairs, after being 'turned upside down', returned to their original position. By 1800 the word had acquired a popular meaning of a great upheaval or disturbance but still with the assumption of an ultimate restoration of some status quo ante. The modern theory of revolution as a conscious attempt to change the social and political order in a permanent and radical fashion was only developed in the middle part of the nineteenth century. Once developed the concept was applied retrospectively as a category of analysis to past events. Thus, the achievement of independence by the American colonies only became widely known as the American Revolution after 1815. This change occurred in response to the French Revolution of 1789, correctly seen by many observers as something unprecedented in human affairs, the concept being used to describe the events of that time.

The French was the archetypal revolution, archetypal in the true sense of being the original model or exemplar of revolution. The response to that event by contemporaries and near-contemporaries was also archetypal and the critique and account of the French Revolution by Burke and others are the origin of all subsequent conservative and classical liberal theorizing on this subject. For progressives of all types and particularly for Marxists revolutions are both benign and inevitable. In Marxist thought revolutions are the moments of crisis which mark the transition from one social system and mode of production to another. For Marx revolutions, although bloody, would be brief, with the overwhelming mass of the population opposed only by a small class of exploiters, the revolution being necessary because of the refusal of any ruling class to give up its power voluntarily. Lenin introduced several new elements, the most significant being the notion of the vanguard which would act on behalf of the mass of society who lacked sufficiently advanced consciousness. In this he was translating into theory the practice of revolutionaries, from the Jacobins onwards.

Conservatives and classical liberals are profoundly hostile to revolution both as theory and reality. From Burke onwards they have attacked both on a variety of grounds. First, there are consequentialist arguments to the effect that the outcome of revolution is necessarily undesirable even in terms of the revolutionaries' own aspirations. The outcome of revolution is disorder and ultimately despotism even worse than the original state of affairs. This happens because the attempt to effect fundamental change in a short space of time disrupts or destroys the informal institutions upon which society depends and abolishes the structure of tacit yet binding rules which govern human interactions, particularly political ones. Consequently there is a state of chaos in which only force is available to settle disputes and maintain order. Violence is also needed to bring about fundamental change because such a process inevitably arouses an extreme response from those affected as well as being unwelcome to the great majority of any population. Since freedom and a peaceful social order depend upon the existence of a settled and strong civil society which a revolution will inevitably undermine no revolution can lead to either peace or freedom.

Second, conservatives and classical liberals have attacked the theoretical basis of revolution. What revolutionaries do is to amend or do away with the traditional and customary institutions of society so as to bring things into line with some abstract model. This is, in Hayek's terminology, constructivist rationalism, a misunderstanding of the limitations of human reason and knowledge. Traditional institutions and beliefs articulate and express the tacit knowledge which is spread throughout society and are for Hayek the product of a process of evolution in which undesirable practices have been eliminated. No person or group can fully comprehend the nature or working of the social order and so it is theoretically impossible to redesign society from a priori principles. Moreover, revolutionaries claim to know what the result of their actions will be, either because they are acting in accordance with absolute reason (e.g. the Jacobins) or else because they are the agent of a deterministic process of historical trans-formation (e.g. Marxist/Leninists). This is arrogant and again theoretically impossible as all human actions have consequences which are unforseeable.

For Burke and many other conservatives there was another reason for hostility to revolution, perhaps the most fundamental: that it was in a very real sense impious. For Burke, society was a contract between the living and both the dead and the unborn, an organic entity which could not be radically transformed by any one generation without a breach of that contract and duty. Moreover, society as the product of long organic development was the child of divine providence and to attempt to remake it in accordance with some human design was to substitute the will of man for that of God. Furthermore, the notion, common to revolutionaries from Saint-Just onwards, that the world is totally and irredeemably corrupt and can only be saved by a sweeping away of all existing institutions and a 'fresh start', is a heresy, derived from the Gnostic belief that the world is the creation of the Devil.

However, conservatives and classical liberals from Burke onwards have not been against all change and many have advocated reform as the most sure defence against revolution. Also, although a critic of the French Revolution, Burke was an ardent defender of the Glorious Revolution of 1688. Much conservative and classical liberal writing on this topic contrasts two kinds of revolution with 1688 and 1789 seen as the rival models. The definitive version of this is found in Macaulay's *History of England*. For Macaulay, 1688 was a limited and preservative revolution which confirmed and perfected an existing constitution and prevented its subversion by the Stuarts. It made no major change in politics or society but rather clarified and strengthened what already existed, so building on the past rather than seeking to replace it. It also created a mechanism which made future peaceful change possible, hence it was the last revolution experienced by England. Two other revolutions are often put in this class of 'conserving revolutions', the American Revolution of 1776 and the Dutch Revolt of 1567–1609. All of these created stable and liberal societies.

There is also a wealth of conservative and classical liberal writing on the cause and nature of actual revolutions. For Burke and many others the origin of revolution is found in the activities of the intelligentsia who, alienated from traditional society, undermine the established order and justify violent revolution as well as often leading it. For Hume all political unrest was the product of a crisis of legitimacy since for him social and political stability depended upon the tacit consent of the governed rather than force. He also emphasized the role of intellectuals as well as the disruptive effect of popular 'enthusiasm'. A sociological account of revolutions was first produced by De Tocqueville in his *The Ancien Régime and the French Revolution*. He pointed out that in 1789 France had never been more prosperous and argued that the revolution was caused by rapid economic development which had undermined the old institutions of the state. This model, of revolution as a result of the social stress consequent upon the move from traditional society to modernity, has been used to explain the Russian, Chinese, and Iranian revolutions among others. Other conservatives, notably Dostoevsky in *The Possessed*, have stressed the widespread occurrence in modern society of a certain type of personality, alienated and disaffected from conventional life, which produces a hatred of existing ways of life and a desire to destroy them.

The main difficulty for the conservative and classical liberal view of revolution can be simply put. All of the above is all very well if, like Burke, you are fortunate enough to live in a polity which has evolved into a humane regime, but what if you are living under a despotic government? In the modern context, what view should you take of revolution against totalitarian regimes, particularly communist ones? Historically some liberals, such as J.S. Mill, have supported the use of force to overthrow despotic regimes either by outside intervention or else by revolution. Even so, such liberals have applied a form of the 'just war' argument, i.e. that revolution is only justified if there is no alternative and the result will be an undoubted increase of liberty. This leaves much room for argument as debate over support for movements such as the Nicaraguan Contras indicated. As regards methods, the dominant liberal view has been to support the idea of a 'counter-society' strategy where the institutions of a free civil society are constructed within the framework of a despotic regime. Poland is sometimes cited as an example of this.

SD

Further reading

Bailyn, B., *The Ideological Origins of the American Revolution*, Cambridge, MA, Harvard University Press, 1967.
Burke, E., *Reflections on the Revolution in France*, Harmondsworth, Penguin, 1968.
Macaulay, T.B., *History of England* (1848–61).

RIGHTS

Following the classic analysis of the American legal theorist Hohfeld, two basic types of rights exist. If someone has a *liberty* right, they are not prohibited from engaging in the activity to which they have a right. If someone has a *claim* right, others are under an obligation not to interfere with them. As an example, if someone is at liberty to speak in Hyde Park, they violate no prohibition by doing so. If they do not have a claim right to speak, others can interfere with them, e.g. by shouting them down or by speaking themselves, denying them the platform. If the person was in their own home, they presumably would have a claim right to speak. Others would then be under an obligation not to interfere with them.

To complete this analysis of rights, one needs to specify what sort of obligations and prohibitions are involved. Generally, legal and moral rights are distinguished from each other. Legal rights answer the question: what rights exist in a particular society? Normally, the permissions and obligations of a legal system are backed by the coercive power of the state. The question raised by moral rights is a different one – what rights ought one to have? The two types are, however, connected in that the political rights someone ought to have usually are held to consist of the rights that ought to be granted them by their legal system.

Much more controversial than the analysis of rights is the proper answer to the question of what moral rights should exist. Here conservatives and classical liberals tend to diverge in their views. The former position usually maintains that moral rights are not for the most part a matter of abstract principles. Instead, the moral rights appropriate to a particular society depend on its history and traditions. Classical liberals, by contrast, *do* view rights as a matter of principle.

One way to bring out the difference more clearly is to compare Burke's *Reflections on the Revolution in France* (1790) with J.S. Mill's *On Liberty* (1859). Burke contrasted the French Revolution with the Glorious Revolution of 1688. The first of these, in Burke's opinion, was based on the arbitrary speculations of philosophers. They wrongly thought that the basic principles of society are open to choice. Instead, custom and prescription are the proper basis of social order. Whether an abstract principle is 'correct' or not cannot be determined, for two reasons: the consequences of a principle can be known only in practice; and the value of the social institutions that the new principle will overthrow is beyond the power of reason to understand fully. Thus, the risks of instituting a new principle are incalculable. The claim that the new principles are supported by reason often serves to cloak destructive passions.

The classical liberal position maintains that because of the existence of conflicting traditions, prescriptive right cannot be a fully adequate guide to social policy. In some instance, e.g. in Mill's *On Liberty*, classical liberals held that the 'tyranny of society' needed to be guarded against as well as political despotism. 'Experiments in living', not adherence to tradition for its own sake, were desirable. Mill contended that the state could interfere with individuals only when their actions harmed others, not for their own benefit. Freedom of speech and religion were subject to few if any limitations. This again contrasts with the conservative view, which usually favours restriction on speech deemed subversive and often supports an established church. Mill, unlike Burke, supported the French Revolution, although he condemned the Jacobins.

Although Mill defended individual rights, he did so on the basis of utilitarian arguments. To allow individuals a wide sphere of autonomy is the best way to promote the general happiness. Many classical liberals favour a different approach, in which individuals have 'natural rights' to liberty and property. In this view, rights of liberty and property possess moral force apart from their value in promoting social welfare. Locke's *Second Treatise on Government* is the most influential example of this view.

Although there are substantial disagreements between conservatives and classical liberals, important similarities exist also. Both strongly support the rights of individuals to own property and oppose socialism as destructive of individual liberty. Classical liberals have always favoured a free market economy, and most contemporary Anglo-American conservatives agree with this. Both positions also support reliance on voluntary associations to provide social services rather than the state. Twentieth-century conservatives have come to share the distrust for the state characteristic of classical liberals.

Nevertheless, some points of disagreement remain even in these areas. Conservatives usually value the preservation of landed estates through primogeniture. Also, many conservatives tend to be sceptical about industrialism. This emphasis is not characteristic of classical liberals, although some 'conservative liberals,' e.g. Ortega y Gasset, share it.

Marxists tend to view rights as part of an order that the future will transcend. The new era will bring about general abundance, and conflicts among people will cease to be significant. No one will need to insist on their 'rights' against others. All varieties of conservative and classical liberal thought resolutely oppose this chiliastic position. It leads to dictatorship and totalitarianism, as regimes attempt to remould human beings to fit the supposed utopia to come.

DG

Further reading

Allison, L. *Right Principles: A Conservative Philosophy of Politics*, Oxford, Blackwell, 1984.
Kirk, R., *The Conservative Mind*, Chicago, IL, Regnery, 1952.
Nozick, R., *Anarchy, State, and Utopia*, Oxford and New York, Blackwell and Basic Books, 1974.
Rand, A., 'Man's rights', in *Capitalism, the Unknown Ideal*, New York, New American Library, 1967.
Rothbard, M., *The Ethics of Liberty*, Atlantic Highlands, NJ, Humanities Press, 1982.
Scruton, R., *The Meaning of Conservatism*, London, Macmillan, 2nd edition 1984.

RULES

A rule, as Kant might have had it, is a kind of imperative. So rules can sensibly be addressed to or followed by only those creatures which are capable of conduct; those creatures, that is to say, which are capable of acting in one way or another, or in any one of several others.

Rules may nevertheless be followed by individual people or by sets of several people who have never formulated those rules, and who were perhaps at the time incapable of producing explicit and adequate formulations. The most persuasive illustration of that truth is provided by the natural languages. For every term in any such language acquires and retains its particular meaning only in so far and for so long as the various rules prescribing and defining the correct usage of that particular term are customarily observed by those who employ that language. Yet the fact is that few of these rules are ever formulated; while even to understand any formulations which have been excogitated it is necessary first to have attained at least some minimum competency in the language employed in that formulation.

If, however, and *per impossible*, people were to succeed in formulating all the rules of correct usage for their entire vocabulary, then this knowledge – that these were indeed the right rules – would become a handicap rather than a help to the retention of their logically prior knowledge – how to communicate in that language. For to communicate with any tolerable degree of fluency they would have to put all these fine formulations out of their minds; relying on their previous purely practical verbal training to ensure that, unconsciously, they followed all the right rules.

So, whatever the merits of legal positivism as an account of established systems of statute law, it remains certain that the legendary or semi-legendary lawgivers of ancient societies must have been codifiers and, hopefully, improvers of often unformulated traditional rules customarily observed. Once this is recognized it becomes easy to appreciate the folly of Voltaire's exhortation: 'If you want good laws, burn those which you have and make new ones.'

That exhortation is an expression of what Hayek has labelled and denounced as constructivistic rationalism. This kind of Cartesian approach can be made to many matters. In the *Discourse on the Method* Descartes himself recommends its application to the problems of legislation: 'the greatness of Sparta was due not to the pre-eminence of each of its laws in particular . . . but to the circumstances that, originated by a single individual, they all tended to a single end'. Later Leibniz was to propose the similarly *ab initio* artificial construction of what would supposedly be the logically perfect language.

Against the constructivistic rationalist the objections of the conservative are in both cases the same. Certainly, as traditional rule systems both of language and of law are confronted with newly arising circumstances – circumstances which were unforeseen and perhaps unforeseeable at the times when their constituent rules first became established – there will be many possibilities of and needs for reform. But the prudent reformer will always remember that traditional systems must embrace, however inadequately, the knowledge of a great many people who lived in the successive generations through which those systems survived. Conservatives will, therefore, be reluctant to reshape any parts, much less the whole, of any such traditional systems – at least, until and unless they have enquired and are sure that they know not only why these rules became established and survived so long but also that the needs which presumably they once met either obtain no longer or else can be better met by the introduction of different rules.

In its most extreme applications constructivistic rationalism demands not some fresh system of rules, artificially created instead of naturally evolved, but rather the total abandonment of all rules, in favour of somehow dealing with every successive situation as it arises on the basis of some estimate of its merits. In the field of morals this abandonment is approached by what calls itself 'situation ethics', while it may be said to culminate completely in the professed 'immoralism' of Keynes and his Bloomsbury set. In the field of politics and government, constructivistic rationalism can lead to a Leninist rejection of the very idea of a transcendent rule of law. For, for the Leninist, the putative interests of the proletariat must always override the at most subordinate and derivative claims of any law, or rule, or regulation whatsoever.

AF

Further reading

Hayek, F.A., *Law, Legislation and Liberty*, Chicago, IL, and London, Chicago University Press and Routledge & Kegan Paul, 1982.
Oakeshott, M., *Rationalism in Politics*, London, Methuen, 1962.
Rawls, J., 'Two concepts of rules', *Philosophical Review* 1955, VI: 3–13.

S

SCEPTICISM

'Scepticism' may be defined as an enquiring inclination to doubt whether knowledge has in fact been obtained or whether it is even attainable. People may, of course, be sceptical on some issues or in some areas but not in others. J.S. Mill suggests that what he describes and deplores as Hume's Toryism in politics might be explained by reference to Hume's general and indeed systematic scepticism. This was a notably insightful observation. For both in Mill's own day and since, it has been Hume's sceptical eschewing of all religious belief and practice which has so often prevented conservatives from recognizing that it was Hume rather than his younger contemporary Burke who was the founding father of the modern conservative intellectual tradition.

But now, why and how far should sceptical considerations lead to conservative conclusions? In so far as the scepticism concerns the objectivity of values, the implications must generally be liberal rather than strictly conservative. For unless my values are somehow objective and endowed with a transcendent authority it is hard to see what justification I might offer for striving to impose these values upon other people. The truth begins to emerge only when conservative is contrasted not with liberal but with socialist. For those things about which conservatives are by their cloth sceptical are all the projects of what Hayek has called 'constructivistic rationalism'. Of these projects socialism itself perhaps constitutes the perfect paradigm case.

Constructivistic rationalists are in their method and approach radically Cartesian. They call always for new beginnings upon foundations swept clear of all the supposedly useless detritus of the past. (We need to recollect that Plato too insisted that, before they embarked upon any exercise of wholesale utopian social engineering, his Guardian elite would require 'a clean canvas'.)

Although most of his successors have been prepared to make way for a more collective leadership, Descartes himself suggested that it would

238

nearly always be best if great projects were directed by a single mind:

> Thus we see that buildings planned and carried out by one architect alone are usually more beautiful and better proportioned than those which many have tried to put in order and improve, making use of old walls which were built with other ends in view. In the same way also, those ancient cities which, originally mere villages, have become in the process of time great towns, are usually badly constructed in comparison with those which are regularly laid out on a plan by a surveyor who is free to follow his own ideas.

The traditional conservative objection to such constructivistic rational-ism in its application to political and social affairs is that in thus proposing to create institutions anew it refuses to take account of the wisdom and experience embodied in institutions which have evolved and survived through several generations. But in our century a further and, surely, more powerfully persuasive and sceptically conservative objection has been developed. It is an objection drawing upon rich experience – rich experience, generally, of the unexpected and often unwelcome outcomes sometimes produced by even the most benevolently intended policies; and rich experience, particularly, of the immense and catastrophic human costs of the success of Lenin's October coup, and of the immediately consequent attempt forcibly to realize the Marxist socialist project over one-sixth of the land surface of the earth.

This further sceptical objection has been deployed most famously by Popper. To appreciate its full force it is necessary first to spell out – as Popper himself has never done – the compelling rationale in both theoretical and practical enquiry for what he calls (not the sceptical but) the critical approach. (This remarkable neglect is, presumably, to be explained by reference to Popper's too charitable reluctance to suggest that any of his intellectual opponents may have been, or may be, acting in bad faith.)

The crux is the almost tautological truism that persons sincerely pursuing any purpose must as such be concerned to monitor their progress in that pursuit; and be ready, if it seems that they are having no success, to adopt any available alternative and apparently more promising tactics. From this it follows, for instance, that a man sincerely concerned to find the Holy Grail will not want either to be deceived or to deceive himself into accepting any fraudulent substitute however seductive. He will instead be constantly anxious to examine all evidence suggesting that what he has in his treasury, and what he so strongly hoped was the genuine article, is in fact, after all, demonstrably not.

Again, a woman who sincerely wishes to know the truth about something must be resolved to accept no substitute belief, however conformable to her interests or consistent with her prejudices. Instead she must be ever ready to attend and to give due weight to upsetting evidence, to falsifying fact. To be ready to do and to do just this is to adopt the sceptical, Popperian, critical approach.

When we turn to matters of practical policy it now becomes equally obvious that, for instance, if and so long as the true purpose of promoting some particular educational policy is to bring it about that all our children achieve higher levels of educational attainment, then the promoters will be concerned to discover whether that objective is in fact being achieved; and ready, if it is not, to change their tactics. If they are not so concerned, and if instead they are eager to suppress any findings suggesting that that policy is in fact failing to accomplish its originally stated purpose, then the inference to be drawn must be either that that never was, or that it has by now ceased to be, their true purpose.

Popper wants to dig a deep divide between wholesale, utopian, social engineering – which he rejects – and piecemeal, reformist, social engineering – which he admits. In the light of what has just been said it is easy to see how a sceptical, conservative, and properly Popperian dividing line is to be drawn. Policies can be admitted as acceptably piecemeal and reformist only so long as it is possible continually to monitor their success or failure in achieving their originally stated objectives; and possible also to change course fairly promptly if it turns out either that those objectives are not being achieved or that, if they are, it is at unacceptable costs.

AF

Further reading

Hume, D., *Essays Moral, Political and Literary*, ed. E.F. Miller, Indianapolis, IN, Liberty Press, 1985.
Popper, K.R., *The Open Society and its Enemies*, London, Routledge & Kegan Paul, 5th edition 1956, Vol. I.

SCIENTISM

This is the belief that the methods used in the study of the natural sciences are equally appropriate when employed in studying all aspects of human behaviour – e.g. in economics, sociology, or psychology. It is the slavish, uncritical, and inapt limitation of the methods and language of science. The practice of scientism is described as *scientistic*, which should not be confused with *scientific*. To be scientific is to start by being open-minded in deciding the most appropriate method of study for a specific problem; to be scientistic is to apply the methods, say, of physics to anything and everything in an unthinking habitual manner.

Scientism assumes that the only true source of factual knowledge is the method of the natural sciences – especially physics. This is in contrast to the view that the social sciences are inherently different from the natural sciences. The term 'scientism' was first introduced in this sense by Hayek in *The Counter-Revolution of Science* (1952) in which he traces the origins of scientism to eighteenth-century France among the scientists of the Ecole Polytechnique, who took the lead in all the important fields of study of the natural world. The spirit of the age in its most extreme form is demonstrated by the teachings of the mathematician Laplace, who envisaged the theoretical possibility that by collecting enough measured data and devising correct models, the movements of all the atoms in the universe, including those of which humans are composed, could, in principle, be known and hence forecast accurately. Today, through developments in modern physics and mathematics such as quantum theory and chaos theory, it appears probable that Laplace's dream is both theoretically and practically impossible even in physics itself.

As applied to the study of society, scientism attained its most influential and clearest formulation in the work of Auguste Comte, who is regarded as the founder of positivism. He rightly predicted that man, having shed attempts to explain natural phenomena in terms of the actions of gods and spirits in favour of scientific method, would then introduce this approach into sociology, ethics, and political economy.

Objections to scientism cannot be well founded on the proposition that scientific method should be reserved for the study of inorganic matter, since biology, physiology, and psychology, for example, are successful fields of enquiry into living things – human and non-human. A better way of looking at it, perhaps, is to concentrate on certain concepts with which scientism is commonly associated: objectivism, holism, and historicism. Objectivism entails measurability, but in the study of society the un-measurable elements may be the most important, as, for example, in the theory of value in economics; holism often pervades the unthinking use of macro-economic data such as the Gross National Product or the Retail Price Index, ignoring the importance of the underlying subjectiveness of individual action; historicism, which exaggerates the possibility of predicting the movement of social 'forces' and 'trends', lends a misleading and spurious simplicity to complex events.

The most significant example in economics of the failure of scientism as a method of giving a true picture of reality is to be seen in equilibrium models of the market. Market forces are often unquantifiable, subjective, and unpredictable. Furthermore – and this is the important point – even those data that are measurable are inherently unpredictable since they do not exist until they have been generated by the market process. It is from this consideration that the theoretical criticisms of the possibility of 'market socialism' are derived.

AS

Further reading

Hayek, F.A., *New Studies*, London, Routledge & Kegan Paul, 1978, Chs 1 and 2.
Hayek, F.A., *The Counter-Revolution of Science*, Indianapolis, IN, Liberty Press, 2nd edition, 1979.
Popper, K.H., *The Poverty of Historicism*, London, Routledge & Kegan Paul, 2nd edition, 1960, repr. 1984, Ch. 23.

SOCIALISM

In English the term 'socialism' appears to have been printed first in 1827 or 1828, characterizing the views of Robert Owen. In France it first appeared a few years later, a description for the teachings of Saint-Simon. By 1840 it was throughout Europe in common use to mean a doctrine that all property, or at least – as Clause IV of the Constitution of the British Labour Party was to have it – all the 'means of production, distribution and exchange', should be socially owned and controlled. What in practice this has been taken to involve is that any firms not owned and run by the national or local state should be of that kind of extended partnerships known as co-operatives. In Israel, for instance, both the state-owned airline and the autonomous *kibbutzim* are acceptably socialist institutions.

By the end of the century, most Continental socialist parties affiliated to what was later to be identified as the Second International – including the Russian, which would shortly be split into Bolshevik and Menshevik factions – called themselves social democratic. Most were in doctrine more or less explicitly Marxist, and all admired and modelled themselves on the German. Lenin's own Marxist admiration for that paradigm social democratic party ceased only with the shock of the news that its deputies in the Reichstag had in 1914 voted for war credits. It was after the establishment of a Leninist collective despotism over the Union of Soviet Socialist Republics, and the formation of The Third International dedicated to the universal extension of such rule, that persons and parties remaining affiliated to the Second International first began to distinguish themselves as democratic socialists.

Due partly to participation in government, and partly to experience of 'actually existing socialism' in the ever more numerous countries under communist rule, the commitment to the socialist ideal in several of the Continental social democratic parties has progressively weakened. The Swedish, for instance, nationalized virtually nothing during its first forty years in office. And at its 1959 conference at Bad Godesberg the German explicitly and categorically repudiated socialism. In that same year, Hugh Gaitskell as Leader of the British Labour Party – tacitly borrowing the key phrase with which, after the catastrophic collapse of his first venture into total socialism, Lenin introduced his New Economic Policy – appealed for a restriction of nationalization to 'the commanding heights of the economy'.

With no British 'economic miracle' to serve as a warning, all Gaitskell got was an insubstantial amendment to that crucial Clause IV.

It is thanks to these developments that the expression 'social democratic' has now come to be used to refer to an unequivocally democratic, strongly egalitarian, non-socialist mixture: a very extensive welfare state, combined with a pluralist, competitive market economy. It was in this understanding that people for whom the Labour Party had both remained too socialist and become too friendly to 'actually existing socialism' formed the British Social Democratic Party.

After the formation of the third Communist International (Comintern), members and supporters of its affiliates used to distinguish communism from socialism, and to this day no Leninist ruling party claims to have established communism. For them communism is a utopia where, after the 'shackles of capitalism' have been struck from the economy, socialism has brought in the Age of Abundance. Then the state 'withers away', and the principle of distribution is: 'From each according to their abilities, to each according to their needs.'

Let others employ the word 'communist' to describe, in the first instance, all members and supporters of Marxist–Leninist parties – whether or not these particular parties are from time to time in or out of communion with Moscow – and, by derivation, socialist regimes of the sort actually imposed and maintained by all such parties if once they are allowed to seize power. If and when such communists claim to have become non-revolutionary democrats and 'Eurocommunists', prudence bids us recall that eagerness to be voted in is no guaranteee of willingness to be voted out: 'There is', as Burke remarked, 'no safety for honest men, but by believing all possible evil of evil men, and by acting with promptitude, decision, and steadiness on that belief.'

Attacks upon the socialist ideal are of two kinds: they concern its practicality, or its desirability. The most sophisticated argument of the former kind was first developed by Mises in his 1919 article, 'Economic calculation in the socialist commonwealth'. Mises claimed to have demonstrated that, since the socialist planning board would have no genuine price system for the means of production, the planners would be unable to calculate rationally the costs or the productivity of these resources, and hence would be unable to allocate them rationally. Crucial to socialism is for central planners to allocate resources to fulfil the planners' goals. Mises strove to show that, even if we set aside the vexed question of whether the planners' goals coincide with the public good, socialism would not permit them to achieve their own goals rationally, let alone to achieve the goals of consumers.

The crux is that the rational planning and allocation of resources requires the exercise of economic calculation, and such calculation in turn requires resource prices to be set in free markets where titles of ownership are exchanged by owners of private property. But, since the very hallmark of socialism is government or collective ownership of all (non-human) means of production, this means that socialism will not be able to calculate or rationally plan a modern economic system.

The thesis that socialism is undesirable, because any country with a socialist command economy is bound to be comprehensively despotic, is an old one; and is often dismissed for this reason – for want, no doubt, of any more rational refutation. Even before Marx became a Marxist, his collaborator Ruge was calling the socialist dream 'a police and slave state'. In 1848 the vice-president of Blanc's party told Engels: 'You are leaning towards despotism.' Similar objections were developed later by Proudhon and by Bakunin. The biographical fact that neither Marx nor Engels ever published any attempt to meet such objections should suggest, what there is sufficient other evidence to show, that neither had much interest in individual liberty.

Socialists who are nevertheless sincerely democratic will want to suggest that, at least for those living in long and firmly established democracies, it is possible to reach full socialism gradually and democratically; and thereafter to retain, and perhaps even extend and improve, democratic institutions.

There is a strong case for concluding that it is not, that economic pluralism is a necessary, although not of course a sufficient, condition of political pluralism. This case was perhaps most famously argued in general by Hayek, and later supplied with post-Second World War British illustrations by Jewkes.

The most decisive possible refutation of this or any other thesis of impossibility is the production of an actual counter-example. But, although there are now a great many states which are as near as makes precious little matter fully socialist, in not one of these has an administration been removed from office as the result of a general election.

Certainly the Institute of Marxism–Leninism in Moscow is happy to recognize that, in a favoured Soviet phrase, 'this is no accident'. In 1971, with eyes most immediately upon Chile and France, it sketched a programme for achieving, through 'United Front' or 'Broad Left' tactics, irreversible communist domination:

> Having once acquired political power, the working class implements the liquidation of the private ownership of the means of production. . . . As a result, under socialism, there remains no ground for the existence of any opposition parties counter-balancing the Communist Party.

AF

Further reading

Hayek, F.A., *The Road to Serfdom*, London, Routledge & Kegan Paul, 1944.
Hayek, F.A., *The Fatal Conceit*, Chicago, IL, and London, Chicago University Press and Routledge & Kegan Paul, 1988.

Hoff, T.J.B., *Economic Calculation in the Socialist Society*, Indianapolis, IN, Liberty Press, 1981.

Mises, L. von, *Socialism*, Indianapolis, IN, Liberty Press, 1981.

Schumpeter, J.A., *Capitalism, Socialism and Democracy*, New York, Harper, 1962.

Shafarevich, I., *The Socialist Phenomenon*, New York, Harper, 1980.

SOCIETY

Although 'society' is the key concept in social philosophy, and the object of study of the empirical social sciences, it is not easy to define. Not the least of the difficulties is that theories of society frequently have a critical, and often ideological, aspect so that purported explanations of the concept are highly contestable.

At its simplest, and least controversial, a society is a set of interacting individuals whose behaviour is governed by general rules. Although in the ontological sense a society consists only of individuals, it may be said to have a history that transcends the biographies of its particular members. Societies acquire a persistence through time not merely because of the enforcement of general rules but through the agreement between its members over at least a minimum of common values. Societies are not necessarily politically organized entities; people may form coherent and persistent organizations for cultural, sporting, commercial, and other activities within the framework of a larger community. Furthermore, societies may be international in that people are often members of organizations that cut across recognized frontiers. Nevertheless, sociologists and political philosophers are interested in societies that are complex, highly organized, and the membership of which is to a greater or lesser extent involuntary.

A distinction should be made between society and the state. The regularities displayed by society exist independently of that agency with a monopoly of coercive power, i.e. the modern state. Anthropologists have described 'stateless' societies: entities which are held together by decentralized rules with no centralized law-enforcing or law-creating power. In modern Africa, tribal societies cut across artificial state boundaries. Societies may then be described in terms of spontaneity while states are constructed by agreement, artifice, and, frequently, force.

It is difficult, however, to conceive of society without law. Even though primitive societies do not have the modern paraphernalia of legislatures, statutes, and courts, they will have traditional rules to regulate behaviour. In 'liberal' social science, such rules, following Hart's analysis in *The Concept of Law*, are called 'primary rules', i.e. rules that prohibit certain actions. Primitive societies become more progressive as they develop 'secondary rules', i.e. rules that make possible the creation of new primary rules and of authoritative adjudication procedures, and provide for the final determination of legal validity.

Although social organizations seem to emerge without conscious design, sociologists sometimes, following Toennies, make a slightly different distinction: that between *Gemeinschaft* (or community) and *Gesellschaft* (society as an association). In a community individuals are held together by emotional ties and a belief in communal values; a society, however, is interpreted as an artifice required by calculating rational self-interested individuals. Once a distinction between society and the state is made, however, the distinction between *Gemeinschaft* and *Gesellschaft* may not be so crucial. Nevertheless, modern industrial societies are often described as types of *Gesellschaft* since in them communal loyalties have been to a great extent attenuated by egoistic values. In them stability, order, and predictability seem to be more a function of contract and artifice than of emotional and extra-legal ties. This, of course, does not preclude the existence of 'communities', identified by such things as race, religion, and culture, existing within legally organized societies. However, although societies might lack the intimacy of communities, modern political theory still distinguishes between the realm of social relationships, characterized by an important element of spontaneity, and that of the state, with its essentially coercive features.

In the history of political and social thought the concept of society has been a battleground for individualist and collectivist interpretations. In the individualist tradition, which begins in its modern form with Hobbes, society is regarded as a 'fiction'; it has no specific reference to 'reality' but is merely a convenient short-hand expression for the description of the interactions of individuals; laws and institutions are in principle the outcome of individual subjective choices since that is all of which social reality consists. This is not necessarily liberal (or individualist in a political sense) since the persistence of authoritarian social structures can in a methodological sense be attributed to subjective choice.

Nevertheless, this method of social analysis was used in a critical way by later utilitarians, especially Bentham and his followers. In this radical utilitarianism inherited social institutions had no intrinsic virtue: they were valued only to the extent that they maximized social utility (itself an aggregate social welfare function derived, allegedly, from individual preferences). This is in fact a critical normative theory of society concerned with how institutions can be improved: it has little to say about their historical evolution or the general conditions of social stability. Its vision of a society as a collection of abstract, atomized individuals concerned only to maximize their utility has been much criticized by socialists, conservatives, and some liberals. To the extent that sociology rests upon the assumption that there are social phenomena that are not reducible to the actions of individuals, its origins may be said to lie as much in conservative as in socialist thought.

There is, however, a crucial difference between the socialist and the conservative conceptions of society. The socialist tends to view social relationships as conflictual rather than consensual and claims that conflicts can only be permanently resolved by a fundamental economic reorganization of society. The conservative views society as a natural harmony of interests: it is a delicate arrangement of interrelated parts that is likely to be disrupted by deliberate plans for economic and political reorganization.

It is from Marxism that the conflict theory of society primarily derives. For Marx all history is described in terms of a struggle between social classes. The social classes themselves are defined exclusively in economic terms, i.e. in terms of the relationship of individuals to the means of production. In capitalist society, for example, the bourgeoisie own the means of production and the proletariat have only their labour power to sell. Hence these two classes must inevitably be in conflict: a conflict that can only be resolved by revolution. In a future classless society institutions such as law, private property, money, and the division of labour will be transcended by arrangements which reflect man's social and co-operative features rather than his egoistic and acquisitive ones. In the Marxist description of the relationship between man and society there is a rejection of that methodological individualism which abstracts man from his environment and attributes to him universal features. In contrast, it is claimed that man is a product of his social environment and that a change in this will eventuate in a change in the person.

Non-socialist sociological theory denies that the class structure of society is accurately described in economic terms. There are many other differences, especially those to do with status and types of occupation, which divide groups irrespective of economic considerations. Furthermore, it is claimed that the emphasis on class and class conflict is inappropriate: a society is a co-operative enterprise in which individuals are held together by common rules of just conduct. It is indeed true historically that revolutionary social change does not fit the class conflict pattern depicted by Marx. Most non-socialists would stress the importance of ideas in social change; ironically, Marxism itself has been crucial here.

Of greatest significance is the non-socialist critique of the collectivist reification of 'society': the view that society can have ends and purposes over and above individual ends and purposes. There are two major arguments here. First, such a conception of society erroneously makes individuals the helpless victims of mysterious historical forces. Second, it undermines individual responsibility for action: society is treated, anthropomorphically, as an entity to which blame and criticism can be attributed. Hence, in socialist thought, crime is often treated as if it were socially caused rather than a product of the actions of responsible individuals. The assumption that society can be understood apart from the actions of individuals underlies much of contemporary social engineering.

In contemporary liberal individualist theory a society is understood in terms of individuals whose actions are co-ordinated by the following of general, impartial rules rather than by direct command. Although this model of society is essentially individualistic it is very different from Benthamite utilitarianism in that it is denied that a social utility function can be computed from individual preferences. Instead, in an indirect utilitarian sense, social well-being emerges accidentally from the actions of decentralized agents. The most important examples of this phenomenon are market exchange processes and common law systems. The advantages that accrue from individual action stem largely from the fact that in modern complex societies central agencies can never have the knowledge that is required to co-ordinate the actions of millions of people. Much of 'social' knowledge is 'tacit' or 'non-articulated' knowledge, i.e. information which is constantly changing (e.g. prices in the market) and which is dispersed across all members of a society. Intervention that goes beyond the main-tenance of rules of just conduct will disrupt the flow of tacit knowledge. The major exponents of this view of society are Popper, Polanyi, and Hayek.

In Popper's 'open society' and Hayek's 'Great Society' the key descriptive feature is anonymity. Members of complex, industrial societies do not know one another and, therefore, if their actions are to be effectively co-ordinated, they have to submit themselves to the discipline of abstract rules. Modern society is largely based on contract rather than status and its fluidity and mobility depend upon the absence of fixed hierarchies and rigid castes or classes. However, many people find these abstract features uncongenial and yearn for the intimacy of 'closed' or primitive societies: societies which are much less mutable and are held together by religion and custom rather than general rules of just conduct. Popper interprets many of the crises and revolutions that occur historically as consequences of the traumas that accompany the transition from the closed to the open society.

In Hayek's social philosophy the doctrine of 'social' justice is seen as a major threat to the stability of the Great Society. In classical liberal theory, justice relates to individual conduct under general and non-discriminatory rules: only individual action in breach of such rules can be criticized as just or unjust. With regard to income distribution concepts such as 'desert' or 'need' are irrelevant: wages simply reflect the value of labour services as revealed in an impersonal market exchange process. Any attempt to alter the distribution of income away from the market's decision will lead to a misallocation of labour resources and, ultimately, transform a free and open society into a totalitarian society.

The liberal and conservative conceptions of society have much in common. Both evince an attitude which rejects the imposition of any particular 'end-state' or rationally designed pattern on a spontaneously evolving organism. In conservative thought this is best exemplified in Oakeshott's idea of a 'civil association'. This is a form of order in which individuals who pursue differing ends and purposes are held together by laws which in themselves have no end or purpose. Such laws prescribe the form in which individuals may pursue varying actions: in Oakeshott's description they are 'adverbial'. The rationalist error of the twentieth century is the supposition that ideal social blueprints can be prescribed for individuals independently of any social and historical experience.

There is, however, an extreme brand of liberalism – libertarianism. This does presuppose that individuals have rights against a social order, however well grounded in experience such an order might be. In Nozick's social philosophy individuals possess rights prior to all experience and no violation of these rights is permissible, even on indirect utilitarian grounds. While this, of course, does not preclude social co-operation it does reject the traditional liberal–conservative view that a social order is prior to the exercise of individual liberty.

NB

Further reading

Flew, A., *Thinking About Social Thinking*, Oxford, Blackwell, 1985.
Hart, H.L.A., *The Concept of Law*, Oxford, Clarendon Press, 1961.
Hayek, F.A., *Studies in Philosophy, Politics and Economics*, London, Routledge & Kegan Paul, 1967.
Popper, K.R., *The Open Society and its Enemies*, London, Routledge & Kegan Paul, 1945.

SOCIOLOGY

Both the classical liberal and conservative traditions of sociological thinking precede modern sociology, although it is impossible to disentangle their origins from the speculations of social philosophers and political theorists concerned to explain the origin of social life or to define the nature of the good society.

Smith is rightly celebrated as a key figure in the classical liberal tradition for it was he who most clearly demonstrated the existence of an alternative to authority as a basis for social order, namely the hidden hand of the market which regulates human activities as decisively as and more effectively than the clenched fist of the warrior or the raised palm of the priest. He did not, however, push the leaders of the hierarchies of church and state as firmly to the margin as his very varied nineteenth-century successors such as J. S. Mill and Spencer did. Spencer is in many ways *the* libertarian sociologist, opposed to all state regulations whether by socialists, conservatives, or those nineteenth-century liberals who put short-term social amelioration before what he saw as the eternal rules of libertarian social evolution. For Spencer the organization of societies tends towards either a militant or an industrial form. The former is characterized by hierarchy and status, obedience and discipline, and by compulsory co-operation, especially in the service of the state, and the latter by voluntary co-operation based on individual liberty and contract, with the state merely there to provide the minimal regulation necessary to guarantee the freedom and integrity of its citizens. The industrial form with its advanced division of labour and highly developed and differentiated institutions is for Spencer inherently the more progressive of the two although he sees all existing societies as containing both forms of organization. Spencer was the last thorough-going libertarian sociologist and it is difficult to believe today how very influential and popular his work once was.

In the twentieth century, liberals have been reluctant to describe and analyse how actual societies work. They have retreated to the abstract ideal worlds of social and political philosophy and to demonstrating how actuality falls short of their models of law and economics based on the interaction of lone individuals. Many of their ideas, though – notably those concerning the necessity and nature of spontaneous as opposed to planned order, the importance of the unintended consequences of human action, the limits to legal regulation, and the phenomenon of secondary deviance (i.e. if you prohibit an activity that others regard as legitimate their response will create more serious crimes and problems than those you are seeking to abolish) – have been incorporated into contemporary sociology, albeit without acknowledgement and in a rather biased way.

The failure of modern liberals to construct a sociology matching their contributions to law, economics, psychology, and philosophy often stems from their rather rigid commitment to methodological individualism which prevents them from making proper use of social variables or seeing societies or institutions as systems. The point is not whether these can or could be reduced to an aggregate of interlocking purposive individual acts, but rather whether there is any point in trying to do so. Perhaps in consequence, too, liberals are apt to see societies as cohering entirely or nearly entirely as a result of the mutual benefits that arise from the contractual links between individuals.

Conservatives, by contrast, see this as an inadequate answer to the central and problematic question of how order is established and main-tained. They perceive modern societies with their marked division of labour, diversity of interests, and pervasive individualism as requiring some kind of overall authority, loyalty, and morality if they are to survive. At the very least there must be some means of preventing individuals or groups of individuals from resorting to force, fraud, or the establishment of an entrenched monopoly and thus subverting a system based on mutual self-interest by the illicit pursuit of a particular self-interest. The more pessimistic (or, as they would say, realistic) conservative sociologists see society as ever likely to collapse into a war of all against all unless there is a generally accepted central authority that can hold it together. Some would go even further and declare that the social ideals of the liberals and even more so of the socialists are absurdly utopian, since the tendency to resort to force and fraud are universal and are to be found even within such central integrative institutions as the nation state and its religious, ideological, and military institutions. For this reason many conservative sociologists distrust as well as respect the state and stress the importance of local and intermediate institutions such as families, churches, professional bodies, voluntary associations, and regional assemblies which both enjoy a degree of independence from the state and have a degree of regulative authority over the conduct of individuals. Where such institutions are weak or absent, then an unstable 'mass society' exists which is all too likely to undergo a transformation into a totalitarian one where no institutions independent of the state and its ruling party are permitted to exist.

In the main, conservative sociology is comparative and anti-utopian. At the core of a conservative sociology lies the recognition that (i) in all societies certain inevitable tasks have to be performed such as economic production, defence, the resolution of disputes, the care and upbringing of children, (ii) all societies are imperfect and characterized to varying extents by inefficiency and deviance, by crime, corruption, negligence, and oppression, and (iii) there are limits to reform and improvement since the undue pursuit of a single value (much as in the case of material goods) has to be purchased at the expense of others. The task of the sociologist is not to contrast the present state of a particular society with some theoretical ideal but to compare actual existing societies or cultures in the hope of being able to explain how and why they differ.

Why is there relatively so little crime in Switzerland? Why is overall life expectancy increasing in the countries of the capitalist industrial world and decreasing in their socialist counterparts? Why do Japanese schoolchildren perform better than their European and American contemporaries? Why did industrialization occur earlier in Western Europe than elsewhere? Why are Irish Americans more likely to have problems with alcohol than Jewish Americans? Why are the majority of the world's stable democracies monarchies? Why do societies differ so much in their patterns of sexual morality? Why do Moslems in India have a higher birth-rate than Hindus? Such questions are or ought to be central to the thinking of the conservative sociologist.

The main difference that seems to set conservative sociologists apart from those of a Marxist or socialist persuasion is their pragmatic refusal to force the answers to social puzzles such as those cited above into a narrow pattern based on economic classes, dichotomous power relations, or some similar and often irrelevant obsession with inequality. Sociologists of an even moderately conservative persuasion are apt to use a greater range of independent explanatory variables. These include religion, cultural traditions and values, and patterns of family life, which they would argue give a fuller and truer picture of a complex social world, one that even in authoritarian socialist countries is rarely completely at the mercy of the powerful.

CD

Further reading

Aron, R., *Main Currents in Sociological Thought*, Harmondsworth, Penguin, 1967, Vols I and II.
Durkheim, E., *The Division of Labor in Society*, New York, Free Press, 1964.
Nisbet, R., *The Sociological Tradition*, London, Heinemann, 1967.
Spencer, H., *The Man Versus the State*, ed. D.G. MacRae, Harmondsworth, Penguin, 1969.

STATE

The role and significance of the state in social life is perhaps the single most important issue that divides liberals and conservatives. Although both schools of political philosophy have objected to the expansion of the state that has occurred in all western democracies in the twentieth century, they have differed over their analysis of the concept, its relation to other concepts, such as has law and society, and in their moral evaluation of it.

In the history of political philosophy there have been persistent attempts to determine 'essentialist' definitions of the state by the use of reason. Thus instead of identifying and describing particular states by normal empirical methods, philosophers have tried to construct definitions of state that capture its necessary features. Normally such definitions conceal a normative attitude, either favourable or unfavourable, towards the state. Such definitions are persuasive, i.e. designed to elicit some response from the reader rather than to convey information about existing states. In Plato's *Republic*, philosophy determines an 'ideal form' of the state (as representative of truth and justice) against which existing states appear to be imperfect copies. By contrast, in Marxist theory, the state is defined as the 'executive committee of the ruling class', whose typical mode of operation is coercive. In Marx's theory the institutions that divide people are private property, money, and the division of labour: once those are transcended, through a historical process of social and economic development, there will be no class rule and therefore no necessity for the state. It will 'wither away', its coercive laws replaced by 'administration' and competition replaced by co-operation.

In contemporary political theory an attempt is normally made to provide a neutral definition, to delineate those features of the state which distinguish it from other social institutions. Its value can then be assessed on some appropriate ethical or economic criteria.

A distinction is made between state and law (although it is much more precisely made by liberals). All societies have rules of some kind to regulate conduct but there is no logical necessity that such rules should be enforced by a monopoly agency. The modern state is distinguished by the public nature of its rules, its centralized authority, its determinate geographical boundaries, and its claim to a monopoly of coercive power. The term 'sovereignty' is usually used to describe the state's supremacy over other associations in a politically organized community, although some political theorists deny the necessity of a determinate sovereign for legal and political order.

By the state acting through public rules it is meant that certain disputes have a social dimension which cannot be incorporated in private law procedures. The public enforcement of criminal law is a quintessential example of state activity. The whole structure of a publicly organized court system, and the rules that govern public agencies, government departments, the police, and so on, constitute state-like phenomena. Even though individuals may settle disputes under a structure of private law, enforcement procedures by a public authority indicate the presence of the state. Societies vary in the nature of the public–private mix: in a highly *dirigiste* society virtually all of social regulation will be through public rules.

The existence of a state implies the centralization of power. Decentralized organizations such as churches and trade unions, which may appear to have power over their members not unlike that of states, are subject to the state's rules. However, states vary in the degree of centralization: some devolve considerable regulatory power to decentralized authorities, such as local governments. Genuine federal states allow great decentralization: thus although the police power is a public function it is exercised by a variety of local institutions.

States claim a monopoly of coercive power in the sense of denying other associations the right to exercise the defence and security functions. The theory of sovereignty presupposes that in the absence of a monopoly of coercive power society will collapse into disorder. However, states are not always successful in this claim.

Geographical integrity is the final feature of the modern state: unlike tribal society, the state has determinate boundaries. These boundaries are artificial and may not coincide with national or racial groupings. The state is then an artefact, a legal association whose public rules apply to whosoever shall reside within its boundaries or travel across them. As an artificial legal association the state may contain many different nationalities, races, and linguistic groups within its boundaries. Modern African states are unstable precisely because they are arbitrary constructions that cut across tribal (natural) human associations.

Anthropologists have traced the emergence of state-like forms in tribal society to the gradual passing of the function of the rule enforcement to a specialized central agency. Changes in agricultural production methods, irrigation, and so on are said to generate this process; also, private enforcement of traditional rules is simply inefficient. In Europe the modern centralized state emerged, especially in England and France, in the sixteenth and seventeenth centuries. The defining characteristics of the modern European state came to be law creation, i.e. the abandonment of Christian natural law, the erosion of common law by statute, and the claim to absolute sovereignty over a given territory.

Although Marxism presupposes the eventual demise of the state, communist regimes are characterized by all-powerful states in which public rules have obliterated private rules and the bulk of decision-making is centralized. Non-Marxist socialists have, however, accepted the role of the state in principle and do not envisage its disappearance. For them the state is not an instrument of pure coercion for it has a legitimate role in the supply of welfare and in the management of the economy. The socialist justification of the state depends upon, ultimately, an economic claim: that in the absence of central direction and public control, an economy cannot generate prosperity.

It is this rationale of the state to which liberals (and, to some extent, conservatives) have reacted. Although classical liberals accept the necessity of some state action they have chiefly emphasized its predatory rather than its productive role. Oppenheimer, in his *The State*, distinguished two methods by which men can gain sustenance: the economics method (production and exchange) and force. The state emerges when a particular group gains sufficient strength to exploit the economically productive groups. The main difficulty of classical liberal theory is that since it admits the legitimacy of the state, how is the institution to be prevented from becoming predatory?

What is distinctive of the modern liberal theory is that it explicates fully the rationale of state action. A state, defined conventionally, is needed because of 'market failure'. Although free exchange between individuals generates most wanted goods and services, there are 'public goods' which are not produced spontaneously. A public good is defined in terms of its being non-rival in consumption (i.e. the consumption of it by one does not reduce the amount available to others) and non-excludability (i.e. once supplied it is impossible to exclude from consumption those who have not paid for it – 'free riders'). This is known as the 'prisoners' dilemma', the situation in which rational self-interest leads to undesirable collective outcomes (as seen from the point of view of the same rational, self-interested agents). The rationale of the state lies in its capacity to supply public goods; it has no value beyond this.

Thus taxation to provide these goods and the regulation of 'negative externalities' (such as air pollution and other damage to the environment which cannot be priced) is permissible on individualistic grounds. Although the state operates necessarily through compulsion, it is thought to respond to the subjective wants of individuals. Thus liberal theory says that individuals 'agree' to state compulsion, in a manner not unlike Rousseau's paradoxical claim that individuals may be 'forced to be free' in obeying the General Will.

This liberal theory of the state derives from welfare economics. The difficulty is that the criteria proposed may permit state action beyond the limits prescribed by liberal individualist philosophy. Interventionist economics have had no difficulty in discovering a whole range of externalities and market failures which require corrective action by the state. The tendency has been to impose collective goods on society, e.g. the expansion of state education, health, and welfare services, on the ground that they benefit the community at large.

The liberal response to this has been to recommend changes in property rights structures so that negative externalities may be 'internalized' by individual actions at law. Furthermore, the welfare economist's notion of the 'social good' has been rejected on the ground that it does not reflect the subjective choices of individuals but the opinions of administrators (and welfare economists). Hence, liberals favour the return of many state-run services to private hands, and the construction of constitutional rules that protect individuals from predatory state action.

Nozick, in *Anarchy, State and Utopia*, is exceptional in claiming both that the state necessarily acts through compulsion and that in so doing it does not violate individual rights. His minimal state is said to emerge, by an 'invisible hand' process, as a kind of natural monopoly from a state of nature characterized by competing protection agencies. Nozick argues that the prohibition on independent agencies that the minimal state imposes is legitimate because their activities are 'risky'. The right to self-defence is not violated, Nozick claims, because independents are 'compensated' by the provision of protection at more or less zero price. Most critics, however, maintain that Nozick's state inevitably violates rights; they also have noted that he provides no constitutional machinery to prevent the expansion of the minimal state. The standard liberal defence of the state is still constructed around utilitarianism and public goods.

The conservative view of the state is complex and its methodological explanation quite different from the individualists', even though in practical terms conservatives often want a small state. The conservative does not normally make an analytical distinction between state and law. The state is not an agency that satisfies the subjective desires of individuals for public goods within a constitutional framework but is an organic entity that comprehends law, the constitution, and public morality. The state is said to embody collective ends and purposes, narrow though those might be.

From Hegel, the conservative holds that the state is an objective reality which, if it does not literally have a 'will' of its own, nevertheless cannot be reduced to individual choices. It has a biography in the sense that its organic growth proceeds independently of the intentions of the particular office-holders. Its spontaneous growth means that it represents immanent wisdom and morality, expressed in institutional form, which is superior to individual reason. Thus although political obligation is derived from a kind of approval, this is not the kind of consent envisaged in liberal rational choice theory: a theory that implies that laws and institutions are entitled to only a provisional acceptance. The state must be an instrument (ultimately) of force since without its overall authority 'civil society', the world of egoistic maximizing individuals, would be fragile. Implicit in this is a distinction between the 'idea' of a state and particular governments.

In conservative political philosophy there are no rational criteria for delimiting the appropriate sphere of state action; what the state should do depends very much on the traditions of particular states. Nevertheless, contemporary conservatives hold that if the state extends too far into the activities of individuals it will depart from its true function, which is to maintain the integrity and unity of a social organism. But since the conservative conception of society is organic, the state may provide welfare, and act paternalistically in matters of personal morality, in order to sustain social harmony.

NB

Further reading

Jasay, A. de, *The State*, Oxford, Blackwell, 1985.

Nozick, R., *Anarchy, State, and Utopia*, Oxford and New York, Blackwell and Basic Books, 1974.

Scruton, R., *The Meaning of Conservatism*, London, Macmillan, 2nd edition, 1982.

Spencer, H., *The Man Versus the State*, ed. D.G. MacRae, Harmondsworth, Penguin, 1970.

Whynes, D. and R. Bowles, *The Economic Theory of the State*, Oxford, Martin Robertson, 1981.

T

TAX

Taxes are exactions extracted under the force of law; and here the word 'force' needs to be stressed, since it is crucially relevant to all consideration of the justice of particular forms of taxation and their purposes. Taxes may be direct or indirect; the distinguishing principle is whether they fall directly upon the capital possessed and the income received by individuals, or whether they diminish its value indirectly by increasing the prices of their purchases of goods and services. Direct taxes may be imposed upon either capital or income. This, however, is a distinction which may sometimes be hard to make. A capital gains tax, for instance, which may at first seem to be a tax on a special sort of income, will, if it is not in an inflationary period indexed to offset that inflation, become a kind of capital levy or wealth tax.

About the legitimacy in principle of taxing in order to finance the provision of public goods, there is little dispute. The egregious exception here is Nozick, who has argued that all taxation of income constitutes a form of forced labour and is, therefore, manifestly unjust. What is more disputable, although nowadays very rarely disputed, is the principle of progressive as opposed to proportionate taxation, which, it may be argued, discriminates unfairly against those who have to pay the higher rates. To this the most promising counter-argument is to appeal to considerations of marginal utility.

There is, again, little dispute about the principle of permitting the lowest incomes, and usually the lowest tranche of all incomes, to be tax exempt; although it is perhaps more rarely recognized that, in practice, the higher the share of GNP seized by the state the lower becomes the threshold of tax liability. The deep and intractable divisions of opinion concern the proper purposes of taxation, and they arise just so soon as it is proposed to raise taxes for any purposes other than to finance the provision of public goods.

We may distinguish two main sorts of such purposes. One is to finance some advance towards the socialist ideal, under which all capital is collectively owned and is, typically, directly in the hands of the state. The limiting case of taxation for this purpose would be, indeed in several countries has been, the outright confiscation of – in the words of the original and unamended Clause IV of the Constitution of the British Labour Party – 'all the means of production, distribution and exchange'. The other sort of purpose is redistributive, to transfer resources – usually on a continuing rather than a once-for-all basis – from one subject or set of subjects to other individuals or sets of individuals. (Some of these others may nowadays be the foreign beneficiaries of what is optimistically described as 'development aid'.)

Since both conservatives and liberals oppose the socialist end they also have to oppose any tax means employed to realize that ideal. But if for any reason they do consent to the public acquisition of any particular enterprise or sort of enterprises, then – since the alternative must be confiscation – they will presumably prefer to raise taxes.

The interesting problems are those of legitimating redistributive taxation. At all times and in all countries some of the transfer payments which have in fact been financed out of the tax take have been of kinds for which no respectably presentable justification could be given or would even be attempted. Such are, for instance, transfers into the personal purses of potentates – or, today, their numbered Swiss bank accounts. Such too are those US agricultural subsidies which benefit mainly the richest and biggest farmers. The tax-financed transfers which are in our time widely held to be not merely licensed but mandatory are those made and to be made in the name of social justice: a conception which is generally identified first with equity and then with a usually qualified equality of outcome.

Against all such programmes for state-sponsored, compulsory redistribution, whether made in the name of social justice or any other, the first, simple but nevertheless significant objection is that (unless we are talking about a completely centralized command economy) there has in fact been no prior and faulty distribution for which a redistribution might supply the needed remedy.

With the exception already mentioned we are not, in Nozick's happy comparison,

> in the position of children who have been given portions of pie by someone who now makes last minute adjustments to rectify careless cutting. There is no *central* distribution, no person or group entitled to control all the resources, jointly deciding how they are to be doled out. . . . There is no more a distributing or distribution of shares than there is a distributing of mates in a society in which persons choose whom they shall marry.

By far the best known and most formidable presentation and defence of this conception of social justice is in a book with the misleading and overambitious title *A Theory of* (without prefix or suffix) *Justice*. Here Rawls begins by asking how hypothetical social contractors, operating behind a veil of ignorance, would agree to allocate among themselves all the wealth either already produced or in the future to be produced within their, to them temporarily unknown, territories. And he concludes by insisting upon what he denominates the Difference Principle – that inequalities are permissible *only* to the extent that either directly or indirectly they redound to the advantage of the least advantaged group in whatever particular society is under consideration.

With characteristic gaiety Nozick has made much, and rightly, both of the observation that the conditions of his thought-experiment commit Rawls to treating all goods as if they 'fell from heaven like manna'; and of the objection that in the real world most goods have in some way to be produced, and are for this or other reasons subject to antecedent claims. 'Things', Nozick insists, 'come into the world already attached to people having entitlements over them.' The force of these criticisms is felt still more strongly when we recall that the goods to be distributed or redistributed at the unfettered discretion of the Rawls's social contractors apparently include not only cash and consumer durables, but also services of every kind. Yet services, typically, are in the most intimate way linked with the people who provide them: they are most often actions which those people perform.

For all advocates of redistributive taxation the primary problem is how validly to delegitimize the taxpayers' previous holdings. How can it be shown to be just to take a part of what one person has honestly acquired – whether as a gift or by fulfilling the terms of some contract of service – in order to transfer this taking to someone else who, however deplorably, possesses no such claim thereto?

This intractable problem is not solved but simply assumed out of existence by all those who so regularly and so unquestioningly speak of the wealth in a non-socialist country as the wealth of that country, or who describe any chancellor of the exchequer who reduces some tax on income or capital as *giving to* rather than *ceasing to extort from* the taxpayers.

AF

Further reading

Flew, A.G.N., *The Politics of Procrustes*, Buffalo, NY, and London, Prometheus and Temple Smith, 1981, Chs. 1–4.

Nozick, R., *Anarchy, State, and Utopia*, New York and Oxford, Basic Books and Blackwell, 1974, Ch. 7.

Rawls, J., *A Theory of Justice*, Cambridge, MA, and Oxford, Harvard University Press and Clarendon, 1971 and 1972.

TECHNOLOGY

Strictly speaking, technology is the study of the technical arts or a discourse concerning them. In popular usage, followed here, technology is the application of knowledge to alter or manipulate the environment especially, but not exclusively, through mechanical devices. Western culture has been from a very early period unusually adept at applying and adapting technological breakthroughs. The windmill, invented by the Chinese in the sixth century AD and transmitted unchanged to western Europe by the Arabs during the Crusades, was radically improved within a short time of its arrival by the shift from a vertical to a horizontal mounting. Technologies are not neutral: they profoundly influence political and social development. Thus changes in military technology in the early modern period played a major part in the rise of the modern state. Political science is concerned with the impact of technology and the relation between technological change and social and political organization.

In general, classical liberals have always taken a favourable view of technology. It is typically seen as a liberating force. Technical innovations, by raising productivity, increase wealth which gives more people greater power over their own lives. Particular technological breakthroughs can empower people in other ways as well. The private motorcar, for example, has made people much more mobile and enabled them to do things that would otherwise be inconceivable. Electronic communications have made it possible for more people to know more about the world in which they live than ever before. Devices such as the washing machine have liberated millions from hours of drudgery. Moreover the wider social and political impact of technological change is often liberating. The invention of printing destroyed a priestly monopoly of the transmission of knowledge and made information more widely available throughout society. This diffused power as well as knowledge. Similarly, many liberals argue that modern developments in communications and information technology are undermining the power of national governments and are creating a more open and flexible world, based on networking (i.e. free association) and the free flow of information.

However, classical liberals do not see technology as an autonomous force. It is explicitly connected with free institutions and economies. The technological opportunism of western civilization is accounted for in two ways. First, the limited nature of political power in western societies meant that rulers could not simply stop technical change by diktat. The division of Europe into separate states meant that there was no single authority which could block change everywhere. Second, the market economy encouraged technical experimentation by rewarding successful innovation with profit. Markets operate as 'discovery procedures' with entrepreneurs trying out new techniques. This accounts for the technological stagnation of command economies in the contemporary world. In contrast China saw great technological advance during inter-dynastic periods or under 'weak' dynasties such as the later Sung. On coming to power in the fifteenth century the Ming dynasty deliberately stopped all technological advance.

Conservatives are more ambivalent. While welcoming individual innovations they are often critical of others. There is, for example, a substantial conservative literature deploring the consequences of television; not the content of the medium but its very nature. Conservatives are also often critical in more general terms of what they regard as the excessive interest in technology as opposed to cultural matters which they discern in modern life. Technology is also feared as being socially disruptive and as creating a dangerous condition of alienation and anomie. Thorough-going anti-technology sentiments are rare among conservatives but there is a flourishing minority tradition of agrarianism, especially in the United States, which is profoundly antipathetic to the whole technological drift of modern society. In general, however, conservatives are more likely to be sceptical about the benefits of technological change and to fear the consequences of uncontrolled innovations.

SD

Further reading

Ellul, J., *The Technological Society*, London, Jonathan Cape, 1965.
Maddox, J., *The Doomsday Syndrome*, London, Macmillan, 1972.
Twelve Southerners, *I'll Take My Stand*, Gloucester, MA, Peter Smith, 1976 (first published New York, 1930).

TOLERATION

Toleration can be of actions, or of the expression of belief or opinion. Various and sometimes conflicting justifications have been offered for it. Toleration is part of the essence of classical liberalism, in that intrinsic to the individualism of the liberal is the conviction that people ought to be free to express their views and to behave as they see fit. The sources of such a conviction lie in a secularized Protestantism, the right of each person to follow their conscience or the conclusions of their own enquiry and not to have beliefs or actions prescribed to them either by the state, by a church, or by any other agency.

For the conservative, toleration is less central, a side-effect of their political outlook rather than a central tenet. The conservative values particular liberties and therefore defends particular areas of tolerance. But their enthusiasm for general toleration is qualified by a recognition of the importance of the ongoing institutions and cultures of which individuals form a part; and by the centrality of tradition, of political authority, and of loyalty to both. The conservative's defence of toleration tends to be in negative terms; it is what has been won from tyrants and dictators. This attitude harks back to the standard conservative suspicion of liberalism, that it is unstable because it offers no moral and spiritual tradition to provide intelligible and acceptable grounds for, and limits to, freedom of action. In the eyes of the conservative, in so far as liberal influences are stable it is because they are supported by traditional values tacitly held.

Any general doctrine of toleration faces certain difficulties, those of reconciling conflicting freedoms, and of setting limits to what is tolerable. For toleration cannot be absolute. The liberal stresses, as a matter of principle, that these limits should be as few and as generous as possible, and in particular that interference with another's liberty should not extend to what is done or said in private. It may be thought that this pays scant regard to the immature or weak in society, and for this reason if for no other the scope of toleration is in practice limited by the liberal.

The conservative is more cautious; they are less abstract in their approach, and less confident that it is possible to distinguish so readily what is private from what is public, and what is individual from what is corporate. However, the conservative is ready to regard toleration as one important way in which power can be diffused throughout a society. Both the liberal and the conservative stress the importance of the rule of law, both civil and criminal, in setting limits to tolerable actions. Moreover, it does not follow that because certain activities are legal, i.e. officially tolerated, that they are in fact tolerated at the popular level.

The general grounds for tolerating diverse and unorthodox views are mainly of two types, person-centred and truth-centred justifications. It is argued that the acquiring of truth requires a plurality of opinions; and people need to hold their beliefs in an authentic, uncoerced way. It is invalid to infer relativism from toleration, or toleration from relativism. The argument for tolerating unconventional activities is based on their harmlessness, or on the intrinsic worthwhileness of a society which contains such variety. Here toleration is closely connected with 'pluralism' in at least one of its meanings, the freedom of individuals and groups to communicate and to organize within the law in pursuit of diverse and even of incompatible ends.

In recent times the general issue of toleration has tended to be focused on two areas: sexual relations and state secrets. Tolerance of sex is often referred to as 'permissiveness'. It is argued by liberals that no sexual activity performed by adults in private ought to be outlawed, and that facts which do not affect the security of the state, however sensitive, may be published. At a time when the media dominate much of popular life it is not surprising that toleration is coming more and more to mean the right of the press to publish without restraint, rather than individuals' right to speak their opinions and act unconventionally.

PH

Further reading

Locke, J., *Letter on Toleration*, 1689.
Mendus, S., and D. Edwards (eds), *On Toleration*, Cambridge, Cambridge University Press. 1987.
Mill, J.S., *On Liberty*, 1859.
Milton, J., *Aeropagetica*, 1644.

TOTALITARIANISM

Few, if any, would today adopt the term 'totalitarian' to describe their own views. This was not always the case: when Benito Mussolini referred to the 'total' state in his famous article on fascism in the *Italian Encyclopedia*, he intended praise for the fascist system of government. The separation between state and civil society, in his view a relic of old-fashioned classical liberalism, had now been overcome. All the major institutions of society must be directed by the state: this, in the Duce's opinion, was true democracy. Mussolini's article was in part written by the neo-Hegelian philosopher Gentile. Gentile and the members of his school elaborated the theory of the total state in works written throughout the Fascist Era.

Although the German lawyer and political theorist Schmitt sometimes discussed the coming of the total state, he was primarily concerned to indict the Weimar system for ineffectual government rather than to support the direction of society by an all-powerful state. Perhaps surprisingly, the propaganda of the National Socialist movement tended to stress the importance of the party rather than the state. Hitler, the Führer of the German people, was the embodiment of the *Volk* rather than the head of an all-powerful state. The Nazis did, however, use the term *Gleichshaltung* (co-ordination) by which was meant the total subordination to Nazi leadership. 'The common interest [which] outweighs the particular interest', as one of their slogans had it, was, of course, the common interest as judged by themselves.

The disastrous outcome of the Nazi regime led to a different use of the term 'totalitarian' after the Second World War. Many theorists saw in the attempt at total control of society the key to the evils of the Third Reich. The quest for total power characterized the regime of Soviet Russia as well, according to these writers. Although supposed to be at opposite ends of the political spectrum, Nazism and communism both relied crucially on complete dominance by the state. The most notable work of this kind was *The Origins of Totalitarianism* by Arendt. Two influential American political scientists, Friedrich and Brezinski, codified and systematized the characteristics of totalitarian government in a way that became standard in the 1960s in the United States. All of these writers, incidentally, regarded Italian fascism as not fully totalitarian.

The term, although hardly in the 1980s a novelty, aroused controversy when Kirkpatrick used it to distinguish communist states from 'authoritarian' dictatorships which left society largely alone while monopolizing government power. Critics accused Mrs Kirkpatrick, who became US Ambassador to the United Nations, of political bias by her use of the distinction between totalitarian and authoritarian governments. She in fact adhered to 'standard' usage in her speeches. Regardless of its use on the current political scene, however, the concept of totalitarianism has proved a useful one in analysing communism and nazism.

DG

Further reading

Arendt, H., *The Origins of Totalitarianism*, New York, Houghton-Mifflin, 1951.
Friedrich, C.J., and Z. Brezinski, *Totalitarian Dictatorship and Autocracy*, Cambridge, MA, Harvard University Press, 1956.
Kirkpatrick, J., *Dictatorships and Double Standards*, Washington, DC, American Enterprise Institute, 1982.

TRADITION

The existence and growth of tradition in any human institution or way of thinking that lasts is inevitable. So that even those modernistic movements in the arts, religion, or politics which ignore or belittle the importance of tradition are all the while developing traditions of their own. The important issues concern whether tradition functions normatively in the present life of the institution or thinking, and whether the tradition has the capacity to renew itself or is 'dead'.

'Tradition' lies ambiguously between the process, the precise ways in which the past affects the present, and the product, what is actually handed on. In political conservative thinking generally, tradition considered as manners and methods of engaging in politics has had a considerably greater influence than has tradition as doctrine or dogma received from the past. Conservatives' emphasis upon the importance of long-established institutions, attitudes, and customs stem from the importance that they attach to what is already in place, familiar, and functioning satisfactorily; to the particular institutions, rather than the general doctrine. And to the importance they attach to the way in which social, shared institutions give meaning and point to the lives of individual human beings.

So the normativeness of tradition, for the conservative, derives not merely from pragmatic, utilitarian considerations about effectiveness, but from the existence of deeper, non-instrumental notions of loyalty, sympathy, authority, and honour. The positive link from the past to the present is also preserved by the concept of good stewardship, the idea that what has been received by the present generation from the past, with all its attendant benefits, should be husbanded and as far as possible passed on intact to the next generation.

In the twentieth century the scope of this stewardship has come to embrace the natural order, though for conservatives this is merely an instance of the way in which an older, rural, paternalistic tradition for the village community is being renewed after being obscured by the dominance of the industrialism and commercialism of the last 150 years, and by the ignorance of what industrial processes may do to the natural order.

In a less overtly theoretical and intellectual way the conservative sees a close connection between the importance of tradition and what is acceptable to ordinary men and women. It is politically as well as personally and psychologically important that men and women have their bearings in society. It is desirable that they are 'at home', at ease, that they know their way around, that they have physical and social 'space' in which they and their children may be safely off-guard and may develop their interests and personalities even to the point of eccentricity. Such vague expressions as these denote those intangibilities – to which the conservative attaches great importance – which require not only a firm tradition in which to flourish, but an awareness of that tradition. In the eyes of the conservative they give a meaning to life which no amount of socialist planning, or of the granting of 'freedoms' in the abstract, can be substitutes for.

A tradition able to renew itself, and which corresponds to some of the central, permanent needs of human nature, is to be contrasted with *traditionalism* which is concerned merely with turning the clock back to an earlier era, and to replicating in the present the attitudes and institutions of that era. The contrast lies in the ready acknowledgement by the conservative that what is inherited cannot avoid interacting with changes which cannot be anticipated.

The conservative view of tradition is diametrically opposed to views of political change which rely upon revolution, and particularly upon its claimed inevitability. For while, for the revolutionary socialist, the past produces the revolutionary situation, that past is violently repudiated in the revolution. What is allegedly the product of class conflict is to guarantee classlessness hereafter. What such a doctrine has meant in practice in socialist countries is a systematic attempt to disinform the public by rewriting history lest, like the children of Israel, the children of socialism hanker after the leeks and garlic of the Egypt left behind.

Equally unacceptable for the conservative is the modernism which asserts the uniqueness of the present epoch, and which may be based upon a historical relativism, and certainly upon a plastic view of human nature. Exclusive concentration upon the present is likely to breed parochialism and a lowering of standards, as the best of the achievements of the past are ignored. At its worst, modernism will dislocate individuals and produce a psychotic and disinherited mind.

In the eyes of the political conservative, liberalism is a powerful expression of the modernistic mind-set. Liberalism manifests itself not in a complete repudiation of the past, for the liberal has a view of history, but in the conviction that the present is the best of what has so far been, and that there is better still to come. So the modernism of liberalism is both a doctrine and an attitude. The doctrine is that of individualism, of individual human rights and of the maximizing of personal freedom, notably in the market-place but also, for example, in permissive sexual morality.

History is seen as the progressive development of such rights and attitudes, and their further development is extrapolated indefinitely into the future. Such progress is held to be inevitable because this is the way in which history is going. The rise of modern liberalism is inseparable from this 'Whig view of history' and the doctrine of inevitable progress – inevitable so long as liberals hold the reins of power – which is an intrinsic part of it.

It follows, therefore, that to the eyes of a Comte or J.S. Mill, tradition is a dead hand, something which the enlightened modernist wishes to be emancipated from, for it stultifies growth as well as foreclosing on some of the indefinite possibilities which the future opens up. In arguing their case liberals appeal to 'human nature' viewed as an abstraction from any of its historical expressions, and 'natural' economic mechanisms of the free market. It is the role of the politician, therefore, to clear away the jungle of inherited laws and practices in so far as they inhibit the enterprise of the individual. And the individual here may be male or female; so the differences between the sexes are incidental and, from a liberal point of view, inconvenient.

The distinctive roles and sensibilities of men and women are the product of conditioning, part of a tradition which regards women as inferior and exploitable. National barriers, the product of past conflict and conquest, are not the visible and tangible boundaries guarding a national identity, but irrational lines inhibiting unrestricted trade and the movement of people in obedience to the pulling power of market forces. Such arguments, pressed to their logical conclusion, foresee the removal of national and other cultural and historical identities, since the nation state represents a set of arrangements from which the individuals that comprise them ought to be emancipated.

While liberals see themselves, in such ways as these, as free from the past, as rational and even scientific in their approach to political and social issues, they are in fact inescapably the product of tradition. For liberalism was not discovered *de novo*, or revealed from heaven, but has arisen from a variety of sources: from the Protestant Reformation, with its emphasis upon the individual conscience, and from later Dissenting movements; from the Enlightenment, and particularly from that strand of the Enlightenment influenced by Locke; and from reaction against war, and persecution, and economic and personal exploitation and inhibition. Conservatives will argue that liberalism developed during a period in which Christian moral values were tacitly accepted, and that it continues to live off this Christian inheritance.

Yet it is becoming less clear that this is so. For it is part of the liberal creed in the late twentieth century that homosexuality and abortion are both legally permissible because they are matters of individual choice over which neither the state nor other people ought to have any decisive influence. These developments vividly illustrate liberal's advocacy of toleration, and their view that the scope of what is to be tolerated ought, in their opinion, to go on increasing, and that society is capable of indefinitely and quickly adapting to such changes.

Liberalism as a successful political movement cannot be understood apart from the opening up of the United States as a refuge for successive generations of oppressed peoples, and from the part played by outstanding individuals, e.g. J.S. Mill, reacting in eloquent and impassioned ways against their personal circumstances. Tradition is so all-pervading that what are supposedly new developments are unintelligible apart from the tradition out of which they spring.

The argument of conservatives is made difficult by the claim that the arrangements which they seek at present to preserve have in the past been the source of great evil; e.g. it is claimed by liberals that paternalism has resulted in elitism and in a stultifying of individual potential; free commercial arrangements have led to the horrors of child labour and unregulated working conditions. But conservatives do not argue that whatever has been has been correct and acceptable in every respect. They in turn will reply that causes should not be confused with accompaniments; they will accept that abuses should be checked, but that the whole social order ought not to be overthrown to do this. And in any case, in comparing the present with the past, like ought to be compared with like.

It is, in turn, a strength of conservatism that the passing of time can sanitize certain issues and positions to the extent that they can become incorporated into the conservative tradition. Notable examples are the rise of constitutional monarchy and the extension of the franchise. So much so that in the case of the former it becomes extremely difficult now to say with any degree of confidence which position prior to the fall of the Stuarts corresponds to that of the modern conservatism. Would the modern conservative have taken the side of the king, or the side of those who wished to limit royal power? The Glorious Revolution of 1688 is only intelligible in the light of the upheavals of the Commonwealth period, which brought about permanent changes. Those changes, embodied in the constitutional arrangements of 1688, quickly became the baseline for all subsequent political debate (except for the nonjurors and radical Dissenters) and part of the tradition to which a conservative could appeal.

A similar argument can be mounted in the case of the United States. The American Constitution was a novelty, and its adoption a radical step. But today's American conservatives may appeal to the Constitution to fend off liberal proposals which in their view compromise or undermine the American way of life.

PH

Further reading

Clark, J.C.D., *English Society 1688–1832*, Cambridge, Cambridge University Press, 1985.
Oakeshott, M., *Rationalism in Politics and Other Essays*, London, Methuen, 1962.
Shils, E., *Tradition*, London, Faber, 1981.
White, R.J. *The Conservative Tradition*, London, Black, 1964.

U

UTOPIANISM

Utopias are a distinctive genre of political writing, consisting of accounts, often fictional, of an imaginary perfect state or society. 'Utopianism' refers both to the methodology involved, i.e. the exploration of political ideas by the construction of such an imaginary state, and to the detailed content of the majority of actual utopian narratives. In popular usage 'utopian' is a pejorative term, meaning impractical or fanciful and naïve. In Marxism it has a technical use, again pejorative, as the name for pre- and non-Marxist varieties of socialism, especially those honest enough to give detailed descriptions of how a socialist society would work. Marx eschewed this, arguing that the details of socialism could be left to the future to settle after the revolution when all would be changed.

J.C. Davis argues that utopian narratives can be distinguished from four other kinds of accounts of perfect societies. These are arcadias in which complex social institutions do not exist and humans live a simple life in harmony with nature; the land of Cockayne, in which people inhabit a fantasy realm of abundance; the millenarian narrative which supposes a total transformation of the world by an act of divine intervention (which in the Christian context usually means the Second Coming); and the perfect moral commonwealth where existing social institutions are made to function perfectly by the moral reformation of people, especially rulers. The issues addressed by all accounts of a perfect society are the natural condition of scarcity, the need to work, human nature, and the nature and role of social institutions. For Davis the distinctive features of utopian narratives are, first, that they are set in the real world where scarcity exists; second, that work is seen to be necessary; third, that human nature is taken as it is, i.e. imperfect; and that institutions are changed or reformed rather than people. The central theses of utopias are: that although humans are imperfect and inhabit a world of scarce resources most ills and social problems such as poverty and crime arise from a faulty social system and can therefore be corrected by the creation of a perfect society; and that such a society can be designed by human reason from first principles.

Although some works of Greek philosophy are often described as utopias the genre really appeared with the publication of More's *Utopia* in 1516. This ambiguous and deeply ironic work had a great impact and led to a plethora of imitations, only a few of which are now remembered. During the eighteenth and nineteenth centuries even more were published, many being best-sellers. Before about 1900 the most striking feature of utopias was their near unanimity of prescription. In all but a few the perfect society had as its main features the abolition of private property and markets, the near or total disappearance of the division of labour, a communal lifestyle with features such as collective eating and the wearing of a standard dress, a strictly organized and structured system of social relations and government, and a strong bias against individualism. The utopian genre appeared at the moment when markets were becoming the dominant form of economic organization in Europe and utopianism is at least partly a response to that process and its perceived consequences. The content of utopias presents both a critique of existing society and an ideal alternative with the implication that this is realizable if only the will existed. Even if the ideal society is defined as implausible or unattainable, the account of it given in the narrative provides a yardstick by which to judge both existing institutions and any changes which take place. Those which move in the direction of the utopia are good and the closer society approximates to the ideal state the better it is.

In general there is a deep hostility between utopianism and conservatism and classical liberalism. Conservative and liberal writers have criticized both the content of utopias and the very idea of a perfect society. Many argue that, human nature being imperfect and fallible, no perfect society can be realized, so to design one is simply otiose. This, however, ignores the fact that most utopias do not assume a perfect human nature. Others, including Nozick, argue that humans are so varied in their nature and desires that no single form of social organization is going to be perfect for everyone. One person's utopia is another's dystopia. For Hayek and the Austrians the very idea of designing a society or describing how a perfect one works is a theoretical impossibility since no one can know all that is needed even to describe a social order, much less design one. Social institutions are the product of unplanned human actions rather than design and no way exists for anyone to discover completely how a complex institution works or has come to be. Also a utopia attempts to fix and define a single, final model of how society should be, so eliminating any prospect of change. Again this is impossible since we cannot tell what the interaction of human beings over time is going to create. Consequently utopia is incompatible with a free society because to prevent human action changing things, with change in a perfect society necessarily causing deterioration, individual actions would have to be rigorously controlled. As Nozick puts it, utopia would have to ban capitalist acts between consenting adults.

Moreover utopias are dangerous in two practical ways. First, attempts may be made to realize utopia, to squeeze the reality of life into the abstract blueprint of utopia. Where this has been done in a limited way, e.g. in town planning, the results have been disastrous. For liberals and conservatives this is an inevitable outcome as the attempt to plan society disrupts the vital networks of tacit knowledge and informal institutions. Second, the presentation of an ideal society where all ills are solved undermines support for actual existing societies and their benefits. Any society is going to suffer by comparison with an ideal alternative. A crucial part of the strategy of the left is always to compare capitalist societies with the ideal alternative but never to treat socialist societies in this way. This reflects the extent to which the socialist utopia is taken to be the *only* ideal society, hence any socialist state, being closer to that ideal, is better than any capitalist state, with faults seen as failures to meet an ideal rather than as a necessary part of socialism.

In response to this conservatives and classical liberals have increasingly attacked the very ideal presented in utopian works. The kind of society portrayed in *Utopia* is criticized as totalitarian, repressive, and inhumane. In this endeavour they have been helped by the collapse of utopian unanimity since 1900. In this century utopian works have had a much more varied content, with many presenting alternative models of the ideal state. Some have described an individualist/libertarian utopia, e.g. Smith, while other writers have developed the sub-genre of dystopia where a society with all the features of the traditional utopia is presented in a fashion which reveals it as repulsive, e.g. Zamyatin. Nozick has argued that the only real utopia is a meta-utopia where a framework of law and rights allows people to pursue a variety of lifestyles and create many competing forms of social organization. This fits in with the liberal argument that one can advocate the pursuit of the good life without prescribing a particular version of it but only a method of pursuit. Nozick's argument allows conservatives and liberals to maintain their critique of the method and content of traditional utopias while using an adapted form of the utopian methodology themselves. This position has also been adopted by Hayek who has argued for the creation and articulation of a liberal utopia as a necessary part of political debate. He has himself made a major contribution in this direction in his later works.

SD

Further reading

Davis, J.C., *Utopia and the Ideal Society*, Cambridge, Cambridge University Press, 1981.

Manuel, F. and F.P. Manuel, *Utopian Thought in the Western World*, Oxford, Oxford University Press, 1982.

More, T., *Utopia*, 1521.

Nozick, R., *Anarchy, State, and Utopia*, Oxford and New York, Blackwell and Basic Books, 1974.

Smith, L.N., *The Probability Broach*, New York, Ace Books, 1980.

V

VOLUNTARISM

1   Voluntarism is a concept of great importance in classical liberal thought, originating in arguments over church government, but applied more generally. In the traditional parochial model of church government the church was organized on a hierarchical basis with power flowing from the top downwards through bishops and priests. The individual Christian belonged to a particular parish by virtue of birth or residence but had no choice in the matter of his fellow parishioners or his priest. The voluntarist model of church government has power flowing from the bottom upwards. The basic unit of the church, the congregation, is a free association of individual believers who have chosen to meet together for worship and the practice of the faith in accordance with a covenant which they freely subscribe to. The congregation is self-governing and choses its minister or pastor and may chose to associate with other self-governing congregations. These two models could be, and were, applied not only to church affairs but to society in general, hence the central importance of debates over church establishment between liberals and conservatives in the last century.

The first model, articulated by conservatives, has society as existing prior to its individual members. Society and its institutions exist as entities in their own right and the individual is born into and lives in and through a whole range of social institutions without any question of their chosing to opt in any more than they can chose their parents. What matters is that these institutions should be ruled by law, not arbitrary will. Society, like the church, has existed for many years and will outlast those now alive; it transcends any single generation. The second model, associated with classical liberalism, has the individual as ontologically primary. Each individual adult is autonomous and so society consists of arrangements voluntarily entered into between consenting individuals. The contract or covenant is thus at the base of society. In fact, in this view society does not exist as a thing-in-itself, it is only the shorthand term for the collection of institutions and arrangements which voluntary agreement has produced. In

273

political philosophy this leads to contractarian theories such as that of Locke. Any institution, including the state, only has authority in so far as individuals have delegated it to the institution under some implicit or explicit contract. Voluntarism is associated with advocacy of a minimal state or even outright anarchism. It is in fact a theory of social organization in general which can be applied to any institution.

2 A specific application of the above principle to the provision of public services and, particularly, welfare or poor relief. Essentially it is the idea that collective social needs and assistance to the less fortunate should be provided through voluntary action and co-operation by and between individuals. It was argued, first, that this was more effective than relying upon the public authority because the administration would be local and small scale and the detailed personal knowledge of the people involved could be used; the administration would be more careful and efficient because people would be spending their own money, and because there would be more room for local variations. Second, that it promoted sociability and cohesion by developing the feeling of 'sympathy' found in most people and encouraging free and equal association with people of varied backgrounds. Last, but not least, that it encouraged virtue because it emphasized the personal responsibility of individuals for those around them rather than relying upon coercion through taxation which enabled people to shrug off their responsibility onto the state.

The voluntary principle was a staple idea for nineteenth-century liberals; indeed voluntary co-operation is referred to far more often than competition in the writings of that time. The practice of Britain and other countries also reflected the importance of the principle, with the Victorian middle class spending at least a tenth of their income on philanthropy, more than they spent on anything else except food. There was a great range of institutions run on the voluntarist basis, notably schools and friendly societies which provided services from entertainment to poor relief to education. Many public services such as libraries were also supplied in this way and in Britain one such service, that of the lifeboats, is still provided on a voluntary basis by a charity, the RNLI, with almost all the crews made up of volunteers. The emphasis on market competition in contemporary classical liberal thought has tended to overshadow the equally important notion of voluntarism, but there are signs that this is starting to change and it may be that this central element of liberalism will be resuscitated.

SD

Further reading

Bradley, I., *The Optimists*, London, Faber, 1980.
Gosden, P.H.J.H., *Self-help*, Manchester, Manchester University Press, 1960.

W

WAR

In the western intellectual tradition there are broadly two ways of looking at war. One sees it as inevitable, even good under certain circumstances. The other sees war as the consequence of particular things or conditions, hence in theory at least not inevitable, and always bad – even if no moral alternative exists. This second school of thought can be further subdivided into the pacifist variety which argues that war is never justified and the 'just war' type wherein war is justified only if certain strict conditions apply and the war is fought in a particular way. Briefly, the war must be fought in self-defence, it must have a just end, it must be the last possible resort, and the expected benefits must exceed the costs. The fighting must be limited in scope and confined to combatants, it must be done according to certain rules, and it cannot include wanton cruelty. Both the pacifist and just war arguments derive mainly from Christian theology.

Today the problem facing all theorists is how to come to terms with the transformation of war in the modern world. With the application of modern industrial technology and organization to warfare the nature of wars has changed. Today entire societies are involved and there is almost no limit to their destructiveness. The evidence of the last century is that once a war has started it is almost impossible to stop it breaching the limits of a just war and that the destruction and loss of life is always greater than anticipated. This casts doubt on the idea of war as a species of politics, fought for precise and limited ends. The end of all rational statesmen has become the prevention of war.

Liberals have always held that war is an evil because of its essential inhumanity, and its consequences are seen rightly as profoundly anti-liberal. There have been many liberal theorists of war and peace, such as Angell and Murray Butler, both Nobel Peace Prize winners. Most liberals have argued that war is an anachronism, a reversion to an older form of society than modern, commercial, capitalist civilization. This liberal faith was severely shaken by the Great War of 1914–18, and especially the popular response to the outbreak of war. Today one can distinguish two liberal attitudes. One argues for changes in politics, economy, and society which will make war impossible. The second, more chastened, one argues that on the evidence of the past century the prime need is to prevent war in the world as it is and that the best way to do this is through collective security and a deterrent defence policy, i.e. one which deters political aggressors by making the cost of war too high for it to be contemplated. This can be seen as a reversion to Kant's idea that eventually the horror of war would be the best guarantee of peace. The attitude of conservative thinkers to war was ambivalent until relatively recently. For much of the nineteenth century many conservatives saw it as an inevitable part of human life which served many useful purposes, e.g. promoting patriotism and the virtues of courage and solidarity. Since 1914 (or even 1860) it has become clear that modern warfare is profoundly inimical to everything that conservatives hold dear, while a nuclear war would make all political argument rather superfluous. In practice most conservatives today adhere to the 'chastened liberal' argument. The problem for both is that, given the consequences of modern war, the failure of deterrence is unthinkable, but the consequences of permanent and successful deterrence for international relations have not been thought out.

SD

Further reading

Aron, R., *Peace and War*, London, Weidenfeld & Nicholson, 1966.
Howard, M., *War and the Liberal Conscience*, Oxford, Oxford University Press, 1978.

WELFARE

'Welfare' is used as a shorthand term to refer to both state welfare and the policy issues arising therefrom, and, more generally, to the entire question of how far society can or should relieve distress and destitution. Today it is widely accepted that there is a collective responsibility on the part of society to relieve poverty and destitution and that this is best done through state action via what has come to be called the welfare state. The notion of public responsibility can be traced back a long way – to the Poor Law of 1601 and other legislation of that period – but it is only in the twentieth century that welfare has become a central part of public policy. For revisionist liberals and most socialists, support for the principle of state welfare is their strongest and most deeply felt commitment. Conversely, classical liberals and most conservatives have always been, and remain, highly critical of both the theory and practice of state welfare.

Some classical liberals, such as Rand, reject the whole notion that the distress of one person creates some kind of claim on the wealth and work of another. For Rand, helping the poor is a matter of voluntary choice, not of obligation. A less extreme view is that put by writers such as Spencer and Nozick that, while there may be a moral obligation upon the individual to aid the less fortunate this cannot be compulsory since to take part of a person's income forcibly and give it to another is to violate their right of self-ownership and ownership of the product of their labour. For Spencer compulsory poor relief means that people are working involuntarily to maintain someone else, which is a form of slavery. An argument commonly put by conservative critics of state welfare is that it constitutes a shuffling off of responsibility from the individual or the family, where it belongs to the state, and that a society with a welfare state is actually less caring than one without one.

However, given the dominance of welfarist theses during the present century, such fundamentalist arguments are found less often than ones which, while accepting the principle of state welfare, are critical of the actual practice of the welfare state. Conservatives and classical liberals criticize the practice of state welfare on many grounds, with certain themes appearing regularly. One frequent argument makes the moral point that many welfare practices demoralize the recipients by destroying their sense of pride and independence and reducing them to a state of dependency upon public assistance. The most frequently mentioned factor in this connection is the poverty trap where because of the withdrawal of benefits as income is earned welfare recipients can find that they are worse off if they work than if they remain wholly dependent upon the state. This is also an example of another common argument, that welfare often has unintended consequences which are bad for the poor themselves and for society in general. The most adverse effect is that the welfare state undermines or destroys institutions such as the family and collective self-help which are much better at helping poor people, as well as creating incentives to behave in ways which are ultimately self-destructive. Often it discourages qualities which are necessary for economic advance, especially self-respect. Much American writing has concentrated upon this point, most notably that of Murray, with an extensive attack being mounted on the consequences of Johnson's Great Society programmes. The most frequently cited example is the Aid to Families with Dependent Children programme which has gone a long way towards destroying the family structure of America's urban poor, especially, though not exclusively, among the black population. Many of these points have also been made on the left, with some going so far as to argue that the welfare state is primarily an instrument of social control, designed to keep the working class powerless and divided.

This last point has been taken up by writers influenced by the Public Choice School as well as left-wing commentators such as Le Grand.

Detailed study reveals that the major beneficiaries of state welfare are the middle classes and that there may even be a net transfer of income from the less well off to the better off. Since the welfare state is a system which politicizes welfare, policy decisions concerning resource allocation will be made on a political basis with groups with political clout, such as the professional middle classes, gaining at the expense of the unorganized and apathetic poor.

This relates to another general argument, that the welfare state is not in the best interests of the poor themselves. State welfare disrupts the market by sending false signals to producers and consumers. The result is to reduce the total efficiency of resource allocation within the economy, hence total wealth is less than it would otherwise be. Some specific welfare measures, such as minimum wage legislation, have a particularly serious effect because they raise the price of some types of labour (e.g. unskilled teenagers) above the market level. The result is to destroy jobs and increase poverty and dependence upon state benefits.

While there is wide agreement among conservatives regarding the failures of the existing welfare state there is no such unanimity on the question of how to reform it. Some suggest a system of strict targeting with aid only going to those in real need. Apart from the vexed question of what constitutes 'need' such a policy inevitably produces or exacerbates the poverty trap. So, others such as Parker have gone to the other extreme and advocated either a universal single benefit to provide a minimum income guarantee (MIG) or else a form of income supplement through a negative income tax (NIT) where income is made up to a set level. Both of these face formidable practical obstacles, not least cost, and can be attacked on the grounds that they constitute a major forced and improper transfer of property which violates any number of rights. Another possibility would be to revive the old distinction between the deserving and the undeserving poor enshrined in the British Poor Law Amendment Act of 1834. Here, apart from the practical problem of defining desert, many follow Hayek in arguing that there is no connection between economic condition and desert, so making the whole concept meaningless.

Faced with these problems, an increasing number of conservatives and classical liberals are looking at more radical alternatives to state welfare and even the outright abolition of the welfare state. Two possible alternatives are philanthropy and mutual aid. Philanthropy can do more than is commonly realized. In the last century the middle classes spent a tenth of their income on charitable giving which if it were revived today would provide a massive transfer of wealth from rich to poor. However, more attention is being paid to the idea of reviving mutual aid, i.e. collective self-help by the poor themselves through friendly societies, credit unions, co-operatives, and other mutual institutions. This would, in contrast to the welfare state, have a positive moralizing effect as it would encourage responsibility, independence, and sociability. It would also give power and control to the poor themselves instead of bureaucrats and professionals. The ultimate goal would be to replace the welfare state with a welfare society with need met by voluntary action.

SD

Further reading

Gray, J., *Limited Government: a Positive Agenda*, London, Institute of Economic Affairs, 1989.
Harris, R., *Beyond the Welfare State*, London, Institute of Economic Affairs, 1988.
Hayek, F.A. *The Constitution of Liberty*, London, Routledge & Kegan Paul, 1960.
Spencer, H., *The Principles of Ethics*, 2 vols, Indianapolis, IN, Liberty Press, 1975.

Conservatives and classical liberals cited in text

Acton, John Emerich Edward Dalberg-Acton, First Lord (1834–1902); English historian. Major works *Essays on the History of Liberty*, *Essays in the Study and Writing of History*, *Essays in Religion, Politics and Morality*.

Adams, John (1735–1826); American conservative politician and writer. Major work *Defence of Constitutions of Government*.

Alchian, Armen (1914–); American economist. Major work *Economic Forces at Work*.

Angell, Norman (1872–1967); English writer, politician, and peace laureate. Major works *The Great Illusion*, *After All*.

Aron, Raymond (1905–83); French sociologist and writer. Major works *On Peace and War*, *Clausewitz, Philosopher of War*, *The Imperial Republic*, *The Opium of the Intellectuals*, *Eighteen Lectures on Industrial Society*.

Babbitt, Irving (1865–1933); American critic. Major works *Democracy and Leadership*, *Rousseau and Romanticism*.

Bagehot, Walter (1826–77); English journalist and political writer. Major works *The English Constitution*, *Lombard Street*, *Physics and Politics*.

Barrès, Maurice (1862–1923); French writer. Major works *Le Culte du moi*, *Le Roman de l'énergie national*.

Bastiat, Frédéric (1801–50); French journalist and economist. Major works *The Law*, *The State*, *Economic Harmonies*, *Economic Sophisms*.

Beccaria, Cesare Bonesana, Marchese di (1738–94); Italian philosopher. Major work *Of Crimes and Punishments*.

Becker, Gary (1930–); American economist. Major works *Human Capital*, *A Treatise on the Family*, *The Economic Approach to Human Behaviour*.

Bell, Daniel (1919–); American sociologist. Major works *The End of Ideology*, *The Cultural Contradictions of Capitalism*, *The Coming of Post-industrial Society*, *Capitalism Today* (with Irving Kristol).

Belloc, Hilaire (1870–1953); English writer and Liberal politician. Major work *The Servile State*.

Benda, Julien (1867–1956); French journalist and philosopher. Major work *The Treason of the Intellectuals*.

Bentham, Jeremy (1748–1832); English philosopher. Major works *Introduction to the Principles of Morals and Legislation*, *A Fragment on Government*, *In Defence of Usury*.

Berlin, Sir Isaiah (1909–); English philosopher and historian. Major works *Two Concepts of Liberty*, *The Hedgehog and the Fox*, *Historical Inevitability*.

Bernanos, Georges (1888–1948); French writer and critic. Major works *Star of Satan*, *Diary of a Country Priest*, *The Fearless Heart*, *Tradition of Freedom*.

Boehm-Bawerk, Eugen von (1851–1914); Austrian economist and politician. Major works *Karl Marx and the Close of His System*, *The Pure Theory of Capital*.

Bohm, Franz (1895–); German economist and writer.

Bolingbroke, Henry St John, First Viscount (1678–1751); English Tory politician and philosopher. Major work *The Idea of a Patriot King*.

Bonald, Louis Gabriel Ambrose, Viscomte de (1754–1840); French political thinker. Major works *Théorie du pouvoir*, *Législation Primitive*.

Bourget, Paul (1852–1935); French writer and political thinker. Major work *Collected Studies*.

Bright, John (1811–89); English Liberal politician.

Brunetière, Ferdinand (1849–1906); French literary critic. Major works *Discours de combat*, *Essays in French Literature*, *L'Evolution des genres dans l'histoire de la literature*.

Buchanan, James M. (1919–); American economist. Major works *The Calculus of Consent* (with G. Tullock), *Limits of Liberty*, *The Theory of Public Choice*.

Buckle, Henry Thomas (1821–62); Scottish historian. Major work *History of Civilisation in England*.

Buckley, William Frank (1925–); American journalist. Major works *God and Man at Yale*, *Up from Liberalism*.

Burke, Edmund (1729–97); Irish politician and political thinker. Major works *A Vindication of Natural Society*, *The Sublime and Beautiful*, *Reflections on the Revolution in France*, *Thoughts and Details on Scarcity*.

Bury, John Bagnell (1861–1927); Irish historian. Major works *History of Freedom of Thought*, *The Idea of Progress: Its Origins and Historical Development*.

Butler, Nicholas Murray (1862–1947); American educationalist and peace laureate. Major works *Across the Busy Years*, *The Path to Peace*, *World in Turmoil*, *Between Two Worlds*.

Calhoun, John Caldwell (1782–1850); American politician. Major work *A Disquisition on Government*.

Cantillon, Richard (1680–1734); Irish/French political economist. Major work *Essay on the Nature of Commerce in General*.

Carey, John (1934–); English literary critic. Major works *Original Copy*, *The Violent Effigy*.

Cassel, Gustav (1866–1945); Swedish economist. Major works *Theory of Social Economics*, *From Protectionism through Planned Economy to Dictatorship*.

Chateaubriand, François Auguste, Vicomte de (1768–1848); French conservative politician and writer. Major work *The Genius of Christianity*.

Chesterton, Gilbert Keith (1874–1936); English writer. Major works *Orthodoxy*, *Heretics*, *Eugenics and Other Essays*, *The Everlasting Man*, *Catholic Essays*, *The Napoleon of Notting Hill*, *The Flying Inn*.

Clark, Stephen Richard Lyster (1950–). Major works *Civil Peace and Sacred Order*, *The Moral Status of Animals*, *The Mysteries of Religion*.

Cobbett, William (1763–1835); English writer. Major works *Rural Rides*, *Cottage Economy*.

Cobden, Richard (1804–65); English Liberal politician. Major works *Russia*, *England, Ireland and America*.

Coleridge, Samuel Taylor (1772–1834); English poet and writer. Major works *On the Constitution of Church and State*, *Biographia Literaria*, *Lay Sermons*, *Aids to Reflection*.

Comte, François Charles Louis (1782–1837); French political and economic theorist. Major works *Traité de legislation*, *Le Censeur européen* (with Charles Dunoyer).

Condorcet, Antoine-Nicolas Caritat, Marquis de (1743–94); French philosopher and mathematician. Major work *Sketch for a Historical Picture of the Progress of the Human Mind*.

Constant de Rebecque, Benjamin (1767–1830); French Liberal politician and writer. Major works *The Spirit of Conquest and Usurpation, Principles of Politics, The Liberty of the Ancients Compared with that of the Moderns*.

Cowling, Maurice (1926–); English historian. Major works *Religion and Public Doctrine in England, Conservative Essays, The Rise of Labour*.

Croce, Benedetto (1866–1952); Italian philosopher, historian and Liberal politician. Major works *History as the Story of Liberty, The Conduct of Life, Poetry, Philosophy, History, History of the Kingdom of Naples, History of Italy*.

Dahlmann, Friedrich Christoph (1785–1860); German historian and Liberal politician. Major work *Die Politik auf den Grund und das Mass der gegebenen Zustände zurückgeführt*.

Destutt de Tracy, Antoine Louis Claude, Comte (1754–1836); French political thinker. Major work *Commentary on Montesquieu's 'Spirit of the Laws'*.

Dicey, Albert Venn (1835–1922); English writer. Major works *Lectures on the Relation between Law and Public Opinion in England, Introduction to the Study of the Law and of the Constitution*.

Diderot, Denis (1713–84); French writer and philosopher. Major works *The Encyclopaedia* (editor), *Supplement to the Voyage of Bougainville*.

Dunoyer, Barthelemy Charles Pierre Joseph (1786–1862); French political writer. Major works *De la liberté du travail, Le Censeur européen* (with Charles Comte).

Eliot, Thomas Stearns (1888–1965); American/English poet. Major works *Notes Towards a Definition of Culture, The Idea of a Christian Society, Ash-Wednesday, Four Quartets, Murder in the Cathedral, The Waste Land*.

Ellul, Jacques (1912–); French theologian. Major works *The Political Illusion, The Technological Society, The Ethics of Freedom, The Betrayal of the West*.

Elton, Geoffrey Rudolph (1921–); English historian. Major works *England under the Tudors, The Tudor Revolution in Government, Political History: Principles and Practice, The Practice of History*.

Eucken, Walter (1891–1950); German economist. Major works *The Foundations of Economics, This Unsuccessful Age*.

Faguet, Emile (1847–1916); French literary critic and political writer. Major works *Liberalism, Politiques et moralistes du dix-neuvième siècle, The Cult of Incompetence*.

Ferguson, Adam (1723–1816); Scottish writer. Major work *An Essay on Civil Society*.

Fichte, Johann Gottlieb (1762–1814); German philosopher. Major works *Addresses to the German Nation, The Closed Commercial State*.

Flynn, John T., (1882–1964); American writer. Major works *The Road Ahead, As We Go Marching*.

Friedman, David (1945–); American writer. Major work *The Machinery of Freedom*.

Friedman, Milton (1912–); American economist. Major works *Capitalism and Freedom, Free to Choose* (with Rose Friedman), *Essays in Positive Economics, A Monetary History of the United States* (with Anna Schwarz).

George, Stefan (1868–1933); German poet and writer. Major works *Year of the Soul, The Seventh Ring, The New Reich*.

Gibbon, Edward (1737–94); English historian. Major work *History of the Decline and Fall of the Roman Empire*.

Gierke, Otto von (1844–1921); German jurist. Major work *German Law of Associations*.

Gilmour, Sir Ian (1926–); English Conservative politician. Major work *Inside Right*.

Glazer, Nathan (1923–); American sociologist. Major works *Ethnic Dilemmas, Clamour at the Gates, Affirmative Discrimination, Beyond the Melting Pot* (with Daniel P. Moynihan).

Gray, John (1948–); English philosopher. Major works *Mill on Liberty: A Defence, Hayek on Liberty, Liberalism, Liberalisms*.

Guizot, François (1787–1874); French historian and liberal politician. Major works *History of the English Revolution, History of the Origins of Representative Government*.

Halévy, Elie (1870–1937); French historian. Major works *The Rise of Philosophic Radicalism, History of the English People in the Nineteenth Century, The Era of Tyrannies*.

Haller, Karl Ludwig von (1768–1854); German writer. Major work *The Restoration of the Social Sciences*.

Hamilton, Alexander (1757–1804); American conservative politician. Major work *The Federalist Papers*.

Hayek, Friedrich August von (1899–); Austrian economist and political thinker. Major works *The Road to Serfdom, The Constitution of Liberty, Law, Legislation and Liberty, Individualism and Economic Order, The Sensory Order, The Fatal Conceit*.

Heath, Spencer (1876–1956); American writer. Major works *Citadel, Market and Altar, Politics versus Proprietorship*.

Hegel, Georg Wilhelm Friedrich (1770–1831); German philosopher. Major works *Phenomenology of Spirit, The Science of Logic, Philosophy of Right, Lectures on the Philosophy of History*.

Himmelfarb, Gertrude (1922–); American historian. Major works *The Old History and the New, The Idea of Poverty, Lord Acton: A Study in Conscience and Politics, On Liberty and Liberalism: The Case of John Stuart Mill*.

Hirst, Francis Wrigley (1873–1953); English writer and Liberal politician. Major works *The Political Economy of War, Liberty and Tyranny, Free Trade and Other Fundamental Doctrines of the Manchester School*.

Hooker, Richard (1554–1600); English divine. Major work *Of the Laws of Ecclesiastical Polity*.

Humboldt, Wilhelm von (1767–1835); German politician and educational reformer. Major work *The Sphere and Duties of the State*.

Hume, David (1711–76); Scottish philosopher. Major works *A Treatise of Human Nature, History of Great Britain*.

Jacobs, Jane (1916–); Canadian writer. Major works *Cities and the Wealth of Nations, The Death and Life of Great American Cities*.

Jevons, William Stanley (1835–82); English economist. Major works *The State in Relation to Labour, The Theory of Political Economy*.

Jewkes, John (1902–89); English economist. Major works *Ordeal by Planning, A Return to Free Market Economics?*

Jouvenel, Bertrand de (1903–87); French political thinker. Major works *Power, Sovereignty, The Pure Theory of Politics, The Art of Conjecture, Ethics of Redistribution*.

Kames, Henry Home, First Lord (1696–1782); Scottish jurist and philosopher. Major work *Essays on the Principles of Natural Morality and Religion*.

Kant, Immanuel (1724–1804); German philosopher. Major works *Critique of Pure Reason, Critique of Practical Reason, Perpetual Peace*.

Kendal, Wilmoore (1909–67); American political scientist. Major works *Wilmoore Kendal Contra Mundum, The Conservative Affirmation, John Locke and the Doctrine of Majority Rule*.

Kirk, Russell (1918–); American writer. Major works *The Conservative Mind*, *Beyond the Dreams of Avarice*, *Confessions of a Bohemian Tory*, *A Program for Conservatives*.

Kirkpatrick, Jeanne (1926–); American politician and writer. Major works *Strategy of Deception*, *Dictatorships and Double Standards*.

Knight, Frank Hyneman (1885–1972); American economist. Major works *Risk, Uncertainty and Profit*, *The Ethics of Competition*, *Freedom and Reform*.

Kristol, Irving (1920–); American writer. Major works *Two Cheers for Capitalism*, *Reflections of a Neo-conservative*, *Capitalism Today* (with Daniel Bell).

Laboulaye, Edouard (1811–83); French lawyer and political writer. Major works *L'Etat et ses limites*, *La Liberté antique et la liberté moderne*.

Lafitte, Jacques (1767–1854); French banker and liberal politician.

Lamennais, Abbé Félicité Robert de (1782–1854); French political theorist. Major works *Paroles d'un croyant*, *L'Avenir*, *Essai sur l'indifférence*.

La Tour du Pin la Charce, Réné de (1858–); French political writer. Major work *Vers un ordre social chrétien*.

Le Bon, Gustave (1841–1931); French psychological theorist. Major work *The Psychology of Crowds*.

Lecky, William Edward Hartpole (1838–1903); Irish historian. Major works *History of the Rise and Influence of the Spirit of Rationalism in Europe*, *Democracy and Liberty*, *European Morals from Augustus to Charlemagne*, *History of England in the Eighteenth Century*.

Leoni, Bruno (1913–67); Italian jurist. Major work *Freedom and the Law*.

Leroy-Beaulieu, Paul (1843–1916); French journalist and economist. Major works *Traité théorique et pratique d'économie politique*, *L'Etat moderne et ses fonctions*.

Lipset, Seymour Martin (1922–); American political scientist. Major works *Revolution and Counter-Revolution*, *The Politics of Unreason*, *Failure of a Dream*, *Dialogues on American Politics*.

Locke, John (1632–1704); English philosopher. Major works *Two Treatises of Civil Government*, *Essay on Human Understanding*, *On the Reasonableness of Christianity*, *Letters Concerning Toleration*.

Macaulay, Thomas Babbington (1800–59); English Whig politician and historian. Major work *The History of England*.

Madison, James (1751–1836); American politician. Major work *The Federalist Papers*.

Maine, Sir Henry Sumner (1822–88); English jurist. Major works *Ancient Law*, *Popular Government*.

Maistre, Joseph de (1753–1821); French political thinker. Major works *Du Pape*, *Les Soirées de St Petersburg*, *Considerations on France*, *Generative Principles of Constitutions*.

Mauriac, François (1885–1970); French writer. Major works *The Knot of Vipers*, *The Frontenac Mystery*, *The Black Notebook*, *Second Thoughts*.

Maurras, Charles Marie Photius (1868–1942); French poet, critic, and conservative political activist. Major works *La Politique religieuse*, *Mes idées politiques*, *Dictionnaire politique et critique*, *Enquête sur la monarchie*.

Menger, Karl (1840–1921); Austrian economist. Major work *Problems of Economics and Sociology*, *Principles of Economics*.

Meyer, Frank (1909–1972); American conservative thinker. Major work *In Defence of Freedom*.

Mill, James (1773–1836); English economist and philosopher. Major works *Elements of Political Economy*, *Essay on Government*.

Mill, John Stuart (1806–73); English philosopher. Major works *On Liberty*, *Principles of Political Economy*, *Considerations on Representative Government*,

Utilitarianism, The Subjection of Women.

Millar, John (1735–1801); Scottish political thinker. Major work *Origin of the Distinction of Ranks.*

Milton, John (1608–74); English poet. Major works *Paradise Lost, Samson Agonistes, Areopagitica, The Tenure of Kings and Magistrates, The Ready and Easy Way to Establish a Free Commonwealth.*

Minogue, Kenneth (1930–); Australian political scientist. Major works *The Liberal Mind, Nationalism, Hidden Powers: The Pure Theory of Ideology.*

Mises, Ludwig Elder von (1881–1973); Austrian economist. Major works *Socialism, Human Action, The Theory of Money and Credit, The Ultimate Foundations of Economic Science.*

Molinari, Gustave de (1819–1912); Belgian/French economist. Major works *The Production of Security, The Society of Tomorrow, Les Soirées de la rue St. Lazare, Les Lois naturelles de l'économie politique.*

Montesquieu, Charles-Louis de Secondat, Baron de (1689–1755); French political thinker. Major work *De l'Esprit des lois.*

Moore, Paul Elmer (1864–1937); American critic. Major work *Shelburne Essays.*

Morley, John (1838–1923); English writer and Liberal politician. Major works *Life of Gladstone, Life of Richard Cobden, On Compromise.*

Motley, John Lothrop (1814–77); American historian. Major works *The Rise of the Dutch Republic, History of the United Netherlands, Life and Death of John of Barneveld.*

Moynihan, Daniel Patrick (1927–); American politician. Major works *The Politics of a Guaranteed Income, Counting our Blessings, Maximum Feasible Misunderstanding, Beyond the Melting Pot* (with Nathan Glazer).

Mueller, Adam Heinrich (1779–1829); German political thinker. Major work *Elemente der Staatskunst.*

Muller-Armack, Alfred (1901–); German economist and social thinker. Major works *Religion und Wirtschaft, Wirtschaftordnung und Wirtschaftpolitik.*

Murray, Charles (1943–); American social scientist. Major works *Losing Ground, In Pursuit of Happiness and Good Government.*

Nisbet, Robert (1913–); American sociologist. Major works *The Quest for Community, The Twilight of Authority, Prejudices, Conservatism.*

Norman, Edward Robert (1938–); English historian. Major works *Christianity and World Order, A History of Modern Ireland, Church and Society in Modern England.*

Novak, Michael (1933–); American writer. Major works *The Spirit of Democratic Capitalism, Freedom with Justice, Will it Liberate?, Free Persons and the Common Good.*

Novalis, pseudonym of Georg Philip Friedrich, Baron von Hardenberg (1772–1801); German writer and poet. Major works *Christenheit oder Europa?, Heinrich van Otterdingen.*

Nozick, Robert (1938–); American philosopher. Major work *Anarchy, State, and Utopia.*

Oakeshott, Michael (1901–); English philosopher. Major works *Experience and its Modes, Rationalism in Politics, On History, On Human Conduct.*

Oppenheimer, Franz (1864–1943); German sociologist. Major work *The State.*

Penn, William (1644–1718); English/American pioneer and religious leader. Major work *An Essay Towards the Present and Future Peace of Europe.*

Pi y Margall, Francisco (1824–1901); Spanish federalist politician. Major works *Reaction and Revolution, Federation.*

Pobedonostev, Konstantin Petrovitch (1827–1907); Russian jurist and politician. Major work *Reflections of a Russian Statesman.*

Podhoretz, Norman (1930–); American writer. Major works *Making It*, *Breaking Ranks*, *The Bloody Crossroads*.

Polanyi, Michael (1891–1976); Hungarian/English chemist and philosopher. Major works *The Contempt of Freedom*, *The Logic of Liberty*, *Personal Knowledge*.

Popper, Sir Karl Raimund (1902–); Austrian/English philosopher. Major works *The Poverty of Historicism*, *The Open Society and its Enemies*, *Logic of Scientific Discovery*, *Objective Knowledge: An Evolutionary Approach*.

Posner, Richard Allen (1939–); American economist. Major work *The Economics of Justice*.

Rand, Ayn, pseudonym of Alice Rosenbaum (1905–82); Russian/American writer. Major works *We the Living*, *The Fountainhead*, *Atlas Shrugged*, *The Virtue of Selfishness*, *Capitalism: The Unknown Ideal*, *Philosophy: Who Needs It?*

Reid, Thomas (1710–96); Scottish philosopher. Major works *Essays on the Intellectual Powers of Man*, *Essays on the Active Powers of Man*.

Ricardo, David (1772–1823); English economist. Major work *Principles of Political Economy and Taxation*.

Richter, Eugen (1838–1906); German Liberal politician. Major work *Picture of the Socialist Future*.

Robertson, John Mackinnon (1856–1933); Scottish Liberal politician, historian, and sociologist. Major works *The Evolution of States*, *Buckle and His Critics*, *The Meaning of Liberalism*.

Roepke, Wilhelm (1899–1966); German/Swiss economist. Major works *The Social Crisis of our Time*, *Civitas Humana*, *A Humane Economy*, *Against the Tide*.

Rossiter, Clinton (1917–); American writer. Major works *Conservatism in America*, *Seedtime of the Republic*.

Rothbard, Murray Newton (1926–); American economist. Major works *Man, Economy and State*, *Power and Market*, *The Ethics of Liberty*, *For a New Liberty*.

Rotteck, Karl von (1775–1840); German writer and political activist. Major works *Allgemeine Weltgeschichte*, *Lehrbuch des Vernunftsrechts*, *Staatslexikon* (with K.T. Welcker).

Royer-Collard, Pierre Paul (1763–1845); French liberal politician.

Rustow, Alexander (1885–1963); German historian. Major work *Freedom and Domination*.

Salisbury, Arthur Talbot Gascoyne-Cecil, Third Marquess of (1830–1903); English Conservative politician.

Santayana, George (1863–1952); Spanish/American philosopher and poet. Major works *Realms of Being*, *Obiter Scripta*, *Dominations and Powers*, *The Birth of Reason and Other Essays*.

Say, Jean Baptiste (1767–1832); French economist. Major works *Treatise on Politican Economy*, *Lettres à Malthus*, *Cours complet d'économie politique*.

Schiller, Johann Friedrich Christoph von (1759–1805); German writer and philosopher. Major works *Wilhelm Tell*, *Maria Stuart*, *Don Carlos*, *History of the Revolt of the Netherlands*, *History of the Thirty Years War*, *Wallenstein*.

Schulze–Delitzsch, Hermann (1808–83); German politician and social reformer.

Schumpeter, Joseph Alois (1883–1950); Czech/American economist. Major works *Theory of Economic Development*, *Business Cycles*, *Capitalism, Socialism and Democracy*.

Scruton, Roger (1944–); English philosopher and writer. Major works *The Aesthetics of Architecture*, *Art and Imagination*, *Dictionary of Political Thought*, *The Meaning of Conservatism*.

Sidgwick, Henry (1838–1900); English philosopher. Major works *Methods of Ethics*, *Elements of Politics*, *Principles of Political Economy*.

Sidney, Algernon (1622–83); English republican politician and martyr. Major work *A Discourse Concerning Government*.

Simons, Henry Calvert (1899–1946); American economist. Major work *Economic Policy for a Free Society*.

Simon Suisse, Jules François (1814–96); French liberal politician. Major work *La Politique radicale*.

Smith, Adam (1723–90); Scottish philosopher and economist. Major works *The Theory of Moral Sentiments, An Inquiry into the Nature and Causes of the Wealth of Nations*.

Sowell, Thomas (1930–); American economist and writer. Major works *Ethnic America, A Conflict of Visions, Compassion versus Guilt, Pink and Brown People, Marxism, Markets and Minorities, Knowledge and Decisions*.

Spencer, Herbert (1820–1903); English sociologist. Major works *Social Statics, The Man versus the State, Principles of Ethics, Education: Intellectual, Moral and Physical*.

Spooner, Lysander (1808–87); American individualist anarchist. Major works *No Treason, A Letter to Thomas F Bayard*.

Staël, Anne Louise Germaine, Madame de (1766–1817); French writer. Major works *The Influence of Literature upon Society, On Germany, Considerations on the French Revolution*.

Stephen, James Fitzjames (1829–94); English lawyer and politician. Major work *Liberty, Equality, Fraternity*.

Strauss, Lee (1899–1973); American philosopher. Major works *National Right and History, History of Political Philosophy, Liberalism, Ancients* and *Moderns*.

Taine, Hippolyte Adolphe (1828–93); French historian. Major work *Origines de la France contemporaine*.

Talmon, Jacob Leib (1916–); historian. Major works *The Origins of Totalitarian Democracy, Political Messianism: The Romantic Phase, The Myth of the Nation and the Vision of Revolution*.

Thierry, Augustin (1795–1856); French historian. Major work *History of the Norman Conquest of England, The Historical Essays, Essai sur l'histoire de la formation et des progrès du tiers état*.

Thiers, Maris Joseph Louis Adolphe (1797–1877); French liberal politician and historian. Major works *Histoire de la révolution, Histoire du consulat et de l'empire*.

Tocqueville, Alexis de (1805–59); French political thinker. Major works *The Ancien Régime and the French Revolution, Democracy in America, Recollections*.

Toennies, Ferdinand (1855–1936); German sociologist. Major works *Community and Association, Custom, On Social Ideas and Ideologies*.

Treitschke, Heinrich von (1834–96); German historian. Major work *Deutsche Geschichte im 19 Jahrhundert*.

Tucker, Benjamin (1854–1939); American individualist anarchist. Major work *Instead of a Book*.

Tullock, Gordon (1922–); American economist. Major works *The Politics of Bureaucracy, Social Dilemmas, The New World of Economics, The Calculus of Consent* (with James Buchanan).

Turgot, Anne Robert Jacques (1727–81); French administrator and economist. Major work *Reflections on the Formation and Distribution of Riches*.

Viereck, Peter (1916–); American writer. Major works *The Shame and Glory of the Intellectuals, Metapolitics: From the Romantics to Hitler, Conservatism Revisited*.

Viner, Jacob (1892–1970); American economist and historian of ideas. Major works *The Long View and the Short, Religious Thought and European Society*.

Voltaire, pseudonym of François-Marie Arouet (1694–1778); French writer. Major works *The Philosophical Dictionary, Essai sur les moeurs, Treatise on Toleration*.

Walras, Léon (1834–1910); Belgian economist. Major work *Elements of Pure Economics*.

Warren, Josiah (1798–1874); American individualist anarchist. Major work *Equitable Commerce*.

Weaver, Richard (1910–63); American writer. Major works *Ideas have Consequences, The Ethics of Rhetoric, The Southern Tradition at Bay*.

Welcker, Karl Theodore (1790–1869); German writer. Major works *The Foundations of Law, State and Penalty, Staatslexikon* (with Karl von Rotteck).

Will, George F. (1941–); American journalist. Major works *Statecraft as Soulcraft, The Pursuit of Happiness and Other Sobering Thoughts, The Pursuit of Virtue and Other Tory Notions*.

Williams, Roger (1603–83); English and American political and religious leader. Major work *The Bloudy Tenet of Persecution*.

Wilson, James Quin (1931–); American political scientist. Major works *Thinking About Crime, Crime and Human Nature*.

Wollstonecraft, Mary (1759–97); English feminist. Major work *A Vindication of the Rights of Woman*.

Worsthorne, Peregrine Gerard (1923–); English journalist. Major works *The Socialist Myth, By the Right*.

Zamyatin, Evgeny Ivanovitch (1884–1937); Russian writer. Major work *We*.